LISP

Patrick Henry Winston
Massachusetts Institute of Technology

Berthold Klaus Paul Horn
Massachusetts Institute of Technology

ADDISON-WESLEY PUBLISHING COMPANY

Reading, Massachusetts · Menlo Park, California
London · Amsterdam · Don Mills, Ontario · Sydney

Reproduced by Addison-Wesley from camera-ready copy supplied by the authors.

ISBN 0-201-08329-9

HIJ-AL-8987654

PREFACE

This book has two parts. The purpose of Part One is to introduce the basics of LISP programming. The first nine chapters of Part One, together with selected material from the remaining three, are appropriate for an introductory subject on LISP. People studying Part One will understand the basic ideas of symbol manipulation and know how to use LISP in contexts that are interesting, albeit simple. Writing programs to do search, for example, will be straightforward.

The purpose of Part Two is to demonstrate how LISP is used in practice. We have selected examples with a view toward illustrating ideas that are well-known in Artificial Intelligence and related fields. In dealing with these examples, we discuss rules of good programming practice, basic debugging tools, data-driven programming, and building embedded interpreters and compilers. The chapters of Part Two, together with selected material from the last three chapters of Part One, are appropriate for an intermediate-to-advanced subject on how to exploit LISP. People studying Part Two will be ready to work on the big systems that are now common in parts of Artificial Intelligence such as problem solving, pattern matching, expert systems, natural language understanding, and frame systems.

MACLISP is the dialect of LISP used in this book. People who have access to INTERLISP but not MACLISP should note that an appendix describes the differences that are relevant to doing the exercises with the help of a computer. Other appendices supply an index of LISP functions, give a sample of terminal interaction using LISP, and provide supplementary notes for some of the more esoteric ideas.

Some of the material in this book is drawn from an earlier book, *Artificial Intelligence*. Occasionally a paragraph or example has been transferred verbatim because we could not think of a better way of doing something. For the most part, however, the borrowed material has been extensively revised, augmented, and generally improved:

iii

Chapter 11 of *Artificial Intelligence,* Basic LISP Programming, has been distributed over the first eight chapters of this book.

Chapter 12, The Blocks World, is now part of Chapters 13 and 16. Chapters 14 and 15 build on the blocks world material in new ways.

Chapter 13, The Games World, which introduced an alpha-beta program, has been replaced by Chapter 11 on search.

Chapter 14, Symbolic Pattern Matching, has become Chapter 17, with the addition of a simple resolution theorem prover for propositional calculus. The material on solving algebra word problems has been omitted and the DOCTOR program appears only in an exercise.

Chapter 15, Implementing Embedded Languages, is hardly recognizable. The ATN compiler is now in Chapter 20, but it is preceded by an ATN interpreter in Chapter 19 and followed by a data-base interface in Chapter 21. The low-level, cognitive-model, production-system interpreter has been replaced by a more general, higher-level, MYCIN-like deduction system, described in Chapter 18. The LISP interpreter, improved to deal with issues of variable scoping and closure, is now in Chapter 23.

Chapter 16, Data Bases and Demons, has been replaced by Chapter 22 on frames.

Certainly this book supersedes Part Two of *Artificial Intelligence,* and someday we will want to revise, augment, improve, and separate out Part One of that book too. At this writing, however, it regrettably looks like that will take a while.

P.H.W.
B.K.P.H.

ACKNOWLEDGEMENTS

The cover design and the drawings are by Karen Prendergast.

Mike Brady, Boris Katz, James Meehan, Robin Stanton, and Guy Steele read various drafts of this book with great care.

In addition, the authors were helped considerably by Harold Abelson, Richard Brown, Will Clinger, Ken Forbus, Bernard Greenberg, Kent Pitman, Karen Prendergast, Charles Rich, Carol Roberts, Richard Stallman, and Clement Wang.

We wish we had sufficient time to incorporate more of their suggestions.

Most of the research work described in the examples in the second part of this book was sponsored by the Defense Advanced Research Projects Agency.

CONTENTS

PART I

PART I

1
UNDERSTANDING
SYMBOL
MANIPULATION

This book has two parts, each written to accomplish a particular purpose:

■ The purpose of Part One of this book is to introduce the ideas of symbol manipulation and to teach the basics of LISP programming.

■ The purpose of Part Two is to demonstrate LISP's muscle and to excite people about what LISP can do.

This brief chapter defines symbol manipulation, explains why LISP is the right symbol-manipulation language to learn, and previews the ideas that will be covered.

Symbol Manipulation is Like Working with Words and Sentences

What exactly is symbol manipulation? Everyone understands that computers can do arithmetic like crazy, but how can they do more? How, for example, can a computer do things that are intelligent or that seem to be? In part, the answer lies in the fact that the numbers stored in a computer can be thought of as a code for other things. It is true that from one perspective everything in a computer is a string of binary digits, ones and zeros, that everyone calls bits. Commonly, these binary digits are interpreted as a code for decimal digits. But from another perspective, groups of those same bits can be interpreted as characters, just as sequences of dots and dashes are interpreted as characters by people who have learned the Morse code.

Then, once it is understood that groups of bits can represent characters, it is clear that groups of characters can represent words. And groups of words can represent sentences, and groups of sentences can represent paragraphs. By more and more grouping, eventually larger and larger structures are possible. Groups of bits eventually become sections, chapters, books, and encyclopedias.

In LISP similar interpretation and grouping notions are at work, although the units go by different names.

■ In LISP, the fundamental things formed from bits are word-like objects called *atoms*.

■ Groups of atoms form *lists*. Lists themselves can be grouped together to form higher-level lists. Indeed, the ability to form hierarchical groups is of fundamental importance.

■ Atoms and lists collectively are called *symbolic expressions*. Working with them is what symbol manipulation using LISP is about. Indeed, symbol manipulation is sometimes called list processing.

A symbol-manipulation program uses symbolic expressions to remember and work with data and procedures, just as people use pencil, paper, and human language to remember and work with data and procedures. A symbol-manipulation program typically has sections that recognize particular symbolic expressions, tear old ones apart, and assemble new ones.

Here are two examples of symbolic expressions. The parentheses mark where lists begin and end. The first is a description of a structure built out of children's blocks. The second is a description of a certain university.

```
(ARCH (PARTS LINTEL POST1 POST2)
      (LINTEL MUST-BE-SUPPORTED-BY POST1)
      (LINTEL MUST-BE-SUPPORTED-BY POST2)
      (LINTEL A-KIND-OF WEDGE)
      (POST1 A-KIND-OF BRICK)
      (POST2 A-KIND-OF BRICK)
      (POST1 MUST-NOT-TOUCH POST2)
      (POST2 MUST-NOT-TOUCH POST1))

(MIT (A-KIND-OF UNIVERSITY)
     (LOCATION (CAMBRIDGE MASSACHUSETTS))
     (PHONE 253-1000)
     (SCHOOLS (ARCHITECTURE
               BUSINESS
               ENGINEERING
               HUMANITIES
               SCIENCE))
     (FOUNDER (WILLIAM BARTON ROGERS)))
```

Certainly these are not very scary. Both just describe something according to some conventions about how to arrange symbols. Here is another example, this time expressing a rule for determining whether some animal is a carnivore:

```
(RULE IDENTIFY6
      (IF (ANIMAL HAS POINTED TEETH)
          (ANIMAL HAS CLAWS)
          (ANIMAL HAS FORWARD EYES))
      (THEN (ANIMAL IS CARNIVORE)))
```

What we see is just another way of expressing the idea that an animal with pointed teeth, claws, and forward-pointing eyes is probably a carnivore. Using such a rule amounts to taking it apart, finding the conditions specified following the IF, checking to see if those pieces are on a list of believed assertions, and adding the conclusion following the THEN to a list of believed assertions. Using such a rule is an example of symbol manipulation.

Symbol Manipulation is Needed to Make Computers Intelligent

These days, there is a growing armamentarium of programs that exhibit what most people consider intelligent behavior. Nearly all of these intelligent or seemingly intelligent programs are written in LISP. Many have the potential of great practical importance. Here are some examples:

■ Expert problem solvers. One of the first LISP programs did calculus problems at the level of university freshmen. Another early program did geometric analogy problems of the sort found in intelligence tests. Since then, newer programs have diagnosed infections of the blood, understood electronic circuits, evaluated geological evidence for mineral prospecting, and invented interesting mathematics. All are written in LISP.

■ Common-sense reasoning. Much of human thinking seems to involve a small amount of reasoning using a large amount of knowledge. Representing knowledge means choosing a vocabulary of symbols and fixing some conventions for arranging them. Good representations make just the right things explicit. LISP is the language in which most research on representation is done.

■ Learning. Not much work has been done on the learning of concepts by computer, but certainly most of what has been done also rests on progress in representation. LISP again dominates.

■ Natural language interfaces. There is a growing need for programs that interact with people in English and other natural languages. Full understanding of natural languages by computer is probably a long time off, but practical systems have been built for asking questions about constrained domains ranging from moon rocks to the ships at sea to the inventory of a carpet company.

■ Education and intelligent support systems. To interact comfortably with computers, people must have computers that know what people know and how to tell them more. No one wants a long-winded explanation after they know a lot. Nor does anyone want a telegram-like explanation when just beginning. LISP-based programs are beginning to make user models by analyzing what the user does. These programs use the models to trim or elaborate explanations.

■ Speech and vision. Understanding how people hear and see has proved fantastically difficult. It seems that we do not know enough about how the physical world constrains what ends up on our ear drums and retinas. Nevertheless, progress is being made and much of it is made in LISP, even though a great deal of straight arithmetic-oriented programming is necessary. To be sure, LISP has no special advantages for arithmetic-oriented programming. But at the same time, LISP has no completely debilitating disadvantages for arithmetic either. This is surprising to some people because LISP was once molasses slow at such work.

Consequently, a person who wants to know about computer intelligence at some point needs to understand LISP if his understanding is to be complete. And there are certainly other applications, some of which are again surprising. At least the following deserve mention:

■ Word processing. EMACS is a powerful text editor. The version that runs on the MULTICS operating system was written entirely in LISP. So was the editor called ZWEI, used on the LISP machine, a modern personal computer. Similarly, a number of text justifiers, programs that arrange text on pages, have been written in LISP.

■ Symbolic mathematics. The MACSYMA system is a giant set of programs for applied mathematicians that enables them to handle algebra that would defy pencil and paper efforts.

■ Systems programming. The LISP machine is a modern personal computer programmed from top to bottom in LISP. The operating system, the user utility programs, the compilers, and the interpreters are all written in LISP with a saving in cost of one or two orders of magnitude.

Given all these examples, it is no surprise that the following is accepted by nearly everyone:

■ Symbol manipulation is an essential tool. Computer scientists and engineers must know about it.

LISP is the Right Symbol-Manipulation Language to Learn

There are too many programming languages. Fortunately, however, only a few are for symbol manipulation, and of these LISP is the most used. After LISP is understood, most of the other symbol-manipulation languages are easy to learn.

Why has LISP become the most used language for symbol manipulation, and lately, much more? There is some disagreement. All of the following arguments have adherents:

■ The interaction argument. LISP is oriented toward programming at a terminal with rapid response. All programs and all data can be displayed or altered at will.

■ The environment argument. LISP has been used by a community that needed and got the best in editing and debugging tools. For over two decades, people at the world's largest artificial intelligence centers have created sophisticated computing environments around LISP, making a combination that is unbeatable for writing big, intelligent programs.

■ The features argument. LISP was designed for symbol manipulation from the start. In fact, LISP is an acronym for list processing language. Consequently, LISP has just the right features.

■ The uniformity argument. LISP functions and LISP data have the same form. One LISP function can analyze another. One LISP function even can put together another and use it.

Happily, LISP is an easy language to learn. A few hours of study is enough to understand some amazing programs. Previous exposure to some other more common language is not necessary. Indeed such experience can be something of a handicap, for there can be a serious danger of developing a bad accent. Other languages do things differently and function-by-function translation leads to awkward constructions.

One reason LISP is easy to learn is that its syntax is extremely simple. Curiously, this came about by accident. John McCarthy, LISP's inventor, originally used a sort of old LISP that is about as hard to read as old English. At one point, however, he wished to use LISP in a context that required both the functions and the data to have the same syntactic form. The resulting form of LISP, which McCarthy intended to use only for developing a piece of mathematics, caught on and quickly became the standard.

Historically, LISP is antedated by IPL, a language developed in the 1950's at Carnegie-Mellon University by Newell, Shaw, and Simon. Having introduced many key ideas, IPL served its purpose with distinction and is now more or less extinct.

The First Part of the Book Introduces LISP

■ CHAPTER 2, Basic LISP Functions. About twenty LISP functions constitute a basic symbol-manipulation vocabulary. This chapter introduces half of them, along with the functions for doing arithmetic.

■ CHAPTER 3, Definitions, Predicates, Conditionals, and Variable Scoping. LISP is more fun when it is possible to make new functions. This chapter shows how to do this while also explaining testing functions called predicates and a way of doing things conditionally.

■ CHAPTER 4, Recursion and Iteration. Sometimes the best way for a function to solve a problem is to first break the problem up into simpler problems and then hand these off to copies of itself. In the copy, the processes of breakup and handoff may be repeated. This is called recursion. On the other hand, sometimes it is best to use explicit test-operate-test sequences. Something is repeated until a condition is met. This is called iteration.

■ CHAPTER 5, Properties, A-lists, and Arrays. There are a number of ways to attach information, always in the form of a symbolic expression, to an atom. This chapter describes three of the most popular: using atom-property-value triples, association lists, and arrays.

■ CHAPTER 6, Using Lambda Definitions. Many times it is useful to define functions that appear only once and hardly deserve a name. This chapter shows how to define such functions.

■ CHAPTER 7, Printing, Reading, and Atom Manipulation. LISP comes with READ and PRINT, two simple functions for getting data into a function and getting results out. This chapter explains them and mentions certain others for people who prefer fancy input and output.

■ CHAPTER 8, Defining Fexprs and Macros. Some functions in LISP are idiomatic in that they do nonstandard things with the symbolic expressions they are given to work on. This chapter explains how users can define such functions.

■ CHAPTER 9, List Storage, Reclamation, and Surgery. Occasionally it is useful to know how lists are actually represented. This chapter explains the box-and-arrow notation and describes certain dangerous, structure-altering functions.

■ CHAPTER 10, Examples Involving Binary Images. LISP is not limited to symbolic computation. This chapter uncovers LISP's ecumenical spirit, showing that is possible to use LISP with a style that is like that of other programming languages if one so chooses. The chapter also demonstrates the use of arrays and shows how simple objects can be identified.

■ CHAPTER 11, Examples Involving Search. Many problem-solving jobs require searching through some kind of network of places and connections. This chapter shows how to implement the most popular techniques. Sorting is also touched upon.

■ CHAPTER 12, Examples from Mathematics. There are some numeric calculations for which LISP is rather well suited, such as those involving the manipulation of sparse arrays. This chapter presents examples involving matrix multiplication and finding roots of algebraic equations.

The Second Part of the Book Demonstrates LISP's Power

■ CHAPTER 13, The Blocks World. Eventually, the time comes to get a feeling for larger systems of functions that do things that are beyond what one or two functions can do. The blocks-world system is such a collection. Its purpose is to move toy blocks from place to place, dealing with such obstacles as it finds. This chapter introduces the system, shows how it works, and establishes it as an example to be exploited in the following few chapters.

■ CHAPTER 14, Rules for Good Programming and Debugging. It is wrong to expect all functions to work the first time. The job of getting things right is a proper thing for LISP itself to help with. This chapter uses the block-world system to introduce break points, tracing, and some rules of good programming practice.

■ CHAPTER 15, Answering Questions about Goals. It is easy to add machinery to the block-world system that enables it to answer questions about its past behavior intelligently. This chapter shows how to arrange for answering questions like "How did you ...," "Why did you ...," and "When did you ...." Complex systems should be able to explain how they reached any decision that they have made.

■ CHAPTER 16, Getting Functions from Data. The proper action for a function is often determined by the type of thing it is working with. The standard way to ensure that things are handled properly is first to test for type as soon as a function is activated and then to jump to that part of the function that handles the given type. The nonstandard way is first to attach functions to the type names and then to fetch them automatically as needed. The standard way is said to be verb centered. The nonstandard way is object centered. The ideas in this chapter are relevant to the creation of object-centered functions that must grow to handle more and more situations.

- CHAPTER 17, Symbolic Pattern Matching and Simple Theorem Proving. The purpose of a matcher is to compare two similar symbolic expressions to determine if they are enough alike to say that one is an instance of another. The chapter begins by developing a simple general pattern matcher in preparation for understanding well-known classic programs like DOCTOR and STUDENT. The chapter ends with a demonstration of matching at work in a resolution theorem prover for propositional calculus.

- CHAPTER 18, Expert Problem Solving Using If-then Rules. Problem solvers have reached the point where they do all sorts of expert things like some forms of medical diagnosis and some forms of engineering design. Many of these problem solvers are based on the use of if-then rules, also known as situation-action rules or productions. This chapter shows how to implement a simple version of such a system. A rule set that enables animals to be identified from properties is used for illustration.

- CHAPTER 19, Interpreting Augmented Transition Networks. One prominent feature of LISP is that functions and the data they work on are both expressed in the form of symbolic expressions. This means that one function can treat another as data or even build up a function from scratch. This chapter introduces the idea by describing a LISP function that accepts functions given in a nonLISP, user-convenient way and follows the nonLISP function statement by statement, doing whatever the nonLISP function asks for. This is called interpreting. The particular functions that are interpreted are called augmented transition networks. They have the purpose of analyzing English sentences in preparation for answering questions or following commands.

- CHAPTER 20, Compiling Augmented Transition Networks. When a function is described in nonLISP, another option is to translate the function into LISP once and for all. This is called compiling. This chapter illuminates the difference between interpreting a function and compiling a function by introducing a compiler for augmented transition networks to compare with the interpreter of the previous chapter.

- CHAPTER 21, Program Writing Programs and Natural Language Interfaces. Translating English into formal data-base queries is an exciting use for LISP's function-writing ability. It is at the heart of many interesting natural language interfaces, including a system that answers questions using a data base of Moon rocks, a system that eases access to a large data base of information about ships, and a system that has been attached to a variety of commercial management information systems, providing English access to them. This chapter illustrates how such systems work, using a toy data base containing information about the tools in a workshop.

■ CHAPTER 22, Implementing Frames. Research has shown that there is great utility in building better tools for representing information. Representing information in packets called frames is one result of this work. In a frame system, the notion of property value is generalized, so that a property can have an ordinary value, a default value, or even a function that can compute a value when one is requested. A frame system also allows values to be inherited, as when we know that a particular person has one heart because all people do. This chapter shows how a frame system can be implemented in LISP.

■ CHAPTER 23, LISP in LISP. Often the best way to describe a procedure is to exhibit a function that is an embodiment of the procedure. English can be a poor second. This means that one good way to describe in detail how a LISP system can interpret a user's LISP functions is to exhibit the LISP interpreter as a function. Curiously, this function itself can be written in LISP, as this chapter shows.

MACLISP and INTERLISP are two principal dialects of LISP. MACLISP is the one discussed in this book. People who have access to INTERLISP but not MACLISP should note that an appendix describes the differences that are relevant to doing the exercises with the help of a computer.

Other appendices supply an index of LISP functions, give a sample of terminal interaction, and provide supplementary notes for some of the more esoteric ideas.

There are some Myths about LISP

There is no perfect computer language, and to be sure, LISP has defects. Many of the original defects have been fixed, even though some people mistakenly cite them even today. Among the most pervasive and unfortunate are the following:

■ Myth: LISP is slow at doing arithmetic. In fact this was true at one time. This historical problem has been corrected by the development of good LISP compilers. (Compilers are programs that reduce the stuff programmers produce into the primitive operations that a computer can do directly, without further decomposition.)

■ Myth: LISP is slow. In fact this also was true at one time. LISP has been used traditionally in research, where interaction is at a premium and high-speed for fully debugged production functions is less important. Making a language fast is generally more a matter of effort than it is a matter of inherent limitations.

- Myth: LISP functions are big. Actually, this is not a myth. They are. But that is only because LISP makes it possible to create big functions that know a lot.

- Myth: LISP is hard to read and debug because of all the parentheses. In fact the parentheses problem goes away as soon as a person learns to put things down on the page properly or has a editing function do it for him. No one finds the following to be particularly clear:

```
(DEFUN FIBONACCI (N) (COND ((ZEROP N) 1) ((EQUAL N 1) 1) (T (PLUS
(FIBONACCI (DIFFERENCE N 1)) (FIBONACCI (DIFFERENCE N 2))))))
```

But the equivalent, formatted version, is fine after a little experience:

```
(DEFUN FIBONACCI (N)
       (COND ((ZEROP N) 1)
             ((EQUAL N 1) 1)
             (T (PLUS (FIBONACCI (DIFFERENCE N 1))
                      (FIBONACCI (DIFFERENCE N 2))))))
```

LISP-oriented editors quickly convert the ugly version into the pretty one. The process is called prettyprinting.

- Myth: LISP is hard to learn. In fact many find LISP easy to learn. LISP earned its bad reputation by being in the company of some hard-to-read books in its youth.

Summary

- Symbol manipulation is like working with words and sentences.

- Symbol manipulation is needed to make computers intelligent.

- LISP is the right symbol-manipulation language to learn.

- LISP is easy to learn.

- The first part of the book introduces LISP.

- The second part of the book demonstrates LISP's power.

- There are some myths about LISP.

References

Slagle [1963] did early work on expert problem solving with his program for symbolic integration. Moses [1966] subsequently wrote a program that performed as well as most experts. Later still, methods were devised that enable integration of all integrable expressions composed of elementary functions. Work on integration was instrumental in promoting the development of systems for symbolic mathematics, as was the thesis of Martin [1967]. For more information on such systems, see papers by Manove [1965], Hearn [1971a, 1971b], Moses [1974], and The Mathlab Group [1977].

Evans [1962] also did early work on expert problem solving with his program for geometric analogy problems. For the particular expert problem solving involved in medicine, see Shortliffe [1976], Szolovits and Pauker [1978], and Weiss, Kulikowski, Amarel, and Safir [1978]. Others have concentrated on the expert problem solving involved in programming. See Green and Barstow [1978] and Bauer [1979]. For still further reading on expert problem solving, see Buchanan and Feigenbaum [1978], Davis [1979a], Davis, Buchanan, and Shortliffe [1977], Duda et al. [1978], Hart, Duda, and Einaudi [1979], Sacerdoti [1974], and Stallman and Sussman [1977]. Goldstein has studied the problem of modeling human problem solving skills [1978].

For work on learning, see Hedrick [1976], Lenat [1976, 1977], Waterman [1970], and Winston [1970, 1978, 1979].

For reading on natural language, look at Bobrow et al. [1977], Bruce [1975], Kaplan [1972], Schank and Rieger [1974], Winograd [1972], and Woods, Kaplan and Nash-Webber [1972]. For work concentrating on natural language interfaces to data bases, see Codd [1974], Grishman and Hirschman [1978], Harris [1977], Hendrix et al. [1978], Minker, Fishman, and McSkimin [1972], and Waltz [1978].

For reading on theorem proving, start with Bledsoe [1971], Chang and Slagle [1979], Fikes and Nilsson [1971], Fikes, Hart, and Nilsson [1972], Luckham and Nilsson [1971], Robinson [1965], Siklossy and Roach [1975], and Wang [1960].

For looking at the history of LISP, McCarthy [1960], and McCarthy et al. [1962] are musts. White [1979] gives a good account of the development of MACLISP and the relation to other dialects. MACLISP itself is documented in Samson [1966], White [1967, 1970], Moon [1974], and Greenberg [1976]. Other, older LISP implementations are described in Blair [1970], Bobrow [1966], Deutsch and Berkeley [1964], Deutsch and Lampson [1965], Hart and Evans [1964], Hearn [1969], Kameny [1965], Martin and Hart [1963], McCarthy et al. [1960], Moses and Fenichel [1966], Saunders [1964], and Smith [1970]. A few recent implementations are covered by Chaitin [1976], Griss and Swanson [1977], LeFaivre [1978], Reboh and Sacerdoti [1973], Urmi [1976a], and White [1978].

Other symbol manipulation languages, some embedded in LISP, are covered in Bobrow [1963, 1974], Burstall [1971], Galley and Pfister [1975], Johnson and Rosin [1965], McDermott and Sussman [1974], Pratt [1976], Roberts and Goldstein [1977a, 1977b], Rulifson, Derken, and Waldinger [1972], Sussman, Winograd, and Charniak [1971], Sussman and McDermott [1972], Warren and Pereira [1977], and

Weizenbaum [1963]. For information on IPL see Newell [1961]. Other discussions of list processing may be found in Bobrow [1964], and Foster [1967].

There are a number of useful books and papers on LISP and its theoretical foundations including the following: Berkeley and Bobrow [1964], Church [1941], Kleene [1950], Landin [1964], McCarthy [1978], Moore [1976], Moses [1970], Sandewall [1978], Steele and Sussman [1978], and White [1977a, 1977b]. Some of the important implementation issues are covered in Baker and Hewitt [1977], Baker [1978a, 1978b, 1979], Bawden et al. [1977], Bobrow and Murphy [1967], Bobrow and Wegbreit [1973], Bobrow and Clark [1979], Cheney [1970], Fenichel and Yochelson [1969], Fenichel [1970], Greenblatt [1974], Greenblatt et al. [1979], Greussay [1976], Hart [1963], Knight et al. [1979], Kung and Song [1977], Steele [1977a, 1977b, 1977c], and Urmi [1976b].

For arguments in favor of LISP as a programming language, see the papers by Pratt [1979] and Allen [1979]. For details about real time editors written in LISP, see Greenberg [1979] and Weinreb [1979].

There are definitive manuals for the principle LISP dialects. The following are particularly noteworthy: MACLISP, Moon [1974]; LISP Machine LISP, Weinreb and Moon [1978]; Franz LISP, Foderaro [1979]; INTERLISP, Teitelman [1975]; INTERLISP/370, Urmi [1976a]; LISP/370, Blair [1979]; Stanford LISP, Quam and Diffie [1972]; UCI LISP, Meehan [1979]; and UNIVAC 1108 LISP, Norman [1978]. A technical report by Ericson [1979] describes software aids for translating from MACLISP to INTERLISP.

There are a number of LISP textbooks. Allen's book [1978] is an advanced book particularly good for its use of LISP as a context for a discussion of certain theoretical issues in modern coputer science. It is a must for anyone who wants to thoroughly understand a LISP implementation or to create one. Siklossy's book [1976] is a recent textbook with many good points, competing with this one. Greenberg's notes [1976] provide a brief, well thought out, data structure oriented introduction. Weissman's book [1967] is a good, but aging, text. It stresses two notions purposely treated more briefly here, namely dotted pairs and EVALQUOTE. We avoid the dotted-pair notation because it is a source of great confusion for beginners. We omit EVALQUOTE because its use is now obsolete. Other books include Friedman [1974], Maurer [1973], Ribbens [1970], and Shapiro [1979]. Still other books on related topics, include Organick, Forsythe, and Plummer [1978], and Pratt [1975].

Books on artificial intelligence include Bobrow and Collins [1975], Boden [1977], Feigenbaum and Feldman [1963], Findler and Meltzer [1971], Hunt [1975], Jackson [1974], McCorduck [1979], Minsky [1968], Nilsson [1971, 1980], Raphael [1976], Schank [1973], Slagle [1971], Shapiro [1979], Wilks and Charniak [1976], and Winston [1977].

2
BASIC
LISP
FUNCTIONS

The purpose of this chapter is to introduce LISP's basic symbol-manipulation functions. To do this, some functions are introduced that work on numbers and others are introduced that work on lists. The list-oriented functions extract parts of lists and build new lists.

LISP Means Symbol Manipulation

As with other computer languages, the best way to learn LISP is bravely, jumping right into interesting programs. We will therefore look occasionally at things that will not be completely understood with a view toward moving as quickly as possible into exciting applications.

To get started, imagine being seated in front of a computer terminal. You begin as if engaging in a conversation, with LISP tossing back results in response to typed input. Suppose, for example, that you would like some help adding numbers. The proper incantation would be this:

```
(PLUS 3.14 2.71)
```

LISP would agreeably respond:

```
5.85
```

This is a simple example of LISP's ability to handle arithmetic. Elementary examples of symbol manipulation are equally straightforward. Suppose, for example, that we are interested in keeping track of some facts needed in connection with understanding a children's story about, say, a robot. It might well be important to remember that certain children are friends of the robot. Typically a name is required to denote such a group, and the name FRIENDS will do as well as any other. If Dick and Jane and Sally are friends of the robot, this fact could be remembered by typing this line:

```
(SET 'FRIENDS '(DICK JANE SALLY))
```

SET associates (DICK JANE SALLY) with FRIENDS. Do not worry about the quote marks that appear. They will be explained later.

Typing FRIENDS now causes the list of friends to be typed in response:

```
FRIENDS
 (DICK JANE SALLY)
```

There could be a similar list established for enemies:

```
(SET 'ENEMIES '(TROLL GRINCH GHOST))
```

Because friends and enemies tend to be dynamic categories in children's worlds, it is often necessary to change the category a particular individual is in. The ghost ceases to be an enemy and becomes a friend after typing two lines like this:

```
(SET 'ENEMIES (DELETE 'GHOST ENEMIES))
```

```
(SET 'FRIENDS (CONS 'GHOST FRIENDS))
```

The first line changes the remembered list of enemies to what it was minus the entry GHOST. The second line would be simpler if CONS were replaced by something more mnemonic like ADD, but we are stuck with historical convention. In any event, FRIENDS and ENEMIES have been changed such that we now get properly altered responses:

```
ENEMIES
 (TROLL GRINCH)
```

```
FRIENDS
 (GHOST DICK JANE SALLY)
```

Later we will see how to write a program that does the same job. In particular we will understand how the following creates a program named NEWFRIEND for changing a person from an enemy into a friend:

```
(DEFUN NEWFRIEND (NAME)
      (SET 'ENEMIES (DELETE NAME ENEMIES))
      (SET 'FRIENDS (CONS NAME FRIENDS)))
```

With NEWFRIEND, the previous elevation of the status of GHOST can be achieved more simply by typing only this:

```
(NEWFRIEND 'GHOST)
```

LISP Programs and Data Are Constructed out of S-expressions

Some important points should be noted. First, when left and right parentheses surround something, we call the result a list and speak of its elements. In our very first example, the list (PLUS 3.14 2.71) has three elements, PLUS, 3.14, and 2.71.

Note the peculiar location of the function PLUS, standing strangely before the two things to be added rather than between them as in ordinary arithmetic notation. In LISP the *function* to be performed is always given first, followed then by the things that the function is to work with, the *arguments*. Thus 3.14 and 2.71 are the arguments given to the function PLUS.

This so-called prefix notation facilitates uniformity and because the function name is always in the same place no matter how many arguments are involved.

Let us look at more examples. We will stick to arithmetic for the moment since arithmetic is initially more familiar to most people than symbol manipulation is. LISP's responses are indented by two spaces in order to distinguish them from the user's typed input:

```
(DIFFERENCE 3.14 2.71)
  0.43

(TIMES 9 3)
  27

(QUOTIENT 9 3)
  3

(MAX 2 4 3)
  4

(MIN 2 4 3)
  2

(ADD1 6)
  7

(SUB1 6)
  5
```

```
(SQRT 4.0)
  2.0

(EXPT 2 3)
  8

(MINUS 8)
  -8

(MINUS -8)
  8

(ABS 5)
  5

(ABS -5)
  5
```

Note that MAX selects the largest of the numbers given as arguments. As with MAX, the functions MIN, PLUS, TIMES can work on more than two arguments. DIFFERENCE will keep on subtracting and QUOTIENT will keep on dividing when given more than two arguments. There is never any confusion because the end of the argument sequence is signaled clearly by the right parenthesis. SQRT, of course, takes the square root, and ABS, the absolute value. EXPT calculates powers. SQRT, MINUS, ADD1, SUB1, and ABS all deal with a single argument.

Now consider this expression, in which PLUS is followed by something other than raw numbers:

```
(PLUS (TIMES 2 2) (QUOTIENT 2 2))
```

If we think of this as directions for something to do, it is easy to see that the subexpression (TIMES 2 2) evaluates to 4, (QUOTIENT 2 2) evaluates to 1, and these results fed in turn to PLUS, give 5 as the result. But if the whole expression is viewed as a kind of list, then we see that PLUS is the first element, the entire expression (TIMES 2 2) is the second element, and (QUOTIENT 2 2) is the third. Thus lists themselves can be elements of other lists. Said another way, we permit lists in which individual elements are lists themselves. In part the representational power of LISP derives from this ability to build nested structures out of lists.

Things like PLUS and 3.14, which have obvious meaning, as well as things like FOO, B27, and 123XYZ, are called atoms. Atoms that are not numbers are called *symbolic atoms*.

■ Both atoms and lists are often called *s-expressions*, *s* being short for symbolic. S-expressions are the *data objects* manipulated by LISP.

Problems

Problem 2-1: Each of the following things may be an atom, a list, an s-expression, some combination, or a malformed expression. Identify each accordingly.

ATOM

(THIS IS AN ATOM)

(THIS IS AN S-EXPRESSION)

((A B) (C D))

3

(3)

(LIST 3)

(QUOTIENT (ADD1 3) (SUB1 3))

)(

((()))

(() ())

((())

())(

((ABC

Problem 2-2: Evaluate the following s-expressions:

(QUOTIENT (ADD1 3) (SUB1 3))

(TIMES (MAX 3 4 5) (MIN 3 4 5))

(MIN (MAX 3 1 4) (MAX 2 7 1))

LISP Handles Both Fixed and Floating Numbers

It would be diversionary to discuss at length the difference between the so-called *fixed-point* and *floating-point* numbers. Like many other programming languages LISP can handle both. Let it suffice to say that fixed-point numbers are used to represent integers, while floating-point numbers are used to represent reals. Programming beginners can ignore the difference for the moment. Others should know that FLOAT converts fixed-point numbers into floating-point ones, while FIX goes the other way, producing the largest integer that is less than or equal to its argument. Further details are given in Note 1 of Appendix 4.

We can now summarize the relationships between the various types of objects manipulated by LISP. This is done graphically in figure 2-1.

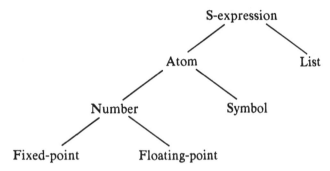

Figure 2-1: The relationships between various types of objects in LISP. An s-expression can be a list or an atom; an atom can be a symbol or a number; a number can be floating-point or fixed-point.

CAR and CDR Take Lists Apart

Examples from arithmetic are simple, but arithmetic does not expose the talent of LISP for manipulating s-expressions. Suppose we have an s-expression like (FAST COMPUTERS ARE NICE). We might like to chip off the first element leaving (COMPUTERS ARE NICE), or we might like to insert a new first element producing something like (BIG FAST COMPUTERS ARE NICE). It is time to look at such manipulations starting with basic techniques for dissecting and constructing lists. In particular we must understand the functions CAR, CDR, APPEND, LIST, and CONS. A regrettable historical convention has left two of these five key functions terribly nonmnemonic — their meaning simply has to be memorized.

Some examples will help explain how the basic CAR and CDR functions work. Again, do not worry about the quote marks that appear. They will be explained soon. To work. CAR returns the first element in a list:

```
(CAR '(FAST COMPUTERS ARE NICE))
    FAST

(CAR '(A B C))
    A
```

In the next example the argument given to CAR is the two-element list ((A B) C). The first element is itself a list, (A B), and being the first element of the argument, (A B) is returned by CAR.

```
(CAR '((A  B) C))
    (A B)
```

CDR does the complementary thing. It returns a list containing all but the first element.

```
(CDR '(FAST COMPUTERS ARE NICE))
    (COMPUTERS ARE NICE)

(CDR '(A B C))
    (B C)

(CDR '((A B) C))
    (C)
```

Note that CDR, unlike CAR, always returns a list. Remembering the following diagram may help keep the asymmetry of CAR and CDR straight:

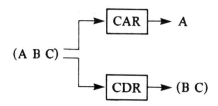

Also note that when CDR is applied to a list with only one element, it returns the *empty list*, sometimes denoted by ().

Evaluation is often Purposely Inhibited by Quoting

Now it is time to understand those quote marks that have been appearing. We will use the fact that CAR and CDR operations can be nested together just like the arithmetic functions. To pick out the second element of some list, the first function to use is CDR and the second is CAR. Thus if we want the second element of (A B C), it might seem reasonable to write this:

```
(CAR (CDR (A B C)))
```

There is a problem, however. We want CDR to take (A B C) and give back (B C). Then CAR would certainly return B, the second element in the original list. But how is LISP to know where the specification of what to do leaves off and the data to be manipulated begins? Look at the embedded list:

```
(A B C)
```

LISP might legitimately think that A is some sort of function, perhaps one defined by the user. Similarly, the following s-expression is certainly a list:

```
(CDR (A B C))
```

And its first element is surely CDR! Thus the following expression could well result in an answer of CDR:

```
(CAR (CDR (A B C)))
```

How far should the evaluation process go into an s-expression? LISP needs help in making this decision. The user specifies where to stop evaluation by supplying an evaluation-inhibiting signal in the form of a quote character, '. Thus the following expression returns B:

```
(CAR (CDR '(A B C)))
```

B is returned because the quote mark prevents LISP from wading in and thinking of (A B C) as an s-expression in which A is a function to be applied to B and C. Instead, (A B C) is given to CDR which then hands (B C) to CAR resulting finally in just plain B.

Moving   the   quote   mark   changes   the   result.   If   we   type (CAR '(CDR (A B C))), then LISP does not try to take the CDR of anything but simply gives the s-expression (CDR (A B C)) to CAR as a list to work on, resulting in CDR since CDR is the first element.

Leaving out the quote mark altogether would result in an effort to use A as a function. There is no function supplied by LISP and if none had been defined by the user, LISP would report a so-called undefined function error.

■ It is important to know that the scope of the quoting mechanism is exactly the immediately following s-expression. A quote in front of a list prevents any attempt at evaluating the list.

Sometimes it is useful to know about another, older way to stop evaluation. The s-expression to be protected against evaluation is simply bracketed on the left by a left parenthesis followed by the atom QUOTE and on the right by a matching right parenthesis. Thus the following stops evaluation of the list (A B C):

```
(QUOTE (A B C))
  (A B C)

(CAR (CDR (QUOTE A B C)))
  B
```

Note then that ' (A B C) is equivalent to (QUOTE (A B C)).

Problems

Problem 2-3: Evaluate the following s-expressions:

```
(CAR '(P H W))

(CDR '(B K P H))

(CAR '((A B) (C D)))

(CDR '((A B) (C D)))

(CAR (CDR '((A B) (C D))))

(CDR (CAR '((A B) (C D))))

(CDR (CAR (CDR '((A B) (C D)))))

(CAR (CDR (CAR '((A B) (C D)))))
```

Problem 2-4: Evaluate the following s-expressions:

```
(CAR (CDR (CAR (CDR '((A B) (C D) (E F))))))

(CAR (CAR (CDR (CDR '((A B) (C D) (E F))))))

(CAR (CAR (CDR '(CDR ((A B) (C D) (E F))))))
```

```
(CAR (CAR '(CDR (CDR ((A B) (C D) (E F))))))

(CAR '(CAR (CDR (CDR ((A B) (C D) (E F))))))

'(CAR (CAR (CDR (CDR ((A B) (C D) (E F))))))
```

Problem 2-5: Write sequences of CARs and CDRs that will pick the atom PEAR out of the following s-expression:

```
(APPLE ORANGE PEAR GRAPEFRUIT)

((APPLE ORANGE) (PEAR GRAPEFRUIT))

(((APPLE) (ORANGE) (PEAR) (GRAPEFRUIT)))

(APPLE (ORANGE) ((PEAR)) (((GRAPEFRUIT))))

((((APPLE))) ((ORANGE)) (PEAR) GRAPEFRUIT)

((((APPLE) ORANGE) PEAR) GRAPEFRUIT)
```

Composing CARs and CDRs Makes Programming Easier

When many CARs and CDRs are needed to dig out some item from deep inside an s-expression, it is usually convenient to substitute a composite function of the form CxR, CxxR, CxxxR, or CxxxxR. Each x is either an A, signifying CAR, or D, signifying CDR. Thus (CADR '(A B C)) is completely equivalent to (CAR (CDR '(A B C))).

Atoms Have Values

So far we have seen how symbolic structures can be taken apart by evaluating lists that begin with CAR or CDR. We have also seen how arithmetic can be done by evaluating lists that begin with PLUS, DIFFERENCE, and other similar functions. Indeed it seems like LISP's goal is always to evaluate something and return a value. This is true for atoms as well as lists. Suppose we type a the name of an atom, followed by a space, and wait for LISP to respond:

X

On seeing X, LISP tries to return a value for it, just as it would if some s-expression like (PLUS 3 4) were typed. But for an atom, the *value* is something looked up somewhere, rather than the result of some computation as when dealing with lists.

The value of a symbolic atom is established by a special function, SET. It causes the value of its second argument to become the value of the first argument. Typing (SET 'L ' (A B)) results in a value of (A B) for the expression. But more importantly, there is a side effect because (A B) becomes the value of L. If we now type L, we see that (A B) comes back:

```
L
  (A B)
```

Thus the expression (SET 'L ' (A B)) is executed mainly for the side effect of giving a value to the atom L.

Now since the value of L is (A B), L can be used in working through some examples of the basic list manipulating functions. These illustrate that LISP seeks out the value of atoms not only when they are typed in by themselves, but also when the atoms appear as arguments to functions.

```
L
  (A B)

'L
  L

(CAR L)
  A

(CAR 'L)
  ERROR

(CDR L)
  (B)

(CDR 'L)
  ERROR
```

Note that both CAR and CDR announce an error if asked to work on an atom. Both expect a list as their argument and both work only when they get one.

■ All numbers are treated specially in that the value of a number is just the number itself.

APPEND, LIST, and CONS Construct Lists

While CAR and CDR take things apart, APPEND, LIST, and CONS put them together. APPEND strings together the elements of all lists supplied as arguments:

```
(SET 'L '(A B))
  (A B)

(APPEND L L)
  (A B A B)

(APPEND L L L)
  (A B A B A B)

(APPEND '(A) '() '(B) '())
  (A B)

(APPEND 'L L)
  ERROR
```

Be sure to understand that APPEND runs the elements of its arguments together, but does nothing to those elements themselves. Note that the value returned in the following example is ((A) (B) (C) (D)), not (A B C D):

```
(APPEND '((A) (B)) '((C) (D)))
  ((A) (B) (C) (D))
```

LIST does not run things together like APPEND does. Instead, it makes a list out of its arguments. Each argument becomes an element of the new list.

```
(LIST L L)
  ((A B) (A B))

(LIST L L L)
  ((A B) (A B) (A B))

(LIST 'L L)
  (L (A B))

(LIST '((A) (B)) '((C) (D)))
  (((A) (B)) ((C) (D)))
```

CONS takes a list and inserts a new first element. CONS is a mnemonic for list constructor.

■ Let us adopt a convention by which the words between angle brackets are taken as descriptions of what should appear in the position occupied.

Then the CONS function can be described as follows:

```
(CONS <new first element> <some list>)
```

Thus we have these:

```
(CAR (CONS 'A '(B C)))
  A

(CDR (CONS 'A '(B C)))
  (B C)
```

And working again with L, whose value was established to be (A B), we have a sort of do-nothing combination of CONS, CAR, and CDR:

```
L
  (A B)

(CONS (CAR L) (CDR L))
  (A B)
```

Representing this inverse relationship between CONS and the pair CAR and CDR in a diagram, we have this:

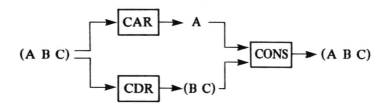

Note that (CONS L '(C D)) yields the result ((A B) C D) in which the list (A B) has become the first element of a list that was just (C D) before. Study how APPEND, LIST, and CONS differ:

```
(APPEND '(A B) '(C D))
  (A B C D)

(LIST '(A B) '(C D))
  ((A B) (C D))
```

```
(CONS '(A B) '(C D))
  ((A B) C D)

(APPEND L L)
  (A B A B)

(LIST L L)
  ((A B) (A B))

(CONS L L)
  ((A B) A B)

(APPEND 'L L)
  ERROR

(LIST 'L L)
  (L (A B))

(CONS 'L L)
  (L A B)
```

Problems

Problem 2-6: Evaluate the following s-expressions in the order given:

```
(SET 'TOOLS (LIST 'HAMMER 'SCREWDRIVER))

(CONS 'PLIERS TOOLS)

TOOLS

(SET 'TOOLS (CONS 'PLIERS TOOLS))

TOOLS

(APPEND '(SAW WRENCH) TOOLS)

TOOLS

(SET 'TOOLS (APPEND '(SAW WRENCH) TOOLS))

TOOLS
```

LENGTH, REVERSE, SUBST, and LAST Round out a Basic Repertoire

LENGTH counts the number of elements in a list. REVERSE turns a list around. Both consider what they get to be a list of elements, not caring whether the elements are atoms or lists. Often they are used on lists that have lists as elements, but they do nothing with the insides of those elements. Assume, in the following examples, that the value of L is still (A B).

```
(LENGTH '(A B))
  2

(LENGTH '((A B) (C D)))
  2

(LENGTH L)
  2

(LENGTH (APPEND L L))
  4

(REVERSE '(A B))
  (B A)

(REVERSE '((A B) (C D)))
  ((C D) (A B))

(REVERSE L)
  (B A)

(REVERSE (APPEND L L))
  (B A B A)
```

SUBST takes three arguments, one of which is an s-expression in which occurences of a specified s-expression are to be replaced. The first argument is the new s-expression to be substituted in; the second is the s-expression to be substituted for; and the third is the s-expression to work on:

```
(SUBST <new s-expression> <old s-expression> <s-expression to work on>)
```

Study the following, in which the s-expressions to be substituted for are atoms:

```
(SUBST 'A 'B '(A B C))
  (A A C)
```

```
(SUBST 'B 'A '(A B C))
  (B B C)

(SUBST 'A 'X (SUBST 'B 'Y '(SQRT (PLUS (TIMES X X) (TIMES Y Y)))))
  (SQRT (PLUS (TIMES A A) (TIMES B B)))
```

LAST returns a list which contains only the last element of the list given as the argument:

```
(LAST '(A B C))
  (C)

(LAST '((A B) (C D)))
  ((C D))

(LAST 'A)
  ERROR
```

Problems

Problem 2-7: Evaluate the following s-expressions:

```
(LENGTH '(PLATO SOCRATES ARISTOTLE))

(LENGTH '((PLATO) (SOCRATES) (ARISTOTLE)))

(LENGTH '((PLATO SOCRATES ARISTOTLE)))

(REVERSE '(PLATO SOCRATES ARISTOTLE))

(REVERSE '((PLATO) (SOCRATES) (ARISTOTLE)))

(REVERSE '((PLATO SOCRATES ARISTOTLE)))
```

Problem 2-8: Evaluate the following s-expressions:

```
(LENGTH '((CAR CHEVROLET) (DRINK COKE) (CEREAL WHEATIES)))

(REVERSE '((CAR CHEVROLET) (DRINK COKE) (CEREAL WHEATIES)))

(APPEND '((CAR CHEVROLET) (DRINK COKE))
        (REVERSE '((CAR CHEVROLET) (DRINK COKE))))
```

Problem 2-9: Evaluate the following s-expressions:

(SUBST 'OUT 'IN '(SHORT SKIRTS ARE IN))

(SUBST 'IN 'OUT '(SHORT SKIRTS ARE IN))

(LAST '(SHORT SKIRTS ARE IN))

The Interpreter Evaluates S-expressions

When an expression is typed by a LISP user, it is automatically handed to the function EVAL. The diagram in figure 2-2 describes how this function works.

Note, in particular, that some functions get special handling. SETQ is such a function because it handles its arguments in a nonstandard way: SETQ is like SET except that SETQ makes no attempt to evaluate the first argument. SETQ is much more popular than SET.

(SETQ ZERO 0)
    0

Sometimes the pairs of arguments to several SETQs are run together and given to a single SETQ. The odd numbered arguments are not evaluated but the even ones are, as would be expected. Thus one SETQ can do the work that would otherwise require many:

(SETQ ZERO 0 ONE 1 TWO 2 THREE 3 FOUR 4
        FIVE 5 SIX 6 SEVEN 7 EIGHT 8 NINE 9)
     9

ZERO
    0

NINE
    9

EVAL Causes Extra Evaluation

Note that one can use the function EVAL explicitly to call for another round of evaluation beyond the one already employed to evaluate the arguments of a function. The following example will illustrate:

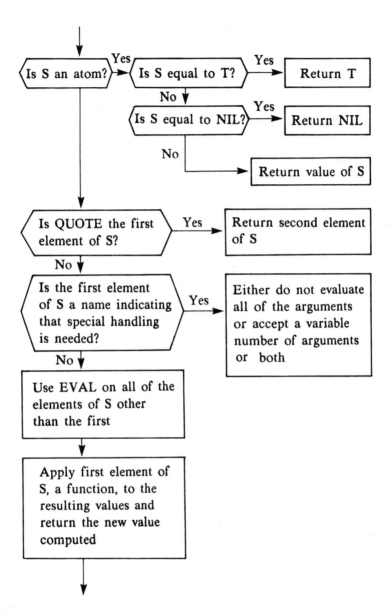

Figure 2-2: Definition of EVAL. This version assumes quoting is done by using (QUOTE <s-expression>) rather than '<s-expression>.

```
(SETQ A 'B)
  B

(SETQ B 'C)
  C

A
  B

B
  C

(EVAL A)
  C
```

The atom A is first evaluated because it is the unquoted argument to a function. The result is then evaluated because the function is EVAL. EVAL causes whatever the value is to be evaluated!

Later on we shall see that EVAL will be used when a program-writing program needs to use what it has written.

Problems

Problem 2-10: Evaluate the following s-expressions in the order given:

```
(SETQ METHOD1 'PLUS)

(SETQ METHOD2 'DIFFERENCE)

(SETQ METHOD METHOD1)

METHOD

(EVAL METHOD)

(SETQ METHOD 'METHOD1)

METHOD

(EVAL METHOD)

(EVAL (EVAL '(QUOTE METHOD)))
```

Summary

■ LISP means symbol manipulation.

■ LISP programs and data are constructed out of s-expressions.

■ LISP handles both fixed and floating numbers.

■ CAR and CDR take lists apart.

■ Evaluation is often purposely inhibited by quoting.

■ Composing CARs and CDRs makes programming easier.

■ Atoms have values.

■ APPEND, LIST, and CONS construct lists.

■ LENGTH, REVERSE, SUBST, and LAST round out a basic repertoire.

■ The interpreter evaluates s-expressions.

■ EVAL causes extra evaluation.

3
DEFINITIONS
PREDICATES
CONDITIONALS
AND
SCOPING

The first purpose of this chapter is to explain how you can create your own functions. The second purpose is to show how tests make it possible to do things conditionally.

Caution: the words *procedure, function,* and *program* will be used throughout this book. For our purpose, it is not necessary to be precise about the differences. Generally speaking, though, a *procedure* is a recipe for action. A *function* is a kind of procedure for which it is convenient to think in terms of an output called the value and inputs called the arguments. Mathematical procedures, in particular, are often called functions. A *program* is an embodiment of a procedure in a particular programming language.

DEFUN Enables a User to Make New Functions

We now have some ingredients. Let us see how they can be combined into new functions using DEFUN. It has the following syntax:

```
(DEFUN <function name>
       (<parameter 1>  <parameter 2> ... <parameter n>)
       <process description>)
```

As before, the angle brackets delineate descriptions of things (the descriptions may denote atoms, lists, or even fragments as appropriate).

DEFUN does not evaluate its arguments. It just looks at them and establishes a function definition, which can later be referred to by having the function name appear as the first element of a list to be evaluated. The function name must be a symbolic atom. When DEFUN is used, like any function, it gives back a value.

The value DEFUN gives back is the function name, but this is of little consequence since the main purpose of DEFUN is to establish a definition, not to return some useful value.

The value a function gives back when used is called the *value returned*. Anything a function has done that persists after it returns its value is called a *side effect*. DEFUN and SETQ both have side effects. The side effect of DEFUN is to set up a function definition. The side effect of SETQ is to give a value to an atom.

The list following the function name is called the function's *parameter list*. Each parameter is a symbolic atom which may appear in the <process description> part of the definition. Its value is determined by the value of one of the arguments when the function is called.

Let us consider an example immediately. Using DEFUN it is easy to define a function that converts temperatures given in degrees Fahrenheit to degrees Celsius:

```
(DEFUN F-TO-C (TEMP)
       (QUOTIENT (DIFFERENCE TEMP 32) 1.8))
  F-TO-C
```

When F-TO-C is used, it appears as the first element in a two-element list. The second element is F-TO-C's argument. After the argument is evaluated, it becomes the temporary value of the function's *parameter*. In this case, TEMP is the parameter, and it is given the value of the argument while F-TO-C is being evaluated. It is as if the operations shown in figure 3-1 are carried out.

Suppose, for example, that the value of SUPER-HOT is 100. Then consider this:

```
(F-TO-C SUPER-HOT)
```

To evaluate this expression, SUPER-HOT is evaluated, handing 100 to the function F-TO-C. On entry to F-TO-C, 100 becomes the temporary value of TEMP. Consequently when the body of the function is evaluated, it is as if the following were evaluated:

```
(QUOTIENT (DIFFERENCE 100 32) 1.8)
```

The value returned is 37.77. If TEMP had a value before F-TO-C was evaluated, that value is restored. If TEMP had no value before F-TO-C was evaluated, it has no value afterward either.

■ Sometimes several functions use the same parameter. If one such function calls another, which calls another, and so on, it is necessary for LISP to keep track of several values of the common parameter. This makes it possible to restore the parameter's values properly as the function evaluations are completed later.

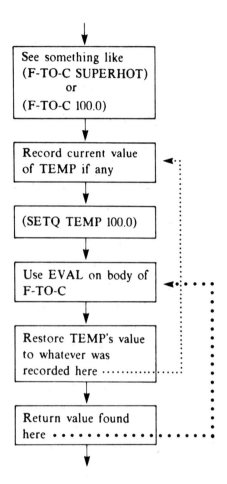

Figure 3-1: When entering a function, the parameters receive values which are used in the evaluation of the body. The old values of these parameters are saved so that they can be restored when leaving.

Now consider another example, this time involving a function that does a symbolic computation, rather than a numerical one. This new function exchanges the first and second elements of a two-element list:

```
(DEFUN EXCHANGE (PAIR)
       (LIST (CADR PAIR) (CAR PAIR)))                    ;Reverse elements.
    EXCHANGE
```

Note the so-called *comment*. LISP totally ignores semicolons and anything that appears after them on the same line. This makes it possible to annotate programs without interfering with their operation. Liberal use of comments is considered good programming practice.

To see how EXCHANGE works, suppose the value of SINNERS is (ADAM EVE). Then to evaluate (EXCHANGE SINNERS), the first thing LISP does is evaluate the argument, SINNERS. The value of SINNERS then becomes the temporary value of PAIR while EXCHANGE is doing its job. Consequently, (CADR PAIR) is EVE, (CAR PAIR) is ADAM, and the following is evident:

```
(EXCHANGE SINNERS)
   (EVE ADAM)
```

The next example introduces a function with two parameters, rather than just one. Its purpose is to compute percentage. More specifically, the value returned is to be the percentage by which the second argument given to the function is greater than the first.

```
(DEFUN INCREASE (X Y)
         (QUOTIENT (TIMES 100.0 (DIFFERENCE Y X)) X))     ;Nested operations.
   INCREASE

(INCREASE 10.0 15.0)
   50.0
```

In the example, the temporary value of X becomes 10.0 on entry, and the temporary value of Y becomes 15.0. Note that there is never any confusion about how to match X and Y with 10.0 and 15.0 — LISP knows the correct way to match them up because DEFUN's parameter list specifies the order in which parameters are to be paired with incoming arguments.

Finally, note that a function definition can employ any number of s-expressions. The last one always determines the value returned. The others therefore are useful only in that they cause some side effect, as in this altered definition of F-TO-C:

```
(DEFUN F-TO-C (TEMP)
         (SETQ TEMP (DIFFERENCE TEMP 32))             ;Subtract.
         (QUOTIENT TEMP 1.8))                         ;Divide.
```

In this second version, TEMP is used as an input parameter and as a temporary anchor for the difference between the input and 32. The DEFUN creates a program that specifies two sequential steps.

Note that one can build up a set of functions incrementally. Each can be entered and tested in turn. If a function is found to be faulty, it can be replaced right away by simply using DEFUN again.

Problems

Problem 3-1: Some people are annoyed by the nonmnemonic character of the critical functions CAR, CDR, and CONS. Define new functions FIRST, REST, and INSERT that do the same things. Note that SECOND, THIRD, and similar functions are equally easy to create.

Problem 3-2: Define ROTATE-L, a function that takes a list as its argument and returns a new list in which the former first element becomes the last. The following illustrates:

```
(ROTATE-L '(A B C))
  (B C A)

(ROTATE-L (ROTATE-L '(A B C))
  (C A B)
```

Problem 3-3: Define ROTATE-R. It is to be like ROTATE-L except that it is to rotate in the other direction.

Problem 3-4: A palindrome is a list that has the same sequence of elements when read from right to left that it does when read from left to right. Define PALINDROMIZE such that it takes a list as its argument and returns a palindrome that is twice as long.

Problem 3-5: When converting between degrees Fahrenheit and degrees Celsius, it is useful to note that —40 Fahrenheit equals —40 Celsius. This observation makes for the following symmetric conversion formulas:

$$C = (F + 40) / 1.8 - 40$$
$$F = (C + 40) * 1.8 - 40$$

Define conversion functions, F-TO-C and C-TO-F, using these formulas.

Problem 3-6: Define ROOTS, a function with three parameters, A, B, and C. ROOTS is to return a list of the two roots of the polynomial $ax^2 + bx + c$, using this formula:

$$x = [-b \pm (b^2 - 4ac)^{1/2}] / (2a)$$

Assume that the roots are real.

A Predicate Is a Function that Returns T or NIL

More complicated definitions require the use of functions called predicates. A *predicate* is a function that returns one of two special atoms, T or NIL. These values of T and NIL correspond to logical true and false.

■   Note that T and NIL are special atoms in that their values are preset to T and NIL. That is, the value of T is T and the value of NIL is NIL.

Consider ATOM, for example. ATOM is a predicate that tests its argument to see if it is an atom. To facilitate showing how ATOM and other important predicates behave, let us make the value of the atom DIGITS be a list of the names of the numbers from zero to nine:

```
(SETQ DIGITS '(ZERO ONE TWO THREE FOUR FIVE SIX SEVEN EIGHT NINE))
   (ZERO ONE TWO THREE FOUR FIVE SIX SEVEN EIGHT NINE)
```

Now ATOM can be demonstrated:

```
(ATOM 'DIGITS)
   T
```

```
(ATOM 'FIVE)
   T
```

```
(ATOM DIGITS)
   NIL
```

```
(ATOM '(ZERO ONE TWO THREE FOUR FIVE SIX SEVEN EIGHT NINE))
   NIL
```

BOUNDP expects a symbolic atom as its argument. It tests if its argument has a value. If it does, it returns T. Otherwise it returns NIL.

```
(BOUNDP 'DIGITS)
   T
```

```
(BOUNDP 'ZERO)
   NIL
```

```
(BOUNDP (CAR DIGITS))
   NIL
```

EQUAL is another fundamental predicate. It takes two arguments and returns T if they are the same. Otherwise it returns NIL:

```
(EQUAL DIGITS DIGITS)
   T

(EQUAL 'DIGITS 'DIGITS)
   T

(EQUAL DIGITS '(ZERO ONE TWO THREE FOUR FIVE SIX SEVEN EIGHT NINE))
   T

(EQUAL DIGITS 'DIGITS)
  NIL
```

NULL checks to see if its argument is an empty list:

```
(NULL '())
   T

(NULL T)
  NIL

(NULL DIGITS)
  NIL

(NULL 'DIGITS)
  NIL
```

MEMBER tests to see if one s-expression is an element of another. It would make sense for MEMBER to return T if the first argument is an element of the following list and NIL otherwise. Actually MEMBER returns the fragment of the list that begins with the first argument if the first argument is indeed an element of the list. This is a special case of a common programming convenience. The general idea is that a function can return either NIL or something that is both nonNIL and useful for feeding further computation.

```
(MEMBER 'FIVE DIGITS)
  (FIVE SIX SEVEN EIGHT NINE)

(MEMBER 'TEN DIGITS)
  NIL
```

The first argument must be an element of the second argument. It is not enough for the first argument to be buried somewhere in the second argument, as in this example:

```
(MEMBER 'FIVE '((ZERO TWO FOUR SIX EIGHT) (ONE TWO THREE FOUR FIVE)))
   NIL
```

The following use of MEMBER exploits the fact that MEMBER returns something other than T when an element is present. It determines the number of digits after the first instance of the atom FIVE in the list DIGITS.

```
(SUB1 (LENGTH (MEMBER 'FIVE DIGITS)))
   4
```

For some further examples, let us establish values for the elements of DIGITS:

```
(SETQ ZERO 0 ONE 1 TWO 2 THREE 3 FOUR 4
      FIVE 5 SIX 6 SEVEN 7 EIGHT 8 NINE 9)
   9
```

Now using these values, we can look at some predicates that work on numbers. NUMBERP tests its argument to see if it is a number:

```
(NUMBERP 3.14)
   T
```

```
(NUMBERP FIVE)
   T
```

```
(NUMBERP 'FIVE)
   NIL
```

```
(NUMBERP DIGITS)
   NIL
```

```
(NUMBERP 'DIGITS)
   NIL
```

GREATERP and LESSP expect their arguments to be numbers. GREATERP tests them to see that they are in strictly descending order. LESSP checks to see that they are in strictly ascending order. Both may be given any number of arguments.

```
(GREATERP FIVE 2)
   T
```

```
(GREATERP 2 FIVE)
   NIL
```

```
(LESSP 2 FIVE)
  T

(LESSP FIVE 2)
  NIL

(LESSP 2 2)
  NIL

(GREATERP FIVE FOUR THREE TWO ONE)
  T

(GREATERP THREE ONE FOUR)
  NIL

(GREATERP 3 1 4)
  NIL
```

ZEROP expects a number. It tests its argument to see if it is zero:

```
(ZEROP ZERO)
  T

(ZEROP 'ZERO)
  ERROR

(ZEROP FIVE)
  NIL
```

MINUSP tests whether a number is negative:

```
(MINUSP ONE)
  NIL

(MINUSP (MINUS ONE))
  T

(MINUSP ZERO)
  NIL
```

Note that several predicates end in P, a mnemonic for predicate. The predicate ATOM is an unfortunate exception that would tend to suggest that LIST is a predicate too.

Problems

Problem 3-7: Define EVENP, a predicate that tests whether a number is even. You will need REMAINDER, a function that returns the remainder produced by dividing the first argument by the second (see Appendix 4, Note 1).

Problem 3-8: Define PALINDROMEP, a predicate that tests its argument to see if it is a list that has the same sequence of elements when read from right to left that it does when read from left to right.

Problem 3-9: Define RIGHTP, a predicate that takes three arguments. The arguments are the lengths of the sides of a triangle that may be a right triangle. RIGHTP is to return T if the sum of the squares of the two shorter sides is within 2% of the square of the longest side. Otherwise RIGHTP is to return NIL. You may assume the longest side is given as the first argument.

Problem 3-10: Define COMPLEXP, a predicate that takes three arguments, A, B, and C, and returns T if $b^2 - 4ac$ is less than zero.

AND, OR, and NOT are used to do Logic

NOT returns T only if its argument is NIL.

```
(NOT NIL)
  T

(NOT T)
  NIL

(NOT 'DOG)
  NIL

(SETQ PETS '(DOG CAT))
  (DOG CAT)

(NOT (MEMBER 'DOG PETS))
  NIL

(NOT (MEMBER 'TIGER PETS))
  T
```

AND and OR make composite tests possible. AND returns nonNIL only if all arguments are nonNIL. OR returns nonNIL if any argument is nonNIL. Both take any number of arguments.

```
(AND T T NIL)
   NIL

(OR T T NIL)
   T

(AND (MEMBER 'DOG PETS) (MEMBER 'TIGER PETS))
   NIL

(OR (MEMBER 'DINGO PETS) (MEMBER 'TIGER PETS))
   NIL
```

AND and OR do not treat all of their arguments the same way:

■ AND evaluates its arguments from left to right. If a NIL is encountered, NIL is returned immediately. Any remaining arguments are not even evaluated. Otherwise AND returns the value of its last argument.

In other words, anything other than NIL behaves like T as far as logical considerations are concerned. This is a great feature. An OR behaves similarly:

■ OR evaluates its arguments from left to right. If something other than NIL is encountered, it is returned immediately. Any remaining arguments are not even evaluated. Otherwise OR returns NIL.

Consider the following examples, remembering that MEMBER returns the remainder of its second argument if it finds its first argument in that argument:

```
(AND (MEMBER 'DOG PETS) (MEMBER 'CAT PETS))
   (CAT)

(OR (MEMBER 'DOG PETS) (MEMBER 'TIGER PETS))
   (DOG CAT)
```

Predicates Help COND Select a Value among Alternatives

The predicates are most often used to determine which of several possible s-expressions should be evaluated. The choice is most often determined by predicates in conjunction with the branching function COND. COND is therefore an extremely common function. Regrettably, it has a somewhat peculiar syntax. The function name COND is followed by a number of lists, each of which contains a test and something to return if the test succeeds. Thus the syntax is as follows:

```
(COND (<test 1> ... <result 1>)
      (<test 2> ... <result 2>)
         .
         .
         .
      (<test n> ... <result n>))
```

Each list is called a *clause*. The idea is to search through the clauses evaluating only the first element of each until one is found whose value is nonNIL. Then everything else in the successful clause is evaluated and the last thing evaluated is returned as the value of the COND. Any expressions standing between the first and the last elements in a COND clause must be there only for side effects since they certainly cannot influence the value of the COND directly. There are two special cases:

■ If no successful clause is found, COND returns NIL.

■ If the successful clause consists of only one element, then the value of that element itself is returned. Said another way, the test and result elements may be the same.

It may seem strange, incidentally, that T is not strictly required to trigger a clause, and anything other than NIL will do. This is a desirable feature because it allows test functions whose outcomes are not limited to T and NIL values. Since nonNIL is the same as T as far as COND is concerned, a test function can often return something that is both nonNIL and potentially useful. MEMBER is such a function.

While on the subject of strange things, one particular one deserves special attention:

■ The empty list, ( ), and NIL are equivalent in all respects. For example, they satisfy the equal predicate: (EQUAL NIL '( )) returns T. (By convention, the empty list is printed out as NIL.)

Some say the reason that the equivalence of ( ), and NIL was originally arranged has to do with the instruction set of the ancient 709 computer. Others believe the identity was always known to be a programming convenience. No one seems to know for sure. In any case, the first element in a COND clause is frequently an atom whose value is a list that may be empty. If the list is empty, it does not trigger the COND clause since it acts like NIL. On the other side, occasional bugs derive from the fact that (ATOM '( )) is T.

Note that NULL and NOT are actually equivalent functions because NULL returns T only if its argument is an empty list and NOT returns T only if its argument is NIL.

Also, while on the subject of the empty list, it is important to know what happens when CAR or CDR gets one. They may or may not be happy depending on the particular LISP implementation. One argument is that CAR returns the first element of a list and should complain if there is none. The same argument holds that CDR returns the rest of a list after the first is removed and should complain if there is nothing to remove.

A better argument is that both CAR and CDR should return NIL if given an empty list by reason of programming convenience. Otherwise it is constantly necessary to test a list before working on it.

■ The CAR and CDR of the LISP used in the programs in this book both return NIL when given an empty list.

COND Enables DEFUN to do More

Now the ingredients are ready so let us bake the cake. Suppose we want to have a function that adds a new element to the front of a list only if it is not already in the list. Otherwise the value returned is to be the unaltered list. Clearly the desired function must do a test and act according to the result. This will do:

```
(DEFUN AUGMENT (ITEM BAG)
        (COND ((MEMBER ITEM BAG) BAG)              ;Already in?
              (T (CONS ITEM BAG))))                ;Add ITEM to front.
    AUGMENT
```

Note again that the list of parameters shows how arguments are to be used by the function. Without displaying the names somewhere in the definition in the order they are to be given to the function, there would be no way of deciding if (AUGMENT '(A B) '(X Y)) should yield ((A B) X Y) or ((X Y) A B).

Problems

Problem 3-11: In some LISPs, trying to take the CAR or CDR of NIL causes an error. Define NILCAR and NILCDR in terms of CAR and CDR such that they work like CAR and CDR, but return NIL if given NIL as their argument no matter what CAR and CDR do.

Problem 3-12: Some people prefer the Fahrenheit scale to the Celsius scale, because they find it aesthetically pleasing that $0°$ and $100°$ are pinned to temperatures that bracket the temperature spectrum of temperate climates, $0°$ being ridiculously cold and $100°$ being ridiculously hot.

Define CHECK-TEMPERATURE, a function that is to take one argument, such that it returns RIDICULOUSLY-HOT if the argument is greater than 100, RIDICULOUSLY-COLD if the argument is less than 0, and OK otherwise.

Variables May Be Free or Bound

In LISP the process of relating arguments to parameters on entering a function is called *lambda binding*. The following function is strangely written in order to clarify some details:

```
(DEFUN INCREMENT (PARAMETER)                    ;PARAMETER is bound.
    (SETQ PARAMETER (PLUS PARAMETER FREE))      ;FREE is free.
    (SETQ OUTPUT PARAMETER))                    ;OUTPUT is free.
  INCREMENT
```

Evidently INCREMENT is to add the value of FREE to its argument, returning the result after arranging for the result to be the value of OUTPUT. Now let us try something:

```
(SETQ PARAMETER 15)
   15

(SETQ FREE 10)
   10

(SETQ OUTPUT 10)
   10

(SETQ ARGUMENT 10)
   10

(INCREMENT ARGUMENT)
   20

OUTPUT
   20

PARAMETER
   15

ARGUMENT
   10
```

The value of OUTPUT was permanently altered while that of PARAMETER was not. PARAMETER was temporarily changed — it became 10 on entry to INCREMENT, and then became 20 by virtue of the SETQ. PARAMETER gets a value on entry and gets restored on exit because it appears in the function's parameter list. We say that PARAMETER is bound with respect to INCREMENT while OUTPUT is free in the same context.

■ A *bound variable*, with respect to a function, is an atom that appears in the function's parameter list.

■ A *free variable*, with respect to a function, is an atom that does not appear in the function's parameter list.

■ It makes no sense to speak of a variable as bound or free unless we also specify with respect to what function the variable is free or bound.

■ Bound variable values must be saved so that they may be restored. If a bound variable is also used as a free variable, its value is the current one, not any that may have been saved.

It is sometimes nontrivial to figure out what the value of a free variable is. This problem is discussed in detail in Chapter 23 and in Note 3 of Appendix 4.

Note also that changing the value of PARAMETER using SETQ did not change the value of ARGUMENT, even though PARAMETER inherited its original value from ARGUMENT. In some programming languages ARGUMENT and PARAMETER would get tied together, and as a result, the value of ARGUMENT would change as well.

Problems

Problem 3-13: Define CIRCLE such that it returns a list of the circumference and area of a circle whose radius is given. Assume PI is to be a free variable with the appropriate value.

LISP is Neither Call-by-reference nor Call-by-value

In LISP, the notion of what a variable involves is somewhat different from that of most programming languages. In LISP, we say that atoms are *bound* to objects. The objects are s-expressions. We may think of these s-expressions as the values and the atoms as the variables. In most other languages, however, things are a little different. The basic entities are variables which can be in different states. In the case of a fixed-point variable, for example, the different states correspond to the different numbers that can be represented.

When the argument to a function is in the form of the name of a variable, there are two common options, referred to as *call by reference* and *call by value*. Strictly speaking, LISP can be neither call by value nor call by reference since the notion of what a LISP variable is does not correspond exactly to the notion of variable for which call by value and call by reference have a natural meaning.

Programming beginners can ignore the subtleties involved for now. The details are explored in Note 2 of Appendix 4.

Free-variable Values are Determined Dynamically, not Lexically

A collection of bindings is called an *environment*. The object to which an atom is bound can be found by looking in the environment. If a language uses *dynamic scoping*, as LISP does, the values of free variables are determined by the so-called activation environment, the environment in force when the function requiring the free-variable values is used. If a language uses *lexical scoping* instead, then the values of free variables are determined by the so-called definition environment, the environment in force when the function requiring the free-variable values was defined.

   Again, programming beginners can ignore the subtleties involved for now. The details are explored in Note 3 of Appendix 4.

Function Names can be Used as Arguments

Sometimes it is useful for the value of an atom to be a function name. Then the function FUNCALL makes it possible to retrieve the value and use the function.

   Let the value of BANKING-FUNCTION be the atom INTEREST, let the value of INTEREST-RATE be 0.1, and let the definition of INTEREST use INTEREST-RATE:

```
(SETQ BANKING-FUNCTION 'INTEREST)
   INTEREST

(SETQ INTEREST-RATE 0.1)
   0.1

(DEFUN INTEREST (BALANCE)
       (TIMES BALANCE INTEREST-RATE))
```

Note that INTEREST-RATE is a free variable with respect to the function INTEREST. Now BANKING-FUNCTION can be used as the first argument to FUNCALL. FUNCALL finds its value, namely INTEREST, and uses the rest of the arguments to feed INTEREST:

```
(FUNCALL BANKING-FUNCTION 100.0)
   10.0
```

Evidently all of the following produce exactly the same result:

```
(INTEREST 100.0)

(FUNCALL 'INTEREST 100.0)

(FUNCALL BANKING-FUNCTION 100.0)
```

Actually, since the first argument to FUNCALL is evaluated, anything at all that is subject to evaluation can be there, including a COND. Thus the following would key the interest function used to the type of account:

```
(SETQ ACCOUNT-TYPE 'NORMAL)
  NORMAL

(FUNCALL (COND ((EQUAL ACCOUNT-TYPE 'NORMAL) 'INTEREST)
               ((EQUAL ACCOUNT-TYPE '90DAY) 'HIGHINTEREST)
               (T 'NOINTEREST))
       100.0)
  10.0
```

Certainly the same effect could be obtained in another way, but there are many situations in which the use of FUNCALL is appropriate, rather than contrived, as we shall see later when talking about data-driven programming.

With two possible banking functions, INTEREST and NEWBALANCE, it is possible to define TRANSACT, a function whose first argument is intended to be the name of a function:

```
(DEFUN TRANSACT (FUNCTION-NAME BALANCE)
       (FUNCALL FUNCTION-NAME BALANCE))
```

This leads to the following examples:

```
(TRANSACT 'INTEREST 100.0)
  10.0

(TRANSACT 'NEWBALANCE 100.0)
  110.0
```

Summary

■ DEFUN enables a user to make new functions.

■ A predicate is a function that returns T or NIL.

■ AND, OR, and NOT are used to do Logic.

■ Predicates help COND select a value among alternatives.

■ COND enables DEFUN to do more.

■ Variables may be free or bound.

- LISP is neither call-by-reference nor call-by-value

- Free variable values are determined dynamically, not lexically.

- Function names can be used as arguments.

4
RECURSION
AND
ITERATION

The first purpose of this chapter is to understand how a function can use itself in its own definition. This proves useful because it enables a procedure to solve a problem by simplifying it slightly and handing the simplified problem off to one or more exact copies of itself, much like people do when working in a mature bureaucracy. This is called recursion. It is one way of doing something repeatedly.

The second purpose is to see how a function can do something repeatedly without using recursion. This is called iteration. Iteration should be done according to rules that ordinarily improve program readability.

Programming Requires Control Structure Selection

A *control structure* is a general scheme by which a program can go about getting things done. Recursion and iteration are examples of control structures. In general, the choice of a control structure should be determined by the problem under consideration. Sometimes a mathematical function is specified in a way that suggests how it should be computed. Sometimes the way a problem is represented determines the proper thing to do. Sometimes either recursion or iteration will do equally well.

Recursion Allows Programs to Use Themselves

To calculate the n-th power of some number, m, it is sufficient to do the job for the $n-1$-th power because this result multiplied by m is the desired result for the n-th power:

$$m^n = m * m^{n-1} \quad \text{for} \quad n > 0$$
$$m^0 = 1$$

Definitions that describe a process partly in terms of fresh starts on simpler arguments are said to be *recursive*. The power function, as just specified, suggests a recursive definition. Let us look at a recursive definition for POWER expressed in LISP. Since it cannot handle fractional exponents, it is somewhat weaker than the EXPT function supplied by LISP itself:

```
(DEFUN POWER (M N)
        (COND ((ZEROP N) 1)                          ;n = 0 ?
              (T (TIMES M (POWER M (SUB1 N))))))      ;Recurse.
```

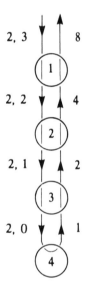

Figure 4-1: A simulation often helps illuminate the strategy of a recursive program. Here each copy of the POWER function reduces the value of N by one and passes it on until N is reduced to zero. The arrows show how control moves from one numbered application of POWER to another. Arguments are shown on the downward pointing arrows; values returned, on the upward.

Using figure 4-1, we can easily follow the history of M and N as LISP evaluates (POWER 2 3). The conventional device used to show how the recursion works is an inverted tree where the branches under a node represent fresh entries to the function as required by the computation. Each entry is listed with its order in the sequence of entries to the function. Downward portions of the flow of control show the argument or arguments carried down while upward portions indicate the values returned.

In the POWER example, each place in the tree sprouts only one new branch because each copy of POWER can create only one new copy. Such recursive programs are generally easy to convert into programs that do not call themselves and therefore are not recursive.

The Fibonacci function provides a different example. The Fibonacci function is defined as follows:

$$f(n) = f(n-1) + f(n-2) \quad \text{for} \quad n > 1$$
$$f(0) = 1$$
$$f(1) = 1$$

Putting this into LISP, we have this:

```
(DEFUN FIBONACCI (N)
       (COND ((ZEROP N) 1)                            ;n = 0
             ((EQUAL N 1) 1)                          ;n = 1
             (T (PLUS (FIBONACCI (DIFFERENCE N 1))
                      (FIBONACCI (DIFFERENCE N 2)))))))
```

Figure 4-2 shows FIBONACCI computing a result when given an argument of 4.

Computing Fibonacci numbers this way is more interesting than computing powers because each copy of FIBONACCI can create two new copies, not just one. Computing Fibonacci numbers is an example of a problem that would be naturally suited to recursion but for the fact that there happens to be a more efficient way to do the computation.

Having seen recursion at work on two simple numerical problems, we next pretend that LISP does not come equipped with the function MEMBER already. We define MEMBER to be a function that tests to see if its first argument is an element of its second.

```
(DEFUN MEMBER (ITEM S)
       (COND ((NULL S) NIL)                    ;List empty?
             ((EQUAL ITEM (CAR S)) S)          ;First element wins?
             (T (MEMBER ITEM (CDR S)))))       ;Recurse.
```

Evidently, MEMBER considers two situations to be basic: either the second argument, S, is an empty list, resulting in a value of NIL for MEMBER; or the first element of S is equal to the first argument, ITEM. If neither of the basic situations is in effect, MEMBER gives up and hands a slightly simplified problem to a copy of itself. The new copy has a list to work with that is one element shorter.

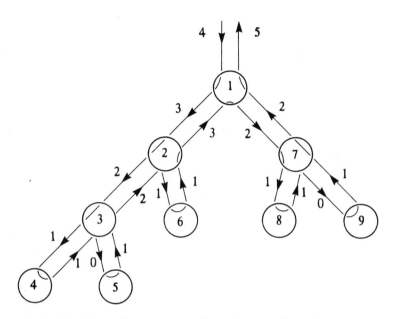

Figure 4-2: A simulation of FIBONACCI. Note that recursion activates two copies each time the argument proves to be hard to handle.

Figure 4-3 shows MEMBER at work on the following problem:

```
(MEMBER 'COMPUTERS '(FAST COMPUTERS ARE NICE))
  (COMPUTERS ARE NICE)
```

Note that presenting the LISP definition of MEMBER is a way of describing what MEMBER does. Describing MEMBER by presenting a definition that uses only more primitive LISP functions is a useful alternative to describing it in English. This amounts to defining part of LISP using LISP itself. In Chapter 23, this idea will be developed to a seemingly impossible extreme, with the whole of LISP evaluation incestuously defined in terms of a LISP program.

Note also that MEMBER delivers a simplified problem to a copy of itself, except in those situations considered basic, but it never does anything to a result produced by a copy. Results are just passed on. Such functions are called tail recursive.

■ A function is *tail recursive* if values are passed upward without alteration as the recursion unwinds.

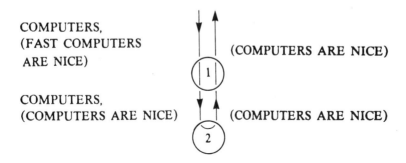

COMPUTERS,
(FAST COMPUTERS
ARE NICE)

COMPUTERS,
(COMPUTERS ARE NICE)

(COMPUTERS ARE NICE)

(COMPUTERS ARE NICE)

Figure 4-3: A simulation of MEMBER at work on the atom COMPUTERS and the list (FAST COMPUTERS ARE NICE).

POWER and FIBONACCI are not tail recursive, nor is COUNTATOMS, the next example. COUNTATOMS counts the atoms in some given s-expression:

```
(DEFUN COUNTATOMS (S)
       (COND ((NULL S) 0)                      ;List empty?
             ((ATOM S) 1)                      ;Atom rather than a list?
             (T (PLUS (COUNTATOMS (CAR S))     ;T forces recursion.
                      (COUNTATOMS (CDR S)))))))
```

The first line announces that the function COUNTATOMS of one argument, S, is about to be defined. The first two clauses of the COND enumerate the very simplest cases, returning 0 for empty lists and 1 for atoms. If COUNTATOMS gets NIL as its argument, then it returns 0 since NIL is equivalent to ( ) and the empty-list test is done before the atom test.

The third clause handles other situations by converting big problems into smaller ones. Lists are broken up using CAR and CDR and COUNTATOMS is applied to both resulting fragments. Since every atom in the list is either in the CAR or the CDR, every atom gets counted. The PLUS combines the results. Eventually, after perhaps many, many applications of itself, COUNTATOMS reduces the hard cases to something that either the first or the second COND clause can handle.

At this point it is helpful to see how COUNTATOMS can take an s-expression apart and reduce it successively to the simple cases. As shown in figure 4-4, the particular expression whose atoms are to be counted is (TIMES X (SQRT 4)). Note that the data expression itself is in the form of an expression one might think of executing for a value. Here then is an example of a program, COUNTATOMS, examining some other piece of program and performing a computation on it.

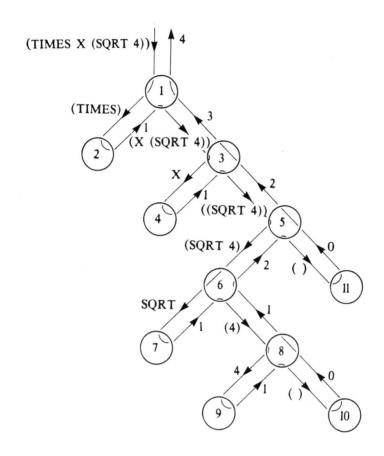

Figure 4-4: Again a simulation helps illuminate the strategy of a recursive program. Here the s-expression (TIMES X (SQRT 4)) is broken up into its constituent pieces by the function COUNTATOMS. The arrows show how control moves from one numbered application of the function to another. Arguments are shown on the downward pointing arrows; values returned, on the upward.

At each stage the argument to COUNTATOMS gets broken into two smaller pieces. Once the answers for both pieces are at hand, PLUS adds the results together and returns the value to a higher-level place further up the tree.

Note that the T in COUNTATOMS insures that the last clause will be triggered if the others are not. A T is often seen in the last clause of a COND where it clearly establishes that the evaluation will not run off the end. The T is not really necessary, however, since the same values would result were it left out.

```
(DEFUN COUNTATOMS (S)
       (COND ((NULL S) 0)                       ;List empty?
             ((ATOM S) 1)                        ;Atom rather than a list?
             ((PLUS (COUNTATOMS (CAR S))         ;No T, first is also last
                    (COUNTATOMS (CDR S)))))))
```

This works because COND triggers on anything but NIL, not just T. PLUS can
never produce a NIL, and the clause therefore triggers just as if the T were there.
Since the clause has only one element, that element is both first and last and
provides both the test and the value returned.

Using a T is better programming practice because it clearly signals the fact that
the programmer expects the last clause to be used when all else fails. Using a T
clearly indicates that there can be no falling through the COND completely with
the default value of NIL.

Problems

Problem 4-1: Describe the evident purpose of the following function:

```
(DEFUN MYSTERY (S)
       (COND ((NULL S) 1)
             ((ATOM S) 0)
             (T (MAX (ADD1 (MYSTERY (CAR S)))
                     (MYSTERY (CDR S))))))
```

Problem 4-2: Describe the evident purpose of the following function:

```
(DEFUN STRANGE (L)
       (COND ((NULL L) NIL)
             ((ATOM L) L)
             (T (CONS (STRANGE (CAR L))
                      (STRANGE (CDR L))))))
```

Problem 4-3: Define SQUASH, a function that takes an s-expression as its
argument and returns a nonnested list of all atoms found in the s-expression. Here
is an example:

```
(SQUASH '(A (A (A (A B))) (((A B) B) B) B))
  (A A A A B A B B B B)
```

Problem 4-4: The version of FIBONACCI given in the text is the obvious, but
wasteful implementation. Many computations are repeated. Write a version
which does not have this flaw. It may help to have an auxiliary function.

Problems about Sets and Binary Trees

The next group of problems involves functions that work with sets. A *set* is a collection of elements, each of which is said to be a member of the set. A set can be represented as a list, with each element of the set represented by an atom. Each atom occurs only once in the list, and no significance is attached to the order of the atoms in the list.

Problem 4-5: Define UNION. The union of two sets is a set containing all the elements that are in either of the two sets.

Problem 4-6: Define INTERSECTION. The intersection of two sets is a set containing only the elements that are in both of the two sets.

Problem 4-7: Define LDIFFERENCE. The difference of two sets, the IN set and the OUT set, is what remains of the set IN after all elements that are also elements of set OUT are removed.

Problem 4-8: Define INTERSECTP, a predicate which tests whether two sets have any elements in common. It is to return NIL if the two sets are disjoint.

Problem 4-9: Define SAMESETP, a predicate which tests whether two sets contain the same elements. Note that the two lists representing the sets may be arranged in different orders.

A *binary tree* can be defined recursively as either a leaf, or a node with two attached binary trees. Such a binary tree can be represented using atoms for the leaves and three-element lists for the nodes. The first element of each list is an atom representing a node, while the other two elements are the sub-trees attached to the node. Thus

```
(N-1 (N-2 L-A L-B) (N-3 (N-4 L-C L-D) (N-5 L-E (N-6 L-F L-G))))
```

is the representation of a particular binary tree with six nodes (N-1 to N-6) and seven leaves (L-A to L-G). The following group of problems make use of this representation.

Problem 4-10: A mobile is a form of abstract sculpture consisting of parts that move. Usually it contains objects suspended in mid-air by fine wires hanging from horizontal beams. We can define a particularly simple type of mobile recursively as either a suspended object, or a beam with a sub-mobile hanging from each end. If we assume that each beam is suspended from its midpoint, we can represent such a mobile as a binary tree. Single suspended objects are represented by numbers equal to their weight, while more complicated mobiles can be represented by a three-element list. The first element is a number equal to the weight of the beam, while the other two elements represent sub-mobiles attached at the two ends of the beam.

A mobile should be balanced. This means that the two mobiles suspended from opposite ends of each beam must be equal in weight. Define MOBILEP, a function which determines whether a mobile is balanced. It returns NIL if it is not, and its total weight if it is. So for example:

```
(MOBILEP '(6 (4 (2 1 1) 4) (2 5 (1 2 2)))))
   30.
```

Problem 4-11: Binary trees can be used to represent arithmetic expressions, as for example:

```
(* (+ A B) (- C (/ D E)))
```

One can write a compiler, or program for translating such an arithmetic expression into the machine language of some computer, using LISP. Suppose for example that the target machine has a set of sequentially numbered registers which can hold temporary results. The machine also has a MOVE instruction for getting values into these registers, and ADD, SUB, MUL and DIV instructions for arithmetically combining values in two registers. The above expression, for example, could be translated into the following:

```
((MOVE 1 A)
 (MOVE 2 B)
 (ADD 1 2)
 (MOVE 2 C)
 (MOVE 3 D)
 (MOVE 4 E)
 (DIV 3 4)
 (SUB 2 3)
 (MUL 1 2))
```

The result is left in register number one. Define COMPILE, which performs this translation.

Problem 4-12: Let the "weight" of a binary tree equal one when it is just a leaf. If the binary tree is not a leaf, its weight is the larger of the weights of the two sub-trees if these are not equal. If the weights of the two sub-trees are equal, the weight of the tree is one larger than the weight of either sub-tree. The tree representing the arithmetic expression shown in the previous problem, for example, has weight three. Define WEIGHT, a function which computes the weight of a tree.

Problem 4-13: The number of registers used to compute an arithmetic function depends on whether one computes the left or the right sub-trees first. The function WEIGHT, defined in the previous problem, actually determines the minimum number of registers required to compute a particular arithmetic expression. It is clear that our compiler is not optimal, since it used four registers for a tree with weight three. Assume that another instruction, COPY, is available for moving the contents of one register into another. Improve COMPILE, using WEIGHT, to minimize the number of registers used.

Problems about "C" Curves and Dragon Curves

William Gosper first drew our attention to certain recursively defined drawings.
    Consider the following recursive program:

```
(DEFUN C-CURVE (LENGTH ANGLE)
      (COND ((LESSP LENGTH MIN-LENGTH) (PLOT-LINE LENGTH ANGLE))
            (T (C-CURVE (QUOTIENT LENGTH (SQRT 2.0))
                        (PLUS ANGLE (QUOTIENT PI 4.0)))
               (C-CURVE (QUOTIENT LENGTH (SQRT 2.0))
                        (DIFFERENCE ANGLE (QUOTIENT PI 4.0)))))))
```

Assume that (PLOT-LINE LENGTH ANGLE) plots a straight line of length LENGTH at an angle ANGLE with respect to some standard reference axis. The line is drawn from wherever the last line ended. Also assume that the value of the free variable PI is π. It may help to simulate the result with paper and pencil for cases where the recursion is only two or three layers deep. Compare the results with figure 4-5.

Problem 4-14: Write the procedure PLOT-LINE using LINE, a procedure which takes four arguments X-START, Y-START, X-END and Y-END, specifying the coordinates of the end points of a line to be drawn. Use the free variables X-OLD and Y-OLD to remember where the previous line ended. Assume that the functions SIN and COS calculate the sine and cosine of their single arguments.

Problem 4-15: Lines end up being drawn in only one of eight directions.(Actually only four for given values of LENGTH and MIN-LENGTH.) Write PSEUDO-SIN which takes an integer and produces the result previously offered up by SIN. The corresponding angle is $\pi/4$ times the integer.

Problem 4-16: One can view the recursive step in C-CURVE as one in which a straight line is replaced by a pair of shorter straight lines at right angles to each other, connecting the end points of the original line. There are two ways of doing this, depending on which side of the original line one decides to place the elbow so formed. In C-CURVE the shorter lines are consistently placed on one side of the

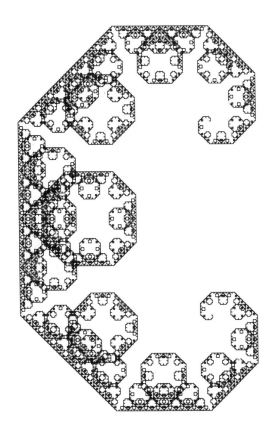

Figure 4-5: The "C" curve, a recursively defined drawing.

line being replaced. Write DRAGON-CURVE, where the first and second recursive calls place the elbows on opposite sides of their respective lines. The drawing produced by such a program is shown in figure 4-6.

Problems about Rewriting Logical Expressions

When working with digital hardware, people often use more than the minimum number of logic element types than are absolutely needed. This is convenient because it is tedious to work in terms of a minimal set. At the same time, only a

Figure 4-6: The "Dragon" curve, another recursively defined drawing.

minimal set may be available for actually building electronic circuits. There is then a need for automatic translation from the form preferred by the designer to that required when actually building something. In particular, designers may prefer to think in terms of logical operations like NOT, AND, OR, and XOR, while the basic hardware modules may be NAND gates.

The function REWRITE will translate from one form to the other by rewriting the logical operation at the head of the expression handed to it. The arguments to this logical operator are translated using recursive calls to REWRITE. Well-known identities between logical expressions are used in the process.

```
(DEFUN REWRITE (L)
     (COND ((ATOM L) L)
           ((EQUAL (CAR L) 'NOT)
            (LIST 'NAND
                  (REWRITE (CADR L)) T))
           ((EQUAL (CAR L) 'AND)
            (LIST 'NAND
                  (LIST 'NAND
                  (REWRITE (CADR L))
                  (REWRITE (CADDR L)))
                  T))
           ((EQUAL (CAR L) 'OR)
            (LIST 'NAND
                  (LIST 'NAND (REWRITE (CADR L)) T)
                  (LIST 'NAND (REWRITE (CADDR L)) T)))
           ((EQUAL (CAR L) 'XOR)
            (LIST 'NAND
                  (LIST 'NAND
                        (LIST 'NAND
                              (LIST 'NAND (REWRITE (CADR L)) T)
                              (LIST 'NAND (REWRITE (CADDR L)) T))
                        (LIST  'NAND
                               (REWRITE (CADR L))
                               (REWRITE (CADDR L)))))
                  T))
           (T (LIST 'ERROR L))))
```

Problem 4-17: The above implementation of REWRITE is sometimes wasteful. In certain cases, composite operands may be rewritten several times. Develop a new version of REWRITE that avoids this by applying REWRITE recursively to lists constructed using NAND and untranslated arguments of the logical operations.

Dealing with Lists often Calls for Iteration using MAPCAR

A somewhat more elegant way to define programs like COUNTATOMS is through the functions MAPCAR and APPLY, two new functions that are very useful and very special in the way they handle their arguments.

Iterate is a technical term meaning to repeat. MAPCAR can be used to iterate when the same function is to be performed over and over again on a whole list of things. Suppose, for example, that it is useful to add one to each number in a list of numbers. Then from (1 2 3) we would want to get (2 3 4).

To accomplish such transformations with MAPCAR, one supplies the name of the function together with a list of things to be handed one after the other to the function.

```
(MAPCAR 'ADD1                    ;Function to work with.
        '(1 2 3))                ;Arguments to be fed to the function.
   (2 3 4)
```

The MAPCAR is said to cause iteration of ADD1 since the MAPCAR causes ADD1 to be used over and over again.

There is no restriction to functions of one variable, but if the function is a function of more than one variable, there must be a corresponding number of lists of things to feed the function. As shown in the following example, MAPCAR works like an assembly machine, taking one element from each list of arguments and assembling them together for the function:

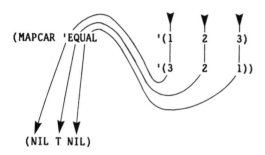

Consider now a common error that shows why the function APPLY is necessary. Suppose we want to add up a list of numbers, L.

```
(SETQ L '(4 7 2))
   (4 7 2)
```

Do we want to evaluate (PLUS L)? No! That would be wrong. PLUS expects arguments that are numbers. But here PLUS is given one argument that is a list of numbers rather than an actual number. PLUS does not know what to do with the unexpected argument. It is as if we tried to evaluate (PLUS '(4 7 2)) instead of (PLUS 4 7 2).

To make PLUS work, we must use APPLY, which takes two arguments, a function name and a list, and arranges to have the function act on the elements in the list as if they appeared as proper arguments. Thus (APPLY 'PLUS L) is a special case of the general form:

```
(APPLY <function description>
       <list of arguments>)
```

Now using APPLY and MAPCAR we can work up a more elegant way of counting atoms:

```
(DEFUN COUNTATOMS (S)
      (COND ((NULL S) 0)
            ((ATOM S) 1)
            (T (APPLY 'PLUS (MAPCAR 'COUNTATOMS S)))))
```

As suggested by the first two COND clauses, simple cases are handled as before. And once again, the objective is to reduce the more complex expressions to the simple ones. Only now MAPCAR is used to simplify s-expressions rather than CAR and CDR. This version of COUNTATOMS takes advantage of MAPCAR's talent in going after every element of a list with a specified function, in this case a recursive application of COUNTATOMS itself.

Now, assuming for a moment that the function works, we see that the MAPCAR comes back with a list of numbers that must be added together. This is why APPLY appears. PLUS wants numbers, not a list of numbers. APPLY does the appropriate interfacing and hands the list of numbers to PLUS as if each element in the list were itself an argument to PLUS.

Simulating this version of COUNTATOMS is easier than simulating the other one since the recursion is less deep and complicated. See figure 4-7.

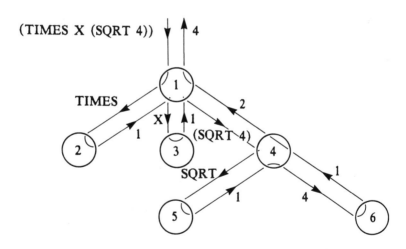

Figure 4-7: A version of COUNTATOMS using MAPCAR instead of CARs and CDRs exhibits less recursion. There are only six entries on three levels rather than eleven on six.

Now it is easy to modify COUNTATOMS to do other things. For example, to determine the depth of an s-expression, the following simple modifications to COUNTATOMS are all that is necessary: change the name to DEPTH, change the empty list and atom results, change PLUS to MAX, and insert ADD1:

```
(DEFUN DEPTH (S)
       (COND ((NULL S) 1)
             ((ATOM S) 0)
             (T (ADD1 (APPLY 'MAX (MAPCAR 'DEPTH S))))))
```

Figure 4-8 shows how DEPTH works on the same expression previously used to illustrate COUNTATOMS. Again, at each branching, we see how MAPCAR splits up an expression into simpler elements to be worked on.

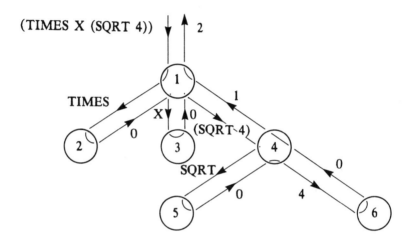

Figure 4-8: The recursion pattern for DEPTH is the same as the one for COUNTATOMS.

The iteration involved in the use of MAPCAR is a special case of iteration since it is restricted to the repeated application of a function to the elements of a list. In the next section we look at PROG, a function that makes it possible to do iteration in general.

Problems

Problem 4-18: Define DYNAMIC-RANGE, a function that takes one argument, a list of numbers, and returns the ratio of the biggest to the smallest.

PROG Creates Variables and Supports Explicit Iteration

PROG is a popular function, particularly with those who do a lot of numerical computation, partly because it creates new variables and partly because it provides one way to write procedures that loop, or said more elegantly, that iterate.

PROG also can be used just to paste together several s-expressions that are to be executed in sequence. This is not done much because DEFUN accepts sequences of s-expressions, not just one. In the old days of early LISP, however, DEFUN and certain other functions were allowed to have only one s-expression. PROG was necessary whenever a sequence was desired.

The syntax for PROG is easier to explain through an immediate example rather than through discussion. We will do the power function, this time specified in a way that suggests iteration rather than recursion:

$$m^n = m * m \quad \ldots \quad m$$

Here, then, is another way to write POWER:

```
(DEFUN POWER (M N)
       (PROG (RESULT EXPONENT)
             (SETQ RESULT 1)                              ;Initialize.
             (SETQ EXPONENT N)                            ;Initialize.
             LOOP                                         ;Start loop.
             (COND ((ZEROP EXPONENT) (RETURN RESULT)))    ;Test.
             (SETQ RESULT (TIMES M RESULT))               ;Reset.
             (SETQ EXPONENT (SUB1 EXPONENT))              ;Reset.
             (GO LOOP)))                                  ;Repeat.
```

Several things must be explained. Keep in mind that the objective is to multiply n m-s together. This will be accomplished by passing repeatedly through the part of the PROG just after LOOP.

■ The arguments to a PROG are mostly s-expressions that are evaluated one after the other. The values are thrown away, so evaluations are only good for side effects. If control runs off the end of a PROG, then NIL is returned, just as with COND.

■ The first position in a PROG is always occupied by a list of parameters that are all bound on entering the PROG and restored to old values on exit. If there are no parameters, NIL or ( ) must be in first position. Each parameter is given an initial value of NIL automatically.

■ Whenever the function RETURN is reached when evaluating a PROG, the PROG is terminated immediately. The value of the terminated PROG is the value of the argument to the RETURN that stopped the PROG.

■ Any atom appearing as an argument to a PROG is considered to be a position marker. These atoms, called *tags*, are not evaluated. They mark places to which control can be transferred by GO functions. (GO <tag>) transfers control to the s-expression following <tag>. A tag can be any atom, by the way; it need not be a symbolic atom.

■ PROGs can be nested, like other functions, but it is only possible to go to a tag that is in the same PROG as the GO.

It is clear that the power function works by looping through the tag named LOOP until the variable N is counted down to zero. Each time through the loop, RESULT is changed through multiplication by *m*. The COND tests for the stop condition, *n*=0, and executes a RETURN when the test succeeds. RESULT starts with a value of NIL as all PROG variables do, but is set to 1 before the loop is entered.

Incidentally, it is sometimes useful to have a way of combining several expressions into a sequence as PROG does, but without the parameters and looping possibilities. PROG2, and PROGN do this. The value returned is the value of the second argument in the case of PROG2, and the last in the case of PROGN. Some LISP implementations provide PROG1, which returns the value of the first argument.

PROG-based Iteration should be done with Care

One reason PROG-based iteration can be hard to understand is that the description of a loop can be too spread out. Variable initialization, variable incrementing SETQs, and termination tests with RETURNs can be scattered everywhere. Worse yet, multiple PROG tags and GOs insure that the actual path a program takes may look like a badly tangled up length of string.

Consequently it is useful to have iteration functions with a syntax that requires all of the loop description to be stated at the beginning, before the body of the loop and not interdigitated with it. PROG begins with a variable list. DO-type functions begin with a variable list, initialization information, descriptions of how to increment the variables each time around the loop, and a loop termination test. There are no tags and no GOs. It can be shown that anything using PROG loops can be rewritten using a DO-type loop.

Most modern LISPs have some sort of DO function built in. If there is no DO, it is easy enough to create one, as we will do in a later chapter. But even without a DO, it is possible to use PROGs in a way that closely adheres to the do-not-misuse-GO philosophy:

■ Initialize PROG variables immediately after the variable list.

■ Then place the PROG's single tag. Let it have some obvious name like LOOP.

■ Then place the PROG's single termination-testing COND. It will have only one clause. That clause will have a RETURN at the end.

■ Then place the body of the loop next.

■ Finally, at the end of the loop, place variable incrementing instructions and conclude with (GO LOOP).

This compresses loop description into two places, one at the beginning of the loop and one at the end, which is as close as PROG can be to the ideal of having everything in one place.

Note that the function POWER, given above, illustrates the suggested semistructuring of PROG loops. Curiously, it has no body. Everything is handled in the variable initialization and incrementing part of the PROG. In fact, this lack of a body is rather common.

Problems and their Representation Determine Proper Control Structure

We can now state some rough guidelines for determining how to select a way to cause repetition from the repertoire of control structures introduced so far.

■ The definition of a mathematical function may suggest an appropriate control structure. If so, use it.

■ If solving a problem involves diving into list structure, recursion probably makes sense.

■ If solving a problem involves doing something to every element in a list, iteration using MAPCAR is usually the right thing.

Keep in mind that these rules are only rough guidelines to be augmented as experience increases. In particular, we will soon add the following:

■ When working with arrays, try iteration using PROGs (or DOs if DO is available).

Problems

Problem 4-19: Define FACTORIAL, using the PROG version of POWER as a model. Factorial of n is to be one if n is zero and n times the factorial of n-1 otherwise.

Problem 4-20: Some elements of a set may be equivalent. Such equivalences can be expressed using a list of pairs of equivalent elements. If A is equivalent to B, then B is equivalent to A. Further, if A is equivalent to B, and B is equivalent to C, then A is also equivalent to C. *Equivalence classes* are subsets, all elements of which are equivalent. In the case just described, the set (A B C) forms an equivalence class. Define COALESCE, a function which takes a set of pairwise equivalences and returns a set of equivalence classes.

A typical application of COALESCE is the following:

```
(COALESCE '((A E) (Z F) (M B) (P K)
            (E I) (F S) (B D) (T P)
            (I O) (S V) (D G) (K P)
            (O U) (V Z) (G M) (P T)))
    ((A E I O U) (F S V Z) (B D G M) (K P T))
```

It may be helpful to employ UNION and INTERSECTP, defined in earlier examples in this chapter. Also, the solution may make use of both recursion and iteration.

Summary

■ Programming requires control structure selection.

■ Recursion allows programs to use themselves.

■ Dealing with lists often calls for iteration using MAPCAR.

■ PROG creates variables and supports explicit iteration.

■ PROG-based iteration should be done with care.

■ Problems and their representation determine proper control structure.

References

The conversion of recursive programs into iterative ones is discussed by Auslander and Strong [1976] as well as Darlington and Burstall [1976], and Burstall and Darlington [1977]. Burge [1975] discusses recursive programming at length.

Algorithms involving sets are analysed by Aho, Hopcroft, and Ullman [1974, pg. 124]. The equivalence class problem can be solved using a transitive closure algorithm found in Aho, Hopcroft, and Ullman [1974, pg. 199]. Binary trees are discussed in the same book [1974, pg. 113].

Knuth [1974] discusses structured programming with GO-TO statements.

5
PROPERTIES
A-LISTS
ARRAYS
AND
ACCESS
FUNCTIONS

So far we only know how to give a symbolic atom a value and to get the value back. The purpose of this chapter is to introduce new methods for remembering and recalling things. Our first objective is to generalize the notion of value, making it possible to give an atom many different values, each of which is associated with an explicitly named property. Then we will work on certain lists called association lists, a-lists for short. One of the features of a-lists is that they enable groups of atom values to be remembered, suppressed, or restored together, all at once. And finally, we will race past the use of arrays, showing that it is possible to store and retrieve information by row and column numbers.

Properties and Property Values Generalize the Notion of Atom and Value

Symbolic atoms can have *properties*. Property names and property values are left to the imagination of the user. An example is the FATHER property. The value of the FATHER property of the atom ROBERT could be JAMES, for example. The PARENTS property of ROBERT could be a list of two atoms, each naming one of ROBERT's parents. In general, the value of a property can be any s-expression.

Note, incidentally, that the word value is being used in two senses: first, we talk of the value of some particular property of an atom; and second, we talk of the value of an atom.

PUTPROP and GET are the Masters of Property Lists

To retrieve property values, GET is used:

```
(GET 'ROBERT 'FATHER)
  JAMES

(GET 'ROBERT 'SURNAME)
  NIL
```

To place or replace a property value, the complementary function, PUTPROP, does the job:

```
(PUTPROP 'ROBERT 'WINSTON 'SURNAME)
  WINSTON

(PUTPROP 'JAMES '(ROBERT ALBERT) 'SONS)
  (ROBERT ALBERT)
```

Note that the value returned by PUTPROP is the same as the value it attaches to the atom given as the first argument. It is also good to know that GET returns NIL if no property with the given name exists yet. This suggests first of all that NIL is a poor choice for the value of a property, since the result returned by GET cannot be distinguished from what GET returns when it does not find the property asked for. It also means that as far as GET is concerned, properties can be removed this way:

```
(PUTPROP <atom name> NIL <property name>)
```

It is clearer to use the function REMPROP with just the atom name and property name as arguments.

```
(REMPROP <atom name> <property name>)
```

DEFPROP is a sort of companion of PUTPROP. It uses the arguments the same way but does not evaluate them. Also, DEFPROP returns its first argument, rather than its second, mostly for obscure historical reasons. Thus the following have equivalent side effects:

```
(PUTPROP 'PATRICK 'WINSTON 'SURNAME)
  WINSTON

(DEFPROP PATRICK WINSTON SURNAME)
  PATRICK
```

After either we get,

```
(GET 'PATRICK 'SURNAME)
  WINSTON
```

Problems

Problem 5-1: Suppose each city in a network of cities and highways is represented by an atom. Further suppose that each city is to have a property named NEIGHBORS. The value of the NEIGHBORS property is to be a list of the other cities for which there is a direct highway connection.

Define a function CONNECT that takes two cities as arguments and puts each on the property list of the other under the NEIGHBORS property. Write CONNECT such that nothing changes if a connection is already in place.

Problem 5-2: Assume that if a person's father is known, the father's name is given as the value of the FATHER property. Define GRANDFATHER, a function that returns the name of a person's paternal grandfather, if known, or NIL otherwise.

Problem 5-3: Define ADAM, a function that returns the most distant male ancestor of a person through the paternal line. If no male ancestor is known, the function is to return the person given as its argument.

Problem 5-4: Define ANCESTORS, a function that returns a list consisting of the person given as its argument together with all known ancestors of the person. It is to work through both the FATHER and MOTHER properties. Assume related people do not have children.

Problem 5-5: Suppose X and Y are properties used to specify the location of cities relative to some reference point. Assuming a flat earth, write a function that calculates the distance between two cities. Remember that SQRT calculates square roots.

ASSOC Retrieves Pairs from Association Lists

An *association list*, a-list for short, is a list of pairs. The following makes TODAY and YESTERDAY into a-lists recording medical facts:

```
(SETQ YESTERDAY '((TEMPERATURE 103) (PRESSURE (120 60)) (PULSE 72)))
    ((TEMPERATURE 103) (PRESSURE (120 60)) (PULSE 72))

(SETQ TODAY '((TEMPERATURE 100) (PRESSURE (120 60)) (PULSE 72)))
    ((TEMPERATURE 100) (PRESSURE (120 60)) (PULSE 72))
```

ASSOC is a function of two arguments. The first argument to ASSOC is often called the *key*. ASSOC looks for its key in the a-list supplied as the second argument. ASSOC moves down the a-list until it finds a list element whose CAR is equal to the key. The value of the ASSOC is the entire element so discovered, key and all, or NIL if the key is never found. These examples illustrate:

```
(SETQ CHART YESTERDAY)
  ((TEMPERATURE 103) (PRESSURE (120 60)) (PULSE 72))

(ASSOC 'TEMPERATURE CHART)
  (TEMPERATURE 103)

(SETQ CHART TODAY)
  ((TEMPERATURE 100) (PRESSURE (120 60)) (PULSE 72))

(ASSOC 'TEMPERATURE CHART)
  (TEMPERATURE 100)

(ASSOC 'COMPLAINTS CHART)
  NIL
```

Problems

Problem 5-6: Write FETCH, a function that takes an atom and an a-list. If the atom is found as the first element of an item on the a-list, then the second item is to be returned. Otherwise FETCH is to return a question mark. (A question mark makes a perfectly good atom.) The following examples illustrate:

```
(SETQ CHART '((TEMPERATURE 100) (PRESSURE (120 60)) (PULSE 72)))
  ((TEMPERATURE 100) (PRESSURE (120 60)) (PULSE 72))

(FETCH 'TEMPERATURE CHART)
  100

(FETCH 'COMPLAINTS CHART)
  ?
```

Problem 5-7: Write LISTKEYS, a function that takes an a-list and returns a list of all the keys in it. Recall that the keys are the things that ASSOC checks its first argument against.

Problem 5-8: Write TREND, a function that takes two a-lists that record temperature, among other things. TREND is to return either IMPROVING or STABLE or SINKING depending on whether the patient's temperature is moving toward normal, at normal, or moving away. Assume the first a-list records the older data. Further assume that there is always an entry for temperature on both a-lists. Use FETCH as defined in a previous problem, if you like.

STORE and ARRAY are used with Arrays

Conceptually, an *array* is a data structure in which information is located in slots, each of which is associated with a particular set of numbers called indices.

Suppose, for illustration, that the measured brightness values at each point of an image are to be stored and retrieved. Any particular point has an *x* and a *y* coordinate, both of which are numbers. It is natural to store the brightness values in an array, using the *x* and *y* coordinates to specify exactly where the values should go.

If an image has been stored in an array named IMAGE, then (IMAGE 314 271) will retrieve the image point whose *x* coordinate is 314 and whose *y* coordinate is 271. Note that the array name is used just as if it were a function. Which index corresponds to which coordinate is, of course, quite arbitrary. In the case of matrices, it is customary to let the first index be the row number and the second the column number.

For arrays, unlike for lists, the size must be announced in advance of use. This is done using the function ARRAY:

```
(ARRAY IMAGE T 1024 1024)
   IMAGE
```

This states that IMAGE is an array, that there are two indices, and that both indices range over 1024 values (from 0 to 1023, oddly enough, not 1 to 1024). (The T signifies that the array slots are to be able to hold arbitrary s-expressions. Instead, we could have used the atoms FIXNUM or FLONUM to indicate that the array will be used only for fixed or floating point numbers respectively.)

Once IMAGE has been created, information can be stored in it. This is done as in the following example which puts 88 in the array location specified:

```
(STORE (IMAGE 314 271) 88)
   88
```

A different syntax, something like (STORE IMAGE 314 271 88) might make more sense, but the actual syntax has advantages that have to do with how arrays are implemented.

Note that while the array in this example happens to hold only numbers, LISP array slots may hold arbitrary s-expressions.

Problems

Problem 5-9: A matrix can be represented as a list, with each row a sublist. Define STUFF-MATRIX, a procedure which makes an array called MATRIX, of appropriate size, and then fills it in from a matrix represented as a list of lists. Here is a test case for STUFF-MATRIX:

```
(STUFF-MATRIX '((0 0 0 0 0 0 0 0 0 0 0 0 0 0 0 0 0 0 0 0)
                (0 0 1 1 1 1 1 1 1 1 1 1 1 1 0 0 0 0 0)
                (0 0 1 1 1 1 1 1 1 1 1 1 1 1 1 0 0 0 0)
                (0 0 0 1 1 0 0 0 0 0 0 0 1 1 0 0 0 0)
                (0 0 0 1 1 0 0 0 0 0 0 0 1 1 0 0 0 0)
                (0 0 0 1 1 1 1 1 1 1 1 1 1 0 0 0 0 0)
                (0 0 0 1 1 1 1 1 1 1 1 1 1 1 0 0 0)
                (0 0 0 1 1 0 0 0 0 0 0 0 1 1 0 0 0)
                (0 0 0 1 1 0 0 0 0 0 0 0 1 1 0 0 0)
                (0 0 0 1 1 0 0 0 0 0 0 0 1 1 0 0 0)
                (0 0 1 1 1 1 1 1 1 1 1 1 1 1 0 0 0)
                (0 0 1 1 1 1 1 1 1 1 1 1 1 1 0 0 0 0)
                (0 0 0 0 0 0 0 0 0 0 0 0 0 0 0 0 0 0 0 0))))
```

Access Functions Simplify Data Interactions

Access functions are functions designed to simplify the chore of retrieving and changing desired data. Access functions for retrieval are built out of LISP primitives like GET, ASSOC, CAR, and CDR. It is often good to get at data by way of access functions, rather than using the LISP primitives directly, for these two reasons:

■ Access functions make programs more transparent. Given mnemonic names, access functions are easier to find and understand than the equivalent combinations of primitives.

■ Access functions make programs easier to modify. Given some need to change the way data is arranged, it is easier to change the definitions of a few access functions than to find and change each place that data is used.

Suppose, for example, that someone has decided that each person's social security number is to be the third item on a list to be found under the NUMBERS key in an a-list to be found under the IDENTIFIERS property of the atom of the same name. To be sure, whenever the social security number of the person whose name is the value EMPLOYEE is needed, it is possible to get it using LISP primitives:

```
(CADDR (ASSOC 'NUMBERS (GET 'IDENTIFIERS EMPLOYEE)))
```

But it is probably better to get away from this by defining an access function:

```
(DEFUN SOCIAL-SECURITY-NUMBER (PERSON)
       (CADDR (ASSOC 'NUMBERS (GET 'IDENTIFIERS PERSON))))
```

Then programs will contain only instances of the access function rather than the possibly confusing combination of a CADDR, ASSOC, and GET:

```
      .
      .
      .
(SOCIAL-SECURITY-NUMBER EMPLOYEE)
      .
      .
      .
```

A set of access functions can become quite elaborate. The so-called frames representation language, discussed in a later chapter, is an example of a set of access functions that is so elaborate that it deserves to be thought of as an embedded language.

Summary

■ Properties and property values generalize the notion of atom and value.

■ PUTPROP and GET are the masters of property lists.

■ ASSOC retrieves pairs from association lists.

■ STORE and ARRAY are used with arrays.

■ Access functions simplify data interactions.

6
USING
LAMBDA
DEFINITIONS

The descriptions of functions are recorded using DEFUN so that they can be recalled later using their name. In this chapter, we will see that it is possible to use a function description in places where ordinarily there would be a function name. This is useful in a variety of ways.

LAMBDA Defines Anonymous Functions

Consider the problem of checking which elements in a list FRUITS are apples. One way would be to start by defining APPLEP:

```
(DEFUN APPLEP (X) (EQUAL X 'APPLE))
```

Then we can write this:

```
(SETQ FRUITS '(ORANGE APPLE APPLE APPLE PEAR GRAPEFRUIT))
   (ORANGE APPLE APPLE APPLE PEAR GRAPEFRUIT)
```

```
(MAPCAR 'APPLEP FRUITS)
   (NIL T T T NIL NIL)
```

This is a little painful if there is only one occasion to test for fruits. Passing over a list with a simple function should not require going off somewhere else to define a function. Why not make the programmer's intention more transparent by laying out the function at the spot where it is to be used.

```
(MAPCAR (DEFUN APPLEP (X) (EQUAL X 'APPLE)) FRUITS)
   (NIL T T T NIL NIL)
```

DEFUN works because MAPCAR wants a function name and the value of DEFUN is the name of the function defined. But to avoid the proliferation of useless names, the name can be dropped if it is used only here! In this event, the lack of a function name is signaled by using something different from DEFUN to define the procedure. For historical reasons this new function definition is called a *lambda expression* and the atom LAMBDA appears instead of DEFUN. The correct way to use a local definition would therefore be as in this example:

```
(MAPCAR '(LAMBDA (X) (EQUAL X 'APPLE)) FRUITS)
   (NIL T T T NIL NIL)
```

■ No one would actually use DEFUN in a MAPCAR anyway since such a practice would be hopelessly inefficient — setting up a function with the inevitable overhead happens each time the section of program is used. The DEFUN was used here only as a way of introducing lambda-style definitions.

A longer but perhaps more informative name for introducing local definitions would be DEFINE-ANONYMOUS. We will stick to LAMBDA for compatibility, but if confusion ever sets in, a good heuristic for understanding LAMBDA is to translate it mentally to DEFINE-ANONYMOUS.

Note that lambda definitions appearing in a MAPCAR require a quote to suppress evaluation, just as a function name does. (Actually, under some circumstances, it is better to use FUNCTION instead of QUOTE. In particular, if a so-called compiler is used to translate raw LISP programs into a machine oriented form, then FUNCTION tells the compiler to translate the surrounded lambda definition, rather than just take it as an s-expression to be left as is.)

Note also that a lambda definition can go just about anywhere a function name can go. In particular, a lambda-style description can be the first element in a list to be evaluated, even though using a function name is vastly more common. The following are exactly equivalent, given the existing definition of APPLEP:

```
(APPLEP 'APPLE)
   T
```

```
((LAMBDA (X) (EQUAL X 'APPLE)) 'APPLE)
   T
```

```
(FUNCALL '(LAMBDA (X) (EQUAL X 'APPLE)) 'APPLE)
   T
```

For further illustration, suppose we want to actually count the number of apples on the list FRUITS. There are several methods involving MAPCAR. The first involves building a new function around APPLEP that returns 1 or 0 instead of T or NIL:

```
(DEFUN APPLEP-1-0 (Y)
       (COND ((APPLEP Y) 1)
             (T 0)))
```

Then it is easy to count the apples by using MAPCAR to run APPLEP-1-0 down the list, adding the results by applying PLUS:

```
(MAPCAR 'APPLEP-1-0 FRUITS)
  (0 1 1 1 0 0)

(APPLY 'PLUS
       (MAPCAR 'APPLEP-1-0 FRUITS))
   3
```

Alternatively, the action now in APPLEP-1-0 can be specified locally, using a lambda-style definition in the MAPCAR:

```
(APPLY 'PLUS
       (MAPCAR '(LAMBDA (Y) (COND ((APPLEP Y) 1)
                                  (T 0)))
               FRUITS))
   3.
```

Indeed, the guts of APPLEP can be brought in too:

```
(APPLY 'PLUS
       (MAPCAR '(LAMBDA (X) (COND ((EQUAL X 'APPLE) 1)
                                  (T 0)))
               FRUITS))
   3.
```

Of course it is easy to bottle all of this up and make a function out of it:

```
(DEFUN COUNTAPPLES (FRUITS)
       (APPLY 'PLUS
              (MAPCAR '(LAMBDA (X) (COND ((EQUAL X 'APPLE) 1)
                                         (T 0)))
                      FRUITS)))

(COUNTAPPLES FRUITS)
   3
```

Incidentally, lambda-style definitions can have any number of s-expressions, just like ordinary definitions. Only the last determines the value. The rest are evaluated for side effects.

LAMBDA is Often Used to Interface Functions to Argument Lists

The next example develops a function that determines how many times atoms with a specified property are found in some given s-expression. Unlike COUNTAPPLES, this new function is expected to work on any s-expression, not just lists of atoms.

The plan is to make a recursive function that can work its way into the s-expression that is given. This preparatory function counts the instances of APPLE:

```
(DEFUN COUNTAPPLES (S)
        (COND ((EQUAL S 'APPLE) 1)        ;It is an apple.
              ((ATOM S) 0)                ;No, it is not.
              (T (APPLY 'PLUS
                     (MAPCAR 'COUNTAPPLES S)))))
```

Now we attempt to generalize this by adding another variable, making a function that will count any item, not just apples. The new function counts the instances of the first argument appearing in the second argument. Our first attempt fails:

```
(DEFUN COUNT (ITEM S)
        (COND ((EQUAL S ITEM) 1)          ;It is one of them.
              ((ATOM S) 0)                ;No, it is not.
              (T (APPLY 'PLUS
                     (MAPCAR 'COUNT S)))))  ;Blunder!
```

This is wrong because COUNT is defined as a function of two arguments, ITEM and S. If it does not get two, it is unhappy. But the MAPCAR only has one list of things to channel into COUNT. Hence disaster. There is a fatal mismatch between the parameter list COUNT is defined with and the arguments it is supplied by the MAPCAR.

The solution is to make a new function, using COUNT, that has only one parameter. Lets call this COUNTAUX:

```
(DEFUN COUNTAUX (S) (COUNT ITEM S))
```

```
(DEFUN COUNT (ITEM S)                          ;Uses auxiliary function.
        (COND ((EQUAL S ITEM) 1)
              ((ATOM S) 0)
              (T (APPLY 'PLUS (MAPCAR 'COUNTAUX S)))))
```

More likely, however, COUNTAUX would not be defined. Instead a local lambda-style definition would be used:

```
(DEFUN COUNT (ITEM S)                        ;Uses LAMBDA.
       (COND ((EQUAL S ITEM) 1)
             ((ATOM S) 0)
             (T (APPLY 'PLUS (MAPCAR '(LAMBDA (E)
                                              (COUNT ITEM E))
                             S)))))
```

Here LAMBDA matches COUNT, a function of two variables, to one list of MAPCAR arguments. Note that ITEM is a free variable with respect to the lambda expression. Using 'COUNT in place of the lambda definition is an example of a common error.

Problems

Problem 6-1: Define PRESENTP, a function that determines if a particular atom exists anywhere in an s-expression. It differs from MEMBER because MEMBER only looks for top-level instances. Symbolic-mathematics systems make use of such a function to determine if an s-expression contains a particular variable. Consider these, for example:

```
(SETQ FORMULA '(SQRT (QUOTIENT (PLUS (EXPT X 2) (EXPT Y 2)) 2)))

(PRESENTP 'X FORMULA)
   T

(PRESENTP 'Z FORMULA)
   NIL
```

MAPCAN Facilitates Filtering

While we are at it, this is a good time to explain MAPCAN, a function closely related to MAPCAR. Often MAPCAN can be used to do *filtered accumulations*. To see what this means, suppose there is a list of groceries, and for some bizarre reason, we want to pick out the fruits and make a list out of them. When defined, the function KEEPFRUITS will do it:

```
(KEEPFRUITS '(BROCCOLI MILK APPLE BREAD BUTTER PEAR STEAK))
   (APPLE PEAR)
```

Assume FRUITP is a predicate that checks to see if an atom is a fruit, perhaps by inspecting its FRUIT property. Assume KEEPFRUITS's variable is named GROCERIES. Then it is natural to think of using FRUITP on every element in GROCERIES. MAPCAR can arrange this for us, but the result is not quite what we want:

```
(MAPCAR 'FRUITP GROCERIES)
  (NIL NIL T NIL NIL T NIL)
```

Another idea is to arrange a local lambda definition so that the actual fruits get into the result. We are on the way with this:

```
(MAPCAR '(LAMBDA (E) (COND ((FRUITP E) E) (T NIL)))
        GROCERIES)
  (NIL NIL APPLE NIL NIL PEAR NIL)
```

It is too bad the result is not a bit different, for then APPLY, working with APPEND, could do a nice thing:

```
(APPLY 'APPEND '(NIL NIL (APPLE) NIL NIL (PEAR) NIL))
  (APPLE PEAR)
```

But of course it is easy to modify the lambda definition to produce what APPEND needs:

```
(MAPCAR '(LAMBDA (E) (COND ((FRUITP E) (LIST E))
                          (T NIL)))
        GROCERIES)
  (NIL NIL (APPLE) NIL NIL (PEAR) NIL)
```

The combination of an APPEND together with a MAPCAR will do the job. The function used by MAPCAR must return the desired elements packaged up by LIST. The function returns NIL when applied to other elements.

Now for MAPCAN, finally. MAPCAN acts much as if it were a combination of MAPCAR and APPEND. (Actually, MAPCAN acts as if it were a combination of MAPCAR and NCONC, a function that will be explained later. This makes MAPCAN a possibly dangerous function for novices since the NCONC can cause unexpected things to happen.) Thus these are equivalent for our present purpose:

```
(APPLY 'APPEND
       (MAPCAR '(LAMBDA (E) (COND ((FRUITP E) (LIST E))
                                 (T NIL)))
               GROCERIES))
  (APPLE PEAR)
```

```
(MAPCAN '(LAMBDA (E) (COND ((FRUITP E) (LIST E))
                          (T NIL)))
        GROCERIES)
    (APPLE PEAR)
```

Thus MAPCAN is convenient when it is good to filter a list. Using it, KEEPFRUITS, the function we started out to define, is done like this:

```
(DEFUN KEEPFRUITS (GROCERIES)
       (MAPCAN '(LAMBDA (E) (COND ((FRUITP E) (LIST E))
                                 (T NIL)))
               GROCERIES))
```

Style is a Personal Matter

When there are choices, people will argue. For example, some people prefer alternatives to the MAPCAN-type filtered accumulation done by KEEPFRUITS. Here are some that do the same job, but with the result in reverse order:

```
(DEFUN KEEPFRUITS (GROCERIES)             ;Recursive instead of iterative.
       (COND ((NULL GROCERIES) NIL)
             ((FRUITP (CAR GROCERIES))
              (CONS (CAR GROCERIES) (KEEPFRUITS (CDR GROCERIES))))
             (T (KEEPFRUITS (CDR GROCERIES)))))

(DEFUN KEEPFRUITS (GROCERIES)             ;Uses PROG for iteration.
       (PROG (RESULT)
             LOOP
             (COND ((NULL GROCERIES) (RETURN RESULT))
                   ((FRUITP (CAR GROCERIES))
                    (SETQ RESULT (CONS (CAR GROCERIES) RESULT))))
             (SETQ GROCERIES (CDR GROCERIES))
             (GO LOOP)))

(DEFUN KEEPFRUITS (GROCERIES)             ;Uses DO (described briefly later).
       (DO ((RESULT)
            (POSSIBILITIES GROCERIES (CDR POSSIBILITIES)))
           ((NULL POSSIBILITIES) RESULT)
           (COND ((FRUITP (CAR POSSIBILITIES))
                  (SETQ RESULT (CONS (CAR POSSIBILITIES) RESULT))))))
```

Similarly, there are a variety of ways to hold values temporarily. Suppose, for example, that LISTFRUITS is to return the fruits in a list if there are fewer than ten. If there are more, it is to return TOO-MANY. The obvious definition is wasteful in that it uses KEEPFRUITS twice:

```
(DEFUN LISTFRUITS (GROCERIES)              ;Uses KEEPFRUITS twice.
      (COND ((GREATERP (LENGTH (KEEPFRUITS GROCERIES)) 10)
             'TOO-MANY)
            (T (KEEPFRUITS GROCERIES)))))
```

The inefficiency can be avoided in a number of ways:

```
(DEFUN LISTFRUITS (GROCERIES)              ;Holds on using PROG parameter.
      (PROG (TEMP)
            (SETQ TEMP (KEEPFRUITS GROCERIES))
            (COND ((GREATERP (LENGTH TEMP) 10) (RETURN 'TOO-MANY))
                  (T (RETURN TEMP)))))
```

```
(DEFUN LISTFRUITS (GROCERIES)              ;Holds on using LAMBDA parameter.
      ((LAMBDA (TEMP)
            (COND ((GREATERP (LENGTH TEMP) 10) 'TOO-MANY)
                  (T TEMP)))
       (KEEPFRUITS GROCERIES)))
```

```
(DEFUN LISTFRUITS (GROCERIES)              ;Uses LET (described briefly later).
      (LET ((TEMP (KEEPFRUITS GROCERIES)))
           (COND ((GREATERP (LENGTH TEMP) 10) 'TOO-MANY)
                 (T TEMP))))
```

In this book, we try to stay flexible, believing that style is often a matter of personal taste and that each style has its rightful place depending on circumstances.

■ We have avoided DO and LET in this book because these functions tend to be less standardized than others at the moment. This is unfortunate since many of the examples would be clearer if DO and LET were used.

Summary

■ LAMBDA defines anonymous functions.

■ LAMBDA is often used to interface functions to argument lists.

■ MAPCAN facilitates filtering.

■ Style is a personal matter.

7
PRINTING
READING
AND
ATOM
MANIPULATION

The purpose of this chapter is to introduce PRINT and READ, functions that help other functions communicate with users. Without PRINT, the only way a user can learn about what a LISP function is doing is to wait for a value to appear. Without READ, the only way a function can get information is through its arguments and free variables. PRINT and READ therefore open the door to much more communication. Happily, both are very simple.

PRINT and READ Facilitate Communication

PRINT evaluates its single argument and prints it on a new line. Thus the following function will print out the squares of the integers until something drops dead:

```
(DEFUN BORE-ME ()
        (PROG (N)
              (SETQ N 0)
              LOOP
              (PRINT (TIMES N N))        ;Print square of integer.
              (SETQ N (ADD1 N))          ;Increment integer.
              (GO LOOP)))                ;Do it forever.
    BORE-ME

(BORE-ME)
    0
    1
```

```
4
9
16
25
36
.
.
.
```

In BORE-ME, the value returned by PRINT is not used. In fact, the value of an application of PRINT is not very useful in this book's LISP because PRINT happens to return T as its value:

```
(PRINT 'EXAMPLE)
   EXAMPLE
   T
```

When (READ) is encountered, LISP stops and waits for the user to type an s-expression. That s-expression, without evaluation, becomes the value of (READ). Using READ by itself therefore causes total inactivity until the user types something. In this example, the user types EXAMPLE (followed by a space):

```
(READ)EXAMPLE
   EXAMPLE
```

Note that READ prints nothing to indicate that it is waiting, not even a carriage return.

Problems about Stacking Disks on Pins

We now tackle the celebrated Tower-of-Hanoi problem. An ancient myth has it that in some temple in the Far East, time is marked off by monks engaged in the transfer of 64 disks from one of three pins to another. The universe as we know it will end when they are done. The reason we do not have to concern ourselves about the cosmological implications of this is that their progress is kept in check by some clever rules: the monks can move only one disk at a time; the disks all have different diameters; and no disk can ever be placed on top of a smaller one.

The insight leading to the correct sequence of moves comes from realizing that a set of n disks can be transferred from pin A to pin B in these stages: first move the top $(n-1)$ disks from A to the spare pin C; then move the large bottom disk from A to B; and finally, move the $(n-1)$ disks from the spare pin, C, onto pin B. Naturally, moving the $(n-1)$ disks can be done by the same trick, using the third pin (not involved in the transfer) as workspace. By means of recursion, we have postponed the actual work until n equals one. It is possible to verify that in each case the transfer of the single disk constitutes a legal move.

```
(DEFUN TOWER-OF-HANOI (N) (TRANSFER 'A 'B 'C N))          ;N disks on A first.

(DEFUN MOVE-DISK (FROM TO)
       (LIST (LIST 'MOVE 'DISK 'FROM FROM 'TO TO)))        ;Build instruction.

(DEFUN TRANSFER (FROM TO SPARE NUMBER)
       (COND ((EQUAL NUMBER 1) (MOVE-DISK FROM TO))        ;Transfer one disk.
             (T (APPEND (TRANSFER FROM                     ;Move from FROM
                                  SPARE                    ;to SPARE
                                  TO                       ;using TO as space
                                  (SUB1 NUMBER))           ;(n-1) disks.
                        (MOVE-DISK FROM TO)                ;Move lowest disk.
                        (TRANSFER SPARE                    ;Move from SPARE
                                  TO                       ;to TO
                                  FROM                     ;using FROM as space
                                  (SUB1 NUMBER)))))))       ;(n-1) disks.
```

This is what the resulting list of instructions looks like for a typical case:

```
(TOWER-OF-HANOI 3)
  ((MOVE DISK FROM A TO B) (MOVE DISK FROM A TO C) (MOVE DISK FROM B TO C)
   (MOVE DISK FROM A TO B) (MOVE DISK FROM C TO A) (MOVE DISK FROM C TO B)
   (MOVE DISK FROM A TO B))
```

Problem 7-1: The above solution may not be very convincing, since everything seems to be done blindly, without checking whether disks are ever placed on smaller disks, or for that matter, whether any disks are left on the pin from which they are supposed to be removed. What is needed is a simulation of the pin transfer steps. Consequently, there is a need to print detailed information about the steps as they are taken.

It would also be more informative if the final instructions included some identification of which disk is being moved. Let us assume that the disks are numbered in order of increasing size. Further, let A, B, and C be lists of numbers representing the stacks of disks currently on each of the three pins. Rewrite MOVE-DISK to include checking on the legality of proposed moves, appropriate modification of the lists A, B, and C, as well as generation of more informative output as suggested by the following:

```
(SETQ A '(1 2 3)  B NIL  C NIL)

(TOWER-OF-HANOI)
```

should print:

```
(MOVE 1 FROM A TO B)
(MOVE 2 FROM A TO C)
(MOVE 1 FROM B TO C)
(MOVE 3 FROM A TO B)
(MOVE 1 FROM C TO A)
(MOVE 2 FROM C TO B)
(MOVE 1 FROM A TO B)
```

Special Conventions Make Weird Atom Names Possible

Sometimes it is useful to have atoms that consist wholly or partly of characters that ordinarily are not allowed in atoms. Spaces and parentheses are examples of such characters. Placing vertical bars around such special characters is the way to do this in our implementation of LISP:

```
(SETQ ATOM1 '|(|)
  |(|

(SETQ ATOM2 '|WEIRD ATOM|)
  |WEIRD ATOM|

(PRINT ATOM1)
  |(|
  T

(PRINT ATOM2)
  |WEIRD ATOM|
  T
```

An older method uses a slash, /, to indicate that the following character is to lose any special properties it might otherwise have had. We could have used '/(for ATOM1 and 'WEIRD/ ATOM for ATOM2 in the above examples. (For output, LISP uses the vertical bar convention, not slashes.)

Atoms can be Broken Apart, Put Together, and Created

It is sometimes useful to take the names of atoms apart or to make new atom names. Later, in another chapter, we will have reason to do this so that patterns read by LISP can be more cosmetically pleasing. In particular, we will use atom-manipulation functions to split up atoms like >RESULT into two new atoms, > and RESULT.

EXPLODE appears in order to break up an atom into a list of its constituent characters, each appearing as a single character atom:

```
(EXPLODE 'ATOM)
  (A T O M)

(EXPLODE 'X)
  (X)
```

IMPLODE performs the complementary operation of running a list of single-character atoms together into a single atom:

```
(IMPLODE '(A B C))
  ABC
```

And if there is a program that wants a fresh atom name without bothering the user to get it, GENSYM should be used. In some sense, GENSYM is an input function that creates new atoms rather than reading them in:

```
(GENSYM)
  G0001

(GENSYM)
  G0002
```

In another chapter, these GENSYMed atoms will be used to build tree structures that record how the functions in a block-world manipulation system call one another to solve problems. The trees will make it possible to answer questions about how things were done, as well as why and when.

Exotic Input/Output Functions Lie Beyond PRINT and READ

It is possible to go through a career of LISP programming without using any printing and reading functions other than PRINT and READ. Eventually, however, most people like to use other functions that enable better-looking, more presentable input and output. It makes no sense to dwell on these other printing and reading functions, however, because they tend to vary from system to system. The following are given mainly to show what is usually available by one name or another.

TERPRI is a function of no arguments that starts a new line. PRIN1 is like PRINT except that PRIN1 does not start a new line. PRINC is like PRIN1 except that vertical bars, if any, are suppressed. Thus:

```
(PRINT ATOM2)
  |WEIRD ATOM|
  T
```

```
(PRIN1 ATOM2)|WEIRD ATOM|
   T

(PRINC ATOM2)WEIRD ATOM
```

Note that since PRIN1 and PRINC do not start a new line, the things they print are on the same line the user types on. READCH reads one character and returns it as an atom:

```
(READCH)X
   X
```

Formatted Printing is Easily Arranged

As an example of what can be done with vertical bars and exotic printing functions, let us consider a program that takes two arguments, a list of atoms to be printed, and a list of columns where printing is to start. This function is named FORTRANPRINT inasmuch as it provides features that are similar to some of those provided by FORTRAN and FORTRAN-like languages.

```
(DEFUN FORTRANPRINT (ATOMS COLUMNS)
      (PROG (N)
            (SETQ N 0)
            (TERPRI)                          ;Print blank line.
            NEXTATOM
            (COND ((OR (NULL ATOMS) (NULL COLUMNS))
                   (RETURN T)))
            NEXTSPACE
            (COND ((LESSP N (CAR COLUMNS))     ;Need another space?
                   (PRINC '| |)
                   (SETQ N (ADD1 N))
                   (GO NEXTSPACE)))
            (PRINC (CAR ATOMS))                ;Print next atom.
            (SETQ N (PLUS N                    ;Allow for atom.
                     (LENGTH (EXPLODE (CAR ATOMS)))))
            (SETQ ATOMS (CDR ATOMS))
            (SETQ COLUMNS (CDR COLUMNS))
            (GO NEXTATOM)))
```

Here is an example in which several FORTRANPRINTs are used to print a timetable in columns determined by the value of TABS:

```
(DEFUN TABLE (TABS)
      (TERPRI)
      (FORTRANPRINT '(CONCORD LINCOLN WALTHAM CAMBRIDGE BOSTON) TABS)
      (TERPRI)
      (FORTRANPRINT '(6:11 6:17 6:29 6:41 6:55) TABS)
      (FORTRANPRINT '(6:46 6:52 7:05 7:17 7:31) TABS))
   TABLE

(TABLE '(0 12 24 36 48))
```

CONCORD	LINCOLN	WALTHAM	CAMBRIDGE	BOSTON
6:11	6:17	6:29	6:41	6:55
6:46	6:52	7:05	7:17	7:31

```
   T
```

Problems

Problem 7-2: Define ECHO1, a function that reads s-expressions and returns them without evaluation, and define ECHO2, a function that returns with evaluation.

Problem 7-3: It is often handy to have a way of printing information without too many parentheses to confuse things. Define a function P that takes one argument and prints the atoms in it as a single nonnested list. This illustrates:

```
(SETQ S '(A (B (C D) E) (F (G (H I) J) K) L))
   (A (B (C D) E) (F (G (H I) J) K) L)

(P (LIST '(THE ATOMS IN S ARE) S))
   (THE ATOMS IN S ARE A B C D E F G H I J K L)
```

Then define PC, a function that takes two arguments and prints only if the first evaluates to nonNIL. When PC does print, it is to print the second argument as a nonnested list. And finally define RQ, a function that prints its argument as a nonnested list, reads an s-expression given by the user, and returns its value. Note that PC is a useful debugging function and RQ is handy for requesting values from the user from deep inside some program. These examples illustrate:

```
(SETQ N 'ROBBIE)
   ROBBIE

(PC (NOT (NUMBERP N)) (LIST 'WARNING N '(IS NOT A NUMBER)))
   (WARNING ROBBIE IS NOT A NUMBER)
```

```
(RQ '(PLEASE SUPPLY A VALUE FOR PI))
  (PLEASE SUPPLY A VALUE FOR PI) 3.14159
  3.14159
```

Problem 7-4: Define P1, a function that behaves like P except that it prints no parentheses at all:

```
(SETQ S '(A B C D E F G H I J K L))
  (A B C D E F G H I J K L)

(P1 (LIST '(THE ATOMS IN S ARE) S))
  THE ATOMS IN S ARE A B C D E F G H I J K L
```

Problem 7-5: The examples throughout this book indicate that PRINT indents two spaces before starting. This is done for clarity only, and in actual LISP systems, PRINT does not indent. Define BOOKPRINT, a function that does.

Problem 7-6: Define ATOMCAR and ATOMCDR. The first returns the first character in a given atom, and the second returns all of the characters but the first.

Problem 7-7: Define PRINT-MATRIX, a procedure which prints each row of the array called MATRIX on a separate line. The two arguments given to the procedure specify the number of rows and the number of columns in the array.

Problem 7-8: A program's requests for information and the user's replies can be arranged neatly on the screen of a display terminal. A list can conveniently describe the desired format by specifying the rows and columns in which input and output is to appear. The form for a sublist specifying where some words are to be printed might be as follows:

```
(<list of words> <row> <column>)
```

Similarly the following sublist would specify the location where information typed by the user is to appear:

```
(<word> <row> <column>)
```

The symbolic atom <word> is set to the number or word typed by the user. Define FORM-ENTRY, a procedure which prints and reads according to such formatting instructions. Assume that items are ordered, so that a cursor can always be positioned by spacing forward and going to the next line (a cursor is a mark that indicates where the next character is to appear on the screen). Further assume that TOP-OF-SCREEN clears the display screen and positions the cursor in the top left hand corner.

The following is a test case for your procedure:

```
(FORM-ENTRY '(((LAST NAME:) 1. 0.)
              (LAST-NAME 1. 11.)
              ((FIRST NAME:) 1. 30.)
              (FIRST-NAME 1. 43.)
              ((AGE:) 3. 0.)
              (AGE 3. 6.)
              ((SEX:) 3. 14.)
              (SEX 3. 20.)
              ((OCCUPATION:) 3. 30.)
              (OCCUPATION 3. 43.)
              ((YOUR ADDRESS NEXT:) 6. 0.)
              ((STREET:) 9. 0.)
              (STREET 9. 9.)
              ((NUMBER:) 9. 30.)
              (NUMBER 9. 39.)
              ((CITY:) 10. 0.)
              (CITY 10. 9.)
              ((STATE:) 10. 30.)
              (STATE 10. 38.)
              ((ZIP CODE:) 10. 52.)
              (ZIP 10. 63.)
              ((THANK YOU VERY MUCH) 13. 0.))
```

Problem 7-9: It is essential, when using LISP, to have some tools to help get the layout of s-expressions right. Otherwise the parentheses become snares. LISP systems therefore have various functions to do what is called prettyprinting. Write a simple PRETTYPRINT, a function that takes one s-expression and prints it neatly by printing the first element, then the second, and then the third, neatly lining up the third and the rest under the second.

```
(<element-1> <element-2>
             <element-3>
                .
                .
                .
             <element-n>)
```

Each element itself should be prettyprinted so that the whole s-expression has a transparent appearance.

Project: Write a simple real time editor in LISP.

Summary

■ PRINT and READ facilitate communication.

■ Special conventions make weird atom names possible.

■ Atoms can be broken apart, put together, and created.

■ Exotic input/output functions lie beyond PRINT and READ.

■ Formatted printing is easily arranged.

References

Pretty-printing is discussed by Goldstein [1973], Oppen [1979], as well as Hearn and Norman [1979]. A powerful real time editor written in LISP is described by Greenberg [1979].

8
DEFINING
FEXPRS
AND
MACROS

So far we know how to define ordinary functions that have a fixed number of parameters, all of which are evaluated before a function is entered. The purpose of this chapter is to show how to define idiomatic functions called FEXPRs and MACROs that take a variable number of parameters and that do not evaluate their arguments. These stand in contrast to the ordinary functions we have worked with so far, the so-called EXPRs. MACROs are particularly useful because they facilitate extensions to LISP such as the introduction of DOWHILE and DOUNTIL functions.

FEXPRs are Functions that do not Evaluate their Arguments

Often it is useful to have functions that differ from the ones seen so far in one or both of the following ways:

- There is an arbitrary number of parameters. PLUS and APPEND are examples of LISP functions that are like this.

- The arguments are not evaluated. DEFUN and DEFPROP are like this.

Evidently something new is needed since ordinary user-defined functions always evaluate their arguments. There must be a way to order DEFUN to create functions that are not ordinary. Here is how it is done:

```
(DEFUN <function name> FEXPR (<single parameter>) <body>)
```

The inserted FEXPR is the signal to DEFUN that orders special treatment. The resulting function is called a FEXPR, which distinguishes it from the ordinary functions, the EXPRs. It is regrettable that these names have only obscure mnemonic content.

The special treatment is limited to the handling of arguments. First, FEXPRs never evaluate any of their arguments. Second, all arguments that appear in a FEXPR application, however many, are formed into a list that then becomes the value of the single symbolic atom that appears in the parameter list. An example will make this clear. Suppose DEMONSTRATE is defined as a FEXPR:

```
(DEFUN DEMONSTRATE FEXPR (PAR) (PRINT PAR) (LENGTH PAR))
```

Now suppose DEMONSTRATE is used as follows:

```
(DEMONSTRATE THIS FUNCTION)
```

No attempt is made to evaluate either THIS or FUNCTION. Instead the list (THIS FUNCTION) becomes the value of PAR. The PRINT therefore causes the list (THIS FUNCTION) to be printed, while LENGTH causes 2 to be returned as the function's value:

```
(DEMONSTRATE THIS FUNCTION)
  (THIS FUNCTION)
  2
```

Consider the function IF, defined below, for further illustration. IF is to have either two or three arguments. If the first evaluates to nonNIL, then the second is evaluated and returned. If the first evaluates to NIL and there is a third, then the third is evaluated and returned. Otherwise NIL is returned.

```
(DEFUN IF FEXPR (X)
       (COND ((EVAL (CAR X)) (EVAL (CADR X)))      ;First arg nonNIL?
             ((CDDR X) (EVAL (CADDR X)))           ;Third arg present?
             (T NIL)))                             ;Otherwise return NIL.
```

The FEXPR style definition is needed for two reasons: first, the number of arguments is not fixed, and second, evaluation of the first argument determines what further evaluation is to take place.

This version of IF does have one serious flaw, however, that can lead to difficult bugs. Suppose we try this:

```
(SETQ X 'ROBBIE)
  ROBBIE

(SETQ SEX (GET X 'SEX))
  MALE
```

And now we evaluate this:

```
(IF (EQUAL SEX 'MALE) X 'SALLY)
  ((EQUAL SEX 'MALE) X 'SALLY)
```

We expected that ROBBIE would be returned since the value of SEX is MALE. In fact the result is ((EQUAL SEX 'MALE) X 'SALLY)! The blunder occurs because X is the FEXPR's parameter as well as a variable that appears in an expression evaluated inside the FEXPR. This *variable conflict* screws things up completely. The inelegant solution is to use an obscure atom instead of X. Something like $%&*! might do. The elegant solution is to define IF as a MACRO.

In fact, FEXPRs are not used that much. They are discussed here nevertheless because they help to explain the behavior of primitives like QUOTE, SETQ, COND and PROG. These do not evaluate their arguments and they take an arbitrary number of arguments.

MACROs Translate and then Execute

MACROs are like FEXPRs in that they do not evaluate their arguments and take any number of arguments. Unlike FEXPRs, they give their single parameter the entire s-expression associated with their call. If IF had been defined as a MACRO and (IF TEST 'YES 'NO) were encountered, then X's value would be (IF TEST 'YES 'NO). Also unlike FEXPRs and everything else, the value of a MACRO is not returned directly. Instead the value is evaluated again. MACROs are defined using this syntax:

```
(DEFUN <function name> MACRO (<single parameter>) <body>)
```

Let us nail this notion down by doing IF as a MACRO. Thinking in terms of MACROs, the overall idea is to translate each IF expression into an equivalent COND. For a three-argument use of IF, we have

```
(IF <first argument> <second argument> <third argument>)
```

translated into

```
(COND (<first argument> <second argument>)
      (T <third argument>)))
```

When evaluated, the equivalent COND yields the desired result. The following MACRO, IF3, builds the required COND using SUBST together with the raw material supplied in IF3's parameter X. The COND is then returned. Then it is evaluated because IF3 is a MACRO and therefore, by special privilege, gets an extra evaluation done on the result returned. This version is called IF3 because it requires exactly three arguments:

```
(DEFUN IF3 MACRO (X)
        (SUBST (CADR X) '1ST                    ; Place first arg.
             (SUBST (CADDR X) '2ND              ; Place second arg.
                  (SUBST (CADDDR X) '3RD         ; Place third arg.
                       '(COND (1ST 2ND) (T 3RD))))))
```

Once this version of IF is understood, it is easy to generalize it, producing a function that handles either two or three arguments. A test on the length of the MACRO's parameter enables the correct analysis:

```
(DEFUN IF MACRO (X)
        (SUBST (CADR X) '1ST                     ; Place first arg.
             (SUBST (CADDR X) '2ND               ; Place second arg.
                  (SUBST (COND ((EQUAL (LENGTH X) 4)   ; Third arg?
                               (CADDDR X))
                              (T NIL))            ; No, just two.
                       '3RD
                       '(COND (1ST 2ND) (T 3RD))))))
```

It is important to understand that the COND is returned and then evaluated after the MACRO is finished. This means that X, the MACRO's parameter, is restored before the COND is evaluated. If X appears inside the COND, the value used when the COND is evaluated is the value it had outside the MACRO. The expression that caused a problem with the FEXPR definition causes no problem here:

```
(SETQ X 'ROBBIE)
   ROBBIE
```

```
(SETQ SEX (GET X 'SEX))
   MALE
```

```
(IF (EQUAL SEX 'MALE) X 'SALLY)
   ROBBIE
```

■ The key idea is that a MACRO is given a piece of program and computes a new piece of program from it. Thus MACROs exploit the fact that LISP programs and data have the same form.

MACROs make it straightforward to extend LISP by introducing DO and LET functions.

Incidentally, other forms of function definition exist. One of them, the so-called LEXPRs, is described briefly in Note 4 of Appendix 4.

Problems

Problem 8-1: The syntax of DEFUN is somewhat unfortunate. It would be prettier to combine the function name with the parameters so that the first argument would be a package that closely resembles what an application of the function looks like. Define DEFINE, a FEXPR that uses DEFUN and defines EXPRs, but that has the following syntax:

```
(DEFINE (<function name> <parameter 1> . . . <parameter n>)
        <body>)
```

Problem 8-2: Define DEFINE as a MACRO.

Problem 8-3: Some people are annoyed by the nonmnemonic character of the critical functions CAR, CDR, and CONS. Define new functions FIRST, REST, and INSERT as MACROs that do the same things. Note that SECOND, THIRD, and similar functions are equally easy to create.

Problem 8-4: Suppose DOWHILE is a function of two arguments that evaluates both arguments over and over until the first one evaluates to NIL. Define DOWHILE as a MACRO. It may help to remember the function GENSYM. Each time (GENSYM) is executed, its value is a new atom in the sequence G0001, G0002, G0003, ...

Problem 8-5: Define DOUNTIL as a MACRO. DOUNTIL is to work like DOWHILE except that it evaluates its arguments until the first is nonNIL rather than NIL.

Problem 8-6: Using DOUNTIL, define FACTORIAL, a function that was defined as an ordinary PROG with a loop in a previous chapter.

Problem 8-7: Suppose (BOOLE 1 A B) computes the bit-wise logical AND of the two binary numbers A and B. Similarly, (BOOLE 7 A B) computes the bit-wise logical OR, and (BOOLE 6 A B) the bit-wise exclusive-or. Define the more mnemonic LOGAND, LOGOR, and LOGXOR as macros. Each is to take two arguments and produce the appropriate result.

Problem 8-8: A *stack* is a linearly ordered set of things which can be accessed using push and pop operations. PUSH adds a new item to the top of the stack, while POP removes the item on top of the stack. A list can be used to represent a stack, with the first element corresponding to the item on top. Define PUSH and POP as MACROs. PUSH takes two arguments, the item to be pushed and the name of a variable whose value is the list representing the stack. The value returned is the enlarged list. POP takes a single argument, the name of the variable whose value is the list. The value returned is the item popped. In both cases the value of the variable is changed to reflect the new state of the stack.

Problem 8-9: In a previous chapter, we noted that lambda parameters can be used to hold on to temporary values so that they need not be recomputed. The function LISTFRUITS was used as an example:

```
(DEFUN LISTFRUITS (GROCERIES)              ;Hold on using lambda parameter.
      ((LAMBDA (TEMP)
              (COND ((GREATERP (LENGTH TEMP) 10) 'TOO-MANY)
                    (T TEMP)))
        (KEEPFRUITS GROCERIES)))
```

The problem with using lambda parameters is that things are too spread out. Variables are named far from where their value computations are given. Use of LET helps because variables and their value computations are together:

```
(DEFUN LISTFRUITS (GROCERIES)            ;Uses LET.
      (LET ((TEMP (KEEPFRUITS GROCERIES)))
            (COND ((GREATERP (LENGTH TEMP) 10) 'TOO-MANY)
                  (T TEMP)))))
```

This pair of definitions for LISTFRUITS correctly suggests that LET can be defined as a MACRO that converts LET forms into LAMBDA forms as follows:

```
(LET ((<parameter 1> <value expression for parameter 1>)
     .
     .
     (<parameter n> <value expression for parameter n>))
     <body>)
```

```
((LAMBDA (<parameter 1> ... <parameter n>)
        <body>)
 <value expression for parameter 1>
 .
 .
 <value expression for parameter n>)
```

Define the LET MACRO.

Summary

■ FEXPRs are functions that do not evaluate their arguments.

■ MACROs translate and then execute.

9
LIST
STORAGE
RECLAMATION
AND
SURGERY

This chapter describes how atoms and lists can be represented in a computer. There are two reasons for knowing about this. First, understanding list representation clears away some of the fog. Second, understanding list representation enables understanding certain functions that can surgically alter existing lists, such as NCONC, RPLACA, RPLACD, and DELETE.

Networks of Memory Cells Represent Lists

Conceptually, the memory of an ordinary computer consists of numbered memory cells. The number of a particular memory cell is called its address. In the following diagram, for example, the address of the first cell is 2001 and its contents is 9100:

Cell Address	Cell Contents
2001	9100
2002	9025
2003	9001
2004	9050

Note that the memory-cell contents are numbers, just as addresses are. Consequently the contents of one memory cell may be said to contain the address of another. If the contents are interpreted this way, then the first memory cell is said to contain a *pointer* to the other. Memory cell 2001, by this terminology, contains a pointer to memory cell 9100.

Sometimes memory cells are large enough to hold two pointers, a left-half pointer and an right-half pointer. Straightforward LISP implementations treat memory cells as two-pointer places.

```
Cell            Cell
Address         Contents

2001            9100|2002
2002            9025|2004
2003            9001|0000
2004            9050|2003
```

Atoms and lists can be represented as collections of memory cells whose contents are mainly pointers to other memory cells. Each LISP system has some set of conventions for interpreting such collections. For example, a list might be represented as a set of memory cells that are threaded together by their right-half pointers. Left-half pointers would specify list elements. Some special reserved number, typically 0, would be in the right-half of the last memory cell in each list to signal its end.

Usually it is convenient to represent the contents of memory in an abstract way that stands above any particular set of implementation choices. Box-and-arrow notation does this. Each pointer is represented by an arrow. Lists are represented by groups of boxes with left and right pointers, connected together by the right pointers, and terminated by a slash. It is not necessary to keep the cells in any particular pattern. They can be arranged to make the connections clear:

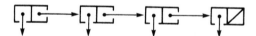

In box-and-arrow notation, an atom is represented by simply writing down its name. When a list element is an atom, a left-half arrow is drawn to the atom's name. An arrow drawn from an atom gives that atom's value. Thus the following is a way of representing the list (THIS IS A LIST), which happens to be the value of the atom EXAMPLE1:

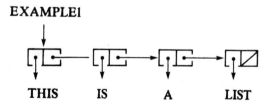

Of course, the elements of a list may be lists rather than atoms. This means that left-half arrows will represent pointers to other lists, as in this example for the list ((THIS IS) (TWO LISTS)), the value of EXAMPLE2:

EXAMPLE2

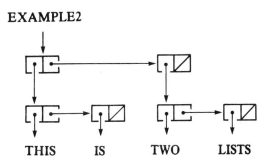

THIS   IS   TWO   LISTS

The key thing is that there are atoms and that there are two-pointer entities, tied together. In computer memory, the atoms actually may be specially marked lists, some consecutive memory cells in a reserved part of memory, or something else. The pointers may be packed two to a memory cell or one each in two consecutive memory cells. Box-and-arrow notation stands above such detail.

   In most LISP implementations, each atom is associated with a pointer to the atom's current value. In other LISP implementations, including a demonstration LISP developed in Chapter 23, each atom is paired with a value on an association list.

Single Quote Marks are a Shorthand Form for the Function QUOTE

At first, it might seem that the single quote mark lies outside of what box-and-arrow notation can handle. But actually, when a LISP system absorbs text from a terminal or from storage, single-quote marks are translated into applications of the function QUOTE. This is necessary because LISP internally requires all data to be expressed strictly and uniformly in s-expression form. The single-quote device does not fit into the s-expression definition although it makes programs clearer and learning easier. LISP is therefore buffered from text prepared by programmers by a reading program that, among other things, effects the following translation:

```
'<s-expression>  —>  (QUOTE <s-expression>)
```

This same reading program also handles any semicolons that appear to mark comments. The reading program discards the semicolons and ignores the text on the rest of the same line.

   Of course, the principal task of the reader is to translate LISP character sequences, full of parentheses, into the corresponding internal representation. Symmetrically, the printing program translates the other way. READ and PRINT give users direct access to these printing and reading programs.

CONS Builds New List Structure by Depositing Pointers in Free Cells

LISP maintains a list of spare memory cells for its own use. This list of spare memory cells is called the free storage list. CONS operates by removing the first cell on the free storage list and by depositing new pointers into this first cell. The following shows what happens when executing

(SETQ EXAMPLE3 (CONS 'A EXAMPLE3))

given that the value of EXAMPLE3 is (A B):

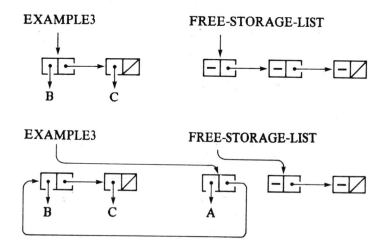

Curiously, CONS need not really have a list as its second argument. Noting that CONS simply connects its two arguments together, there is no reason to panic if the second is an atom. Here is the result of doing (CONS 'A 'B).

There is, of course, the issue of how to represent such structures in printed form.

The fact is, they are neither atoms nor lists. Historically, they have been called dotted pairs and they are written, indeed, with a dot:

```
(CONS 'A 'B)
  (A . B)
```

Sometimes dotted pairs make sense. For example, representing the coordinates of a point is a natural thing for dotted pairs, particularly if memory space is a problem. It is clear that (A . B) takes one memory cell less than does (A B):

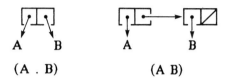

Forthe most part, however, dotted pairs are mainly a source of confusion and insidious bugs. Most programmers avoid them completely and still lead worthwhile lives.

Garbage Collection Reclaims Memory Cells for the Free Storage List

Consider this sequence:

```
(SETQ EXAMPLE4 (LIST 'A 'B 'C))
  (A B C)
```

```
(SETQ EXAMPLE4 (LIST 'X 'Y 'Z)
  (X Y Z)
```

Like CONS, the function LIST builds a new list by taking material from the free storage list. The structure is accessible via the value of EXAMPLE4. But the value of EXAMPLE4 is then changed immediately. The previous structure is no longer accessible. To be sure, the value of EXAMPLE4 can be made to be (A B C) again, but only by taking new cells from the free storage list and rebuilding.

There is no point in wasting the cells previously used in the now inaccessible list. Somehow they should be returned to the free storage list so that they can be used again. *Garbage collection* is the technical term for what needs to be done.

Typical garbage collectors have two phases. In the first phase, the garbage collector runs through memory, starting from the values, properties, and function definitions of all atoms, somehow marking all of the memory cells representing the s-expressions encountered.

The marking may be done by altering one of the bits in the memory cells, if any are unused, or by maintaining a table containing one bit per word of list storage. The choice is influenced strongly by the architecture of the computer.

The following illustrates what the garbage collector's marker does in an area that contains the cells representing the current value of EXAMPLE4 and nothing else:

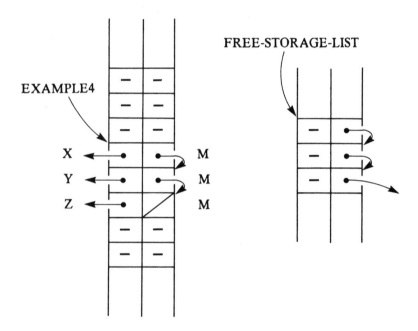

Once the marking phase is finished, a sweep phase passes through memory sequentially, taking note of unmarked cells, returning them to the free storage list. The figure on the next page illustrates how the sweep phase handles a previously marked area.

To clarify exactly what happens in garbage collection, it may be helpful to see a simple garbage collector specified by a LISP program. Assume that there is a predicate named MARKEDP that tells us whether a cell is marked. Further, let MARKIT set the mark on a cell, while UNMARKIT resets the mark. Finally, we need a way to access cells sequentially, rather than by following list structures. Let (CELL I) give us a pointer to the cell in memory whose address is the value of I. The variable FREE points to the head of the free storage list, from which CONS grabs words when it combines pointers to existing list structures.

The first step is to trace along all active list structures and mark all cells encountered. Naturally, cells already marked need not be further considered.

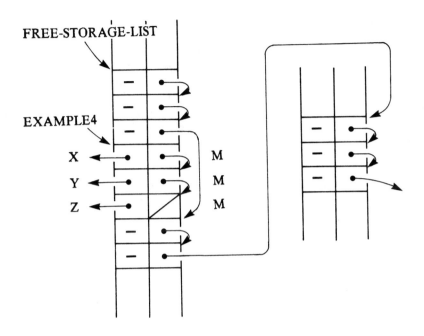

```
(DEFUN MARK (L)
      (COND ((MARKEDP L))                        ;Already marked.
            ((ATOM L) (MARKIT L))                ;Just mark atom.
            (T (MARKIT L)                        ;Mark cell
               (MARK (CAR L))                    ;and trace CAR
               (MARK (CDR L))))))                ;and trace CDR.
```

When everything of importance has been protected by marking it, a linear sweep through memory can pick up words that were not reached by the marking phase.

```
(DEFUN SWEEP ()
      (PROG (I)
            (SETQ I 0)                                    ;Start at first cell.
            LOOP
            (COND ((GREATERP I TOP) (RETURN NIL)))        ;Reached top yet?
            (COND ((MARKEDP (CELL I))                     ;If cell is marked
                   (UNMARK (CELL I)))                     ;then unmark it.
                  (T (RPLACD (CELL I) FREE)               ;If unmarked,
                     (SETQ FREE (CELL I))))               ;add to free list.
            (SETQ I (ADD1 I))                             ;Advance to next cell.
            (GO LOOP)))
```

Here TOP is a free variable whose value is the total number of cells in memory. (The function RPLACD, used here to splice free cells back into the free storage list, will be explained in the section after the next.) Naturally, these program fragments should not be taken too seriously, since a lot depends on details of particular implementations of LISP. In any case, suppose for simplicity that KEEP-LIST contains pointers to all structures currently relevant, as determined by looking at the values, properties, and function definitions of all atoms. Then the following will work: (DEFUN GC () (MARK KEEP-LIST) (SWEEP))

Typically, a garbage collector is invoked automatically when the free storage list is near exhaustion. Users never know, unless they become suspicious because the computer seems to drop dead suddenly, but temporarily. Some newer garbage collectors do not use the sweep-and-mark idea. Instead they do a little garbage collection with each CONS. They never stop for a complete purge.

APPEND Builds New List Structure by Copying

In a moment we consider how APPEND actually works. First let us set up some values that will help. For mnemonic value, let the atoms ABC and XYZ have the lists (A B C) and (X Y X) as their values:

```
(SETQ ABC '(A B C))
  (A B C)

(SETQ XYZ '(X Y Z))
  (X Y Z)
```

The box-and-arrow diagrams for ABC and XYZ are as follows:

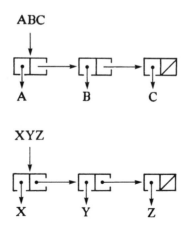

At first, then, it might seem that (SETQ ABCXYZ (APPEND ABC XYZ)) should require alteration of the last memory cell in the representation of the list (A B C):

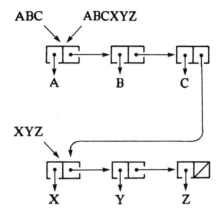

As far as the atom ABCXYZ is concerned, the result is just fine: the newly revised list structure would represent the list (A B C X Y Z) as desired. Also, the value of XYZ is unchanged. The trouble is, the value of ABC has been changed. It is now, unexpectedly, (A B C X Y Z), not (A B C)! Given that APPEND should leave the values of its arguments intact, it must work in some other way.

The following diagram illustrates what APPEND actually does. A copy is made of the first list, using spare memory cells from the free storage list, and then the second list is attached to the copy:

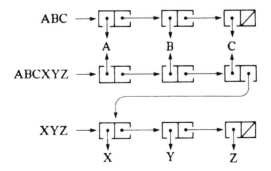

NCONC, RPLACA, RPLACD, and DELETE Dangerously Replace Memory-cell Contents

NCONC does exactly what was just described as what APPEND should not do. It smashes two lists together by a surgical change to the last cell in the first list, altering the value of any atom whose value is represented by a pointer into that first list. Note the following contrast:

```
(SETQ ABC '(A B C))
  (A B C)

(SETQ XYZ '(X Y Z))
  (X Y Z)

(SETQ BC (CDR ABC))
  (B C)

(SETQ YZ (CDR XYZ))
  (Y Z)

(SETQ ABCXYZ (APPEND ABC XYZ))
  (A B C X Y Z)

ABC
  (A B C)

XYZ
  (X Y Z)

BC
  (B C)

YZ
  (Y Z)

(SETQ ABCXYZ (NCONC ABC XYZ))
  (A B C X Y Z)

ABC
  (A B C X Y Z)

XYZ
  (X Y Z)
```

BC
  (B C X Y Z)

YZ
  (Y Z)

NCONC, like APPEND, can take more than two lists. All but the last gets its last cell changed. (MAPCAN does an NCONC-like operation after making up a list of results as MAPCAR does. Hence MAPCAN also requires careful use.)

RPLACA, like NCONC, does surgery. It takes two arguments, the first of which must be a list. It alters this list by replacing the left half of its first cell by a pointer to the second argument. Consider, for example, what happens when we do the following:

```
(SETQ FACT1 '(BIG COMPUTERS ARE NICE))
  (BIG COMPUTERS ARE NICE)

(RPLACA FACT1 'FAST))
  (FAST COMPUTERS ARE NICE)
```

The first cell representing (BIG COMPUTERS ARE NICE) has the pointer to BIG replaced by one to FAST:

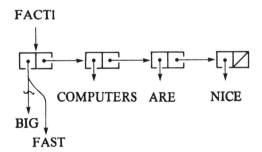

From the memory-cell diagram, we see that the value of FACT1 is changed even though there is no SETQ. Note that the following yields the same value, even though it is produced in a very different way, without a structure-altering side effect.

```
(CONS 'FAST (CDR FACT1))
  (FAST COMPUTERS ARE NICE)
```

RPLACA, incidentally, is a mnemonic for replace CAR. RPLACD, its complement, is a mnemonic for replace CDR. Like RPLACA, the function RPLACD surgically alters its first argument. The alteration is to the other half, however. Consider:

```
(SETQ FACT2 '(APPLES ARE GOOD FOR YOU))
  (APPLES ARE GOOD FOR YOU)

(RPLACD FACT2 '(WERE BAD FOR ADAM))
  (APPLES WERE BAD FOR ADAM)
```

Now only APPLES is retained from FACT2, as the following diagram shows:

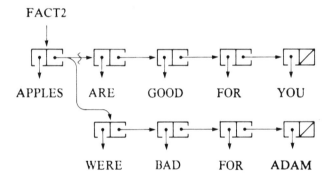

Note that the following yields the same value, even though the value is produced in a very different way:

```
(CONS (CAR FACT2) '(WERE BAD FOR ADAM))
  (APPLES WERE BAD FOR ADAM)
```

DELETE gets rid of instances of its first argument that appear in its second. The first argument can be any s-expression. Here it is an atom:

```
(DELETE 'HEADS '(HEADS TAILS TAILS HEADS TAILS))
  (TAILS TAILS TAILS)
```

If the first element in the list is a matching element, DELETE simply skips over it when handing back a value. Otherwise, DELETE does its job by splicing the matching elements out of list structure. Consequently, DELETE can alter atom values peculiarly as a side effect:

```
(SETQ TOSSES '(HEADS TAILS TAILS HEADS TAILS))
  (HEADS TAILS TAILS HEADS TAILS)
```

```
(DELETE 'HEADS TOSSES)
  (TAILS TAILS TAILS)

TOSSES
  (HEADS TAILS TAILS TAILS)
```

It is best to combine the DELETE with a SETQ to insure that the value of TOSSES is properly changed no matter what elements are deleted.

   The idiosyncracies of DELETE can be avoided by defining a function that does not alter list structure:

```
(DEFUN REMOVE (E L)
       (COND ((NULL L) NIL)
             ((EQUAL E (CAR L)) (REMOVE E (CDR L)))      ;Skip first element.
             (T (CONS (CAR L) (REMOVE E (CDR L)))))))    ;Keep it.
```

Now let us look at the issue of why NCONC, RPLACA, RPLACD, and DELETE can, on occasion, be useful and warranted. Suppose a function is desired that substitutes the atom PERSON for every instance of MAN in any s-expression given as an argument. Call this function LIBERATE1. It can be defined as follows using CAR, CDR, and CONS:

```
(DEFUN LIBERATE1 (S)
       (COND ((EQUAL S 'MAN) 'PERSON)        ;Replace MAN.
             ((ATOM S) S)                     ;Keep other atoms.
             (T (CONS (LIBERATE1 (CAR S))     ;Recurse on CAR
                      (LIBERATE1 (CDR S)))))) ;and CDR.
```

The CAR and CDR rip the given argument apart again and again until the atoms are reached and then reassemble a near copy using CONS to build it. If the list structure is deeply nested, this can take a lot of time even if there are few instances of MAN to replace. The CONS operation itself takes time. In addition, CONS depletes free storage, and the more it is used, the more reclamation is needed.

   In the next version RPLACA is used, not CONS. The original list structure is not copied. Instead, local surgery is performed whenever an instance of MAN is encountered. If a lot of liberation is to be done, time can be saved.

```
(DEFUN LIBERATE2 (S)
       (COND ((ATOM S) S)             ;Leave atoms alone.
             ((EQUAL (CAR S) 'MAN)    ;If MAN spotted
              (RPLACA S 'PERSON))     ;replace.
             (T (LIBERATE2 (CAR S))   ;Recurse on CAR.
                (LIBERATE2 (CDR S))   ;Recurse on CDR.
                S)))
```

However, using this version of LIBERATE can be dangerous because it alters the list structure that is supplied by an argument. Examples using LIBERATE1 and LIBERATE2 show how:

```
(SETQ TEST '(CHAIR MAN))
   (CHAIR MAN)

(LIBERATE1 TEST)
   (CHAIR PERSON)

TEST
   (CHAIR MAN)
```

This is sensible: doing (LIBERATE1 TEST) should not change the value of TEST. Now consider this:

```
(LIBERATE2 TEST)
   (CHAIR PERSON)

TEST
   (CHAIR PERSON)
```

The value of TEST changed because LIBERATE2 was allowed to alter list structure. When either version of LIBERATE is first entered, S and TEST both are bound to the same list structure.

The value of S then changes as recursion takes place. In LIBERATE1, this does not change the value of TEST. This is because SETQ and function call leave existing list structure intact. Not so with LIBERATE2. The recursion causes no problem, but the RPLACA does. If two atoms have the same value by virtue of the fact that they point to the same list structure, changing the value of one, using one of the dangerous functions, changes the other as well. Thus the following observation is indicated:

■ LISP does not completely prevent the abuse of arguments. Efficiency considerations may argue in favor of using the dangerous functions. Flexibility sometimes provides hanging rope.

To further illustrate some of the ideas in this chapter, we present the following marking algorithm used in garbage collection. It is Floyd's modification of a method independently discovered in 1965 by Deutsch and by Schorr and Waite. This algorithm avoids recursive calls by modifying the list structure being marked. LISP pointers are reversed on the way downwards, only to be restored on the way up.

```
(DEFUN MARK (P)
     (PROG (N Q)
           (COND ((NULL P) (RETURN P))             ;Easy cases.
                 ((ATOM P) (RETURN P)))
           LOOPCAR
           (SETQ Q (CAR P))                         ;Track down CAR.
           (COND ((NULL Q))
                 ((ATOM Q))
                 ((MARKEDP Q))
                 (T (RPLACA P N)                    ;Reverse pointer.
                    (SETQ N P P Q)
                    (GO LOOPCAR)))                  ;Continue down CAR.
           LOOPCDR
           (MARKIT P)                               ;Indicate that CAR is done.
           (SETQ Q (CDR P))                         ;Track down CDR.
           (COND ((NULL Q))
                 ((ATOM Q))
                 ((MARKEDP Q))
                 (T (RPLACD P N)                    ;Reverse pointer.
                    (SETQ N P P Q)
                    (GO LOOPCAR)))                  ;Go down CAR first.
           LOOPCONS
           (COND ((NULL N) (RETURN P))              ;Finished marking?
                 (T (SETQ Q N)))
           (COND ((MARKEDP Q)                       ;Was CAR of this done?.
                  (SETQ N (CDR Q))
                  (RPLACD Q P)                      ;Undo pointer reversal.
                  (SETQ P Q)
                  (GO LOOPCONS))                    ;Continue upwards.
                 (T (MARKIT Q)
                    (SETQ N (CAR Q))
                    (RPLACA Q P)                    ;Undo pointer reversal.
                    (SETQ P Q)
                    (GO LOOPCDR)))))                ;Still have to do CDR.
```

Debugging a procedure like this is difficult, because it extensively alters existing list structures.

In general, the use of NCONC, RPLACA, RPLACD, and DELETE is to be discouraged because of unexpected side effects:

■ It is a good idea to leave the use of NCONC, RPLACA, RPLACD, and DELETE to risk-loving programmers. Unless desperate for time or space saving, using them just leads to unnecessary bugs.

Problems

Problem 9-1: A *queue* is a linearly ordered set of things which can be accessed using enqueue and dequeue operations. ENQUEUE adds a new item to the tail of the queue, while DEQUEUE removes an item from the head of the queue. A list can be used to represent a queue, with the first element corresponding to the item at the head of the queue. Define ENQUEUE and DEQUEUE as MACROs. ENQUEUE takes two arguments, the item to be enqueued, and the name of a variable whose value is the list representing the queue. The value returned is the enlarged list. DEQUEUE takes a single argument, the name of the variable whose value is the list. The value returned is the item dequeued. In both cases the value of the variable is changed to reflect the new contents of the queue. Do not copy the list when enqueuing a new item.

EQUAL is Not the Same as EQ

EQ takes two arguments and returns T when both are the same atom. In this respect EQ is similar to EQUAL. When given two lists to compare, however, things are more complicated. Consider the following:

```
(SETQ L1 (LIST 'A 'B 'C))
  (A B C)

(SETQ L2 (LIST 'A 'B 'C))
  (A B C)

(SETQ L3 L2)
  (A B C)
```

Each time LIST is used, it assembles a list using memory cells drawn from the free storage list repository. Consequently, while the values of L1 and L2 are both (A B C), the two values are represented by distinct memory cells. SETQ, on the other hand, simply attaches a pointer from its first argument to the structure that is pointed to by its second. Hence the values of L2 and L3 are not only both (A B C), the two values are represented by the same memory cells. All of this is illustrated by the diagram on the next page.

Now certainly both (EQUAL L1 L2) and (EQUAL L2 L3) return T because on one hand, the values of L1 and L2 are exact copies of one another, and on the other hand, the values of L2 and L3 are represented by exactly the same memory-cell structure. They are equal in a slightly different sense, but EQUAL could not care less.

The function EQ does care. For EQ, two lists are equal only if they are represented by the same memory cells. Copies are not considered equal in the EQ sense. Thus (EQ L1 L2) returns NIL while (EQ L2 L3) returns T!

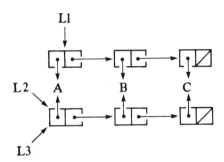

■ Two lists that are EQUAL may not be EQ. In contrast, atoms that are EQUAL are always EQ as well.

■ Any two lists or atoms that are EQ are always EQUAL.

Why use EQ? The answer again is a matter of efficiency. It takes longer to see if a structure is a copy than to see if it is exactly the same. Still, using EQ is best avoided by beginners. In the examples in this book, EQUAL is always used whether strictly necessary or not, just to avoid raising the question of what sense of equal is appropriate. After all, if two values are EQ, they will certainly be EQUAL as well.

Summary

■ Networks of memory cells represent lists.

■ Single quote marks are a shorthand form for the function QUOTE.

■ CONS builds new list structure by depositing pointers in free cells.

■ Garbage collection reclaims memory cells for the free storage list.

■ APPEND builds new list structure by copying.

■ NCONC, RPLACA, RPLACD, and DELETE dangerously replace memory-cell contents.

■ EQUAL is not the same as EQ.

References

Knuth [1969] discusses representations for lists.

Garbage collection is covered by Pratt [1975, chapter 7] and Knuth [1969, pp. 414-422]. See also, Baker [1977, 1979], Conrad [1974], Fenichel [1969], Hansen [1969], Kung [1977], Minsky [1963], Morris [1978], Schorr and Waite [1967], and Steele [1975].

Queues are discussed in Aho, Hopcroft, and Ullman [1974, pg. 155].

10
EXAMPLES
INVOLVING
BINARY
IMAGES

In previous chapters, the purpose was to introduce LISP. With this chapter, we turn to the purpose of showing LISP in use by exploring algorithms used in binary image processing. We deal with binary image processing for three reasons: first, the programs involved illustrate some of the features of arrays, a subject previously skimmed; second, the programs demonstrate that it is possible to use LISP in a style that is like that of other programming languages if one so chooses; and third, simple programs allow one to get to a point where interesting things happen. Specifically, the programs find the position and orientation of an object, as well as doing classification. Even binary images with multiple objects can be analyzed.

Binary Images are Easy to Process

An image is a two-dimensional distribution of brightness such as might be sensed by a TV camera. Sometimes the lighting on an object can be arranged so that there is a clear separation in image brightness between the object and the background. In this case a simple threshold operation can turn measured brightness values into 0's and 1's depending on whether a point is judged to be part of the image of the object or not. If the image is sampled on a square grid of points, one obtains a two-dimensional array of binary numbers as shown in figure 10-1 for example. This so-called binary image is quantized both spatially and in brightness level. If significant information about the object is contained in this compressed, two-dimensional representation, then binary image processing techniques are appropriate.

Suppose, for example, that we want to find out where in the field of view a single object lies and how it is oriented. This is useful if the object is passing by

Figure 10-1: Binary image of an object. The black squares correspond to 1's, while the white squares correspond to 0's.

an image sensor on a conveyor belt because information about the position and orientation of the object then can be used to direct a mechanical manipulator to pick it up. We will assume initially that there is only one object in the field of view. Methods for labeling multiple objects will be explored later.

An Object can be Found Using Binary Image Analysis

We will refer to the set of points in the binary image that have the value 1 as the points of an object. The center of area of these points provides a reasonable definition of the position of the object.

How can we find the center of area from the binary image? Let $p_{i,j}$ be the value of the binary image at a point in the i-th row and j-th column. The total number of points in the object, its area, is simply

$$n = \Sigma_i \, \Sigma_j \, p_{i,j}$$

while the center of area is at

$$i_0 = (1/n) \sum_i \sum_j i\, p_{i,j} \quad \text{and} \quad j_0 = (1/n) \sum_i \sum_j j\, p_{i,j}$$

The sums are to be taken over the whole binary image. If the LISP array IMAGE contains the binary image, then the center of area can be computed as follows:

```
(DEFUN CENTER (N M)                              ;n rows, m columns.
    (PROG (I J SUM SUM-I SUM-J)
        (SETQ SUM 0 SUM-I 0 SUM-J 0)             ;Reset sum accumulators.
        (SETQ I 0)
        LOOP-ROW
        (COND ((EQUAL I N) (GO FINISH)))         ;Done all rows?
        (SETQ J 0)
        LOOP-COLUMN
        (COND ((EQUAL J M) (GO NEXT-ROW)))       ;Finished this row?
        (COND ((ZEROP (IMAGE I J)))              ;Ignore 0's in image.
              (T (SETQ SUM (ADD1 SUM)            ;Total up p(i,j)
                      SUM-I (PLUS SUM-I I)       ;Total up i * p(i,j)
                      SUM-J (PLUS SUM-J J))))     ;Total up j * p(i,j)
        (SETQ J (ADD1 J))                        ;Advance to next column.
        (GO LOOP-COLUMN)
        NEXT-ROW
        (SETQ I (ADD1 I))                        ;Advance to next row.
        (GO LOOP-ROW)
        FINISH
        (COND ((ZEROP SUM) (RETURN 'NO-OBJECT)))
        (RETURN (LIST (QUOTIENT (FLOAT SUM-I)    ;Calculate i(0)
                                (FLOAT SUM))
                      (QUOTIENT (FLOAT SUM-J)    ;Calculate j(0)
                                (FLOAT SUM))))))
```

Orientation is not quite so easy. If the object is elongated it will have a natural axis lying in the direction of elongation. In fact, there will be an axis about which the points in the image have least inertia. Mechanical engineers refer to the axes of least and most inertia as the principal axes of an object. We can use the direction of the axis of least inertia to define the orientation of the object. This will fail only if the object has no axis of least inertia, as will be the case with a centrally symmetric object like a circular disk.

Finding this axis requires mathematical manipulations which we will only hint at here. The axis of least inertia passes through the center of area. It is convenient therefore to change to a new coordinate system, parallel to the old one, but with the origin on top of the center of area,

$$i' = i - i_0 \quad \text{and} \quad j' = j - j_0$$

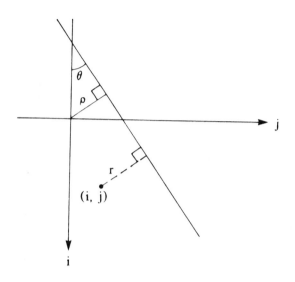

Figure 10-2: The distance of a point (i, j) from a line is

$$i \sin \theta - j \cos \theta + \rho$$

where θ is the inclination of the line with respect to the i-axis, while ρ is the perpendicular distance of the line from the origin.

The inertia about a line is just the sum of squares of the distances of points from the line. This distance can be found as shown in figure 10-2. The inertia about a line inclined θ relative to the i'-axis, through the center of area is:

$$I = \Sigma_i \, \Sigma_j \, p_{i,j} \, (i' \sin \theta - j' \cos \theta \,)^2$$

or,
$$I = a \sin^2\theta - b \sin \theta \cos \theta + c \cos^2\theta$$

where,

$$a = \Sigma_i \, \Sigma_j \, (i')^2 \, p_{i,j}$$
$$b = 2 \, \Sigma_i \, \Sigma_j \, (i' j') \, p_{i,j}$$
$$c = \Sigma_i \, \Sigma_j \, (j')^2 \, p_{i,j}$$

We can find the orientation, θ_0, of the axes of maximum and minimum moment of inertia by differentiating with respect to θ and setting the result equal to zero. This way one finds the following:

$$\tan 2\theta_0 = b / (a - c).$$

The function ORIENTATION will return a list containing the center of area and the angle of the axis of least inertia.

```
(DEFUN ORIENTATION (N M)                              ;n rows & m columns.
      (PROG (C-O-A I0 J0 A B C I J)
            (SETQ C-O-A (CENTER N M)                  ;Find center of area first.
                  I0 (CAR C-O-A)
                  J0 (CADR C-O-A))
            (SETQ A 0.0 B 0.0 C 0.0)                  ;Reset sum accumulators.
            (SETQ I 0)
            LOOP-ROW
            (COND ((EQUAL I N) (GO FINISH)))          ;Done last row?
            (SETQ J 0)
            LOOP-COLUMN
            (COND ((EQUAL J M) (GO NEXT-ROW)))        ;Done last in row?
            (COND ((ZEROP (IMAGE I J)))               ;Ignore 0's in image.
                  (T (SETQ A (PLUS A
                               (TIMES (DIFFERENCE I I0)
                                      (DIFFERENCE I I0)))
                        B (PLUS B
                               (TIMES 2
                                      (DIFFERENCE I I0)
                                      (DIFFERENCE J J0)))
                        C (PLUS C
                               (TIMES (DIFFERENCE J J0)
                                      (DIFFERENCE J J0)))))))
            (SETQ J (ADD1 J))
            (GO LOOP-COLUMN)
            NEXT-ROW
            (SETQ I (ADD1 I))
            (GO LOOP-ROW)
            FINISH
            (COND ((AND (ZEROP B) (EQUAL A C))        ;Check if symmetrical.
                   (RETURN (APPEND C-O-A
                               '(SYMMETRICAL)))))
            (RETURN (APPEND C-O-A                     ;Compute orientation.
                        (LIST (QUOTIENT (ATAN B
                                        (DIFFERENCE A C))
                                 2.0))))))
```

The value of (ATAN Y X) is an angle θ, say, such that $y = r \sin(\theta)$ and $x = r \cos(\theta)$ for some r. That is, this function finds the arc tangent of y/x in the quadrant determined by the signs of x and y (This is just like ATAN2 in

FORTRAN.) Unlike the usual arc tangent function, it has no trouble when the angle tends to plus or minus ninety degrees. The result is undefined, however, if both x and y are zero. This only happens when the object has no axis of least inertia. In this case, the answer contains the atom SYMMETRICAL.

Problems

Problem 10-1: Simplify ORIENTATION by use of the following identities:

$$a = \sum_i \sum_j i^2 \, p_{i,j} - n \, i_o^2,$$
$$b = 2 \sum_i \sum_j i \, j \, p_{i,j} - 2 \, n \, i_o \, j_o,$$
$$c = \sum_i \sum_j j^2 \, p_{i,j} - n \, j_o^2.$$

These formulas allow one to calculate a, b, and c directly, without resorting to the transformed coordinates i' and j'.

Problem 10-2: In order to get adequate accuracy, an image should be sampled finely, producing a huge array of bits. We therefore should be a little sensitive to issues of computational efficiency. While the equations given correctly define the center of area, they suggest algorithms that are unnecessarily slow.

It turns out that the position of the center of area along the i-direction is not altered by projecting the image onto a line parallel to this direction. That is, i_o can be found from the one dimensional array of row sums. A similar projection can be made onto a line parallel to the j-direction, and j_o can be found from the one dimensional array of column sums. If we let the row and column sums be

$$r_i = \sum_j p_{i,j} \quad \text{and} \quad c_j = \sum_i p_{i,j},$$

then, the center of area can be computed using

$$i_o = (1/n) \sum_i i \, r_i \quad \text{and} \quad j_o = (1/n) \sum_j j \, c_j.$$

Note that the row and column sums can be found using nothing more sophisticated than counting. A tremendous data reduction occurs once the row and column sums are known and we need pay less attention to issues of speed. By the way,

$$n = \sum_j c_j \quad \text{and} \quad n = \sum_i r_i.$$

Rewrite CENTER to first determine the row and column sums and store them in the one-dimensional arrays ROW and COLUMN.

Problem 10-3: It would be useful to speed up the calculation of orientation as well by using row and column sums. Here we need to calculate the sums a, b, and c. Two of these, a and b, can be obtained easily from the row and column sums using the following identities:

$$\Sigma_i \, \Sigma_j \, i^2 \, P_{i,j} = \Sigma_i \, i^2 \, \Sigma_j \, P_{i,j} = \Sigma_i \, i^2 \, r_i$$
$$\Sigma_i \, \Sigma_j \, j^2 \, P_{i,j} = \Sigma_j \, j^2 \, \Sigma_i \, P_{i,j} = \Sigma_j \, j^2 \, c_j$$

But what about the sum of the product of i and j needed to calculate b? Another projection of the binary image is needed. Note that,

$$(i + j)^2 = i^2 + 2\,i\,j + j^2$$

This suggests the use of a diagonal projection:

$$d_k = \Sigma_i \, P_{i,k-i} = \Sigma_j \, P_{k-j,j}$$

where i and j are restricted so that only points in the binary image are accessed.

$$\Sigma_i \, \Sigma_j \, (i+j)^2 \, P_{i,j} = \Sigma_k \, k^2 \, d_k$$

and
$$2 \, \Sigma_i \, \Sigma_j \, i \, j \, P_{i,j} = \Sigma_k \, k^2 \, d_k - [\, \Sigma_i \, i^2 \, r_i + \Sigma_j \, j^2 \, c_j \,]$$

The last two terms have been calculated already while finding a and c.

Rewrite ORIENTATION to make use of row, column, and diagonal sums. Assume that the array DIAGONAL contains the sums of the diagonals.

Problem 10-4: Because binary images tend to be so large, they are often packed into computer words so that several bits appear in one array element. Assume that adjacent binary image values of a row are packed left-to-right in groups of 36. Write IMAGE, a function of two arguments that unpacks bits from an array called PACKED. (IMAGE I J) is to pick the appropriate bit from the array element (PACKED I JD), where JD equals J divided by 36.

Note that the functions developed so far can then be used without alteration, since the calls for elements of the *array* IMAGE now are taken care of by the *function* IMAGE. Assume that a LISP function LSH is available for shifting a binary number left by a specified number of bits. Bits shifted out are lost, while zeros enter at the other end of the word. Shifting right is accomplished by specifying a negative argument.

Features found in Binary Images can be used for Classificaton

In many cases more than one type of object may appear in the field of view of a machine vision system. How can we distinguish these? We have already calculated some information that might be useful. Different objects may differ in their total image area and in the least and most moments of inertia.

Using the direction θ_0 of the axis of least inertia one finds that the extreme values of the moment of inertia are,

$$2\,I = (a+c) \pm [b^2 + (a-c)^2]^{1/2}.$$

The sum of the smallest and the largest inertia is

$$(I_{max} + I_{min}) = (a + c),$$

while the difference comes to

$$(I_{max} - I_{min}) = [b^2 + (a-c)^2]^{1/2}.$$

Dividing the sum of the smallest and largest inertia by the area squared provides a measure of how spread out the points of the object are. A circular disk has the least possible value for this quantity, $1/(2\pi)$. Dividing the difference of the maximum and the minimum moment of inertia by the sum provides a measure of how elongated the object appears to be. In many cases, area and these two quantities may be sufficient to differentiate between objects.

If these features do not provide enough discrimination, it is necessary to measure a few more. Some useful measurements can be obtained by counting the outcomes of simple local logical operations. Parameters that can be obtained this way include area, perimeter, and the so-called Euler number. The Euler number is the difference between the number of objects and the number of holes. Thus a single blob has Euler number 1, the object shown in figure 10-1 has Euler number 0, while a binary image of the capital letter B would have Euler number -1.

We already know how to calculate the area:

```
(DEFUN AREA (N M)
       (PROG (I J SUM)
             (SETQ SUM 0)
             (SETQ I 0)
             LOOP-ROW
             (COND ((EQUAL I N) (RETURN SUM)))
             (SETQ J 0)
             LOOP-COLUMN
             (COND ((EQUAL J M) (GO NEXT-ROW)))
             (SETQ SUM (PLUS SUM (IMAGE I J)))
             (SETQ J (ADD1 J))
             (GO LOOP-COLUMN)
             NEXT-ROW
             (SETQ I (ADD1 I))
             (GO LOOP-ROW)))
```

This kind of program, with so much looping, would be much more readable and less like what one would see in some other programming languages if we permitted ourselves to use certain DO-type functions that are now gaining currency. But, since we avoid functions that are not yet standardized, we use a PROG instead.

The perimeter can be estimated by counting the number of places where 0's are adjacent to 1's.

```
(DEFUN PERIMETER (N M)
      (PROG (I J SUM)
            (SETQ SUM 0)
            (SETQ I 1)
            LOOP-ROW
            (COND ((EQUAL I N) (RETURN SUM)))
            (SETQ J 1)
            LOOP-COLUMN
            (COND ((EQUAL J M) (GO NEXT-ROW)))
            (COND ((NOT (EQUAL (IMAGE I J)            ;Ignore 0-0 or 1-1
                               (IMAGE I (SUB1 J))))
                   (SETQ SUM (ADD1 SUM))))
            (COND ((NOT (EQUAL (IMAGE I J)            ;Ignore 0-0 or 1-1
                               (IMAGE (SUB1 I) J)))
                   (SETQ SUM (ADD1 SUM))))
            (SETQ J (ADD1 J))
            (GO LOOP-COLUMN)
            NEXT-ROW
            (SETQ I (ADD1 I))
            (GO LOOP-ROW)))
```

The number calculated here will tend to overestimate the true perimeter of the binary image because of the jaggedness of the outline in a quantized image. The number computed will still be useful, however, to distinguish among objects differing greatly in perimeter.

The Euler number is found by looking for the distinctive patterns:

```
0 0        0 1
0 1        1 1
```

The Euler number is the difference of the number of occurrences of the first pattern and the number of occurrences of the second pattern. In figure 10-1, for example, each pattern occurs fifteen times. For that object the Euler number is zero, as already noted.

The Euler number is sensitive to isolated noise points, but provides useful information in a clean, smoothed binary image. It is computed as follows:

```
(DEFUN EULER (N M)
      (PROG (I J SUM)
            (SETQ SUM 0)
            (SETQ I 1)
            LOOP-ROW
            (COND ((EQUAL I N) (RETURN SUM)))
            (SETQ J 1)
            LOOP-COLUMN
            (COND ((EQUAL J M) (GO NEXT-ROW)))
            (COND ((ZEROP (IMAGE I J)))                      ;Ignore if 0
                  ((NOT (ZEROP (IMAGE (SUB1 I) (SUB1 J)))))  ;Ignore if 1
                  ((AND (ZEROP (IMAGE I (SUB1 J)))
                        (ZEROP (IMAGE (SUB1 I) J)))
                   (SETQ SUM (ADD1 SUM)))                     ;First pattern.
                  ((OR (ZEROP (IMAGE I (SUB1 J)))
                       (ZEROP (IMAGE (SUB1 I) J))))
                  (T (SETQ SUM (SUB1 SUM))))                  ;Second pattern.
            (SETQ J (ADD1 J))
            (GO LOOP-COLUMN)
            NEXT-ROW
            (SETQ I (ADD1 I))
            (GO LOOP-ROW)))
```

At this point we will assume that a list of such measurements can be derived from a binary image. The recognition system can be trained by presenting it with examples of each of the classes and asking it to remember the feature measurements. A list of classes and feature vectors might look like this:

```
((BOLT (25.0 2.3 0.2 9.0 1.0))
 (NUT (12.0 1.1 1.0 3.9 0.0))
 (WRENCH (65.0 3.1 0.75 25.0 1.0))
 (PRETZEL (40.0 1.1 0.5 12.0 -1.0)))
```

Each feature list can be thought of as a point in an n-dimensional space. In figure 10-3 only two dimensions are used, corresponding to the third and fifth elements in the lists above. An unknown object can then be classified by comparing its feature vector with the known ones. While very sophisticated methods have been developed to carry out this classification, in some cases it is enough to measure the distance between two feature vectors. The unknown is assigned to the class whose representative has the closest feature vector. In figure 10-3, for example, the unknown indicated by the question mark would be assigned to class N.

The following function will do the trick:

```
(DEFUN CLASSIFY (CLASSES UNKNOWN)
      (PROG (BEST BEST-D NEW NEW-D)
            (COND ((NULL CLASSES) (RETURN 'NO-CLASSES)))
            (SETQ BEST (CAAR CLASSES)
                  BEST-D (DISTANCE (CADAR CLASSES)
                                   UNKNOWN)
                  CLASSES (CDR CLASSES))
      LOOP
            (COND ((NULL CLASSES) (RETURN BEST)))
            (SETQ NEW (CAAR CLASSES)
                  NEW-D (DISTANCE (CADAR CLASSES)
                                  UNKNOWN))
            (COND ((LESSP NEW-D BEST-D) (SETQ BEST NEW
                                              BEST-D NEW-D)))
            (SETQ CLASSES (CDR CLASSES))
            (GO LOOP)))
```

Problems

Problem 10-5: Write DISTANCE, a function for calculating the distance between two feature vectors. Since the result is only used in comparisons, it is reasonable to calculate the square of the distance instead.

Problem 10-6: The classification can be improved considerably if information is available on the variability of each of the components of the feature vector. Modify the representation of classes to include variance in addition to mean and modify the function DISTANCE to weight the square of the difference of two components inversely with the stored variance value.

Components of a Binary Images can be Labeled in Two Passes

So far we have assumed that there is only one object in the field of view. If there are several we may want to assign a label to each one and perform the sort of calculation discussed so far separately for each component of the image. The idea is to assign a different number to every connected component of the image. The labeling operation can be performed by scanning a little 2 by 2 window over the binary image and observing the pattern found therein.

```
C B
D A
```

We scan along each row from left to right starting at the top. When we inspect cell A, cells B, C, and D have already been labeled with a number. This number

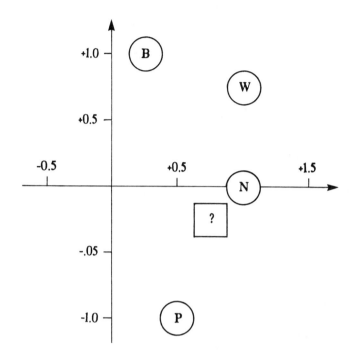

Figure 10-3: Four classes of objects represented by positions of points in feature space. A simple classification algorithm assigns the unknown indicated by the question mark to class **N**. This illustrates how measurements on binary images can be used to identify an object.

will be 0 if the binary image was 0 at the corresponding point. Otherwise it identifies the image component. Let us carefully analyze all possible cases:

First of all, if the three neighbors of A are all zero, a new label is assigned to A. Next, if C has been labeled, we label A similarly. It does not matter in this case whether B or D have been labeled since these two cells touch C and would therefore have the same label in any case. If C is zero and either B or D has been labeled, we label A similarly.

The most difficult case arises when both B and D have labels. The problem is that they may be different. This occurs at a place where two components of an object, thought of as parts of separate objects, are seen to be connected. In figure 10-4, for example, the top right-hand arm of the object has been labeled 1, while the left-hand arm appeared to be part of another object and was labeled 2. When the algorithm attempts to label the point marked with a question mark, it becomes apparent that the two pieces are connected and belong to one object.

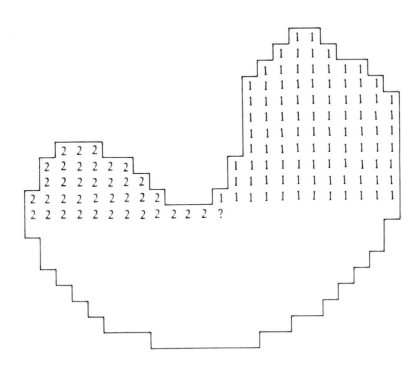

Figure 10-4: When objects in a binary image are labeled, it may be found that pieces with different labels actually are connected. In this case an entry must be made in a list which records the equivalence of the two labels. Here the program notes when attempting to label the point marked with a question mark that the two arms are connected.

Not only must one of the two labels be used to label A, but a note must be made to remember that the two labels seen are in fact equivalent. Later, a second pass over the labeled image will map each label into the smallest equivalent one. These rules can be summarized as follows:

If A is 0, it remains 0, otherwise,
if B, C, and D are 0, A is assigned a new label, otherwise
if C is labeled n, so is A, otherwise
if D is 0 and B is labeled n, so is A, otherwise
if B is 0 and D is labeled m, so is A, otherwise
if B and D are labeled n, so is A, otherwise
if B is labeled n and D is labeled m, then label A as n,
    and note that the m is equivalent to n.

To simplify matters we will assume that the edges of the array are 0's. Then the following program will work:

```
(DEFUN LABEL-COMPONENTS (N M)
      (PROG (I J A B C D EQ-LIST NEXT)
            (SETQ NEXT 1)                                    ;Next free label.
            (SETQ I 1)
            LOOP-ROW
            (COND ((EQUAL I N) (RETURN (LIST (SUB1 NEXT)     ;Done?
                                     EQ-LIST))))
            (SETQ J 1)
            LOOP-COLUMN
            (COND ((EQUAL J M) (GO NEXT-ROW)))
            (SETQ A (IMAGE I J)                              ;Pick up window.
                  B (IMAGE (SUB1 I) J)
                  C (IMAGE (SUB1 I) (SUB1 J))
                  D (IMAGE I (SUB1 J)))
            (COND ((ZEROP A))                                ;Not on object.
                  ((NOT (ZEROP C)) (STORE (IMAGE I J) C))    ;Copy A from C.
                  ((AND (ZEROP B) (ZEROP D))
                   (STORE (IMAGE I J) NEXT)
                   (SETQ NEXT (ADD1 NEXT)))                  ;Use next label.
                  ((ZEROP D) (STORE (IMAGE I J) B))          ;Copy A from B.
                  ((ZEROP B) (STORE (IMAGE I J) D))          ;Copy A from D.
                  ((EQUAL B D) (STORE (IMAGE I J) B))        ;Copy A from B.
                  (T (STORE (IMAGE I J) B)
                     (SETQ EQ-LIST (CONS (LIST D B)
                                   EQ-LIST))))               ;Note equivalence.
            (SETQ J (ADD1 J))
            (GO LOOP-COLUMN)
            NEXT-ROW
            (SETQ I (ADD1 I))
            (GO LOOP-ROW)))
```

At this point some objects may be labeled with a number of equivalent labels. Another pass will solve this problem. First a lookup table, MAPPING, for labels is constructed. The lookup table is then used to reassign each picture cell to the smallest equivalent label.

```
(DEFUN REASSIGN (N M)
    (PROG (I J)
        (SETQ I 0)
        LOOP-ROW
        (COND ((EQUAL I N) (RETURN NIL)))
        (SETQ J 0)
        LOOP-COLUMN
        (COND ((EQUAL J M) (GO NEXT-ROW)))
        (STORE (IMAGE I J)                    ;Replace label
            (MAPPING (IMAGE I J)))            ;by equivalent.
        (SETQ J (ADD1 J))
        (GO LOOP-COLUMN)
        NEXT-ROW
        (SETQ I (ADD1 I))
        (GO LOOP-ROW)))
```

Problems

Problem 10-7: Define MAKE-TABLE, a procedure which uses the equivalence list returned by LABEL to construct a look-up table called MAPPING.

Project: If the edge of an object is near horizontal and very jagged, it may give rise to several false starts. A large number of labels will be used. In fact it is possible that the largest number used cannot be stored in the image array. Combine the functions above so that label equivalence is resolved after each row has been labeled.

Summary

■ Binary images are easy to process.

■ An object can be found using binary image analysis.

■ Features found in binary images can be used for classificaton.

■ Components of a binary images can be labeled in two passes.

References

The text of Duda and Hart [1973] is an excellent introduction to the methods of pattern recognition.
    Gray [1971] gives an excellent discussion of what can and cannot be done using binary image processing methods. Minsky and Papert [1969] also discuss the

limitations of so-called local methods on binary images. Work on hexagonal image arrays is described in Golay [1969] and Preston [1971]. Also of interest are Nagy [1969], Stefanelli and Rosenfeld [1971], Deutsch [1972], and Levialdi [1972].

Industrial applications of these methods can be found in Baird [1978], Ejiri *et al.* [1973], Gleason and Agin [1979], Holland, Rossol, and Ward [1979], and Horn [1975].

For papers on machine vision in general see Winston [1974, 1975], Hanson and Riseman [1978], and Winston and Brown [1979a, 1979b]. Other approaches to machine vision are discussed by Horn [1970, 1974, 1977, 1979, 1980].

11
EXAMPLES
INVOLVING
SEARCH

In the last chapter, we turned our attention to showing LISP in use. We continue here with the well-known problem of search because search is ubiquitous in one form or another.

The search problem is illustrated in figure 11-1. In each of the versions shown, there is a starting place, many intermediate places, and some number of finish places, from zero to many. The problem is to find a path from the starting place, through some of the intermediate places, to a finish place. We will see that various strategies for search look much alike when reduced to program form.

Breadth-first and Depth-first Search are Basic Strategies

Places are called nodes. The connections between nodes are called arcs. Arrowheads on arcs indicate that only one-way travel is permitted. If it is possible to go from a node P to node C, then P is called a parent of C and C is called a child of P.

■ Collections of arcs and nodes are called networks. Figure 11-1a shows a network with loops which make it possible to leave a node and return to it again. Figure 11-1b shows a network without any loops.

■ If every node in a network has a unique parent, with only one exception, then the network is called a tree. The exception node, which has no parent, is called the root node. Figure 11-1c shows a tree.

(a)

(b)

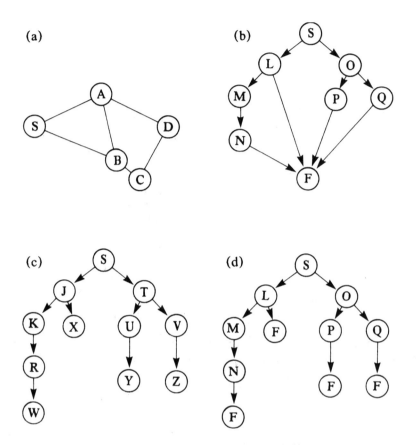

(c)

(d)

Figure 11-1: The search problem. In *a* and *b* the problem is to move through a network. In *c*, the problem is to move through a tree. The tree in *d* was made from the network of *b* by drawing multiple copies of nodes that are reached from different paths.

■ We will have occasion to transform networks into related trees in two steps: first by drawing more than one copy of those nodes that can be reached in more than one way; and second by terminating paths that are about to close on themselves. Figure 11-1d illustrates.

We open our discussion of search strategies by considering *breadth-first* search on the network in figure 11-2. Note that several copies of node F are drawn, making the network look like a tree. Movement is level-by-level, with each node at one level examined before looking at those on the next level.

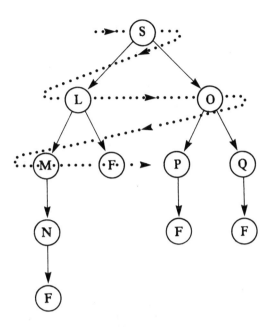

Figure 11-2: Breadth-first search. All nodes on one level are examined before any on the next lower level are considered.

Figure 11-3 illustrates *depth-first* search on the same tree. At first only one of the children of the starting node is examined. If it is not the finish node, one of its children is examined, again ignoring the rest. At each level, the idea is to pick an exit from each node arbitrarily when there is a choice, always moving down. If there are no exits left to explore at some node attention moves back to the last place where there was a choice. Then downward motion begins again.

A Node Queue Facilitates Depth-first Search and Breadth-first Search

It is particularly easy to write a program for depth-first search. In fact, there have been many examples already of recursive functions that rip into list structure, moving in depth-first fashion. The structure of LISP made depth-first the easy way to go.

Unfortunately, it is not easy to modify those functions to implement breadth-first and other varieties of search. We will therefore develop a queue-oriented depth-first search program. Using a queue will make things harder at first, but once we have done depth-first search, modification to do other searches will be easy. Figure 11-4 shows the structure of a basic queue-oriented search program.

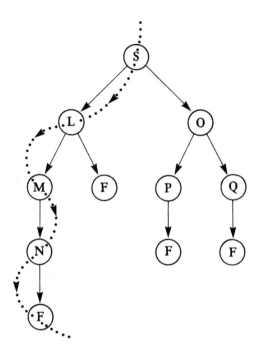

Figure 11-3: Depth-first search. Only one node at each level is examined unless failure requires the search to back up to explore alternatives previously ignored.

Using a PROG loop is one way to translate the flow-chart description into LISP. A queue of encountered but untested nodes is maintained inside the PROG. One node is tested each time around the loop in the PROG.

```
(DEFUN SEARCH (START FINISH)
      (PROG (QUEUE EXPANSION)
            (SETQ QUEUE (LIST START))              ;Initialize.
            TRYAGAIN                               ;Start loop.
            (COND ((NULL QUEUE) (RETURN NIL))      ;Queue empty?
                  ((EQUAL FINISH (CAR QUEUE))      ;Success?
                   (RETURN T)))
            (SETQ EXPANSION (EXPAND (CAR QUEUE)))  ;Get children.
            (SETQ QUEUE (CDR QUEUE))               ;Move on.
            (SETQ QUEUE                            ;Augment queue
                <appropriate merge of
                 expansion and queue>)
            (GO TRYAGAIN)))
```

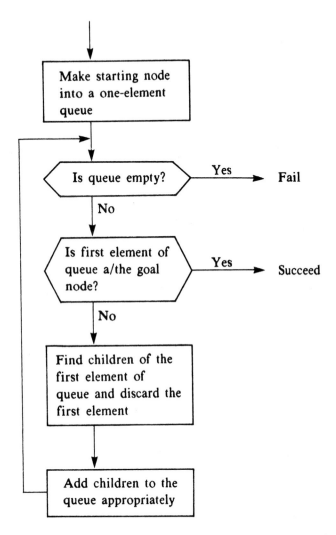

Figure 11-4: The basic search algorithm. Minor changes make a variety of searches possible.

Note that EXPAND is presumed to return the children of a node, given that node as its argument.

Before the EXPAND program can be written, we must deal with the problem of representing the data. Nested lists would do nicely if we were only interested in trees. For networks, it is better to use atoms and properties. The atoms can represent nodes and their CHILDREN properties can represent arcs. Thus the following interactions capture the structure of the tree shown in figure 11-1d.

```
(DEFPROP S (L O) CHILDREN)
  S

(DEFPROP L (M F) CHILDREN)
  L

(DEFPROP M (N) CHILDREN)
  M

(DEFPROP N (F) CHILDREN)
  N

(DEFPROP O (P Q) CHILDREN)
  O

(DEFPROP P (F) CHILDREN)
  P

(DEFPROP Q (F) CHILDREN)
  Q
```

Having recorded the node connections as entries on property lists, EXPAND is easy to write:

```
(DEFUN EXPAND (NODE) (GET NODE 'CHILDREN))
```

The method of merging the new children into the old queue depends, of course, on the search strategy involved. For simple depth-first search, the appropriate line is just this:

```
(SETQ QUEUE (APPEND EXPANSION QUEUE))
```

Thus depth-first search is done by the following program:

```
(DEFUN DEPTH (START FINISH)
      (PROG (QUEUE EXPANSION)
            (SETQ QUEUE (LIST START))
            TRYAGAIN
            (COND ((NULL QUEUE) (RETURN NIL))
                  ((EQUAL FINISH (CAR QUEUE)) (RETURN T)))
            (SETQ EXPANSION (EXPAND (CAR QUEUE)))
            (SETQ QUEUE (CDR QUEUE))
            (SETQ QUEUE (APPEND EXPANSION QUEUE))        ;New nodes in front.
            (GO TRYAGAIN)))
```

While there is nothing wrong with this PROG-based search program, certainly some improvements can be made. For one thing, it only returns T or NIL, and it might be desirable to have some clue about the path if the search is successful. Moreover, while it works fine on trees, it cannot handle networks because there is no check to prevent it from getting stuck in endless loop traversal.

Let us first arrange for a successful path to be returned, if there is one, rather than just T or NIL. One way to do this that minimizes the disruption to what we have seen so far involves packing more information into the elements of QUEUE. Heretofore the elements have been the nodes remaining to be tested. Given the nodes in figure 11-1d, the QUEUE would develop like this:

```
(S)
(L O)
(M F O)
(N F O)
(F F O)
```

Now the elements will consist of paths rather than just nodes. Each path will extend from the starting node to a node whose children have not yet been explored. The QUEUE will develop like this:

```
((S))
((L S) (O S))
((M L S) (F L S) (O S))
((N M L S) (F L S) (O S))
((F N M L S) (F L S) (O S))
```

Thus each element in QUEUE is now a list. The elements in reverse order give the path from the starting node to some other node. The search proceeds as the first path on the QUEUE is extended through the children of the last node on the path.

The changes required in DEPTH to use and exploit the new format for the QUEUE are very simple. First, FINISH is compared with (CAAR QUEUE) rather than (CAR QUEUE). Second, if the finish node is reached, the path on which it was found is returned instead of T:

```
(DEFUN DEPTH (START FINISH)
    (PROG (QUEUE EXPANSION)
        (SETQ QUEUE (LIST (LIST START)))          ;Note slight change.
        TRYAGAIN
        (COND ((NULL QUEUE) (RETURN NIL))
              ((EQUAL FINISH (CAAR QUEUE))          ;Another slight change.
               (RETURN (REVERSE (CAR QUEUE)))))     ;Return path.
        (SETQ EXPANSION (EXPAND (CAR QUEUE)))
        (SETQ QUEUE (CDR QUEUE))
        (SETQ QUEUE (APPEND EXPANSION QUEUE))
        (GO TRYAGAIN)))
```

Of course EXPAND also must be changed. Rather than take a node and return a list of its children, it must take a path, find the children of the node at the end of the path, and return a list of new paths. Each new path will consist of the original path with one of the children tacked on. The number of new paths will equal the number of children.

```
(DEFUN EXPAND (PATH)
    (MAPCAR '(LAMBDA (E)
                 (CONS E PATH))
            (GET (CAR PATH) 'CHILDREN)))
```

The MAPCAR arranges for the new path construction to happen once for each element in the list of children found hanging from the first node on the path that EXPAND receives as its argument.

Lamentably, our programs still risk disaster if given a network with closed loops since there is nothing to prevent going around them again and again. For networks to be handled, if any path offered up by the EXPAND operation has a new node that is already present elsewhere in the path, then that path should be purged. To arrange for this to happen, we could rename EXPAND, call it OLD-EXPAND, and prune the results it gives with a new program, NEW-EXPAND. In place of (EXPAND (CAR QUEUE)), the depth-first-search program would have the following:

```
(NEW-EXPAND (OLD-EXPAND (CAR QUEUE)))
```

Definitions are as follows:

```
(DEFUN OLD-EXPAND (PATH)
    (MAPCAR '(LAMBDA (E)
                 (CONS E PATH))
            (GET (CAR PATH) 'NEIGHBORS)))
```

```
(DEFUN NEW-EXPAND (NEW-PATHS)
     (COND ((NULL NEW-PATHS) NIL)
           ((MEMBER (CAAR NEW-PATHS)
                  (CDAR NEW-PATHS))
            (NEW-EXPAND (CDR NEW-PATHS)))         ;Prune out circular paths.
           (T (CONS (CAR NEW-PATHS)
                  (NEW-EXPAND (CDR NEW-PATHS))))))
```

Note that CHILDREN has been renamed NEIGHBORS to emphasize that we are now working with networks, not just trees. NEW-EXPAND can be defined as follows:

```
(DEFUN NEW-EXPAND (NEW-PATHS)
     (MAPCAN '(LAMBDA (E)
                  (COND ((MEMBER (CAR E) (CDR E)) NIL)
                        (T (LIST E))))
             NEW-PATHS))
```

The MAPCAR works on the list of new paths. Each path is either turned into NIL or made the element of a one-element list. The resulting list of NILs and lists is collapsed into a list of good paths by the application of APPEND.

It is easy now to combine NEW-EXPAND and OLD-EXPAND into a single function by replacing the list that the MAPCAR works on in NEW-EXPAND with the guts of OLD-EXPAND:

```
(DEFUN EXPAND (PATH)
     (MAPCAN '(LAMBDA (E)
                  (COND ((MEMBER (CAR E) (CDR E)) NIL)
                        (T (LIST E))))
             (MAPCAR '(LAMBDA (E)
                          (CONS E PATH))
                     (GET (CAR PATH) 'NEIGHBORS))))
```

Perhaps a better way to get the same effect involves packing the path-building and path-testing operations into the same MAPCAR:

```
(DEFUN EXPAND (X)
     (MAPCAN '(LAMBDA (E)
                  (COND ((MEMBER E X) NIL)
                        (T (LIST (CONS E X)))))
             (GET (CAR X) 'NEIGHBORS)))
```

The COND returns NIL if the path is about to bite itself. The APPEND makes the survivors into a list, getting rid of the spurious NILs.

With this new version of EXPAND, DEPTH will work on networks such as the one shown in figure 11-1a and captured by the DEFPROPs here:

```
(DEFPROP S (A B) NEIGHBORS)
   S

(DEFPROP A (S B F) NEIGHBORS)
   A

(DEFPROP B (S A C) NEIGHBORS)
   B

(DEFPROP C (B F) NEIGHBORS)
   C

(DEFPROP F (A C) NEIGHBORS)
   F
```

For this, the queue develops as follows:

```
((S))
((A S) (B S))
((B A S) (F A S) (B S))
((C B A S) (F A S) (B S))
((F C B A S) (F A S) (B S))
```

Note that the expansion is much like that for the tree in figure 11-1d. Indeed, the tree in figure 11-1d can be made from the network in figure 11-1a by doing the following: first, tracing out all paths leading from the starting node; and second, giving separate names to each instance of nodes A, B, and C encountered (node A became L and P, B became M and O, and C became Q).

This has been a lot of work, but now it is simple to make modifications that capture other search ideas. For example, by making the new paths the last elements on the QUEUE instead of the first, we have breadth-first search, as defined earlier:

```
(DEFUN BREADTH (START FINISH)
     (PROG (QUEUE EXPANSION)
          (SETQ QUEUE (LIST (LIST START)))
          TRYAGAIN
          (COND ((NULL QUEUE) (RETURN NIL))
                ((EQUAL FINISH (CAAR QUEUE))
                 (RETURN (REVERSE (CAR QUEUE)))))
          (SETQ EXPANSION (EXPAND (CAR QUEUE)))
          (SETQ QUEUE (CDR QUEUE))
          (SETQ QUEUE (APPEND QUEUE EXPANSION))      ;New nodes to rear.
          (GO TRYAGAIN)))
```

Best-first Search and Hill-climbing Require Sorting

Sometimes it is possible to make a good guess about how far a given node is from the finish. This means that it may make sense, on each trip around the loop, to extend the path that leads to a place closest to the finish. This strategy is called best-first search.

Identifying the path that leads to the best place so far can be done, albeit somewhat wastefully, by ordering the paths completely. This is done here using SORT, a function available in most LISP systems. Assume SORT orders a list on the basis of any two-argument predicate that can handle any two of the elements on the list.

```
(DEFUN BEST (START FINISH)
       (PROG (QUEUE EXPANSION)
             (SETQ QUEUE (LIST (LIST START)))
             TRYAGAIN
             (COND ((NULL QUEUE) (RETURN NIL))
                   ((EQUAL FINISH (CAAR QUEUE))
                    (RETURN (REVERSE (CAR QUEUE)))))
             (SETQ EXPANSION (EXPAND (CAR QUEUE)))
             (SETQ QUEUE (CDR QUEUE))
             (SETQ QUEUE (SORT (APPEND EXPANSION QUEUE) ;Sort whole queue.
                               'CLOSERP))
             (GO TRYAGAIN)))
```

Now let us work on CLOSERP. First we will need a way of estimating the distance remaining. For a map traversal problem, the straight-line distance is good enough for illustration:

```
(DEFUN DISTANCE (N1 N2)
       (SQRT (PLUS (SQUARE (DIFFERENCE (GET N1 'X) (GET N2 'X)))
                   (SQUARE (DIFFERENCE (GET N1 'Y) (GET N2 'Y))))))
```

Given DISTANCE, it is easy to decide if one partial path terminates closer to the finish than another:

```
(DEFUN CLOSERP (A B)
       (LESSP (DISTANCE (CAR A) FINISH) (DISTANCE (CAR B) FINISH)))
```

For hill-climbing in a tree, the necessary program differs from the one for best-first search in that the new neighbors are sorted and placed at the front of the queue. The whole queue is no longer sorted.

Problems

Problem 11-1: Define HILL, a search program that does hill climbing in a tree, such that the new elements of the queue are sorted and then added to the front.

Problem 11-2: Define PATHLENGTH such that it returns the length of a path through a list of cities, assuming that the distance between adjacent cities on the list is the straight line distance.

Then define SHORTERP, a predicate on two paths that holds if the first path is shorter than the second.

Finally, define BB, a search program that extends the shortest path on the queue. BB stands for branch-and-bound. It is guaranteed to produce the shortest path from start to finish, even though all paths are usually not fully extended to the finish.

Problem 11-3: Define BEAM such that one step in the search process consists of expanding the best n paths on the queue and making the results into a new queue after sorting. (Best means ends closest to the goal.)

Problems about Sorting

In the previous section we needed a function for sorting a list. There are many different methods for sorting things. Naturally we will be tempted to think here in terms of a recursive, divide-and-conquer strategy. One such algorithm is called the radix exchange sorting method. It sorts numbers by looking at them one digit at a time, starting at the high order digit. Having sorted on one digit, the process is repeated on the next lower one, after dividing the list of numbers according to the digit just sorted. Each sublist so formed contains numbers with the same high order digits. This makes it possible to sort each sublist separately according to its low order digits without disturbing the order already created.

The following list of numbers has been sorted on the left-most digit and is ready to be broken up into four lists to be sorted on the next digit to the right:

```
521
543
542
451
467
371
332
318
337
121
172
```

If we choose to use binary representation for numbers (radix equals two), the list of numbers will be divided into two sublists at each step. One sublist contains numbers that have a one in the bit just sorted on, the other containing numbers with a zero in that bit position.

Let us assume that the numbers are stored in an array called TABLE. The function RADIX-SORT will sort the part of the array between BOTTOM and TOP on the bit specified by BIT (a binary number with one non-zero bit). After sorting on this bit the function calls itself to sort the array on the next bit to the right. The recursive calls include the correct boundary positions, so that the part of the array where the bit specified in BIT is zero, is sorted separately from that part of the array where this bit is one.

```
(DEFUN RADIX-SORT (BOTTOM TOP BIT)
     (PROG (BOTTOM-N TOP-N TEMP-B TEMP-T)
          (COND ((ZEROP BIT) (RETURN NIL)))      ;Terminating condition.
          (SETQ BOTTOM-N BOTTOM                   ;Starting value.
                TOP-N TOP)                        ;Starting value.
          UP
          (COND ((GREATERP BOTTOM-N TOP)          ;Scan up for bit on.
                 (GO SIMPLE))                     ;Hit the top.
                ((NOT (ZEROP (BOOLE 1 (TABLE BOTTOM-N) BIT)))
                 (GO DOWN))                       ;Found number with bit on.
           (T (SETQ BOTTOM-N (ADD1 BOTTOM-N))
                 (GO UP)))                        ;Continue scanning up.
          DOWN
          (COND ((LESSP TOP-N BOTTOM)             ;Scan down for bit off.
                 (GO SIMPLE))                     ;Hit the bottom.
                ((ZEROP (BOOLE 1 (TABLE TOP-N) BIT))
                 (GO OUT))                        ;Found number with bit off.
                (T (SETQ TOP-N (SUB1 TOP-N))
                 (GO DOWN)))                      ;Continue scanning down.
          OUT
          (COND ((LESSP TOP-N BOTTOM-N)
                 (GO FINISH))                     ;Pointers have collided.
                (T (SETQ TEMP-B (TABLE BOTTOM-N)
                         TEMP-T (TABLE TOP-N))
                   (STORE (TABLE BOTTOM-N) TEMP-T) ;Exchange.
                   (STORE (TABLE TOP-N) TEMP-B)    ;Exchange.
                   (GO UP)))
          SIMPLE
          (RADIX-SORT BOTTOM TOP (QUOTIENT BIT 2))    ;Whole thing.
          (RETURN NIL)
          FINISH
          (RADIX-SORT BOTTOM TOP-N (QUOTIENT BIT 2))  ;Split array
          (RADIX-SORT BOTTOM-N TOP (QUOTIENT BIT 2)))) ;and recurse.
```

In this function we have to test a number to see if a particular bit is on. The bit-wise logical AND of the number and BIT is required. In some implementations of LISP the sixteen logical operations on two variables are available using the function BOOLE. In particular (BOOLE 1 X Y) is the bit-wise AND of the two numbers X and Y. In other LISP implementations the same result can be achieved using the function LOGAND. Note that the LISP function AND is not suitable, since it does not perform a bit-wise operation on numbers. Similarly, the result of the boolean operation cannot be used directly in a COND-clause, since it is a number. What COND wants is something that is NIL or nonNIL.

In the initial call, BOTTOM and TOP should point to the beginning and end of the array, while BIT should be a power of two larger than half the largest number in the array. For convenience this value may be fixed as half of the smallest number that is too large to be represented.

Problem 11-4: Check that all special cases are properly dealt with. What if all the numbers have the bit in the position being sorted on equal to zero? What if these bits are all one? What happens if BOTTOM is equal to TOP? Add a special test to avoid unnecessary computations in this case.

Problem 11-5: One of many other ways of sorting a list of things depends on a method called merging. Two ordered lists are combined into a single ordered list by the function MERGE. Sorting is then accomplished by breaking a list into two parts, sorting each, and merging the results. Define SORT-MERGE and MERGE. Assume that the list given to SORT-MERGE contains sublists which are to be sorted on their first element. Here is a test case for SORT-MERGE:

```
(SORT-MERGE '((1.0 'AVOCADO)
              (5.0 'MANGO)
              (2.0 'PAWPAW)
              (4.0 'PINEAPPLE)
              (3.0 'COCONUT)
              (6.0 'BANANA)
              (0.0 'ORANGE))
```

Problem 11-6: Define SORT, introduced in the previous section. The first argument is a list to be sorted using the predicate given as the second argument. Start by defining SPLICEIN, a recursive function that takes three arguments, an element to be spliced in, a list to splice it into, and a predicate that takes two arguments. The new element is to be spliced in just before the first element on the list for which the following evaluates to T:

```
(FUNCALL <predicate> <old element> <existing element>)
```

Then, using SPLICEIN, write SORT, a function of two arguments, a list to be sorted and a predicate that takes two arguments.

Project: Change the radix exchange sorting routine to operate base 4. That is, sort on two bits of the number at each level.

Problems about Measuring out a Volume of Water

Imagine being given two crocks, of different volumes, A and B. The crocks may be filled from a source or emptied into a sink. In addition, water can be poured from one into the other until it is filled or until the crock from which water is being poured is emptied. The problem is to measure out a given volume, C.

First of all, we will insist that this volume fit into one or the other of the two crocks. Thinking about it carefully, it is clear that only certain volumes can be measured out this way. For example, if B is twice A, it is not possible to measure out amounts other than A and twice A. In fact, if both A and B are multiples of X, only multiples of X can be measured out. We can now deduce the general rule that only multiples of the greatest common divisor of A and B can be achieved.

```
(DEFUN WATER-CROCK (A B C)
       (COND ((AND (GREATERP C A) (GREATERP C B)) 'C-TOO-LARGE)
             ((NOT (ZEROP (REMAINDER C (GCD A B)))) 'C-NOT-POSSIBLE)
             (T (WATER-MAKE 0 0))))
```

We now define the function GCD since it is not available in some implementations of LISP. We will use Euclid's algorithm for finding the greatest common divisor of two numbers. If one of the numbers is zero, their greatest common divisor equals the other. Otherwise, it equals the greatest common divisor of the remainder obtained by dividing the second number by the first, and the first number. Sound mysterious? Here is the LISP function:

```
(DEFUN GCD (X Y)
       (COND ((ZEROP X) Y)             ; Termination test.
             (T (GCD (REMAINDER Y X) X))))   ; Recursive call.
```

It took Euclid many sentences to describe the method, in part because proof by induction, the mathematical analog of the concept of recursion, was not then recognized as an acceptable mathematical argument.

Now let us return to the water-crock problem. Assuming that C is achievable, let us proceed to consider sequences of possible moves. A little thought makes it clear that it makes no sense to ever back up, undoing what has been achieved so far. As a result, water always moves in one direction: from the source it goes into one crock; from there, into the other; and from there, it is finally poured out. We do not have to search a huge tree of possible moves because most moves do not make sense. It is sufficient to repeat a series of transfers in one direction, checking at each step whether one of the two crocks happens to contain the correct amount of water.

```
(DEFUN WATER-MAKE (X Y)                                  ;A & B contain X & Y.
       (COND ((EQUAL X C) '((CORRECT AMOUNT IN A)))      ;Right amount in A.
             ((EQUAL Y C) '((CORRECT AMOUNT IN B)))      ;Right amount in B.
             ((EQUAL X A) (CONS '(EMPTY A)               ;A is full, empty it.
                                (WATER-MAKE 0 Y)))
             ((EQUAL Y 0) (CONS '(FILL B)                ;B is empty, fill it.
                                (WATER-MAKE X B)))
             ((GREATERP (DIFFERENCE A X) Y)              ;Will B fit into A?
              (CONS '(EMPTY B INTO A)                    ;Yes, empty B.
                    (WATER-MAKE (PLUS X Y) 0.)))
             (T (CONS '(FILL A FROM B)                   ;No, fill A.
                      (WATER-MAKE A (DIFFERENCE Y
                                   (DIFFERENCE A X)))))))
```

Note the recursion when WATER-MAKE is called with arguments reflecting the
current contents of the two crocks. The function shown will return a list of
instructions which lead to the desired result. Consider this:

```
(WATER-CROCK 3 5 2)
  ((FILL B) (FILL A FROM B) (CORRECT AMOUNT IN B))
```

Problem 11-7: The list of instructions produced by WATER-CROCK may not be the
shortest possible one. Note, for example, that interchanging A and B leads to this:

```
(WATER-CROCK 5 3 2)
  ((FILL B) (EMPTY B INTO A) (FILL B) (FILL A FROM B)
   (EMPTY A) (EMPTY B INTO A) (FILL B) (EMPTY B INTO A)
   (FILL B) (FILL A FROM B) (CORRECT AMOUNT IN B))
```

This happens because we arbitrarily chose to transfer water in the direction:

$$SOURCE \rightarrow crock\ B \rightarrow crock\ A \rightarrow SINK$$

Half the time it is better to go the other way:

$$SINK \leftarrow crock\ B \leftarrow crock\ A \leftarrow SOURCE$$

Write WATER-CROCK-OPTIMUM which returns the shorter of the two possible
sequences of instructions. Avoid using two different versions of WATER-CROCK.

Project: Write a program which finds the greatest common divisor of two
polynomials. Assume that the polynomials are represented by lists of their
coefficients. Naturally functions for adding, subtracting, multiplying, and dividing
polynomials will be needed.

Problems about Placing Queens on a Chess Board

How is it possible to place eight queens on a chess board so that they do not
threaten each other? This well-known problem can be solved conveniently by a
tree-search method. First, we have to write a function that will determine
whether two queens threaten each other. Queens in chess can move along the
columns, rows, and two diagonals through their present position. We can encode
the positions on the board if we number the rows and columns. The following
function then will do:

```
(DEFUN THREAT (I J A B)
     (OR (EQUAL I A)                                    ;Same row.
         (EQUAL J B)                                    ;Same column.
         (EQUAL (DIFFERENCE I J) (DIFFERENCE A B))      ;SW-NE diagonal.
         (EQUAL (PLUS I J) (PLUS A B)))))               ;NW-SE diagonal.
```

Next, we can represent a configuration of queens on the board using a list of
pairs, each sublist being the row and column code of one queen on the board.
Suppose now that we plan to add a queen to a board. The following function will
tell us whether the position (N M) for the new queen is safe:

```
(DEFUN CONFLICT (N M BOARD)
     (COND ((NULL BOARD) NIL)
           ((OR (THREAT N M (CAAR BOARD) (CADAR BOARD))
                (CONFLICT N M (CDR BOARD))))))
```

With these preliminaries out of the way we can tackle the search problem.

Problem 11-8: Write QUEEN such that starting at row one, an attempt is made to
place a queen in column one. Let N and M be the row and column numbers.
After placing the first queen, it does not make sense to place another queen in the
same row, so N is to be incremented. A safe square is then found in this row.
This process is to continue until all queens are placed on the board. If at some
stage all squares on a particular row are threatened, the program has to back up.
It is to do this by removing the last queen placed on the board. Let the single
argument, SIZE, specify the size of the board. This will be eight for a full chess
board, but it is interesting to watch the program at work on smaller boards too.
There are no solutions for 2 by 2 and 3 by 3 boards, for example, but there are
two for a 4 by 4 board:

```
(QUEENS 4)
   ((1 2) (2 4) (3 1) (4 3))
   ((4 2) (3 4) (2 1) (1 3))
   FINISH
```

There are 92 solutions, by the way, for the full 8 by 8 board.

Problem 11-9: Write BOARD-PRINT, a procedure to print out a board configuration given as a list of pairs of row and column numbers:

```
(BOARD-PRINT '((1 1) (2 5) (3 8) (4 6) (5 3) (6 7) (7 2) (8 4)))
```

```
Q . . . . . . .
. . . . Q . . .
. . . . . . . Q
. . . . . Q . .
. . Q . . . . .
. . . . . . Q .
. Q . . . . . .
. . . Q . . . .
```

Summary

■ Breadth-first and depth-first search are basic strategies.

■ A node queue facilitates depth-first search and breadth-first search.

■ Best-first search and hill-climbing require sorting.

References

For more information on search, see Chapter 4 of *Artificial Intelligence,* by Patrick H. Winston [1977]. Knuth [1973] and Aho, Hopcroft, and Ullman [1974, pg. 176] cover methods for searching. Both books also provide extensive discussion of sorting methods. The radix exchange sorting method is discussed by Knuth [1973, pp. 123-129]. The LISP function SORT, when used on arrays, employs an algorithm called quicksort, mentioned by Knuth [1973, pp. 114-116], and Aho, Hopcroft, and Ullman [1974, pg. 92]. For lists, LISP uses a merge sort, discussed by Knuth [1973, pp. 159-170]. See also Cohen and Levitt [1965].

For work on games, start with the review paper by Berliner [1978] or the book edited by Frey [1977]. Also see Gillogly [1972], Simon and Kadane [1975], and Stockman [1979]. Euclid's algorithm for finding the greatest common divisor is discussed in Brown [1971].

12
EXAMPLES
FROM
MATHEMATICS

The purpose of this chapter is to illustrate some of the features of LISP by exploring algorithms for numerical computations. For many, the first exposure to programming is through examples of this kind. We therefore believe it may be helpful to see LISP in action on certain of these problems. Those who find the mathematical details of the examples here distracting, however, should omit this chapter on first reading.

It is Easy to Translate Infix Notation to Prefix

Many find it inconvenient and error-prone to translate mathematical formulas into prefix notation. Therefore let us develop a simple LISP function that performs this translation automatically.

An arithmetic expression will be represented as a list of operands and operators, as in this example:

(A + B * C)

The usual precedence among arithmetic operators will be enforced. This can be explicitly overridden by enclosing a subexpression in parentheses, making it a sublist. Consider this for example:

((A + B) * (C + D))

We start by exhibiting WEIGHT, a function that returns the precedence weighting of an operator.

```
(DEFUN WEIGHT (OPERATOR)                          ;Determine weight of operator.
       (COND ((EQUAL OPERATOR 'DUMMY) -1)
             ((EQUAL OPERATOR '=) 0)
             ((EQUAL OPERATOR '+) 1)
             ((EQUAL OPERATOR '-) 1)
             ((EQUAL OPERATOR '*) 2)
             ((EQUAL OPERATOR '//) 2)
             ((EQUAL OPERATOR '\) 2)
             ((EQUAL OPERATOR '^) 3)
             (T (PRINT (LIST OPERATOR 'NOT 'AN 'OPERATOR)) 'NOP)))
```

The pseudo-operator DUMMY is used to mark the beginning of a list of operators — it has less weight than any of the other operators. Operators that are not recognized are arbitrarily given the greatest weight.

Note that in some LISP implementations the slash, /, is used to signal an unusual treatment for the next character — it is a way to prevent a space from being interpreted as a separator, for example. As a result it is necessary in the above function to use // to get the equivalent of a single /.

Next, we will have to look up the appropriate LISP function to implement each of the operators.

```
(DEFUN OPCODE (OPERATOR)                          ;Get appropriate LISP function.
       (COND ((EQUAL OPERATOR 'DUMMY) (PRINT 'HIT-DUMMY) 'DUMMY)
             ((EQUAL OPERATOR '=) 'SETQ)
             ((EQUAL OPERATOR '+) 'PLUS)
             ((EQUAL OPERATOR '-) 'DIFFERENCE)
             ((EQUAL OPERATOR '*) 'TIMES)
             ((EQUAL OPERATOR '//) 'QUOTIENT)
             ((EQUAL OPERATOR '\) 'REMAINDER)
             ((EQUAL OPERATOR '^) 'EXPT)
             (T (PRINT (LIST OPERATOR 'NOT 'AN 'OPERATOR)) 'NOP)))
```

Note that a message is printed when an error occurs. It would be better to provide the user with more information about the computation going on at the time the error happened. In fact, he should be allowed to inspect the variable bindings in effect at that point as well. Techniques for debugging which make this possible will be introduced in Chapter 14. Here we shall be content with simple messages indicating the general nature of the error.

The *prefix* form of an arithmetic expression can be represented as a tree. Figure 12-1, for example, shows the tree corresponding to the expression:

```
(SETQ TOTAL (TIMES PRINCIPAL (EXPT (PLUS 1.0 INTEREST) YEARS)))
```

The *infix* form is essentially a linear string obtained by a depth-first exploration of the tree representing the arithmetic expression. By tracing along the outer

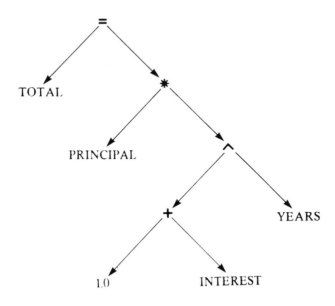

Figure 12-1: An arithmetic expression in prefix form can be represented as a tree. The operators lie at the nodes, while the leaves are the operands. The equivalent infix form can be found by a simple depth-first exploration of this tree.

boundary of the tree in figure 12-1, for example, one obtains:

```
(TOTAL = PRINCIPAL * (1.0 + INTEREST) ^ YEARS)
```

There are many parsing methods for translating from one form to the other. We will employ a linear left-to-right scan, where operands and operators not yet used in producing the output are kept on a list. For clarity, we actually use two separate lists, OPERANDS and OPERATORS, to stack up operands and operators.

Things are added to the front of the lists when the operator at the head of what remains of the arithmetic expression, AE, has a larger weight than the operator at the head of the list OPERATORS. Otherwise, the operator at the head of OPERATORS is combined with the two top operands at the head of OPERANDS. Whenever a piece of code has been assembled in this fashion, it is added to the front of the operand list as a new, composite operand.

The following simple example illustrates some of this by showing successive stages in the translation of the arithmetic expression (A + B * C):

OPERATORS	OPERANDS	AE
(DUMMY)	()	(A + B * C)
(DUMMY)	(A)	(+ B * C)
(+ DUMMY)	(A)	(B * C)
(+ DUMMY)	(B A)	(* C)
(* + DUMMY)	(B A)	(C)
(* + DUMMY)	(C B A)	()
(+ DUMMY)	((TIMES B C) A)	()
(DUMMY)	((PLUS A (TIMES B C)))	()

When precedence is forced using sublists, the function simply calls itself recursively on the sublist. The value returned is the translated result. Here is the function INF-TO-PRE which does the translation:

```
(DEFUN INF-TO-PRE (AE)
    (PROG (OPERANDS OPERATORS)                              ;The two lists.
          (COND ((ATOM AE) (RETURN AE)))                    ;Special case.
          (SETQ OPERATORS (LIST 'DUMMY))                    ;Dummy terminator.
          STUFF
          (COND ((NULL AE)                                  ;Scan for operand.
                 (RETURN 'UNEXPECTED-END)))                 ;Ends on operator.
          (SETQ OPERANDS (CONS (COND ((ATOM (CAR AE)) (CAR AE))
                                     (T (INF-TO-PRE (CAR AE))))   ;Recurse.
                               OPERANDS)                     ;PUSH operand.
                AE (CDR AE))                                 ;Peel off operand.
          SCAN
          (COND ((AND (NULL AE)                              ;Scan for operator.
                      (EQUAL (CAR OPERATORS) 'DUMMY))        ;AE & list empty.
                 (RETURN (CAR OPERANDS))))                   ;Return result.
          (COND ((OR (NULL AE)                               ;End of AE or
                     (NOT (GREATERP (WEIGHT (CAR AE))        ;nesting order.
                                    (WEIGHT (CAR OPERATORS)))))
                 (SETQ OPERANDS                              ;Construct code.
                       (CONS (LIST (OPCODE (CAR OPERATORS))
                                   (CADR OPERANDS)
                                   (CAR OPERANDS))
                             (CDDR OPERANDS))                ;POP two operands.
                       OPERATORS (CDR OPERATORS))            ;POP operator.
                 (GO SCAN))                                  ;Look for operator.
                (T (SETQ OPERATORS (CONS (CAR AE)
                                         OPERATORS)          ;PUSH operator.
                         AE (CDR AE))                        ;Peel off operator.
                   (GO STUFF))))))                           ;Look for operand.
```

Here is an example of INF-TO-PRE in action:

```
(INF-TO-PRE '(TOTAL = PRINCIPAL * (1.0 + INTEREST) ^ YEARS))
  (SETQ TOTAL (TIMES PRINCIPAL (EXPT (PLUS 1.0 INTEREST) YEARS)))
```

Problems

Problem 12-1: It is simple to translate from prefix to infix. Write PRE-TO-INF without worrying about removing unnecessary parentheses.

Problem 12-2: Improve PRE-TO-INF so it will not put in redundant levels of parentheses. It should do the following for example:

```
(PRE-TO-INF '(SETQ TOTAL (TIMES PRINCIPAL (EXPT (PLUS 1.0 INTEREST) YEARS))))
  (TOTAL = PRINCIPAL * (1.0 + INTEREST) ^ YEARS)
```

Problem 12-3: Add a tracing mechanism to INF-TO-PRE that prints the values of AE, OPERANDS and OPERATORS whenever they change. Let the tracing operation be under the control of TRACE-FLG, a free variable.

Problem 12-4: Operators of the same weight now lead to code which nests left to right. While this is the usual convention for most languages able to accept arithmetic expressions, it may at times be desirable to have operations nested right to left. Change one line to modify INF-TO-PRE appropriately.

Problem 12-5: Sometimes it is convenient to indicate multiplication by simply justaposing two operands without an intervening *. Modify INF-TO-PRE to permit implicit multiplication by checking for the presence of an operand where an operator is expected. Note that the operand may be atomic or a sublist.

Problem 12-6: To make it possible to add new operators easily, it is better to store information on their property lists instead of encasing them in functions like WEIGHT and OPCODE. Make INF-TO-PRE extensible by looking these things up on the property lists of the operators.

Problem 12-7: Add comparison operators, like < and >, and logical operators, like & (for AND) and | (for OR), noting the convention that logical operators have less weight than comparison operators, which in turn have less weight than the usual arithmetic operators. (However, the assignment operator, =, has least weight of all.) Also, & has more weight than |. Here is an example of the modified program at work:

```
(INF-TO-PRE '(A + B < C + D  &  A + C > B + D))
  (AND (LESSP (PLUS A B) (PLUS C D)) (GREATERP (PLUS A C) (PLUS B D)))
```

Project: We have not allowed unary operators like -, SQRT, SIN. Add a check for the presence of an operator where INF-TO-PRE is looking for an operand, to implement this extension. Unary operators have highest precedence weight.

It is Useful to Represent Sparse Matrices as S-expressions

Matrices are conveniently represented using arrays. When they get large this becomes unwieldy. In the case of sparse matrices storage is wasted on the large number of zero entries, which also lead to useless arithmetic operations. Adding and multiplying by zero can be avoided if only the nonzero elements are stored. Lists are well suited to this task.

A sparse vector can be conveniently represented as a list of pairs. Each sublist contains an index and the corresponding component. So the vector [1.2, 0.0, 3.4, 0.0, 0.0, -6.7, 0.0] could be represented by the list

```
((1 1.2) (3 3.4) (6 -6.7)).
```

Locating a particular component requires additional work, but storage and computation is conserved when large sparse vectors are manipulated.

First, let us develop a function that multiplies a sparse vector by a scalar. This can be done easily by multiplying one component and recursively applying the same function to the rest of the vector.

```
(DEFUN SPARSE-SCALE-V (SCALE V)
    (COND ((ZEROP SCALE) NIL)              ;Special case.
          ((NULL V) NIL)                   ;Termination ?
          (T (CONS (LIST (CAAR V)          ;Copy index.
                         (TIMES SCALE (CADAR V)))    ;Scale component.
                   (SPARSE-SCALE-V SCALE (CDR V)))))))
```

Note the special treatment of the case when the scale factor equals zero. Next we apply a similar program structure to the problem of calculating the dot product of two sparse vectors. At each step we check whether the components at the head of the lists have matching indices. If they do, the product of the corresponding components is calculated. Otherwise the component with the lower index is discarded, and the function is applied recursively to what remains.

```
(DEFUN SPARSE-DOT-PRODUCT (A B)
       (COND ((NULL A) 0)                              ;Termination?
             ((NULL B) 0)                              ;Termination?
             ((LESSP (CAAR A) (CAAR B))
              (SPARSE-DOT-PRODUCT (CDR A) B))          ;Discard A component.
             ((LESSP (CAAR B) (CAAR A))
              (SPARSE-DOT-PRODUCT (CDR B) A))          ;Discard B component.
             (T (PLUS (TIMES (CADAR A) (CADAR B))      ;Multiply components.
                      (SPARSE-DOT-PRODUCT (CDR A) (CDR B))))))
```

We do not need much more than this to add two sparse vectors, as long as we are careful to construct the representation of the result correctly.

```
(DEFUN SPARSE-V-PLUS (A B)
       (COND ((NULL A) B)
             ((NULL B) A)
             ((LESSP (CAAR A) (CAAR B))
              (CONS (CAR A)                            ;Copy A component.
                    (SPARSE-V-PLUS (CDR A) B)))
             ((LESSP (CAAR B) (CAAR A))
              (CONS (CAR B)                            ;Copy B component.
                    (SPARSE-V-PLUS (CDR B) A)))
             (T (CONS (LIST (CAAR A)
                            (PLUS (CADAR A) (CADAR B))) ;Add components.
                      (SPARSE-V-PLUS (CDR A) (CDR B))))))
```

Sparse matrices can be represented as lists of sublists too. Now each sublist contains a row index and a sparse vector representing the corresponding row. So for example,

```
((1 ((1 1.0)))
 (2 ((2 1.0)))
 (3 ((3 1.0))))
```

is the representation for the 3 by 3 identity matrix.

The product of a vector by a matrix is a vector obtained by listing the dotproducts of the vector with each of the columns of the matrix. Our representation is organized around rows, so to make use of this definition we would first have to transpose the matrix. This may be inefficient or inconvenient, so we look for an alternative. If we scale each row of the matrix by the corresponding component of the vector, and then add up the rows, treating each as a vector, we also obtain the product of the vector and the matrix. The next program will clarify this:

```
(DEFUN SPARSE-V-TIMES-M (V M)
       (COND ((NULL V) NIL)
             ((NULL M) NIL)
             ((LESSP (CAAR V) (CAAR M))
              (SPARSE-V-TIMES-M (CDR V) M))        ;Discard piece of V.
             ((LESSP (CAAR M) (CAAR V))
              (SPARSE-V-TIMES-M V (CDR M)))         ;Discard piece of M.
             (T (SPARSE-V-PLUS (SPARSE-SCALE-V (CADAR V)
                                               (CADAR M))
                               (SPARSE-V-TIMES-M (CDR V)
                                                 (CDR M)))))))
```

Now we are ready for matrix multiplication. There are a number of ways of looking at the product, C, of two matrices A and B. The (i, j)-th element of C is the dotproduct of the i-th row of A and the j-th column of B, for example. Thus the i-th row of C is the product of the i-th row of A and the matrix B.

```
(DEFUN SPARSE-M-TIMES (A B)
       (COND ((NULL A) NIL)
             (T (CONS (LIST (CAAR A)
                            (SPARSE-V-TIMES-M (CADAR A) B))
                      (SPARSE-M-TIMES (CDR A) B)))))
```

We see that multiplication of sparse matrices is simple given all the auxiliary functions.

Problems

Problem 12-8: Write a function to extract the n-th component of a sparse vector.

Problem 12-9: There is no special provision in SPARSE-V-PLUS for the situation when the sum of two components happens to be zero. Change the function SPARSE-V-PLUS so that this component is not inserted in the result.

Problem 12-10: Does it matter whether we let the indices of the component of a sparse vector run from 0 to $(n-1)$ or from 1 to n?

Problem 12-11: Write SPARSE-M-PRINT, a function that prints each row of a sparse matrix on a separate line.

Problem 12-12: Using SPARSE-V-PLUS as a model, write SPARSE-M-PLUS for adding two sparse matrices.

Problem 12-13: The product of a matrix by a vector is a vector obtained by listing the dotproducts of each row of the matrix with the vector. Write SPARSE-M-TIMES-V.

Problem 12-14: Write SPARSE-M-TRANSPOSE, a function for transposing a sparse matrix.

Problem 12-15: The j-th column of C, the product of two matrices A and B, is the product of A and the j-th column of B. Write another version of SPARSE-M-TIMES based on this observation. Use SPARSE-M-TRANSPOSE and SPARSE-M-TIMES-V defined in earlier problems.

Project: Extend the above set of functions to deal with objects of higher dimensionality.

Roots of Numbers can be Found Using Tail Recursion

Typically LISP comes equipped with SQRT, a function that takes the square root of a floating point number. Suppose we wanted to write a function specially suited for fixed point numbers. One approach would be to implement the digit by digit method, similar to long division, that was once taught in school. It turns out however that other methods are faster. One such alternative is based on the so-called Newton-Raphson iteration:

$$x_{n+1} = [x_n + y/x_n] / 2.$$

The argument is y, while x_n is the current estimate of the square-root, and the new estimate is x_{n+1}. This method is usually viewed as one for obtaining increasingly better approximations, and some terminating test must be included to prevent the iteration from running on indefinitely. In the case of integer arithmetic, however, a result, x, is found in a finite number of steps which satisfies:

$$x^2 \leqslant y < (x+1)^2.$$

In most cases this solution is at hand when $x_{n+1} = x_n$. However, if y happens to be one less than a perfect square, successive values of x will cycle between the correct answer and a number one larger. This condition can be detected by checking whether $x_{n+1} = y/x_n$.

We can now write the functions SQUARE-ROOT for integer arguments:

```
(DEFUN SQUARE-ROOT (Y)
        (COND ((MINUSP Y) 'NEGATIVE-SQUARE-ROOT)        ;Error.
               (T (SQUARE-ROOT-AUX Y                     ;Argument.
                        1                                 ;First estimate.
                        (QUOTIENT (PLUS 1 Y)    ;Second estimate.
                                  2)))))

(DEFUN SQUARE-ROOT-AUX (Y XO XN)
        (COND ((EQUAL XN XO) XN)                          ;y, x(n), x(n+1)
               ((EQUAL XN (QUOTIENT Y XO)) XN)            ;x(n+1) = x(n) ?
               (T (SQUARE-ROOT-AUX Y                      ;x(n+1) = y/x(n) ?
                        XN                                ;Argument.
                        (QUOTIENT (PLUS XN        ;Old estimate.
                                  (QUOTIENT Y XN))  ;New estimate.
                        2)))))
```

When given an argument of 15, successive values of x_n are 1, 7, 4, 3, and 3. Note the use of tail recursion in the above implementation.

Problems

Problem 12-16: What happens if SQUARE-ROOT is given a floating point argument?

Problem 12-17: Write CUBE-ROOT, a function to compute the cube root of a fixed point number. Be careful about negative arguments. Use the Newton-Raphson iteration:

$$x_{n+1} = [2x_n + y/x_n^2] / 3.$$

Problem 12-18: Write C-SQRT, a function that takes the square root of a complex number. LISP does not have a way of representing complex numbers directly. Use lists containing a pair of floating point numbers to represent the real and imaginary parts. If

$$(a + i\,b)^2 = c + i\,d,$$

then, since $c = (a^2 - b^2)$ and $d = 2ab$:

$$a = \pm [((c^2+d^2)^{\frac{1}{2}} + c)/2]^{\frac{1}{2}},$$
$$b = \pm [((c^2+d^2)^{\frac{1}{2}} - c)/2]^{\frac{1}{2}}.$$

The signs of a and b must be chosen so that $2ab = d$. Return the square root with the positive real part.

Problems about Calculating Impedances of Electrical Networks

Two-terminal networks of resistors, inductors, and capacitors can be conveniently represented as list structures. Components are denoted by pairs, a component type (R, L, or C), and the component value (in ohms, henries, and farads). Series connections of two components can be indicated by a list containing the code SERIES and the two things connected in series. Similarly, the code PARALLEL indicates parallel connection. The following describes the simple circuit shown in figure 12-2:

```
(SETQ CIRCUIT-A '(SERIES (R 1.0)
                  (PARALLEL (SERIES (R 100.0)
                                    (L 0.2))
                            (PARALLEL (C 0.000001)
                                      (R 1000000.0)))))
```

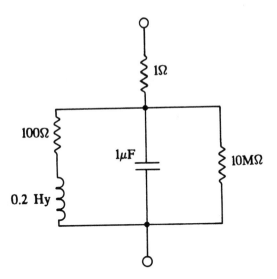

Figure 12-2: A two-terminal network of resistors, capacitors, and inductors can be represented as a list structure. The impedance of the circuit can then be calculated easily.

Suppose now that we wish to compute the impedance of a circuit. This is simple if the circuit consists of just one component:

```
(DEFUN R (X) (LIST X 0.0))

(DEFUN L (X) (LIST 0.0 (TIMES OMEGA X)))

(DEFUN C (X) (LIST 0.0 (QUOTIENT -1.0 (TIMES OMEGA X))))
```

Here OMEGA, a free variable, is the angular frequency in radians per second. Lists containing real and imaginary parts are used since impedance is a complex quantity. The series and parallel connections are treated next:

```
(DEFUN SERIES (A B) (C-PLUS A B))

(DEFUN PARALLEL (A B) (C-INVERSE (C-PLUS (C-INVERSE A) (C-INVERSE B))))
```

Here C-PLUS and C-INVERSE are addition and multiplicative-inverse operations on complex numbers.

The following function will compute the impedance of a given circuit at an arbitrary frequency:

```
(DEFUN IMPEDANCE (CIRCUIT OMEGA)  (EVAL CIRCUIT))
```

So for example, near the resonance of CIRCUIT-A one finds these results:

```
(IMPEDANCE CIRCUIT-A 2179.44)
  (1997.09 0.0)

(IMPEDANCE CIRCUIT-A 2207.99)
  (2022.27 -223.08)
```

The big point here is that we have embedded a problem-solving language in LISP.

Problem 12-19: Write C-PLUS and C-INVERSE. Note that

$$1/(a + i\,b) = (a - i\,b)/(a^2 + b^2).$$

Problem 12-20: Write ADMITTANCE, a function which will calculate the admittance of a circuit described as above.

Project: Develop a representation for networks with one input and one output port. Write a function which will calculate the transfer function of such a network.

Roots of Algebraic Equations can be Found Using Nested Functions

Now, let us construct a series of functions for finding the roots of algebraic equations with real coefficients. Since these roots may be complex, the functions should return a list, with each root represented as a two-component sublist containing the real and imaginary parts. Finding the roots of an equation from its coefficients by means of a finite number of rational operations and extraction of roots is called solution by radicals. The solutions by radicals of algebraic equations of the third and fourth degree were discovered in the sixteenth century.

Early in the nineteenth century P. Ruffini and N. H. Abel showed that the general algebraic equation whose degree is greater than four cannot be solved by radicals. We will confine our attention to equations of degree four or less so that we will be able to find the roots without resorting to approximation or iteration. It may help to remember at this point that complex roots, if any, will occur in conjugate pairs, if we allow only algebraic equations with real coefficients.

We will have to be careful about special cases that arise when some of the coefficients are zero. Naturally, COND will be useful in sorting out these exceptions. We start with the innocent-looking linear equation in one unknown, x,

$$ax + b = 0.$$

If both a and b are zero, this is not much of an equation. The equation is said to be homogeneous and any value of x is a solution. The user should be warned and an empty list should be returned. If a is zero, but b is not, the equation is inconsistent. There are no solutions, and again a warning is called for. Finally, if neither a nor b are zero, we have the obvious result,

$$x = -b/a.$$

Remembering that the value returned should be a list of roots, each a list of the real and imaginary parts, we arrive at the following:

```
(DEFUN LINEAR (A B)
     (COND ((ZEROP A)
          (COND ((ZEROP B) (PRINT 'HOMOGENEOUS) NIL)      ; a = 0 & b = 0
                (T (PRINT 'INCONSISTENT) NIL)))            ; a = 0 & b ≠ 0
        ((ZEROP B) '((0.0 0.0)))                           ; a ≠ 0 & b = 0
        (T (LIST (LIST (MINUS (QUOTIENT B A)) 0.0)))))))   ; a ≠ 0 & b ≠ 0
```

Note that the penultimate line could be omitted at the cost of a few unneccessary arithmetic operations in the case that b is zero. Also, simple messages are printed when the equation does not have roots or has an infinite number of roots. Instead of returning an empty list in these cases, the user could be permitted more elaborate interaction using the debugging techniques to be introduced in Chapter 14.

We are now ready to tackle quadratic equations like

$$ax^2 + bx + c = 0.$$

If a is zero, this is not really a quadratic equation and the solutions are those of the remaining linear equation $bx + c = 0$. If c is zero, one of the roots is zero and the other can be found by solving the linear equation $ax + b = 0$. In these two cases we can call on the function already defined. If neither a nor c are zero we can remove the linear term using the transformation $y = 2ax + b$ and get this equation:

$$y^2 + (4ac - b^2) = 0.$$

To find out if the roots will be real or complex we check the sign of the discriminant:

$$b^2 - 4ac.$$

We can now write the part of the program which deals with the special cases and computes the discriminant.

```
(DEFUN QUADRATIC (A B C)
        (COND ((ZEROP A) (LINEAR B C))                          ;a = 0
              ((ZEROP C) (CONS '(0.0 0.0) (LINEAR A B)))        ;c = 0
              (T (QUADRATIC-AUX A
                      B
                      C
                      (DIFFERENCE (TIMES B B)        ;Discriminant.
                                  (TIMES 4.0 A C))))))
```

Now $x = (y - b)/(2a)$, so if the discriminant is negative, the original equation has the complex conjugate pair of solutions:

$$(-b/(2a),\ \pm\ (4ac-b^2)^{1/2}/(2a)).$$

If the discriminant happens to be zero, the two roots coincide at $-b/(2a)$. Finally, when it is positive, there are two real roots, usually given in the form:

$$[-b \pm (b^2 - 4ac)^{1/2}] / (2a).$$

Curiously, by viewing the original equation as an equation in the variable $1/x$, one finds an alternate form:

$$(2c) / [-b \mp (b^2 - 4ac)^{1/2}].$$

This is quickly verified by noting that the sum of the roots must equal b/a, while their product must equal c/a. Why bother with the second form if both are correct? It is a question of numerical accuracy: if b^2 is much larger than the magnitude of $4ac$, the square root of the discriminant will be only a little different from the magnitude of b. The methods used to represent real numbers in a computer have only limited accuracy, so that precision is lost when two nearly equal quantities are subtracted. Thus one of the two roots will be known with considerably less precision if we recklessly apply either of the two formulations alone. We can avoid this problem by judiciously picking between the possibilities.

We are now ready to write the rest. To make it easier to see what is going on, the work will be divided among three functions.

```
(DEFUN QUADRATIC-CONJUGATE (REAL IMAGINARY)
       (LIST (LIST REAL IMAGINARY)
             (LIST REAL (MINUS IMAGINARY)))))

(DEFUN QUADRATIC-REAL (A TERM C)
       (LIST (LIST (QUOTIENT TERM (TIMES 2.0 A)) 0.0)
             (LIST (QUOTIENT (TIMES 2.0 C) TERM) 0.0)))

(DEFUN QUADRATIC-AUX (A B C DISCRIMINANT)
       (COND ((MINUSP DISCRIMINANT)                        ;Conjugate pair.
              (QUADRATIC-CONJUGATE (MINUS (QUOTIENT B
                                                   (TIMES 2.0 A)))
                                   (QUOTIENT (SQRT (MINUS DISCRIMINANT))
                                             (TIMES 2.0 A))))
             ((ZEROP DISCRIMINANT)                         ;Double root.
              (LIST (LIST (MINUS (QUOTIENT B (TIMES 2.0 A)))
                          0.0)
                    (LIST (MINUS (QUOTIENT B (TIMES 2.0 A)))
                          0.0)))
             ((MINUSP B)                                   ;Real roots b < 0
              (QUADRATIC-REAL A
                              (DIFFERENCE (SQRT DISCRIMINANT) B)
                              C))
             (T (QUADRATIC-REAL A                          ;Real roots b ≥ 0
                                (MINUS (PLUS (SQRT DISCRIMINANT) B))
                                C))))
```

Note that the special treatment of the case when the discriminant is zero can be omitted if the cost of taking the square root of zero is of no concern and exact equality of the two roots is not imperative. Similarly, special treatment of the case when c is zero can be removed with only minor loss in precision of the result.

The amount of programming required for this simple exercise may be surprising. This results from the careful attention to the special cases, use of the best methods for numerical accuracy, a desire to avoid repeating calculations, and the use of mnemonic, but long, function and variable names. Most languages intended for numerical calculations provide single character arithmetic operators such as + instead of full names like PLUS. So do some LISP implementations.

Someone familiar with certain other languages would no doubt have written this procedure quite differently, perhaps as a single function using a large PROG. Several local variables would have been declared and set using SETQ. The other way, illustrated here, is by means of function definition and call. It is quite common to find LISP programs predominantly employing this definition-and-call method. This leads to a division of programs into a large number of subprograms, each short enough to be easy to understand.

Next we tackle cubic equations:

$$ax^3 + bx^2 + cx + d = 0.$$

These either have one real root and a complex conjugate pair or three real roots. It is helpful to remove the quadratic term using the substitution, $y = 3ax + b$. This produces the equation:

$$y^3 + 3(3ac - b^2)\,y + (2b^3 - 9abc + 27a^2d) = 0.$$

In order to find the roots of this simplified cubic, one first finds the roots of the quadratic resolvent:

$$t^2 + (2b^3 - 9abc + 27a^2d)\,t - (3ac - b^2)^3 = 0.$$

```
(DEFUN CUBIC (A B C D)
        (COND ((ZEROP A) (QUADRATIC B C D))            ;a = 0
              (T (CUBIC-AUX A
                  B
                  (QUADRATIC 1.0                        ;Resolvent.
                      (PLUS (TIMES 2.0 B B B)
                            (TIMES 9.0
                                A
                                (DIFFERENCE
                                  (TIMES 3.0 A D)
                                  (TIMES B C))))
                      (EXPT (DIFFERENCE
                              (TIMES B B)
                              (TIMES 3.0 A C))
                            3))))))
```

If the roots of this resolvent are complex, the cubic has three real roots. If the roots of the resolvent are real, the cubic has one real and a complex conjugate pair of roots.

```
(DEFUN CUBIC-AUX (A B ROOTS)
      (COND ((ZEROP (CADAR ROOTS))
            (CUBIC-CONJUGATE A                          ;Resolvent roots real.
                             B
                             (CURT (CAAR ROOTS))        ;Pick out real parts.
                             (CURT (CAADR ROOTS))))
            (T (CUBIC-REAL A                            ;Roots complex.
                           B
                           (SQRT (PLUS (TIMES (CAAR ROOTS)
                                              (CAAR ROOTS))    ;Modulus.
                                       (TIMES (CADAR ROOTS)
                                              (CADAR ROOTS))))
                           (ATAN (CADAR ROOTS)          ;Argument.
                                 (CAAR ROOTS))))))
```

Here we have used CURT, a function that calculates the cube root of a number. This is not usually available in LISP and will need to be defined. The function ATAN fails if both arguments are zero. This cannot happen above because the first clause of the COND is triggered if (CADAR ROOTS) is zero.

Now we can use Cardano's formula. If the roots of the quadratic resolvent are α and β, then the roots of the simplified cubic are as follows, where ω is one of the three cube roots of unity:

$$y = \omega\, \alpha^{(1/3)} + \omega^2\, \beta^{(1/3)}.$$

The complex number ω is given by this:

$$\omega = [\cos\,(2\pi k/3),\ \sin\,(2\pi k/3)] \quad \text{for} \quad k = 0, 1, \text{and } 2.$$

Expanding this result and using the substitution $x = (y - b)/(3a)$, we can make the following program:

```
(DEFUN CUBIC-CONJUGATE (A B R S)                        ;r & s are cube roots.
      (CUBIC-CONJUGATE-AUX (QUOTIENT (DIFFERENCE (PLUS R S) B)
                                     (TIMES A 3.0))
                           (QUOTIENT (DIFFERENCE (MINUS
                                                  (QUOTIENT (PLUS R S)
                                                            2.0))
                                                 B)
                                     (TIMES A 3.0))
                           (QUOTIENT (TIMES (DIFFERENCE R S)
                                            (QUOTIENT (SQRT 3.0) 2.0))
                                     (TIMES A 3.0)))))
```

```
(DEFUN CUBIC-CONJUGATE-AUX (REAL-ROOT REAL IMAGINARY)
    (LIST (LIST REAL-ROOT 0.0)                        ;Real root first.
          (LIST REAL IMAGINARY)
          (LIST REAL (MINUS IMAGINARY)))))
```

We could, but did not, treat specially the case when the two roots of the resolvent quadratic are equal. In this case two of the roots of the cubic are equal too. If the roots of the quadratic resolvent are complex, the cubic has three real roots. This is the celebrated *casus irreducibilis* which cannot be solved using only rational operations and real roots. We proceed trignometrically and find the roots given by the following, where ρ is the modulus of one of the complex roots of the resolvent and θ is the argument of this complex root:

$$y = 2\,\rho^{(1/3)}\cos[(\theta + 2\pi k)/3] \quad \text{for} \quad k = 0, 1, \text{ and } 2.$$

Expanding this result and using the substitution $x = (y - b)/(3a)$, we can write this:

```
(DEFUN CUBIC-REAL (A B RHO THETA)                    ;Rho & theta of complex root.
    (CUBIC-REAL-AUX A
                    B
                    (TIMES 2.0 (CURT RHO))
                    (TIMES (COS (QUOTIENT THETA 3.0)) -0.5)
                    (TIMES (SIN (QUOTIENT THETA 3.0)) -0.5 (SQRT 3.0)))))
```

The functions SIN and COS calculate the sine and cosine of their single argument.

```
(DEFUN CUBIC-REAL-AUX (A B RD CD SD)                 ;If a > 0, most positive first.
    (LIST (LIST (QUOTIENT (DIFFERENCE (TIMES -2.0 RD CD) B)
                          (TIMES 3.0 A))
                0.0)
          (LIST (QUOTIENT (DIFFERENCE (TIMES RD (PLUS CD SD)) B)
                          (TIMES 3.0 A))
                0.0)
          (LIST (QUOTIENT (DIFFERENCE (TIMES RD (DIFFERENCE CD SD)) B)
                          (TIMES 3.0 A))
                0.0)))
```

We now, with our last breath of air, proceed to quartic equations:

$$ax^4 + bx^3 + cx^2 + dx + e = 0.$$

Textbooks advertize several solutions to this type of equation. Unfortunately most, like Ferrari's formula, suffer from poor numerical stability. That is, while formally correct, the results are of low precision. This, once again, has to do with the inexact nature of the computer's representation for real numbers. One method that does not suffer from this problem has us reduce the quartic to a product of two quadratics with real coefficients. In order to find these quadratics, it is first necessary to solve the cubic resolvent,

$$t^3 - c\,t^2 + (bd - 4ae)\,t - (ad^2 + b^2e - 4ace) = 0.$$

If s is the most positive real root of this resolvent, then the quadratics are as follows:

$$2ax^2 + (b \pm [b^2 - 4a\,(c-s)]^{\frac{1}{2}})\,x + [s \pm (s^2 - 4ae)^{\frac{1}{2}}],$$

The signs of the two square roots must be picked carefully so that their product equals $bs - 2ad$. (The product of the two quadratics is actually a constant times the original quartic, but that does not change the roots.) Fortunately we arranged for CUBIC to return the real root first in the list if there is only one, and to return the most positive root first if there are three real roots. Finally, we can write this:

```
(DEFUN QUARTIC (A B C D E)
   (COND ((ZEROP A) (CUBIC B C D E))                    ;a = 0
         ((ZEROP E) (CONS '(0.0 0.0) (CUBIC A B C D)))) ;e = 0
         (T (QUARTIC-AUX A
                         B
                         C
                         D
                         E
                         (CAAR (CUBIC 1.0              ;Resolvent cubic.
                                      (MINUS C)
                                      (DIFFERENCE (TIMES B D)
                                                  (TIMES 4.0 A E))
                                      (DIFFERENCE (TIMES 4.0 A C E)
                                                  (PLUS (TIMES A D D)
                                                        (TIMES B B E)))))))))

(DEFUN QUARTIC-AUX (A B C D E S)                        ;s is root of resolvent.
       (QUARTIC-SPLIT A
                      B
                      (SQRT (DIFFERENCE (TIMES B B)
                                        (TIMES 4.0 A (DIFFERENCE C S))))
                      S
                      (SQRT (DIFFERENCE (TIMES S S)
                                        (TIMES 4.0 A E)))
                      (DIFFERENCE (TIMES B S) (TIMES 2.0 A D))))
```

```
(DEFUN QUARTIC-SPLIT (A B R1 S R2 BS-2AD)
    (COND ((MINUSP (TIMES R1 R2 BS-2AD))              ;r1 r2 same as bs-2ad?
           (APPEND (QUADRATIC (TIMES 2.0 A)           ;No.
                              (DIFFERENCE B R1)
                              (PLUS S R2))
                   (QUADRATIC (TIMES 2.0 A)
                              (PLUS B R1)
                              (DIFFERENCE S R2))))
          (T (APPEND (QUADRATIC (TIMES 2.0 A)         ;Yes.
                                (DIFFERENCE B R1)
                                (DIFFERENCE S R2))
                     (QUADRATIC (TIMES 2.0 A)
                                (PLUS B R1)
                                (PLUS S R2)))))))
```

Problems

Problem 12-21: Write CURT using the functions LOG and EXP, which produce the natural logarithm and natural anti-logarithm respectively. The result will not be as accurate as one might hope for. Add one step of the Newton-Raphson iteration for the cube-root:

$$x_{n+1} = [2x_n + y/x_n^2] \, / \, 3.$$

Problem 12-22: To check the roots of algebraic equations, it is helpful to have a function that finds the coefficients of a polynomial given its roots. Write MAKE-POLY which produces a list of sublists containing real and imaginary parts of the coefficients of a polynomial given a list of sublists containing the real and imaginary parts of its roots. Arrange for the higher order coefficients to appear first in the list. It may help to first write functions for multiplying and subtracting complex numbers.

Problem 12-23: Another way to check a root is to plug it into the original polynomial and see if the polynomial evaluates to zero. Write POLY-VALUE, a function that will evaluate a polynomial at a complex value given as a second argument. Assume the polynomial is given as a list of sublists of complex coefficients, with the high order coefficients appearing first.

Problem 12-24: In the solutions above we sometimes needed only one root of a resolvent equation in order to proceed, yet all roots were calculated and the unused ones discarded. Write CUBIC-S, which only returns the most positive real root.

Project: Write a program to find the solutions of a pair of algebraic equations of the second degree in two unknowns, x and y. The combined degree of any term is less than or equal to two, as in this:

$$a_{00} + a_{01}\,x + a_{10}\,y + a_{02}\,x^2 + a_{11}\,xy + a_{20}\,y^2 = 0$$
$$b_{00} + b_{01}\,x + b_{10}\,y + b_{02}\,x^2 + b_{11}\,xy + b_{20}\,y^2 = 0$$

Consider the equations first as two second order polynomials in x,

$$ax^2 + bx + c = 0,$$
$$dx^2 + ex + f = 0,$$

where a and d are constants, b and e are linear in y, and c and f are quadratic in y. Now use Sylvester's elimination method to get rid of x. That is, either a and b are both zero, or the resultant equals the determinant of the following matrix,

```
| a b c 0 |
| 0 a b c |
| d e f 0 |
| 0 d e f |
```

That is,

$$a^2f^2 + b^2df - abef - 2acdf - bcde + ace^2 + c^2d^2 = 0.$$

You will need the functions defined above for finding roots of algebraic equations. Deal carefully with the special cases that can occur; for example when both a and d are zero. In that case,

$$ce - bf = 0$$

The program you develop can be used for finding the points of intersection of two conic sections in the plane.

Summary

- It is easy to translate infix notation to prefix.

- It is useful to represent sparse matrices as s-expressions.

- Roots of numbers can be found using tail recursion.

- Roots of algebraic equations can be found using nested functions.

References

Methods for numerical computations in general are discussed by Conte and de Boor [1972], Hamming [1962], and Hildebrand [1974]. Matrix operations are analysed in Aho, Hopcroft, and Ullman [1974, pp. 226-251].

Methods for solving algebraic equations can be found in Burington [1973], Abramowitz and Stegan [1964], and Iyanga and Kawada [1977]. Polynomial arithmetic is discussed by Aho, Hopcroft, and Ullman [1974, pp. 278-317].

Seminumerical algorithms are treated in detail in Knuth [1969].

PART II

13
THE
BLOCKS
WORLD

So far the programming examples have been a single function or perhaps a small collection of cooperating functions. Here we turn to the world of blocks with the purpose of seeing a larger system and learning about some points of good programming style and practice. The task of the system is to create plans by which blocks-world commands can be carried out. The commands involve picking up an object or putting one object on another.

The Blocks-World System Creates a Plan

In the course of moving things, it is often necessary to move obstructions out of the way and to make sure every object is properly supported at all times. It is assumed that the hand can grasp only objects that do not support anything. Furthermore, all objects rest on only one support. The plan is created by either of two functions, PICKUP and PUTON:

```
(PICKUP <object name>)
```

```
(PUTON <object name> <support name>)
```

The plan has the form of a list of instructions for a physical arm or a simulated one. It is a series of MOVEOBJECT, GRASP, and UNGRASP instructions like the following one created for the situation in figure 13-1 in response to the command (PUTON 'A 'C):

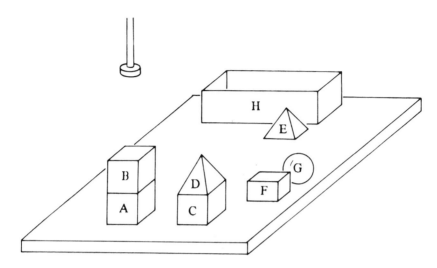

Figure 13-1: A particular situation in the blocks world.

```
((GRASP D)
 (MOVEOBJECT D <space above TABLE for D>)
 (UNGRASP D)
 (GRASP B)
 (MOVEOBJECT B <space above TABLE for B>)
 (UNGRASP B)
 (GRASP A)
 (MOVEOBJECT A <space above C for A>)
 (UNGRASP A))
```

The possible objects are bricks, boxes, pyramids, and balls. Each particular object is represented by an atom that carries a lot of information in the form of property-value pairs. This is a typical property list for a brick:

ATOM	PROPERTY	VALUE
A	TYPE	BRICK
	POSITION	(1 1 0)
	SIZE	(2 2 2)
	SUPPORTED-BY	TABLE
	DIRECTLY-SUPPORTS	(B)
	COLOR	RED

For the hand, we have something like this:

ATOM	PROPERTY	VALUE
HAND	GRASPING	NIL
	POSITION	<some position>

The Blocks-World System Requires some Number-crunching Functions

Shortly we will look at the functions required by the plan-creating system. First we list some auxiliary functions for which program definitions will not be given:

■ FINDSPACE is a function that tries to find a place for a given object on top of a given support.

■ GETOBJECTUNDER is a function that looks at the size and position properties of all objects to determine if there is one lying directly under a given object.

■ TOPCENTER is a function that determines the position of the top of a given block.

■ NEWTOPCENTER is a function that determines the position of the top of a given block after it is moved to a given place.

The Blocks-World System's Functions are Relatively Transparent

The plan itself is manufactured using the functions shown in figure 13-2 along with those listed above. The solid arrows represent function calls that always happen. Dotted-line arrows represent function calls that may or may not happen depending on the state of the blocks world. Let us examine these functions.

The goal of PUTON is to place one object on another. The work is done by finding a place and then putting the object at that place. If FINDSPACE cannot locate a suitable place, then MAKESPACE gets a chance. MAKESPACE is more powerful than FINDSPACE because it can clear away obstructions to make room.

```
(DEFUN PUTON (OBJECT SUPPORT)
    (PROG (PLACE PLAN)
        (COND ((SETQ PLACE (FINDSPACE SUPPORT OBJECT))    ;Space?
                (PUTAT OBJECT PLACE))
              ((SETQ PLACE (MAKESPACE SUPPORT OBJECT))    ;Make some.
                (PUTAT OBJECT PLACE)))
        (RETURN (REVERSE PLAN)))))
```

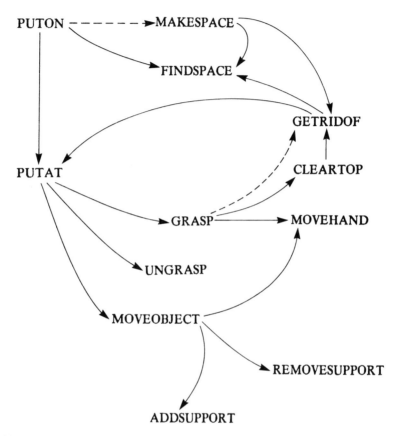

Figure 13-2: The robot's planning program uses many short goal-oriented procedures. PUTON means put one block on another. PUTAT means put a block at a specified location. PUTAT is used both to accomplish the main goal and to help clear away obstacles on the block to be moved and the target block. MAKESPACE is more powerful than FINDSPACE because it will move things if no room is available otherwise. REMOVESUPPORT and ADDSUPPORT are auxiliary functions that do bookkeeping. ADDSUPPORT refuses to act if the supporting object is a ball or pyramid.

PUTAT differs from PUTON in that its second argument is a specific point in space rather than the name of an object. The work is accomplished straightforwardly by the commands GRASP, MOVEOBJECT, and UNGRASP.

```
(DEFUN PUTAT (OBJECT PLACE)
        (GRASP OBJECT)                    ;Get it.
        (MOVEOBJECT OBJECT PLACE)         ;Move it.
        (UNGRASP OBJECT))                 ;Drop it.
```

Note that PUTAT must certainly accomplish its purpose through side effects. As with most of the functions in the system, the value returned is ignored by the higher-level calling function.

Moving on, one might be surprised at GRASP's complexity, but GRASP has many responsibilities.

■ First it checks if the object to be grasped is already held, in which case there is an immediate return.

■ Next, the property list of the object is examined to see if the property DIRECTLY-SUPPORTS indicates that the top is free to be grasped by the hand. If it is not, a call is made to CLEAR-TOP.

■ And finally, it may be that the hand is currently grasping something else that of course must be dispensed with. GET-RID-OF does the job.

After all of these tests are done and responses are made, GRASP passes off its responsibility to MOVEHAND, which moves the hand into position over the object to be grasped. Finally, GRASP makes a note that the hand is grasping the object by appropriately modifying the GRASPING property of HAND.

```
(DEFUN GRASP (OBJECT)
   (PROG (KRUFT)
         (COND ((EQUAL OBJECT (GET 'HAND 'GRASPING))     ;Holding it?
                (RETURN NIL)))
         (COND ((GET OBJECT 'DIRECTLY-SUPPORTS)          ;Top Clear?
                (CLEARTOP OBJECT)))
         (COND ((SETQ KRUFT (GET 'HAND 'GRASPING))       ;Holding something?
                (GETRIDOF KRUFT)))
         (MOVEHAND (TOPCENTER OBJECT))                   ;Position hand.
         (PUTPROP 'HAND OBJECT 'GRASPING)                ;Grab.
         (SETQ PLAN (CONS (LIST 'GRASP OBJECT) PLAN))))
```

Once an object has been grasped, PUTAT uses MOVEOBJECT to get it into position. REMOVESUPPORT and ADDSUPPORT take care of keeping the SUPPORTED-BY properties up-to-date.

```
(DEFUN MOVEOBJECT (OBJECT NEWPLACE)
       (REMOVESUPPORT OBJECT)                            ;Bookkeeping.
       (MOVEHAND (NEWTOPCENTER OBJECT NEWPLACE))
       (PUTPROP OBJECT NEWPLACE 'POSITION)
       (ADDSUPPORT OBJECT NEWPLACE)                      ;Bookkeeping.
       (SETQ PLAN (CONS (LIST 'MOVEOBJECT OBJECT NEWPLACE) PLAN)))
```

MOVEHAND simply changes the POSITION property of the hand.

```
(DEFUN MOVEHAND (POSITION)
       (PUTPROP 'HAND POSITION 'POSITION))
```

UNGRASP proceeds to let go by modifying the GRASPING property. Note, however, that these changes happen only if UNGRASP is sure there is a support. If the SUPPORTED-BY property has a NIL value, then UNGRASP does nothing but return NIL.

```
(DEFUN UNGRASP (OBJECT)
       (COND ((NOT (GET OBJECT 'SUPPORTED-BY)) NIL)      ;Be careful!
             (T (PUTPROP 'HAND NIL 'GRASPING)
                (SETQ PLAN (CONS (LIST 'UNGRASP OBJECT) PLAN)))))
```

GETRIDOF is simple. It puts an object on the table by finding a place for it and moving it to that place. Note the use of PUTAT, which completes a loop in the network of functions, giving the system thoroughly recursive behavior.

```
(DEFUN GETRIDOF (OBJECT)
       (PUTAT OBJECT (FINDSPACE 'TABLE OBJECT)))
```

Now we turn to CLEARTOP. Its purpose is to remove all the objects directly supported by something the hand is supposed to grasp. This is done by looping until each object found under the DIRECTLY-SUPPORTS property is placed on the table by GETRIDOF.

```
(DEFUN CLEARTOP (OBJECT)
       (PROG (NEXT JUNK)
             (SETQ JUNK (GET OBJECT 'DIRECTLY-SUPPORTS))
             REPEAT
             (COND ((NULL JUNK) (RETURN NIL)))
             (SETQ NEXT (CAR JUNK))           ;Select next thing.
             (SETQ JUNK (CDR JUNK))
             (GETRIDOF NEXT)                  ;Move it.
             (GO REPEAT)))
```

Some people prefer a version that uses MAPCAR to do the iteration:

```
(DEFUN CLEARTOP (OBJECT)
       (MAPCAR 'GETRIDOF
               (GET OBJECT 'DIRECTLY-SUPPORTS)))
```

REMOVESUPPORT changes the support relationships that existed at the old place.

```
(DEFUN REMOVESUPPORT (OBJECT)
      (PROG (SUPPORT)
            (PUTPROP (SETQ SUPPORT (GET OBJECT 'SUPPORTED-BY))
                     (DELETE OBJECT (GET SUPPORT 'DIRECTLY-SUPPORTS))
                     'DIRECTLY-SUPPORTS)
            (PUTPROP OBJECT NIL 'SUPPORTED-BY)))
```

ADDSUPPORT is more complicated. Its purpose is to put in new support relationships corresponding to the new position of the object just moved. It refuses to do this, however, if there is no object in a position to do some supporting or if the object proposed as a support fails to be either the table or a box or a brick. Pyramids and balls will not do.

```
(DEFUN ADDSUPPORT (OBJECT PLACE)
   (PROG (SUPPORT)
        (SETQ SUPPORT (GETOBJECTUNDER PLACE))
        (COND ((OR (EQUAL SUPPORT 'TABLE)              ;Support ok?
                   (EQUAL (GET SUPPORT 'TYPE) 'BOX)
                   (EQUAL (GET SUPPORT 'TYPE) 'BRICK))
              (PUTPROP SUPPORT                         ;Update supported
                       (CONS OBJECT                    ;things.
                             (GET SUPPORT
                                  'DIRECTLY-SUPPORTS))
                       'DIRECTLY-SUPPORTS)
              (PUTPROP OBJECT                          ;Update supports.
                       SUPPORT
                       'SUPPORTED-BY)))))
```

MAKESPACE is nothing more than a repeated appeal to GETRIDOF to clear away space for a new object. The loop containing GETRIDOF returns as soon as enough clutter has been cleared away to make room enough for FINDSPACE to succeed.

```
(DEFUN MAKESPACE (SUPPORT OBJECT)
   (PROG (PLACE NEXT JUNK)
        (SETQ JUNK (GET SUPPORT 'DIRECTLY-SUPPORTS))
        REPEAT
        (SETQ NEXT (CAR JUNK))
        (SETQ JUNK (CDR JUNK))
        (GETRIDOF NEXT)                                 ;Remove something.
        (COND ((SETQ PLACE (FINDSPACE SUPPORT OBJECT)) ;Space now?
               (RETURN PLACE)))
        (GO REPEAT)))
```

The Number-crunching Functions can be Faked

Actually writing FINDSPACE and the other functions that deal with geometry is a big job. If only the planning is of interest, as it is here, the big job can be avoided by deflecting certain functions away from geometry toward a simulation of the geometry. The faked data-base functions enable the others to be run, debugged, and experimented with.

By one approach, FINDSPACE would ask some human partner to supply the coordinates that it itself is supposed to find. In the following version, even this is avoided. Instead of working with numbers, the system is led to work with descriptions. Instead of returning a list of three numbers, FINDSPACE returns a description of what the numbers would be:

```
(FINDSPACE 'A 'C)
 (SPACE ABOVE C FOR A)
```

Of course if the support has anything on it, FINDSPACE may not be expected to succeed. The human partner decides.

```
(DEFUN FINDSPACE (SUPPORT OBJECT)
       (PROG (KRUFT)
             (COND ((EQUAL SUPPORT 'TABLE))
                   ((SETQ KRUFT (GET SUPPORT 'DIRECTLY-SUPPORTS))
                    (PRINT (LIST SUPPORT 'SUPPORTS KRUFT))
                    (PRINT '(TYPE T IF FINDSPACE SHOULD WIN))
                    (COND ((NOT (EQUAL T (READ))) (RETURN NIL)))))
             (RETURN (LIST 'SPACE 'ABOVE SUPPORT 'FOR OBJECT))))
```

Given this version of FINDSPACE, the GETOBJECTUNDER function will get places that are represented by lists in which the third element is the object GETOBJECTUNDER is after.

```
(DEFUN GETOBJECTUNDER (PLACE)
       (CADDR PLACE))
```

TOPCENTER and NEWTOPCENTER also can be arranged to return descriptions of places rather than coordinates:

```
(DEFUN TOPCENTER (OBJECT)
       (LIST 'TOPCENTER OBJECT))
```

```
(DEFUN NEWTOPCENTER (OBJECT PLACE)
       (LIST 'NEWTOPCENTER OBJECT PLACE))
```

It is often a good idea to have the access to the data-base portion of a system go

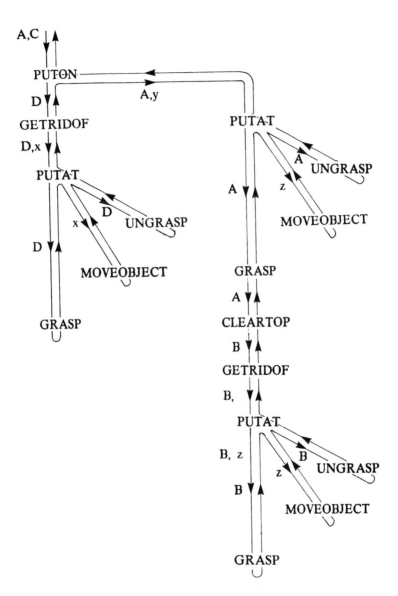

Figure 13-3: The functions and arguments involved in doing (PUTON A C). The x, y, and z are to be read as follows: x as (SPACE ABOVE TABLE FOR D); y as (SPACE ABOVE C FOR A); and z as (SPACE ABOVE TABLE FOR B).

through just a few access functions as it does here. There are two reasons:

- The actual activity in the data base can be simulated, thus allowing independent debugging of the thinking programs and the data-base programs.

- The data base and the data-base functions can be changed easily, thus enabling thinking programs to work with more than one data base.

Simulation is Straightforward

At this point it is helpful to walk through and simulate the actions that follow from an effort to place brick A on brick C given the situation in figure 13-1. Both the functions themselves and the connections shown in figure 13-2 are helpful. The diagram in figure 13-3 gives the result.

Problems

Project: Implement the FINDSPACE, GETOBJECTUNDER, TOPCENTER, and NEWTOPCENTER functions that actually do geometric calculations.

Summary

- The blocks-world system creates a plan.

- The blocks-world system requires some number-crunching functions.

- The blocks-world system's functions are relatively transparent.

- The number-crunching functions can be faked.

- Simulation is straightforward.

References

The blocks world appeared as the domain of discourse in Winograd's thesis [1972] on natural language. Winograd worked with a simulated world. not a real one with real blocks, a vision system, and a manipulator. Work on a system which manipulates real blocks is described in Winston [1972].

Fahlman [1974] describes a much more sophisticated blocks-construction program. Fikes and Nilsson [1971] and Fikes, Hart, and Nilsson [1972] describe the related STRIPS problem solver.

14
RULES
FOR
GOOD
PROGRAMMING
AND
DEBUGGING

Good programming and debugging go hand in hand because attention to some basic rules of good programming practice both eliminates some debugging and simplifies the rest. We begin by enumerating some of our favorite rules of good programming practice and finish by discussing two key debugging functions, BREAK and TRACE. The versions of BREAK and TRACE described here are similar to those available in typical LISP systems.

The Blocks-World System Illustrates some Rules of Good Programming Practice

Some languages make such a big fuss out of procedure interaction that having one procedure call on another is a major event. The connections among procedures written in such languages tend to resemble the example of figure 14-1, where there is one major procedure with a few subprocedures shallowly arrayed under it.

In other languages, the notion of subprocedure is so intimately involved with the language's fundamental structure that essentially everything is best thought of as a subprocedure call. A deep hierarchy of subprocedure arrangements is very natural. Symbol-manipulation languages are usually like that, producing connections among procedures like those suggested back in figure 13-2. Superior procedures accept tasks and hand them to subordinate procedures. Along the way the original task is perhaps simplified a bit or at least is divided up. When all of the subordinates are through, the superior passes the results upward, perhaps adding a bit of embellishment.

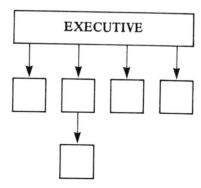

Figure 14-1: Most programming languages encourage shallow system organization with little subprocedure depth.

Facilitating smooth subprocedure call in turn facilitates the use of the following rules, all of which are illustrated by the blocks-world system:

■ Procedures should be short. In the blocks-world system, the modules interact like a community of experts.

■ Procedures should be built around goals. In the blocks-world system, goals are satisfied by invoking a small number of subgoals for other procedures to handle or by calling directly a few primitives.

■ Procedures should presume as little as possible about the situation in effect when they are called. In the blocks-world system, the procedures themselves contain some of the necessary machinery to set up conditions that are required before they do their jobs. This is done through specifications lying near the beginning of each procedure. Typically, simple references to the data base ensure that the world is in a proper state to go ahead, but if not, the appropriate introductory procedures are called.

Two more rules that make sense are these:

■ Procedures should be commented liberally. Put descriptive paragraphs before definitions and staccato notes inside them.

■ Procedures should signal when bad but predictable situations occur. The next section explains.

It is Often Useful to Stop Procedure Execution using BREAK

Recall that the function ADDSUPPORT in the blocks-world system keeps DIRECTLY-SUPPORTS and SUPPORTED-BY properties up to date:

```
(DEFUN ADDSUPPORT (OBJECT PLACE)
       (PROG (SUPPORT)
             (SETQ SUPPORT (GETOBJECTUNDER PLACE))
             (COND ((OR (EQUAL SUPPORT 'TABLE)
                        (EQUAL (GET SUPPORT 'TYPE) 'BRICK))
                    (PUTPROP SUPPORT
                             (CONS OBJECT
                                   (GET SUPPORT 'DIRECTLY-SUPPORTS))
                             'DIRECTLY-SUPPORTS)
                    (PUTPROP OBJECT
                             SUPPORT
                             'SUPPORTED-BY)))))
```

As it stands, ADDSUPPORT does nothing and returns if the value of SUPPORT is an object that is neither the table nor a brick. The following version, responding to the same situation, calls the function BREAK with what appears to be an error message:

```
(DEFUN ADDSUPPORT (OBJECT PLACE)
       (PROG (SUPPORT)
             (SETQ SUPPORT (GETOBJECTUNDER PLACE))
             (COND ((OR (EQUAL SUPPORT 'TABLE)
                        (EQUAL (GET SUPPORT 'TYPE) 'BRICK))
                    (PUTPROP SUPPORT
                             (CONS OBJECT
                                   (GET SUPPORT 'DIRECTLY-SUPPORTS))
                             'DIRECTLY-SUPPORTS)
                    (PUTPROP OBJECT
                             SUPPORT
                             'SUPPORTED-BY))
                   (T (BREAK (ADDSUPPORT CANNOT ARRANGE FOR SUPPORT))))))
```

BREAK, if encountered, prints its argument and enters a loop:

```
(DEFUN BREAK FEXPR (MESSAGE)
     (PROG (QUERY)
           (PRINT MESSAGE)                        ;Print message.
           LOOP
           (PRINT '>)                             ;Prompt user.
           (SETQ QUERY (READ))                    ;Read users s-expression.
           (COND ((AND (NOT (ATOM QUERY))         ;Stop?
                       (EQUAL (CAR QUERY) 'RETURN))
                  (RETURN (EVAL (CADR QUERY))))
                 (T (PRINT (EVAL QUERY))))        ;Print value.
           (GO LOOP)))
```

Within the loop, the user supplies s-expressions that he is curious about. BREAK prints their value. The user types (RETURN <s-expression>) to get out of the loop. BREAK then terminates, returning the value of the s-expression as its value.

To see how BREAK is used, suppose we try to put a brick on top of a pyramid:

```
(PUTON 'A 'D)
  (ADDSUPPORT CANNOT ARRANGE FOR SUPPORT)
  >
```

At this point, the blocks-world system is inside a call to BREAK waiting for the user to type something. Here is how the user might discover what is wrong:

```
(PUTON 'A 'D)
  (ADDSUPPORT CANNOT ARRANGE FOR SUPPORT)
  > OBJECT
  A
  > SUPPORT
  D
  > (GET SUPPORT 'TYPE)
  PYRAMID
  > (RETURN NIL)
```

Evidently the user wanted to know the values for the variables OBJECT and SUPPORT. Finding that SUPPORT has the value D, he elects to find out what D is. Discovering that its TYPE property has the value PYRAMID, he is satisfied that he understands why ADDSUPPORT stumbled and decides to go on. He arranges for BREAK to terminate by typing an s-expression beginning with RETURN.

■ The BREAK function given here is similar to those used in actual LISP systems, but it is not exactly the same as any one of them.

Problems

Problem 14-1: PUTON was defined to have two arguments, OBJECT and SUPPORT. If the values of OBJECT and SUPPORT are the same, then PUTON would attempt to put one block on top of itself. This clearly would be cause for alarm. Define PUTON such that BREAK is called if OBJECT and SUPPORT have the same value and such that BREAK is called if space cannot be found.

Problem 14-2: Define BREAK2 such that it takes two arguments. If the second has the value NIL, then BREAK2 is to return NIL directly. Otherwise it is to behave like BREAK using the first argument as a message to be printed.

TRACE Causes Functions to Print their Arguments and their Values

Suppose for some reason that things are just not working out. Things drop dead, perhaps with an error message that is too opaque to help. For the sake of illustration, suppose the user is suspicious about REMOVESUPPORT. He thinks it may not be getting called or that it is called with a strange argument.

A primitive approach to testing such a theory would be to modify REMOVESUPPORT so that it prints useful information on entry and exit:

```
(DEFUN REMOVESUPPORT (OBJECT)
  (PROG (RESULT)
        (PRINT (LIST 'ENTERING 'REMOVESUPPORT OBJECT))
        (SETQ RESULT (PROG (SUPPORT)
              (PUTPROP (SETQ SUPPORT (GET OBJECT 'SUPPORTED-BY))
                       (DELETE OBJECT (GET SUPPORT 'DIRECTLY-SUPPORTS))
                       'DIRECTLY-SUPPORTS)
              (PUTPROP OBJECT NIL 'SUPPORTED-BY)))
        (PRINT (LIST 'EXITING 'REMOVESUPPORT RESULT))))
```

In the next chapter, we will define a function named TRACE that will arrange for entry and exit information to be printed for a list of functions supplied as arguments. This TRACE will have the additional feature of indenting lines in proportion to depth of function call. The following illustrates its use on FACTORIAL:

```
(DEFUN FACTORIAL (N)
        (COND ((ZEROP N) 1)
              (T (TIMES N (FACTORIAL (SUB1 N))))))
   FACTORIAL

(TRACE FACTORIAL)
  (FACTORIAL)
```

```
(FACTORIAL 10.)
  (ENTERING FACTORIAL 10.)
   (ENTERING FACTORIAL 9.)
    (ENTERING FACTORIAL 8.)
     (ENTERING FACTORIAL 7.)
      (ENTERING FACTORIAL 6.)
       (ENTERING FACTORIAL 5.)
        (ENTERING FACTORIAL 4.)
         (ENTERING FACTORIAL 3.)
          (ENTERING FACTORIAL 2.)
           (ENTERING FACTORIAL 1.)
            (ENTERING FACTORIAL 0.)
            (EXITING FACTORIAL 1.)
           (EXITING FACTORIAL 1.)
          (EXITING FACTORIAL 2.)
         (EXITING FACTORIAL 6.)
        (EXITING FACTORIAL 24.)
       (EXITING FACTORIAL 120.)
      (EXITING FACTORIAL 720.)
     (EXITING FACTORIAL 5040.)
    (EXITING FACTORIAL 40320.)
   (EXITING FACTORIAL 362880.)
  (EXITING FACTORIAL 3628800.)
3628800.
```

The blocks world supplies another illustration. Consider again the use of PUTON in the situation shown back in figure 13-1, this time with some tracing. Returned values are suppressed as they are both verbose and dull.

```
(TRACE PUTON PUTAT GRASP MOVEOBJECT UNGRASP CLEARTOP GETRIDOF)
  (PUTON PUTAT GRASP MOVEOBJECT UNGRASP CLEARTOP GETRIDOF)

(PUTON 'A 'C)
  (ENTERING PUTON A C)
  (C SUPPORTS (D))
  (TYPE T IF FINDSPACE SHOULD WIN)
NIL
    (ENTERING GETRIDOF D)
     (ENTERING PUTAT D (SPACE ABOVE TABLE FOR D))
      (ENTERING GRASP D)
      (EXITING GRASP)
      (ENTERING MOVEOBJECT D (SPACE ABOVE TABLE FOR D))
      (EXITING MOVEOBJECT)
      (ENTERING UNGRASP D)
      (EXITING UNGRASP)
```

```
 (EXITING PUTAT)
(EXITING GETRIDOF)
(ENTERING PUTAT A (SPACE ABOVE C FOR A))
 (ENTERING GRASP A)
  (ENTERING CLEARTOP A)
   (ENTERING GETRIDOF B)
    (ENTERING PUTAT B (SPACE ABOVE TABLE FOR B))
     (ENTERING GRASP B)
     (EXITING GRASP)
     (ENTERING MOVEOBJECT B (SPACE ABOVE TABLE FOR B))
     (EXITING MOVEOBJECT)
     (ENTERING UNGRASP B)
     (EXITING UNGRASP)
    (EXITING PUTAT)
   (EXITING GETRIDOF)
  (EXITING CLEARTOP)
 (EXITING GRASP)
 (ENTERING MOVEOBJECT A (SPACE ABOVE C FOR A))
 (EXITING MOVEOBJECT)
 (ENTERING UNGRASP A)
 (EXITING UNGRASP)
(EXITING PUTAT)
(EXITING PUTON)
((GRASP D) (MOVEOBJECT D (SPACE ABOVE TABLE FOR D))
          (UNGRASP D)
          (GRASP B)
          (MOVEOBJECT B (SPACE ABOVE TABLE FOR B))
          (UNGRASP B)
          (GRASP A)
          (MOVEOBJECT A (SPACE ABOVE C FOR A))
          (UNGRASP A))
```

UNTRACE will stop the tracing of the functions supplied as arguments.

■ The TRACE function described here is similar to those used in actual LISP systems, but it is not exactly the same as any one of them.

LISP Systems Offer many Debugging Features

BREAK and TRACE scratch only the surface of what can be done with interactive debugging in LISP systems. Unfortunately debugging functions tend to be system-specific and therefore inappropriate for detailed discussion here. We must be content with the following overview of functions and features that are typically available:

◘ More general BREAK and TRACE functions that act only when specified conditions hold.

■ Handling of errors in built-in LISP functions as if BREAK had been encountered. After receiving an error message, the user has the full power of LISP at his disposal and can find variable values and evaluate arbitrary s-expressions.

◘ A way of interrupting an ongoing evaluation by typing a special character such as <control B> (made by holding down the control key while pressing B). The result is as if BREAK had been encountered.

◘ A way of interrupting an ongoing evaluation by typing another character such as <control G>, such that all ongoing computation is terminated. This is useful when a program appears to be running for an excessive amount of time.

■ A BAKTRACE function that displays the sequence of function calls leading to an error. This is often helpful when the message printed out is not sufficient to pinpoint the problem.

■ A STEP function that makes it possible to walk through the execution of a function. In stepping mode each s-expression is printed out before evaluation, and the returned value is printed out after evaluation.

◘ Features that make it possible to stop a computation, edit a function, and resume.

More on debugging, with a typical debugging scenario, is found in Appendix 3.

Summary

■ The blocks-world system illustrates some rules of good programming practice.

■ It is often useful to stop procedure execution using BREAK.

■ TRACE causes functions to print their arguments and their values.

■ LISP systems offer many debugging features.

15
ANSWERING
QUESTIONS
ABOUT
GOALS

The plan produced by the blocks-world system is only a list of sequential instructions for a real or simulated hand. It does not offer any insight into how and why those instructions were given. If how and why questions are likely to come up, then it is useful for the system itself to have access to a tree structure showing how the system has moved from one function to another. Since the system is organized around functions that each work toward an identifiable goal, it is easy for the system to answer many questions about its own behavior by looking into the tree structure and performing a sort of introspection.

The Blocks-World System can Introspect to a Degree

Figure 15-1 shows why some introspection is possible. It is another representation of the goal tree, similar to the one given back in figure 13-3. Each node represents an instance in which the named function was invoked. A node branches out into other nodes that represent the functions called to help out.

The question "Why did you put B on the table?" is correctly answered by finding a suitable instance of PUTON in the goal tree, looking up to the next higher node, and answering that the action was performed in order to get rid of B. The question, "Why did you do that?" then requires one more step up the tree, producing a remark about clearing off A. Repeating the question eventually gets to an answer involving the need to put A on C, and repeating again leads to the universal, top-level response, "Because you told me to."

Questions about how go the other way. "How did you put A on C?" causes a response of, "I put it at space above C for A." Repeating causes recitation of the goals listed directly under the node that causes A to be put at space above C for A, namely, "First I grasped A; then I moved A; finally I let go of A."

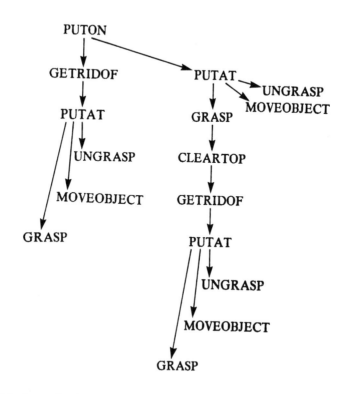

Figure 15-1: Answering how, why, and when questions requires building a goal tree. The goal tree shown here is one built by the block-world system. In general, moving one level down handles questions about how; one level up, why; and all the way to the top, when.

Questions about when can be handled also. The trick is to trace up the tree from the node asked about, all the way to the node at the top, which represents the originating command. Thus "When did you grasp B?" can be answered, "While I was putting A on C." If the question refers to a top-level node, then of course no upward tracing is possible and it is necessary to nail down the time by reference to the next top-level command or the one done just before. "When did you put A on C?" might well be answered, "After I put B on A and before I picked up D."

The following summarizes:

■ *Why* questions are answered either by moving one step up the goal tree and describing the goal found there or by saying, "Because you told me to."

■ *How* questions are answered by either enumerating the goals found one step down in the goal tree or by saying, "I just did it!"

■ *When* questions are answered by either reference to a top-level goal or by reference to adjacent top-level goals in the recorded history.

Thus it is clear that a tree of function calls is a key element in answering how, why, and when questions related to accomplished actions. How can such a tree be constructed? One way is to build some slight extra machinery into the functions in the existing blocks-world system. So far all of the action is focused on creating the plan.

Remembering Function Calls Creates a Useful History

Each time a function is used, we want to record several associated things such as who called it, whom it calls, and the values of the arguments. The natural place to put such information is on the property list of some atom. Consequently, we will arrange to create a new atom each time a function is called. As illustrated, in part, in figure 15-2, created atoms and their property lists represent the history desired.

A call to PUTAT, for example, does three things via calls to GRASP, MOVEOBJECT, and UNGRASP. The node for one call to PUTAT therefore has nodes representing calls to GRASP, MOVEOBJECT, and UNGRASP on its property list under the property CHILDREN. In addition, the node for one call to PUTAT will have a node representing PUTON on its property list under PARENT.

The overall result in complicated cases will be a deep structure in which each level corresponds to a layer of goals. The structure terminates at functions that make no interesting calls to other functions. The nodes representing calls to UNGRASP, for example, have no nodes listed under their CHILDREN property.

Now we must understand how the blocks-world system can be modified to generate such goal trees as it does its work. For illustration, we will continue to work with PUTAT, but certainly any other function would do as well.

```
(DEFUN PUTAT (OBJECT PLACE)
       (GRASP OBJECT)
       (MOVEOBJECT OBJECT PLACE)
       (UNGRASP OBJECT))
```

Modifications will add two variables, PARENT and CHILD. Once this is accomplished and the two variables are given appropriate values, it is easy to put the right things on their property lists. An auxiliary function, ATTACH, helps take care of details and keeps the main function free of clutter:

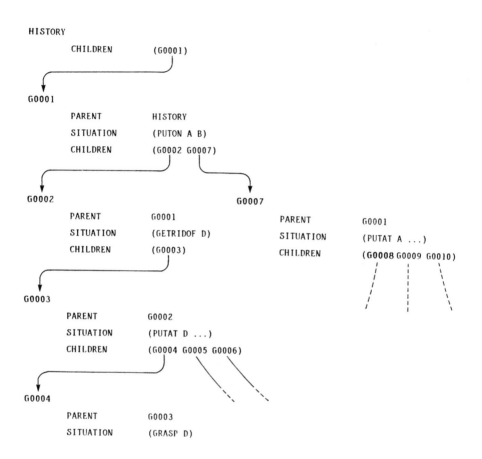

Figure 15-2: A goal tree can be stored by hanging appropriate properties and property values on atoms generated by GENSYM. This is a fragment of the same goal tree given before in a different form.

```
(DEFUN ATTACH (C P)
       (PUTPROP C P 'PARENT)       ;Work on child.
       (PUTPROP P                  ;Work on parent.
              (APPEND (GET P 'CHILDREN) (LIST C))
              'CHILDREN))
```

Using ATTACH, the necessary modification to PUTAT involves only two new function calls:

```
(ATTACH CHILD PARENT)
(PUTPROP CHILD
          (CONS 'PUTAT (LIST OBJECT PLACE))
          'SITUATION)
```

There is no problem creating new atoms for each function call as desired. The function GENSYM can do that. The problem is to embed the GENSYM in a context where the following steps happen as one function calls another. For the situation in which PUTON calls PUTAT, for example, we want the following to happen:

■ The atom that was the value of CHILD inside PUTON becomes the value of PARENT inside PUTAT.

■ Inside PUTAT, the value of CHILD becomes a new atom generated by GENSYM.

These things are done conveniently by surrounding the body of PUTAT by a lambda expression that binds PARENT and CHILD to the correct values:

```
(DEFUN PUTAT (OBJECT PLACE)
     ((LAMBDA (PARENT CHILD)
               <manipulation of PARENT and CHILD>
               <previous body of PUTAT>)
        CHILD
        (GENSYM)))
```

Remember how these lambda expressions are evaluated. First the arguments are evaluated, offering up the current value for CHILD and a new atom via the call to GENSYM. Then the new value for PARENT becomes the value of CHILD, and the new value for CHILD becomes the value supplied by GENSYM. The value returned by PUTAT is not changed by this maneuver since the value returned by the lambda expression is the value returned by the last s-expression in the body of the lambda, which is certainly the same as the last s-expression in the previous body of PUTAT.

Putting all of this together, we have the new, tree-building version of PUTAT:

```
(DEFUN PUTAT (OBJECT PLACE)
     ((LAMBDA (PARENT CHILD)
               (ATTACH CHILD PARENT)
               (PUTPROP CHILD
                        (CONS 'PUTAT (LIST OBJECT PLACE))
                        'SITUATION)
               (GRASP OBJECT)                        ;Old body.
               (MOVEOBJECT OBJECT PLACE)
               (UNGRASP OBJECT))
        CHILD
        (GENSYM)))
```

All other functions that add nodes must have this modification done except PUTON. The modification to PUTON is slightly different since PUTON is the first function called and hence it is the first to produce a value for CHILD. Consequently, there is no value for CHILD at the time PUTON is called. PARENT is bound to the atom HISTORY instead:

```
(DEFUN PUTON (OBJECT SUPPORT)
       ((LAMBDA (PARENT CHILD)
               (ATTACH CHILD PARENT)
               (PUTPROP CHILD
                       (CONS 'PUTON (LIST OBJECT SUPPORT))
                       'SITUATION)
               (PROG (PLACE PLAN)
                     (COND ((SETQ PLACE (FINDSPACE SUPPORT OBJECT))
                            (PUTAT OBJECT PLACE))
                           ((SETQ PLACE (MAKESPACE SUPPORT OBJECT))
                            (PUTAT OBJECT PLACE)))
                     (RETURN (REVERSE PLAN))))
        'HISTORY
        (GENSYM)))
```

Problems

Problem 15-1: Define HOW. It is to have one argument, a description of a function call. It is to look for the given description on the property lists of the nodes in the tree hanging from the node HISTORY. If the given description is found, it is to print descriptions of the nodes immediately below and return T. If the given description is not found, it returns NIL. Thus the following example describes HOW:

```
(HOW '(PUTAT A (SPACE ABOVE C FOR A)))
  (GRASP A)
  (MOVEOBJECT A (SPACE ABOVE C FOR A))
  (UNGRASP A)
  T
```

Assume that the properties PARENT, CHILDREN, and SITUATION are maintained as described before. It may help to adapt a search function from the chapter on search.

Problem 15-2: Define WHY. It also is to have one argument, again a description of a function call. If it finds the given description, it is to print the description of the node immediately above and return T. Otherwise it is to return NIL. Thus the following example describes WHY:

```
(WHY '(PUTAT A (SPACE ABOVE C FOR A)))
  (PUTON A C)
  T
```

Problem 15-3: Define WHEN. It also is to have one argument, again a description of a function call. If it finds the given description, it is to print the description of the node above corresponding to the user command that led to the successful completion of the search and return T. Otherwise it is to return NIL. Thus the following examples describe WHEN:

```
(WHEN '(PUTAT A (SPACE ABOVE C FOR A)))
  (PUTON A C)
  T

(WHEN '(GRASP A))
  (PUTON A C)
  T
```

It can be Convenient to Make a new Function-defining Function

It would be tiresome to modify all blocks-world functions by hand since all of them need the same basic modification. The modification should be done by a function instead. To accomplish this, we will create a new function-defining function, DEFUN+. When DEFUN+ is used instead of DEFUN, the function definition supplied will be surrounded by the node-building machinery just developed. At first the details will seem tortuous, as much will be LISTed, APPENDed, and CONSed together, so let us clearly understand the goal. We assume that this creates a desired function:

```
(DEFUN ⟨function name⟩ (⟨parameter 1⟩ ... ⟨parameter n⟩)
       ⟨function description⟩)
```

Now suppose DEFUN+ is substituted for DEFUN:

```
(DEFUN+ ⟨function name⟩ (⟨parameter 1⟩ ... ⟨parameter n⟩)
       ⟨function description⟩)
```

We then want DEFUN+ to behave as if we had this:

```
(DEFUN <function name> (<parameter 1> ... <parameter n>)
      ((LAMBDA (PARENT CHILD)
              (ATTACH CHILD PARENT)
              (PUTPROP CHILD
                      (CONS '<function name>
                            (LIST <parameter 1> ... <parameter n>))
                      'SITUATION)
              <function description>)
      CHILD
      (GENSYM)))
```

All of the apparent complexity soon encountered has to do with building up a structure like this from raw material. Let us proceed. We begin the definition of DEFUN+, making it a MACRO-type function with the single parameter X:

```
(DEFUN DEFUN+ MACRO (X) ...)
```

Now consider this:

```
(DEFUN+ <function name> (<parameter 1> ... <parameter n>)
       <function description>)
```

Since DEFUN+ is defined as a MACRO, the value of X inside DEFUN+ is as follows:

```
(DEFUN+ <function name>
        (<parameter 1> ... <parameter n>)
        <function description>)
```

Consider PUTAT, for example. Using DEFUN+ instead of DEFUN, we have this:

```
(DEFUN+ PUTAT (OBJECT PLACE)
        (GRASP OBJECT)
        (MOVEOBJECT OBJECT PLACE)
        (UNGRASP OBJECT))
```

Inside DEFUN+, the value of X is therefore:

```
(DEFUN+ PUTAT (OBJECT PLACE)
        (GRASP OBJECT)
        (MOVEOBJECT OBJECT PLACE)
        (UNGRASP OBJECT))
```

Thus X yields the pieces needed to build a version of the given function. The CADR is the function name; the CADDR is the list of parameters; and the CDDDR is the list of the s-expressions that constitute the function description.

The first piece to worry about is found deep inside the structure to be built:

```
(PUTPROP CHILD
         (CONS '<function name>
               (LIST <parameter 1> ... <parameter n>))
         'SITUATION)
```

The CAR of this is PUTPROP, the CADR is CHILD, and so on. This makes it:

```
(LIST 'PUTPROP
      'CHILD
      (LIST 'CONS
            (LIST 'QUOTE (CADR X))
            (CONS 'LIST (CADDR X)))
      ''SITUATION)
```

Note that the quoted instances of CONS, QUOTE, and LIST are necessarily quoted because the purpose is to build a structure with CONS, QUOTE, and LIST in it. Those particular instances of CONS, QUOTE, and LIST are executed later, not now. Also note the two quote marks in front of SITUATION. For PUTAT, the result is:

```
(PUTPROP CHILD
         (CONS 'PUTAT (LIST OBJECT PLACE))
         'SITUATION)
```

Once this is understood, the rest is relatively easy. First it goes into a larger chunk that uses CONS and APPEND to build it into a lambda expression, together with the basic function description, lifted out of X. Then the resulting lambda definition is combined with parameters using LIST.

```
(LIST
 (APPEND '(LAMBDA (PARENT CHILD)
                  (ATTACH CHILD PARENT))
         (CONS
          (LIST 'PUTPROP
                'CHILD
                (LIST 'CONS
                      (LIST 'QUOTE (CADR X))
                      (CONS 'LIST (CADDR X)))
                ''SITUATION)
          (CDDDR X)))
 'CHILD
 '(GENSYM))
```

For PUTAT, the result is as follows:

```
((LAMBDA (PARENT CHILD)
         (ATTACH CHILD PARENT)
         (PUTPROP CHILD
                  (CONS 'PUTAT (LIST OBJECT PLACE))
                  'SITUATION)
         (GRASP OBJECT)
         (MOVEOBJECT OBJECT PLACE)
         (UNGRASP OBJECT))
  CHILD
  (GENSYM))
```

Now one further combination step, using another call to LIST, completes the preparation of the desired form for definition by adding DEFUN, the function name, and the parameter list:

```
(LIST 'DEFUN
      (CADR X)
      (CADDR X)
      (LIST
       (APPEND '(LAMBDA (PARENT CHILD)
                        (ATTACH CHILD PARENT))
              (CONS
               (LIST 'PUTPROP
                     'CHILD
                     (LIST 'CONS
                           (LIST 'QUOTE (CADR X))
                           (CONS 'LIST (CADDR X)))
                     ''SITUATION)
               (CDDDR X)))
       'CHILD
       '(GENSYM)))
```

Evaluating this has a result as if DEFUN were used as follows:

```
(DEFUN PUTAT (OBJECT PLACE)
       ((LAMBDA (PARENT CHILD)
                (ATTACH CHILD PARENT)
                (PUTPROP CHILD
                         (CONS 'PUTAT (LIST OBJECT PLACE))
                         'SITUATION)
                (GRASP OBJECT)
                (MOVEOBJECT OBJECT PLACE)
                (UNGRASP OBJECT))
        'CHILD
        (GENSYM)))
```

This being the desired result, we have evidently discovered most of a definition for DEFUN+. Completing the definition, we have the following:

```
(DEFUN DEFUN+ MACRO (X)
        (LIST 'DEFUN
              (CADR X)                    ;Function name.
              (CADDR X)                   ;Parameters.
              (LIST
               (APPEND '(LAMBDA (PARENT CHILD)
                                (ATTACH CHILD PARENT))
                      (CONS
                       (LIST 'PUTPROP
                             'CHILD
                             (LIST 'CONS
                                   (LIST 'QUOTE (CADR X))
                                   (CONS 'LIST (CADDR X)))
                             ''SITUATION)
                      (CDDDR X)))         ;Body.
              'CHILD
              '(GENSYM)))))
```

Problems

Problem 15-4: Modify DEFUN+ such that it defines functions that work equally well when entered with no value bound to CHILD. Assume that if CHILD has no value, the atom HISTORY is to be used. You will need the function BOUNDP.

Problem 15-5: Define a tracing function, TRACE1. It is to take one parameter, a function to be traced. A traced function will behave as described in the previous chapter. On entry it will print this:

```
(ENTERING <function name> <evaluated arguments>)
```

And on exit it will print this:

```
(EXITING <function name> <value returned>)
```

Each line is to be indented in proportion to the depth of function calls that are traced.

This is a hard problem. The following suggestions therefore should be of great help:

■ Assume that there is a function named INDENT-PRINT that takes two arguments, a number and something to be printed. The number determines how far to indent before printing.

■ Assume that DEFUN operates by placing a lambda definition on the property list of the function being defined. Thus the following are equivalent methods for defining FACTORIAL:

```
(DEFUN FACTORIAL (N)
       (COND ((ZEROP N) 1)
             (T (TIMES N (FACTORIAL (SUB1 N)))))))
   FACTORIAL

(DEFPROP FACTORIAL
        (LAMBDA (N) (COND ((ZEROP N) 1)
                          (T (TIMES N (FACTORIAL (SUB1 N))))))
        EXPR)
   FACTORIAL
```

■ Assume that TRACE1 is to move the lambda definition from the EXPR property to the TRACED-EXPR property. Further assume that it replaces the EXPR property with the necessary function for printing the tracing information and using the definition to be found under the TRACED-EXPR property. For FACTORIAL, the new value of the EXPR property is to be as follows:

```
(DEFUN FACTORIAL (N)
       ((LAMBDA (TRACE-RESULT TRACE-DEPTH EVALUATED-ARGUMENTS)
                (INDENT-PRINT TRACE-DEPTH
                              (APPEND '(ENTERING FACTORIAL)
                                      EVALUATED-ARGUMENTS))
                (SETQ TRACE-RESULT (APPLY (GET 'FACTORIAL 'TRACED-EXPR)
                                          EVALUATED-ARGUMENTS))
                (INDENT-PRINT TRACE-DEPTH
                              (LIST 'EXITING 'FACTORIAL TRACE-RESULT))
                TRACE-RESULT)
        NIL
        (ADD1 TRACE-DEPTH)
        (LIST N)))
```

Finally, it is recommended that you use the following partial solution to get started. The function SUBST should be helpful.

```
(DEFUN TRACE1 (NAME)
     (PROG (PARAMETERS LAMBDA-EXPRESSION)
           (SETQ LAMBDA-EXPRESSION (GET NAME 'EXPR))
           (SETQ PARAMETERS (CADR LAMBDA-EXPRESSION))
           (PUTPROP NAME LAMBDA-EXPRESSION 'TRACED-EXPR)
           (PUTPROP NAME
                    (SUBST (CONS 'LIST PARAMETERS) 'LIST-PARAMETERS
                           (SUBST PARAMETERS 'PARAMETERS
                                  (SUBST NAME 'NAME
                                         <s-expression to be supplied>)))
                    'EXPR)
           (RETURN NAME)))
```

Problem 15-6: Define INDENT-PRINT. It is to take two arguments, a number and something to be printed. The number determines how far to indent before printing.

Problem 15-7: Once TRACE1 is defined, it is relatively easy to write TRACE and UNTRACE. Do so. TRACE and UNTRACE are to get as arguments the functions to be traced and untraced. If UNTRACE has no arguments, it untraces all traced functions. TRACE is to return a list of those functions supplied as its arguments that are not already traced. UNTRACE is to return a list of those functions supplied as its arguments that are traced. Assume that the atom TRACED-FUNCTIONS is a free variable whose value is a list of functions currently traced.

Summary

■ The blocks-world system can introspect to a degree.

■ Remembering function calls creates a useful history.

■ It can be convenient to make a new function-defining function.

16
GETTING
FUNCTIONS
FROM
DATA

Many functions can be applied to a variety of arguments with the details of what happens depending strongly on the types of the particular things involved. Addition and multiplication, for example, are defined differently for numbers, complex numbers, matrices, and many other mathematical entities. Similarly, and perhaps more familiarly, the things a person does to greet someone or to buy someone a present depend on whether the other person involved is a relative, an ordinary friend, a romantic friend, a professor, or a robot.

Functions and Object Types Form a Table

Still another example, easy to develop in the blocks-world context, concerns putting the blocks away. Assume that there is a toy box for each type of block: box BRICKS is for rectangular bricks; box PYRAMIDS is for pyramids; and box BALLS is for balls. The function PUT-AWAY is to take some block as its argument and put it in the right box. Thus (PUT-AWAY 'A) should arrange for execution of (PUTON 'A 'BRICKS) if A is a brick. Conceptually PUT-AWAY and its possible argument types form part of a table as shown in figure 16-1.

The embodiment of the table can be done in many ways. The simplest, and perhaps the worst, is to concatenate the name of the operation and the name of the object type for each viable combination making a new function for each pair. One would then have PUT-AWAY-BRICK, PUT-AWAY-PYRAMID, and PUT-AWAY-BALL.

One reason this solution is bad is that the programmer must know the type of the argument in order to select the right specialized function. This is usually inconvenient and may be impossible. It is better to ask the programmed function

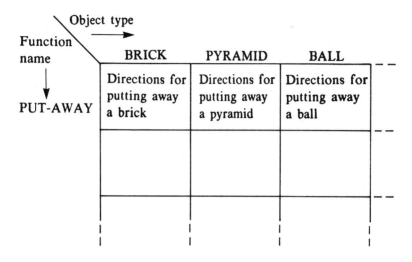

Figure 16-1: Things to do, and things to do to them, form a table. In some circumstances it is better to record the table vertically, putting function information on the property lists of the data types, rather than horizontally, putting object type information into functions.

to figure out the type while it is running.

An obvious improvement is to have a general PUT-AWAY function that defers to special-purpose functions. For this to work, each possible object must reveal its type through a TYPE property on its property list. Then the particular special-purpose function selected depends on the result of examining the argument's TYPE property:

```
(DEFUN PUT-AWAY (OBJECT)
       (COND ((EQUAL 'BRICK (GET OBJECT 'TYPE))        ;Type determines action.
              (PUT-AWAY-BRICK OBJECT))
             ((EQUAL 'PYRAMID (GET OBJECT 'TYPE))
              (PUT-AWAY-PYRAMID OBJECT))
             ((EQUAL 'BALL (GET OBJECT 'TYPE))
              (PUT-AWAY-BALL OBJECT))))
```

Arguments may Supply their Own Procedures

Another solution considerably changes the way the general function is connected to the special-purpose ones. The special-purpose function names are not reached by checking object types in the COND clause. Instead, the special-purpose function names are accessed through the property lists of the type names. The type BRICK, for example, has a property named PUT-AWAY-FUNCTION. The general PUT-AWAY function can therefore decide that some object, say A, should be put away using PUT-AWAY-BRICK through the following steps:

- Object A has a TYPE property.

- The value of the TYPE property is BRICK.

- BRICK has a PUT-AWAY-FUNCTION property.

- The value of the property is PUT-AWAY-BRICK.

FUNCALL Enables Function Names or Descriptions to be Computed

Recall that FUNCALL uses its first argument to compute a function name or lambda expression and then applies the result to the other arguments. Thus the following are equivalent:

```
(PUT-AWAY-BRICK 'A)
```

```
(FUNCALL 'PUT-AWAY-BRICK 'A)
```

But the FUNCALL form allows the following alternatives that have the same result:

```
(FUNCALL (GET 'BRICK 'PUT-AWAY-FUNCTION) 'A)
```

```
(FUNCALL (GET (GET 'A 'TYPE) 'PUT-AWAY-FUNCTION) 'A)
```

Thus PUT-AWAY can be defined as follows:

```
(DEFUN PUT-AWAY (OBJECT)
       (FUNCALL (GET (GET OBJECT 'TYPE)      ;Get function from type atom.
                     'PUT-AWAY-FUNCTION)
                OBJECT))
```

Importantly, the general idea works as well if lambda expressions are placed in the PUT-AWAY-FUNCTION property slots instead of function names! There is no need to have function names for the special-purpose functions unless they are referenced more than once and storage efficiency is of interest. Thus the following arrange for equivalent results when PUT-AWAY is used on a block:

Method 1:

```
(DEFUN PUT-AWAY-BRICK (OBJECT) (PUTON OBJECT 'BRICKS))

(DEFUN PUT-AWAY-PYRAMID (OBJECT) (PUTON OBJECT 'PYRAMIDS))

(DEFUN PUT-AWAY-BALL (OBJECT) (PUTON OBJECT 'BALLS))

(DEFPROP BRICK PUT-AWAY-BRICK PUT-AWAY-FUNCTION)

(DEFPROP PYRAMID PUT-AWAY-PYRAMID PUT-AWAY-FUNCTION)

(DEFPROP BALL PUT-AWAY-BALL PUT-AWAY-FUNCTION)
```

Method 2:

```
(DEFPROP BRICK
        (LAMBDA (OBJECT) (PUTON OBJECT 'BRICKS))
        PUT-AWAY-FUNCTION)

(DEFPROP PYRAMID
        (LAMBDA (OBJECT) (PUTON OBJECT 'PYRAMIDS))
        PUT-AWAY-FUNCTION)

(DEFPROP BALL
        (LAMBDA (OBJECT) (PUTON OBJECT 'BALLS))
        PUT-AWAY-FUNCTION)
```

Using one method, the function body is right there under the PUT-AWAY-FUNCTION property. In the other, it is found one step removed through an intervening function name.

One speaks of the general function *dispatching* to a special-purpose function name or lambda description on the basis of the argument type observed. Conceptually this happens as if there were a table with general things to do on one axis, argument types on the other, and special-purpose functions in the cells. This abstract table is called a *dispatch table* when it is used to access data-dependent functions through TYPE properties.

Data-driven Programming is becoming Popular

Note that the two major alternatives amount to recording the function-object table either horizontally, by stuffing type information into general-purpose functions, or vertically, by stuffing procedural information into the types' property lists. Some people refer to traditional horizontal recording as *verb centered* and to vertical recording as *object centered.*

Keeping the information in the body of general-purpose functions requires function surgery whenever additions are to be made. Keeping it on property lists requires additions to the data base instead. Which is better depends on details of circumstance. Both techniques should be in the tool bag.

The data-driven style of programming has been promoted through a number of very successful systems using it. These include systems whose purpose ranges from electronic circuit analysis to printing bibliographies.

Problems

Problem 16-1: Suppose that particular geometric objects such as circles and squares are represented as LISP atoms with appropriate property lists. For example:

ATOM	PROPERTY	VALUE
C	TYPE	CIRCLE
	RADIUS	3
S	TYPE	SQUARE
	LENGTH	1

Define two data-driven functions, AREA and PERIMETER, that compute the area and perimeter of an object. They are to do their job by finding and using an appropriate lambda description on the property list of the type of the object involved. Place lambda descriptions on the property lists of CIRCLE and SQUARE under the properties AREA-FUNCTION and PERIMETER-FUNCTION so that AREA and PERIMETER will work on the examples given.

Problem 16-2: In calculus, differentiation is defined recursively in the following way for constants, sums, differences, products, and powers:

$$dc/dx = 0$$

$$dx/dx = 1$$

$$d(u + v)/dx = du/dx + dv/dx$$

$$d(u - v)/dx = du/dx - dv/dx$$

$$d(uv)/dx = u\ dv/dx + v\ du/dx$$

$$d(u/v)/dx = d(uv^{-1})/dx$$

$$d(u^n)/dx = n\ u^{n-1}\ du/dx$$

D1, below, is a LISP function that captures these formulas and makes it possible to differentiate expressions that are given in LISP prefix notation. Note that FUNC, ARG1, and ARG2 are equivalent to CAR, CADR, and CADDR. They are used only to make the function somewhat clearer. Note also that D1 expects all the arithmetic functions it sees to have exactly two arguments.

```
(DEFUN D1 (E X)
        (COND ((ATOM E) (COND ((EQUAL E X) 1)      ;Expression is x.
                              (T 0)))               ;Expression is constant.
              ((OR (EQUAL (FUNC E) 'PLUS)
                   (EQUAL (FUNC E) 'DIFFERENCE))
               (LIST (FUNC E)
                     (D1 (ARG1 E) X)
                     (D1 (ARG2 E) X)))
              ((EQUAL (FUNC E) 'TIMES)
               (LIST 'PLUS
                     (LIST 'TIMES
                           (ARG1 E)
                           (D1 (ARG2 E) X))
                     (LIST 'TIMES
                           (ARG2 E)
                           (D1 (ARG1 E) X))))
              ((EQUAL (FUNC E) 'QUOTIENT)
               (D1 (LIST 'TIMES
                         (ARG1 E)
                         (LIST 'EXPT (ARG2 E) -1)) X))
              ((EQUAL (FUNC E) 'EXPT)
               (LIST 'TIMES
                     (ARG2 E)
                     (LIST 'TIMES
                           (LIST 'EXPT
                                 (ARG1 E)
                                 (DIFFERENCE (ARG2 E) 1))
                           (D1 (ARG1 E) X))))))
```

Write a data-driven version of D1 that does its job by finding the appropriate lambda descriptions on the property lists of the functions PLUS, DIFFERENCE, TIMES, QUOTIENT, and EXPT. Assume the descriptions are under the property D2FUNCTION. Write lambda descriptions for PLUS and TIMES.

Summary

■ Functions and object types form a table.

■ Arguments may supply their own procedures.

■ FUNCALL enables function names or descriptions to be computed.

■ Data-driven programming is becoming popular.

References

Stallman and Sussman [1977] describe a data-driven program that works out quiescent voltages and currents in electrical networks. Sandewall [1977] describes a data-driven program written by David McDonald for generating bibliographies.

17
SYMBOLIC
PATTERN
MATCHING
AND
SIMPLE
THEOREM
PROVING

Pattern matching is the process of comparing symbolic expressions to see if one is similar to another. The purpose of this chapter is to develop some pattern-matching functions and to look at some examples. We will see that matching capability makes it easy to implement things like Bobrow's STUDENT and Weizenbaum's DOCTOR, two well-known early programs. Similarly, we will see that matching is central to the operation of a simple theorem prover for proofs in the propositional calculus.

Basic Pattern Matching is Easy to Implement in LISP

The DOCTOR program engages in dialogues like the following:

```
(DOCTOR)
  (SPEAK UP!)

(I AM WORRIED ABOUT THE WEATHER)
  (HOW LONG HAVE YOU BEEN WORRIED ABOUT THE WEATHER)

(SINCE MY MOTHER PASSED AWAY)
  (TELL ME MORE ABOUT YOUR FAMILY)

(THEY ARE ALL INTO COMPUTERS THESE DAYS)
  (DO MACHINES FRIGHTEN YOU)

(NO)
  (PLEASE DO NOT BE SO SHORT WITH ME)
```

```
(GO TO HELL AND DAMN YOU)
  (PLEASE DO NOT USE WORDS LIKE THAT)

(YOU ARE FRUSTRATING ME)
  (EARLIER YOU SPOKE OF YOUR MOTHER)

(NOT NOW -- TELL ME ABOUT MY PROBLEM)
  (I AM SORRY OUR TIME IS UP)
  GOODBYE
```

One might think that writing such a program would be a big undertaking. However, the appearance of understanding is derived from a clever use of key words rather than from genuine analysis and appreciation of what is said. Pattern-matching functions reduce things like the basic DOCTOR program to a simple exercise.

Although LISP itself has no pattern matching built in, it is easy to write pattern-matching functions in LISP. Hence, we say that LISP is a good implementation language for pattern matchers. Many of the matching sublanguages that have been embedded in LISP exhibit the sort of features developed here.

Matching Involves Comparison of Similar S-Expressions

Let us begin by thinking in terms of pattern lists and assertion lists. Often assertion lists will be used to represent facts about some real or supposed world. For the moment, both patterns and assertions will be restricted to be lists of atoms. Patterns, however, can contain certain special atoms not allowed in assertions, the single character atoms > and +, for example:

```
Assertions:     (THIS IS AN ASSERTION)
                (COLOR APPLE RED)
                (SUPPORTS TABLE BLOCK12)

Patterns:       (THIS + PATTERN)
                (COLOR > RED)
                (SUPPORTS TABLE BLOCK12)
```

Soon we will develop a function named MATCH that will compare one pattern and one assertion. This function will be used to illustrate matching-function implementation and use. First, however, let us see what basic things MATCH is to look for.

When a pattern containing no special atoms is compared to an assertion, the two match only if they are exactly the same, with each corresponding position occupied by the same atom. If we match the pattern (COLOR APPLE RED) against the identical assertion (COLOR APPLE RED), the match will of course succeed:

```
(MATCH '(COLOR APPLE RED) '(COLOR APPLE RED))
    T
```

But matching (COLOR APPLE RED) against (COLOR APPLE GREEN) fails:

```
(MATCH '(COLOR APPLE RED) '(COLOR APPLE GREEN))
    NIL
```

The special atom > has the privilege of matching any atom. This greatly expands the usefulness of MATCH:

```
(MATCH '(COLOR APPLE >) '(COLOR APPLE GREEN))
    T
```

```
(MATCH '(COLOR > RED) '(COLOR APPLE RED))
    T
```

The + similarly expands the flexibility of MATCH by matching one or more atoms. Patterns with a + can match against assertions that have more atoms in them than the pattern:

```
(MATCH '(+ MOTHER +) '(SINCE MY MOTHER PASSED AWAY))
    T
```

Note that the matcher pays no attention to whether an assertion is a true fact in some real or imagined world. It tests only for form, ignoring meaning.

Now let us see how to implement MATCH. We adopt a strategy of moving down both the pattern and the assertion, atom by atom, making sure that the pattern atom and the assertion atom match in every position. Translated into LISP terms, we create a function that checks the first elements of two lists, and if satisfied, moves on by calling itself recursively on the CDR of the lists:

```
(DEFUN MATCH (P D)
        (COND ((AND (NULL P) (NULL D)) T)       ;P & D both empty?
              ((EQUAL (CAR P) (CAR D))           ;First elements same?
               (MATCH (CDR P) (CDR D)))))        ;Recurse if so.
```

The first clause in the COND checks for when the end of the lists is reached, thus terminating the recursion. Now since we want to proceed not only if the pattern atom and assertion atom are the same, but also if the pattern atom is a >, we generalize slightly:

```
(DEFUN MATCH (P D)
      (COND ((AND (NULL P) (NULL D)) T)
            ((OR (EQUAL (CAR P) '>)          ;First element is >?
                 (EQUAL (CAR P) (CAR D)))
             (MATCH (CDR P) (CDR D)))))
```

But we also should check for the case in which one of the two lists is shorter than the other:

```
(DEFUN MATCH (P D)
      (COND ((AND (NULL P) (NULL D)) T)
            ((OR (NULL P) (NULL D)) NIL)     ;One list shorter?
            ((OR (EQUAL (CAR P) '>)
                 (EQUAL (CAR P) (CAR D)))
             (MATCH (CDR P) (CDR D)))))
```

Suppose we try some examples.

```
(MATCH '(COLOR > RED) '(COLOR APPLE RED))
```

We get a T as the ultimate result as indicated in figure 17-1. But consider this:

```
(MATCH '(COLOR ORANGE RED) '(COLOR APPLE RED))
```

The result is NIL as shown in figure 17-2.

Now to expand greatly the power of the matching function, we incorporate a feature by which a + will match against one or more atoms. This is one way:

```
(DEFUN MATCH (P D)
      (COND ((AND (NULL P) (NULL D)) T)
            ((OR (NULL P) (NULL D)) NIL)
            ((OR (EQUAL (CAR P) '>)
                 (EQUAL (CAR P) (CAR D)))
             (MATCH (CDR P) (CDR D)))
            ((EQUAL (CAR P) '+)              ;First element +?
             (COND ((MATCH (CDR P) (CDR D))) ;Drop +.
                   ((MATCH P (CDR D)))))))    ;Keep +.
```

The COND clause testing for + initiates recursive calls to MATCH to see if one of two possibilities works out: the + matches one atom, in which case we chip off both the + and the atom it matches; or the + matches two or more atoms, in which case we work forward in the recursive spirit by retaining the + in the pattern while discarding the first of the atoms it matches before recursing.

A simulation helps clarify how the recursion works under these circumstances. See figure 17-3.

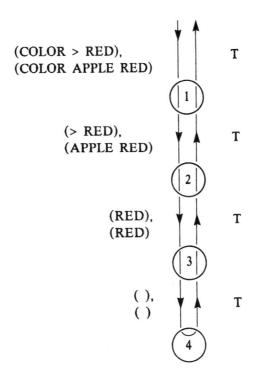

Figure 17-1: MATCH recurses as long as the first atom in the pattern is a > or is the same as the first atom in the fact. On reaching the end of the pattern and the fact simultaneously, T is returned by the lowest level and passes up to the top.

Problems

Some experimental programming languages maintain a data base of assertions. Suppose the list ASSERTIONS is a list of assertions. At some moment an assertion list recording some facts about trees might look like this:

```
ASSERTIONS
  ((FRUIT PEAR) (SHADE MAPLE) (FRUIT APPLE) (SHADE OAK))
```

Problem 17-1: Write ADD, a function that puts a new assertion on the assertion list after first checking to be sure it is not there already. Let it return T if it is successful, and NIL otherwise.

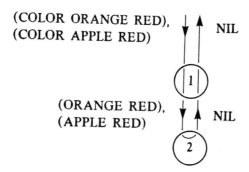

Figure 17-2: As soon as MATCH recurses to a pattern and fact which do not agree in the first position, NIL is returned by the lowest level and passes up to the top.

```
(ADD '(FRUIT CHERRY))
   T
```

ASSERTIONS
   ((FRUIT CHERRY) (FRUIT PEAR) (SHADE MAPLE) (FRUIT APPLE) (SHADE OAK))

Problem 17-2: Write FETCH, a function that looks for a pattern on the assertion list, returning all that match.

```
(FETCH '(FRUIT >))
   ((FRUIT CHERRY) (FRUIT PEAR) (FRUIT APPLE))
```

Problem 17-3: Write FLUSH, a function that deletes all facts from the assertion list that match a given pattern. Let it return T if anything is removed, and NIL otherwise.

```
(FLUSH '(FRUIT >))
   T
```

ASSERTIONS
   ((SHADE MAPLE) (SHADE OAK))

Simultaneous Binding Adds Expressive Power to Matching Operations

The next dimension of improvement lies in generalizing MATCH so that certain

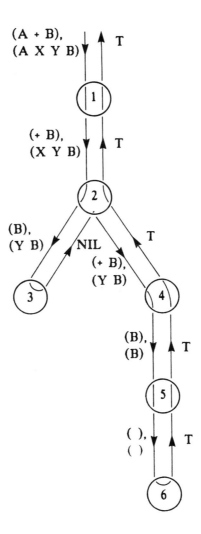

Figure 17-3: When a + appears in a pattern, it substitutes for one or more fact items.

pattern atoms get values if match is successful. Atoms that begin with > and +
act as > and + for matching purposes, but if match succeeds, their values are
made to be whatever they matched. We say that the *pattern variables* are bound
to the matching *assertion items*.

The > variables are to come out bound to atomic values while the + variables
come out bound to lists of atoms. The > notation used here is intended to suggest
shoving values into the variables which begin with the >. Designers of matching

languages are often quite baroque in their selection of syntax.

```
(MATCH '(PLUS >A >B) '(PLUS 2 3))
   T

A
   2

B
   3

(MATCH '(+L MOTHER +R) '(SINCE MY MOTHER PASSED AWAY))
   T

L
   (SINCE MY)

R
   (PASSED AWAY)
```

The > match and bind feature can be implemented by using two new functions, ATOMCAR and ATOMCDR, and adding a clause to the COND in which ATOMCAR peels off the first character in the atom for inspection. Note the use of SET to bind the pattern variable's value to the item it matches in the data.

```
((AND (EQUAL (ATOMCAR (CAR P)) '>)
      (MATCH (CDR P) (CDR D)))
 (SET (ATOMCDR (CAR P)) (CAR D))
 T)
```

Thus we first see if the pattern atom begins with a > and if the rest of the match succeeds. If so, we do the indicated variable binding and pass a T to the next level up.

In fact, most LISP systems do not have ATOMCAR and ATOMCDR, but often something like EXPLODE and IMPLODE instead. ATOMCAR and ATOMCDR are easy to define using EXPLODE and IMPLODE, as demonstrated in the problems of an earlier chapter.

■ This implementation of the simultaneous binding feature suffers from inefficiency because the EXPLODE and IMPLODE operations happen very often. It would clearly be faster to use a more awkward syntax where the atom >XYZ is represented as the list, (> XYZ). Instead of writing

```
(MATCH '(PLUS >A >B) '(PLUS 2 3))
```

one would write

```
(MATCH '(PLUS (> A) (> B)) '(PLUS 2 3))
```

■ The best of both alternatives can be had in advanced LISP systems which permit characters to be declared to have certain special properties when moving from a file or a keyboard into active memory. Then it can be arranged that atoms beginning with the character > are converted into two-element lists beginning with >. The user sees only nice syntax, but internally, LISP exploits the ugly, efficient syntax.

The + variables are handled in the same spirit as the > variables, this time setting their values to a list of the atoms matched by using the following:

```
((EQUAL (ATOMCAR (CAR P)) '+)
 (COND ((MATCH (CDR P) (CDR D))
        (SET (ATOMCDR (CAR P)) (LIST (CAR D)))
        T)
       ((MATCH P (CDR D))
        (SET (ATOMCDR (CAR P))
             (CONS (CAR D) (EVAL (ATOMCDR (CAR P)))))
        T)))
```

Note that no binding takes place and no SETs are executed until all recursion has happened and it is definitely known that the match has succeeded. Then as T values return through higher and higher levels, the relevant SETs are executed and build the appropriate list. The process begins with the construction of the list at the point where the + is matched finally against the last atom it represents and is no longer carried forward in the recursion:

```
(SET (ATOMCDR (CAR P)) (LIST (CAR D)))
```

Then, as unwinding proceeds through levels where the + was retained to match atoms further down the list, we find this:

```
(SET (ATOMCDR (CAR P))
     (CONS (CAR D) (EVAL (ATOMCDR (CAR P)))))
```

The EVAL obtains the list of atoms seen so far using (ATOMCDR (CAR P)), the CONS adds the atom matched at the current level, and the SET causes the augmented list to become the new value of the + variable. Look carefully at this example.

```
(MATCH '(A +L B) '(A X Y B))
```

Figure 17-4 shows that +L should match with X and Y, binding L to (X Y) in the process.

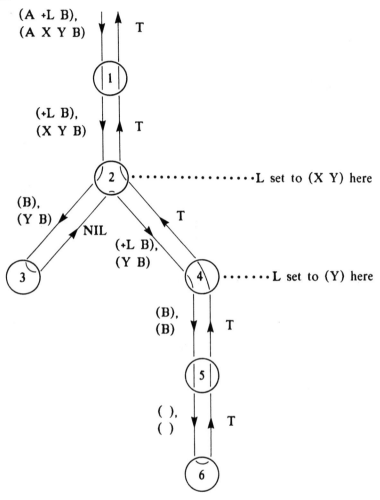

Figure 17-4: Variables prefaced by + substitute for one or more fact items. Successful matching leads to setting the + variables to the fact items they account for.

Restrictions Limit what a Pattern Variable can Match

Another improvement may be made if we wish neither to specify a particular

atom in a position nor to permit anything at all. Rather we demand a member of
some class of atoms like the numbers or the atoms of a particular length or the
atoms with a particular property on their property list. We therefore introduce
the restriction feature. To use it, one substitutes a descriptive list into the pattern
where previously only atoms were expected. The list has the form:

```
(RESTRICT <either ">" or a ">" variable>
          <a predicate>
          .
          .
          .)
```

The idea is that the corresponding position in the assertion must be occupied by
an atom that satisfies all of the predicates listed in the restriction. Thus, we
might define a predicate that has the value T only on atoms of four letters:

```
(DEFUN 4LETTERP (WORD) (EQUAL (LENGTH (EXPLODE WORD)) 4))
```

Or, we might define another that examines an atom's property list:

```
(DEFUN BADWORDP (WORD) (GET WORD 'BADWORD))
```

Such predicates then could be used in pattern restrictions to limit the class of
acceptable atoms in the corresponding assertion positions. One simple restriction
is:

```
(RESTRICT > 4LETTERP)
```

This could be used as in the following example, where we use >V instead of a > to
allow a look at what the restriction matches. V will come out bound to BLUE.

```
(MATCH '(+ (RESTRICT >V 4LETTERP) +)
       '(THE HOUSE IS BLUE AND WHITE))
   T
```

Restrictions can be implemented for the > as follows:

```
((AND (NOT (ATOM (CAR P)))
      (EQUAL (CAAR P) 'RESTRICT)
      (EQUAL (CADAR P) '>)
      (TEST (CDDAR P) (CAR D)))
 (MATCH (CDR P) (CDR D)))
```

TEST is defined this way:

```
(DEFUN TEST (PREDICATES ARGUMENT)
       (PROG ()
             LOOP
             (COND ((NULL PREDICATES) (RETURN T)))      ;All tests T?
             (COND ((FUNCALL (CAR PREDICATES) ARGUMENT) ;This test T?
                    (SETQ PREDICATES (CDR PREDICATES))
                    (GO LOOP))                          ;Then repeat.
                   (T (RETURN NIL)))))                  ;Or else fail.
```

A definition for MATCH follows that does not include restricted + variables:

```
(DEFUN MATCH (P D)
       (COND ((AND (NULL P) (NULL D)) T)
             ((OR (NULL P) (NULL D)) NIL)
             ((AND (NOT (ATOM (CAR P)))            ;Restricted >.
                   (EQUAL (CAAR P) 'RESTRICT)
                   (EQUAL (CADAR P) '>)
                   (TEST (CDDAR P) (CAR D)))
              (MATCH (CDR P) (CDR D)))
             ((AND (NOT (ATOM (CAR P)))            ;Restricted > variable.
                   (EQUAL (CAAR P) 'RESTRICT)
                   (EQUAL (ATOMCAR (CADAR P)) '>)
                   (TEST (CDDAR P) (CAR D))
                   (MATCH (CDR P) (CDR D)))
              (SET (ATOMCDR (CADAR P)) (CAR D))
              T)
             ((OR (EQUAL (CAR P) '>)               ;Equality or >.
                  (EQUAL (CAR P) (CAR D)))
              (MATCH (CDR P) (CDR D)))
             ((AND (EQUAL (ATOMCAR (CAR P)) '>)    ;> variable.
                   (MATCH (CDR P) (CDR D)))
              (SET (ATOMCDR (CAR P)) (CAR D))
              T)
             ((EQUAL (CAR P) '+)                   ;+
              (COND ((MATCH (CDR P) (CDR D)))
                    ((MATCH P (CDR D)))))
             ((EQUAL (ATOMCAR (CAR P)) '+)         ;+ variable.
              (COND ((MATCH (CDR P) (CDR D))
                     (SET (ATOMCDR (CAR P)) (LIST (CAR D)))
                     T)
                    ((MATCH P (CDR D))
                     (SET (ATOMCDR (CAR P))
                          (CONS (CAR D) (EVAL (ATOMCDR (CAR P)))))
                     T)))))
```

There are, incidentally, other things of value in a matcher. For one thing, it is often useful to get values out of pattern variables as well as in. In the following example, an atom beginning with < demands that the assertion element must correspond to the value of the data element, not the data element itself.

```
(MATCH '(>THIS) '(A))
   T

(MATCH '(<THIS) '(A))
   T

(MATCH '(<THIS) '(B))
   NIL
```

With this addition, the > and < characters form a nicely mnemonic and complementary pair. One means *shove* a value into the variable after match; the other means *pull* a value out before match.

Problems

Problem 17-4: Many people do not like prefix notation for arithmetic expressions. They prefer this:

```
(A ^ B / (C * D) - E + F)
```

They dislike this:

```
(PLUS (DIFFERENCE (QUOTIENT (EXPT A B)
                            (TIMES C D))
                  E)
      F)
```

Write INF-TO-PRE, a translation function that converts infix notation into prefix notation using MATCH. Assume the precedence of operations is exponentiation, division, multiplication, subtraction, and then addition unless parentheses force something else. You will probably find that you need a restriction using the following function:

```
(DEFUN ONEPLUS (X)
       (EQUAL X '+))
```

Explain why.

Problem 17-5: Write a function, using MATCH that converts English-like algebraic expressions into LISP-like prefix form. Use the following example as a guide. The expression

```
(THE NUMBER OF CUSTOMERS TOM GETS IS TWICE THE
   SQUARE OF 20. PERCENT OF THE NUMBER OF ADS HE RUNS)
```

should become

```
(EQUAL (THE NUMBER OF CUSTOMERS TOM GETS)
       (TIMES 2.
              (EXPT (TIMES 0.2
                           (THE NUMBER OF ADS HE RUNS))
                    2.)))
```

Your function will be similar to one in STUDENT, an early program that solved high-school algebra problems.

Problem 17-6: With just what we have so far, it is easy to write a simple version of a function which seems to interact with people at a terminal much like the way one type of psychiatrist interacts with people on the couch. Write DOCTOR as a loop through a COND which contains tests for key words and phrases, together with appropriate responses. It should handle the dialog given at the beginning of this chapter.

Various versions of DOCTOR have been elaborated greatly. They typically have functions that replace instances of MY with YOUR in the matched patterns, so that something like the following statement-response pair is possible:

```
(I AM WORRIED ABOUT MY HEALTH)
   (YOU SAY YOU ARE WORRIED ABOUT YOUR HEALTH)
```

It is important to note that the DOCTOR function has no real understanding of the user. It builds no model of the problems it seems to discuss, but depends instead on superficial key-word observations.

Resolution is one way to Prove Theorems in Propositional Calculus

Theorem Proving is a highly developed field that requires considerable mathematical sophistication to understand fully. Still, if we limit ourselves to proofs in the propositional calculus, we can build a simple theorem prover. It will be based on the so-called *resolution principle* (which can be extended to deal with the more difficult problems of the predicate calculus). The key to this theorem prover, again, is a matcher.

A theorem in the propositional calculus, for our purpose, consists of a *premise* and a *conclusion*, both expressed in LISP-like prefix notation. The following sets up a typical premise and conclusion:

```
(SETQ PREMISE
      '(AND (OR Q (NOT P))
            (OR R (NOT Q))
            (OR S (NOT R))
            (OR (NOT U) (NOT S))))

(SETQ CONCLUSION
      '(AND (OR (NOT P) (NOT U))))
```

These are examples of *conjunctive normal form* since only atoms appear inside NOTs, only NOTs or atoms appear inside ORs, and only ORs appear inside ANDs. Each of the OR lists is called a *clause*. Each atom or atom with a NOT is called a *literal*.

Our theorem prover will use the assumption that all inputs are in conjunctive normal form because it can be shown that anything written in terms of ANDs, ORs, and NOTs can be placed in equivalent conjunctive normal form.

■ To prove a theorem, it must be shown that the premise implies the conclusion. For a premise to imply a conclusion, it must be that any combination of T and NIL values for the atoms in the premise that make the premise evaluate to T also makes the conclusion evaluate to T. Or said another way, to prove a theorem, it must be shown that any combination of literal values that makes the premise true also makes the conclusion true.

Clearly, theorems can be proved by simply trying all ways to bind the atoms to T and NIL, checking that no combination causes the premise to evaluate to T and the conclusion to NIL.

Resolution offers an alternative. We first list the steps involved to give a general feel for what is involved, and then we will explain why they work.

■ Step 1: Negate the conclusion, put it into conjunctive normal form, and combine it with the premise.

In our example, negating the conclusion yields the following:

```
(AND (OR P) (OR U))
```

Combining this with the premise produces the following result:

```
(AND (OR P)
     (OR U)
     (OR Q (NOT P))
     (OR R (NOT Q))
     (OR S (NOT R))
     (OR (NOT U) (NOT S)))
```

■ Step 2: Search for two clauses in which the same atom appears naked in one and negated in the other. Form a new clause by combining everything in the two clauses except for the naked atom and its negation. The two clauses involved are said to *resolve*. The new clause is called a *resolvent*. Combine the resolvent with the other clauses.

For the example, the first and the third clauses resolve, producing a resolvent. That is, (OR P) and (OR Q (NOT P)) yield (OR Q). Combining this with the rest of the clauses yields this:

```
(AND (OR Q)
     (OR P)
     (OR U)
     (OR Q (NOT P))
     (OR R (NOT Q))
     (OR S (NOT R))
     (OR (NOT U) (NOT S)))
```

■ Step 3: Repeat step 2 until no two clauses resolve or two clauses resolve to (OR). If no two clauses resolve, report failure. If two resolve to (OR), report success.

The key step clearly is a matching process, the one that produces resolvents of two clauses. The following matching function does the job:

```
(DEFUN RESOLVE (X Y)
   (PROG (REST-X REST-Y)
         (SETQ REST-Y (CDR Y))            ;Get rid of OR.
         (SETQ REST-X (CDR X))            ;Get rid of OR.
         LOOP
         (COND ((NULL REST-X) (RETURN 'NO-RESOLVENT))    ;Any atom left to try?
               ((MEMBER (INVERT (CAR REST-X)) REST-Y)    ;Is negation in Y?
                (RETURN (CONS 'OR                        ;Add OR.
                              (COMBINE (CAR REST-X)       ;Tidy up.
                                       (APPEND (CDR X) (CDR Y)))))))
         (SETQ REST-X (CDR REST-X))
         (GO LOOP)))
```

Note that two auxiliary functions are needed. INVERT returns a bare atom if the argument is in the form of (NOT <atom>). It wraps its argument in a NOT if the argument is an atom. COMBINE gets rid of the match-causing atom and its negation and makes sure there are no repeated elements in the resulting clause:

```
(DEFUN INVERT (X)
       (COND ((ATOM X) (LIST 'NOT X))
             (T (CADR X))))

(DEFUN COMBINE (A L)
       (COND ((NULL L) NIL)
             ((OR (EQUAL A (CAR L))                    ;Is it there?
                  (EQUAL (INVERT A) (CAR L))           ;Is negation there?
                  (MEMBER (CAR L) (CDR L)))            ;Is it there twice?
              (COMBINE A (CDR L)))                     ;Then get rid of it.
             (T (CONS (CAR L) (COMBINE A (CDR L)))))))  ;Otherwise keep it.
```

The function PROVE, shown on the next page, consists of nested loops that search for resolvable clauses and add resolvents to the clause list. Here we show it applied to an example:

```
(PROVE PREMISE NEGATION)
  (THE CLAUSE (OR Q (NOT P)))
  (AND THE CLAUSE (OR R (NOT Q)))
  (PRODUCE A RESOLVENT: (OR (NOT P) R))
  (THE CLAUSE (OR (NOT P) R))
  (AND THE CLAUSE (OR S (NOT R)))
  (PRODUCE A RESOLVENT: (OR (NOT P) S))
  (THE CLAUSE (OR (NOT P) S))
  (AND THE CLAUSE (OR (NOT U) (NOT S)))
  (PRODUCE A RESOLVENT: (OR (NOT P) (NOT U)))
  (THE CLAUSE (OR (NOT P) (NOT U)))
  (AND THE CLAUSE (OR P))
  (PRODUCE A RESOLVENT: (OR (NOT U)))
  (THE CLAUSE (OR (NOT U)))
  (AND THE CLAUSE (OR U))
  (PRODUCE THE EMPTY RESOLVENT)
  (THEOREM PROVED)
```

There are, incidentally, many ways to make resolution more efficient by limiting the attempts at resolving clauses. For example, any clause containing an atom and its negation can be ignored.

```
(DEFUN PROVE (PREMISE NEGATION)
  (PROG (FIRST REST REMAINDER RESOLVENT CLAUSES)
    (SETQ CLAUSES (APPEND (CDR PREMISE)              ;Purge ANDs
                          (CDR NEGATION)))
    FIND-CLAUSE
    (SETQ REMAINDER CLAUSES)
    TRY-NEXT-X-CLAUSE
    (COND ((NULL REMAINDER) (RETURN '(THEOREM NOT PROVED))))
    (SETQ FIRST (CAR REMAINDER))
    (SETQ REST (CDR REMAINDER))
    TRY-NEXT-Y-CLAUSE
    (COND ((NULL REST) (SETQ REMAINDER (CDR REMAINDER)) ;Doesn't resolve.
                       (GO TRY-NEXT-X-CLAUSE)))
    (SETQ RESOLVENT (RESOLVE FIRST (CAR REST)))       ;Try resolving.
    (COND ((OR (EQUAL RESOLVENT 'NO-RESOLVENT)        ;Fail.
               (MEMBER RESOLVENT CLAUSES))            ;Resolvent known.
           (SETQ REST (CDR REST))
           (GO TRY-NEXT-Y-CLAUSE))
          ((NULL (CDR RESOLVENT))                     ;Resolvent empty.
           (PRINT (APPEND '(THE CLAUSE) (LIST FIRST)))
           (PRINT (APPEND '(AND THE CLAUSE) (LIST (CAR REST))))
           (PRINT '(PRODUCE THE EMPTY RESOLVENT))
           (RETURN '(THEOREM PROVED)))
          (T (SETQ CLAUSES (CONS RESOLVENT CLAUSES))  ;Resolvent is new.
             (PRINT (APPEND '(THE CLAUSE) (LIST FIRST)))
             (PRINT (APPEND '(AND THE CLAUSE) (LIST (CAR REST))))
             (PRINT (APPEND '(PRODUCE A RESOLVENT:) (LIST RESOLVENT)))
             (GO FIND-CLAUSE)))))
```

Resolution Proves Theorems by Showing they Cannot be False

Now let us see why resolution works. Recall that a theorem is true if the premise implies the conclusion. Thus a theorem is true if and only if any combination of literal values that makes the premise true also makes the conclusion true. Therefore, we can make the following observation:

■ A theorem is false if and only if there is some combination of literal values that makes the premise true and the conclusion false simultaneously. Equivalently, a theorem is false if and only if there is some combination of literal values that makes the premise and the negation of the conclusion true simultaneously.

Thus a theorem is false if and only if there is some combination of literal values that make all clauses in the premise and in the negation of the conclusion simultaneously true. All clauses must be simultaneously true for the combination of values since we assume the premise and the negation of the conclusion are both in the form of a giant AND, as conjunctive normal form requires.

■ If the combined clauses of the premise and the negation of the conclusion contain one clause that consists of just a literal and another that consists of just the negation of that same literal, then there is no way that all of the clauses can be true simultaneously. Hence the theorem cannot be false. Therefore it must be true.

Thus it is possible to show that a theorem is true by finding two clauses that resolve to an empty resolvent.

■ If two resolvable clauses are both true for some combination of literal values, then their resolvent must be true for the same combination. Said another way, two resolvable clauses imply their resolvent.

Consequently, if there is some combination of literal values that makes the theorem false by making all clauses simultaneously true, then the combination will still make all clauses simultaneously true as resolvents are added.

Why do two resolving clauses imply the resolvent? Consider two clauses from the example:

```
(OR Q (NOT P))
(OR R (NOT Q))
```

If there is some combination of P, Q, and R that make both of these true, then either (NOT P) or R must be true. This is because Q and (NOT Q) cannot simultaneously cause the two clauses to be true.

Clearly then, the OR of two resolvable clauses that have their resolution-enabling elements removed must be true for any combination of literal values that makes the two clauses individually true. But this is the same as saying that the resolving clauses imply the resolvent.

The Q in the example causes the clauses to resolve to (OR (NOT P) R) which must be true when the resolving clauses are true. There is no harm in adding this new clause to the list of clauses.

In summary, adding resolvents to a list of clauses that are all true for some combination of literal values produces an enlarged list of clauses that are still all true for the same combination. If any pair of clauses resolves to the empty clause, there cannot be a combination of literal values that makes all clauses simultanteously true. If all clauses of the premise and the negated conclusion cannot be simultaneously true, the theorem cannot be false. If it cannot be false, it must be true. Therefore producing an empty resolvent constitutes a proof.

Many Matching Problems Remain

The matching described in this chapter is simple because no such thing as close match has been involved. The matchers either succeed or fail. Dealing with matching in general may be much harder since the following possibilities arise:

■ The matcher must deal with more general data structures. There is flexibility in how parts may correspond.

■ The matcher is to report how the match scores on a scale ranging from not at all through poor and good all the way to perfect, perhaps giving a summary description of the match.

Building in these capabilities can be hard. The literature offers little guidance.

Summary

■ Basic pattern matching is easy to implement in LISP.

■ Matching involves comparison of similar s-expressions.

■ Simultaneous binding adds expressive power to matching operations.

■ Restrictions limit what a pattern variable can match.

■ Resolution is one way to prove theorems in propositional calculus.

■ Resolution proves theorems by showing they cannot be false.

■ Many matching problems remain.

References

For more information on these issues, see Chapters 14 and 16 of *Artificial Intelligence*, by Patrick H. Winston [1977]. See also McDermott [1974], McDermott and Sussman [1975], and Kornfeld [1979].

The STUDENT program was done by Bobrow [1962, 1964]. The DOCTOR program was done by Weizenbaum [1965].

For more information on theorem proving, look at one of the basic texts on Artificial Intelligence. Nilsson [1971] and Raphael [1976] have particularly good treatments. See also Bledsoe [1977], Chang and Slagle [1979], Fikes and Nilsson [1971], Fikes, Hart, and, Nilsson [1972], Luckham and Nilsson [1971], Minker, Fishman, and McSkimin [1972], Robinson [1965], Siklossy and Roach [1975].

18
EXPERT
PROBLEM
SOLVING
USING
IF-THEN
RULES

There are many problem-solving systems that are based on matching simple rules to given problems. These are often called if-then systems and sometimes called situation-action systems or production systems. The purpose of this chapter is to summarize what if-then systems are and to show how they can be implemented in LISP. This will be done using a toy animal identification problem.

Identification World Illustrates how If-then Systems Work

The following rules are typical of the things we learn as we become expert problem solvers:

■ If an animal has pointed teeth, claws, and forward-pointing eyes, then it is a carnivore.

■ If a tree is green in the winter, then it is a conifer.

■ If an infection is a primary bacteremia, and it entered by way of the gastrointestinal tract, then there is evidence that the infecting organism is bacteroides.

■ If an automobile engine will not start and fuel reaches the cylinders, then the ignition system is not working properly.

■ If the voltage at the base of a silicon NPN transistor is V, then the voltage at the emitter is V—0.6 if the transistor is on.

Evidently much expert knowledge can be represented as collections of rules, all of
which have the following form:

```
IF       <trigger fact 1 is true>
         <trigger fact 2 is true>
         .
         .
         .
THEN     <conclusion fact 1 is true>
         <conclusion fact 2 is true>
         .
         .
```

These rules are called *if-then* rules, *situation-action* rules, or *production* rules.
Systems based on such rules do convincing medical diagnosis, understand electronic
circuits, and even interpret the squiggles that come from instruments that people
drop in oil wells. Let us see how they can be implemented by working with a
simple animal-identification world.

Facts and Rules can be Represented Easily

Let us agree that facts are represented as lists of atoms. All of them are collected
together in a list that is the value of FACTS. Here is what the value of FACTS
might look like:

```
(Setq FACTS
  '((ANIMAL IS CHEETAH)
    (ANIMAL HAS DARK SPOTS)
    (ANIMAL HAS TAWNY COLOR)
    (ANIMAL IS CARNIVORE)
    (ANIMAL EATS MEAT)
    (ANIMAL IS MAMMAL)
    (ANIMAL HAS HAIR)))
```

We need some functions to get new facts onto the facts list and to look for them.
Let us call these functions REMEMBER and RECALL. Since they work on a simple
list, they are easily built around CONS and MEMBER.

Getting new facts onto FACTS is the job of REMEMBER. It uses FACTS as a
free variable. It returns the fact if it manages to add it on and NIL if it is
already there:

```
(DEFUN REMEMBER (NEW)
        (COND ((MEMBER NEW FACTS) NIL)          ;If present, do nothing.
              (T (SETQ FACTS (CONS NEW FACTS))   ;Otherwise, add
                 NEW)))                          ;and return added fact.
```

RECALL is just as simple:

```
(DEFUN RECALL (FACT)
        (COND ((MEMBER FACT FACTS) FACT)         ;If there, return it.
              (T NIL)))
```

Note that RECALL tests for exact match only. In a more sophisticated if-then system than the one we are building, it would be necessary to be more general, perhaps by using the matching ideas introduced in the previous chapter.

There are many ways to represent rules. The one illustrated below enables easy access to the rule parts. The atoms RULE, IF, and THEN are only to lend perspicuity to the representation.

```
(RULE <name>
      (IF <trigger fact 1>
          <trigger fact 2>
              .
          <trigger fact n>)
      (THEN <conclusion fact 1>
            <conclusion fact 2>
                .
            <conclusion fact n>))
```

Now if an animal eats meat, it is a carnivore. Alternatively, if it has pointed teeth, claws, and forward-pointing eyes, it is a carnivore. This knowledge, represented as if-then rules, looks like this:

```
(RULE IDENTIFY5
      (IF (ANIMAL EATS MEAT))
      (THEN (ANIMAL IS CARNIVORE)))

(RULE IDENTIFY6
      (IF (ANIMAL HAS POINTED TEETH)
          (ANIMAL HAS CLAWS)
          (ANIMAL HAS FORWARD EYES))
      (THEN (ANIMAL IS CARNIVORE)))
```

These are drawn from the following list that is to be the value of RULES for the simulations accompanying our discussion:

```
(SETQ RULES
      '((RULE IDENTIFY1
             (IF (ANIMAL HAS HAIR))
             (THEN (ANIMAL IS MAMMAL)))
        (RULE IDENTIFY2
             (IF (ANIMAL GIVES MILK))
             (THEN (ANIMAL IS MAMMAL)))
        (RULE IDENTIFY3
             (IF (ANIMAL HAS FEATHERS))
             (THEN (ANIMAL IS BIRD)))
        (RULE IDENTIFY4
             (IF (ANIMAL FLIES)
                 (ANIMAL LAYS EGGS))
             (THEN (ANIMAL IS BIRD)))
        (RULE IDENTIFY5
             (IF (ANIMAL EATS MEAT))
             (THEN (ANIMAL IS CARNIVORE)))
        (RULE IDENTIFY6
             (IF (ANIMAL HAS POINTED TEETH)
                 (ANIMAL HAS CLAWS)
                 (ANIMAL HAS FORWARD EYES))
             (THEN (ANIMAL IS CARNIVORE)))
        (RULE IDENTIFY7
             (IF (ANIMAL IS MAMMAL)
                 (ANIMAL HAS HOOFS))
             (THEN (ANIMAL IS UNGULATE)))
        (RULE IDENTIFY8
             (IF (ANIMAL IS MAMMAL)
                 (ANIMAL CHEWS CUD))
             (THEN (ANIMAL IS UNGULATE)
                   (EVEN TOED)))
        (RULE IDENTIFY9
             (IF (ANIMAL IS MAMMAL)
                 (ANIMAL IS CARNIVORE)
                 (ANIMAL HAS TAWNY COLOR)
                 (ANIMAL HAS DARK SPOTS))
             (THEN (ANIMAL IS CHEETAH)))
        (RULE IDENTIFY10
             (IF (ANIMAL IS MAMMAL)
                 (ANIMAL IS CARNIVORE)
                 (ANIMAL HAS TAWNY COLOR)
                 (ANIMAL HAS BLACK STRIPES))
             (THEN (ANIMAL IS TIGER)))
```

```
(RULE IDENTIFY11
        (IF (ANIMAL IS UNGULATE)
            (ANIMAL HAS LONG NECK)
            (ANIMAL HAS LONG LEGS)
            (ANIMAL HAS DARK SPOTS))
        (THEN (ANIMAL IS GIRAFFE)))
 (RULE IDENTIFY12
        (IF (ANIMAL IS UNGULATE)
            (ANIMAL HAS BLACK STRIPES))
        (THEN (ANIMAL IS ZEBRA)))
 (RULE IDENTIFY13
        (IF (ANIMAL IS BIRD)
            (ANIMAL DOES NOT FLY)
            (ANIMAL HAS LONG NECK)
            (ANIMAL HAS LONG LEGS)
            (ANIMAL IS BLACK AND WHITE))
        (THEN (ANIMAL IS OSTRICH)))
 (RULE IDENTIFY14
        (IF (ANIMAL IS BIRD)
            (ANIMAL DOES NOT FLY)
            (ANIMAL SWIMS)
            (ANIMAL IS BLACK AND WHITE))
        (THEN (ANIMAL IS PENGUIN)))
 (RULE IDENTIFY15
        (IF (ANIMAL IS BIRD)
            (ANIMAL FLYS WELL))
        (THEN (ANIMAL IS ALBATROSS)))))
```

Given this form for rules plus the fact-checking function RECALL, it is easy to see if the conditions for a rule are satisfied. TESTIF does the job by looping through all of the elements in a rule's IF part, testing each with RECALL:

```
(DEFUN TESTIF (RULE)
        (PROG (IFS)
              (SETQ IFS (CDADDR RULE))
              LOOP
              (COND ((NULL IFS) (RETURN T))        ;All facts found?
                    ((RECALL (CAR IFS)))           ;Is this fact there?
                    (T (RETURN NIL)))
              (SETQ IFS (CDR IFS))
              (GO LOOP)))
```

Handling a rule's THEN part is the job of USETHEN. Like TESTIF, it is a simple loop. It attempts a REMEMBER on each element in the THEN part, setting SUCCESS to T if any of the REMEMBERs are successful. None will be if all the facts in a rule's THEN section are already on the facts list:

```
(DEFUN USETHEN (RULE)
      (PROG (THENS SUCCESS)
            (SETQ THENS (CDR (CADDDR RULE))))
            LOOP
            (COND ((NULL THENS) (RETURN SUCCESS))     ; All facts added?
                  ((REMEMBER (CAR THENS))             ; Add new fact.
                   (P '|Rule| (CADR RULE)
                      '|deduces| (CAR THENS))
                   (SETQ SUCCESS T)))
            (SETQ THENS (CDR THENS))
            (GO LOOP)))
```

Note the use of the printing function P which was introduced in problem 7-3. With some slight loss of elegance all of the functions using P can be rewritten using only PRINT, together with some APPENDs to put everything together.

Gluing TESTIF and USETHEN together gives TRYRULE. It returns T only if all of the facts in the IF part are on the facts list and at least one of the facts in the THEN part is not. It returns NIL if one of the tests fails or if all of the conclusions are already known.

```
(DEFUN TRYRULE (RULE)
      (AND (TESTIF RULE) (USETHEN RULE)))
```

(DEFUN TRYRULE+ (ROLE)
(AND (TESTIF RULE) (USETHEN ROLE)))

Forward Chaining Means Working from Facts to Conclusions

A problem solver is doing *forward chaining* if it starts with a collection of facts and tries all available rules over and over, adding new facts as it goes, until no rule applies.

The forward-chaining problem solver looks for rules that depend only on already known facts. If it is known that an animal eats meat, then the problem solver notes the following rule:

```
(RULE IDENTIFY5
      (IF (ANIMAL EATS MEAT))
      (THEN (ANIMAL IS CARNIVORE)))
```

The problem solver concludes that the animal is a carnivore. Henceforward, this fact also is available for use and can help trigger other rules.

One step in forward chaining involves scanning down the rule list until a rule is found that works. STEPFORWARD does this:

Tryrule

Rulelist

```
(DEFUN STEPFORWARD ()
     (PROG (RULELIST)
          (SETQ RULELIST RULES)
          LOOP
          (COND ((NULL RULELIST) (RETURN NIL))      ;No more rules?
                ((TESTRULE (CAR RULE)) (RETURN T)))  ;Try this rule.
          (SETQ RULELIST (CDR RULELIST))
          (GO LOOP)))
```

Doing this repeatedly is arranged by DEDUCE. It uses STEPFORWARD until it can do no more:

```
(DEFUN DEDUCE ()
     (PROG (PROGRESS)
          LOOP
          (COND ((STEPFORWARD) (SETQ PROGRESS T))
                (T (RETURN PROGRESS)))
          (GO LOOP)))
```

Backward Chaining Means Working from Hypotheses to Facts

A problem solver is doing *backward chaining* if it starts with an unsubstantiated hypothesis and tries to prove it. The strategy involves finding rules that demonstrate the hypothesis and then verifying the facts that enable the rule to work.

   If the problem solver is trying to verify that an animal is a carnivore, it notes the following rule:

```
(RULE IDENTIFY5
     (IF (ANIMAL EATS MEAT))
     (THEN (ANIMAL IS CARNIVORE)))
```

Using the rule, the problem solver observes that an animal is a carnivore if it eats meat. Eating meat becomes a new hypothesis to be shown. The rules are run backwards, in some sense.

   Backward chaining is a little harder to arrange than forward chaining was. The program that does it will be called VERIFY. The strategy used by VERIFY is as follows:

■ See if the hypothesis fact is already known. If it is, VERIFY returns immediately.

■ See if there is a rule that can deduce the fact directly from other facts already known. If there is such a rule, use it.

■ See if there is a rule that can deduce the fact from other facts that are themselves not yet known. If there is such a rule, try to verify the missing facts using VERIFY. This makes VERIFY recursive.

The general form of VERIFY therefore looks like this:

```
(DEFUN VERIFY (FACT)
      (PROG (...)
              <see if FACT is on the facts list>
              <make a list of rules with FACT in their THEN section>
              <if none give up and ask the human user>
              <use TRYRULE to see if FACT is directly deducible>
              <use TRYRULE+ to see if FACT is indirectly deducible>
```

TRYRULE+ works with TESTIF+ rather than TESTIF. The difference is that TESTIF+ uses VERIFY where TESTIF uses RECALL. This means that VERIFY typically will use itself recursively as it does its job.

```
(DEFUN TESTIF+ (RULE)
      (PROG (IFS)
              (SETQ IFS (CDADDR RULE))
              LOOP
              (COND ((NULL IFS) (RETURN T))
                    ((VERIFY (CAR IFS)))              ;Differs from TESTIF.
                    (T (RETURN NIL)))
              (SETQ IFS (CDR IFS))
              (GO LOOP)))
```

Now look at VERIFY:

```
(DEFUN VERIFY (FACT)
      (PROG (RELEVANT1 RELEVANT2)
              (COND ((RECALL FACT) (RETURN T)))
              (SETQ RELEVANT1 (INTHEN FACT))
              (SETQ RELEVANT2 RELEVANT1)
              (COND ((NULL RELEVANT1)
                     (COND ((MEMBER FACT ASKED) (RETURN NIL))
                           ((AND (P '|Is this true:| FACT) (READ))
                            (REMEMBER FACT)
                            (RETURN T))
                           (T (SETQ ASKED (CONS FACT ASKED))
                              (RETURN NIL)))))
```

```
LOOP1
(COND ((NULL RELEVANT1) (GO LOOP2))
      ((TRYRULE (CAR RELEVANT1)) (RETURN T)))
(SETQ RELEVANT1 (CDR RELEVANT1))
(GO LOOP1)
LOOP2
(COND ((NULL RELEVANT2) (GO EXIT))
      ((TRYRULE+ (CAR RELEVANT2)) (RETURN T)))
(SETQ RELEVANT2 (CDR RELEVANT2))
(GO LOOP2)
EXIT
(RETURN NIL)))
```

The function INTHEN checks each rule to see if the fact is in the THEN part. It collects the rules that pass the check. It uses THENP, a predicate that tests a fact against a given rule:

```
(DEFUN INTHEN (FACT)
       (MAPCAN '(LAMBDA (R)
                        (COND ((THENP FACT R)
                               (LIST R))))
               RULES))

(DEFUN THENP (FACT RULE)
       (MEMBER FACT (CADDDR RULE)))
```

The variable ASKED is maintained by VERIFY so that VERIFY will not ask the same question over and over again. ASKED is bound in the function DIAGNOSE, the function that moves down a list of hypotheses using VERIFY until one of the hypotheses is confirmed:

```
(DEFUN DIAGNOSE ()
       (PROG (POSSIBILITIES ASKED)
             (SETQ POSSIBILITIES HYPOTHESES)
             LOOP
             (COND ((NULL POSSIBILITIES)
                    (P '|No hypothesis can be confirmed.|)
                    (RETURN NIL))
                   ((VERIFY (CAR POSSIBILITIES))
                    (P '|Hypothesis| (CAR POSSIBILITIES) '|is true.|)
                    (RETURN (CAR POSSIBILITIES))))
             (SETQ POSSIBILITIES (CDR POSSIBILITIES))
             (GO LOOP)))
```

Note that HYPOTHESES is a third free variable that joins FACTS and RULES.

Suppose HYPOTHESES is given a value:

```
(SETQ HYPOTHESES
      '((ANIMAL IS ALBATROSS)
        (ANIMAL IS PENGUIN)
        (ANIMAL IS OSTRICH)
        (ANIMAL IS ZEBRA)
        (ANIMAL IS GIRAFFE)
        (ANIMAL IS TIGER)
        (ANIMAL IS CHEETAH)))
```

Then the following interaction takes place on using DIAGNOSE, given that the unknown animal is a cheetah:

```
(DIAGNOSE)
Is this true: ANIMAL HAS FEATHERS
> NO
Is this true: ANIMAL FLIES
> NO
Is this true: ANIMAL HAS HAIR
> YES
Rule IDENTIFY1 deduces ANIMAL IS MAMMAL
Is this true: ANIMAL HAS HOOFS
> NO
Is this true: ANIMAL CHEWS CUD
> NO
Is this true: ANIMAL EATS MEAT
> YES
Rule IDENTIFY5 deduces ANIMAL IS CARNIVORE
Is this true: ANIMAL HAS TAWNY COLOR
> YES
Is this true: ANIMAL HAS BLACK STRIPES
> NO
Is this true: ANIMAL HAS DARK SPOTS
> YES
Rule IDENTIFY9 deduces ANIMAL IS CHEETAH
Hypothesis ANIMAL IS CHEETAH is true.
(ANIMAL IS CHEETAH)
```

If the value of HYPOTHESES is reversed, the DIAGNOSE will get the answer faster since CHEETAH will be the first thing tried:

```
Is this true: ANIMAL HAS HAIR
> YES
Rule IDENTIFY1 deduces ANIMAL IS MAMMAL
Is this true: ANIMAL EATS MEAT
> YES
Rule IDENTIFY5 deduces ANIMAL IS CARNIVORE
Is this true: ANIMAL HAS TAWNY COLOR
> YES
Is this true: ANIMAL HAS DARK SPOTS
> YES
Rule IDENTIFY9 deduces ANIMAL IS CHEETAH
Hypothesis ANIMAL IS CHEETAH is true.
(ANIMAL IS CHEETAH)
```

Problems

Problem 18-1: The function INTHEN finds all the rules that have a given fact in their THEN part. INTHEN therefore answers the question "Do you have any rules that conclude ...?" Define INIF, a function that answers the question "Do you have any rules that use the fact that ...?"

Problem 18-2: Modify TRYRULE (and TRYRULE+) so that it maintains a list of rules successfully used, RULESUSED. Then define USEDP, a predicate that answers the question "Have you use used rule ...?"

Problem 18-3: Define a function HOW that uses RULESUSED, as described in the previous problem, to answer questions like "How did you deduce that ...?" HOW is to get a fact as its argument, it is to print the facts that allowed its deduction, and it is to return T. If the fact was not deduced, but was given, HOW should say so. If neither, HOW should return NIL.

Problem 18-4: Define a function WHY, similar to HOW worked out in the last problem, to answer questions like "Why did you need the fact ...?" WHY is to get a fact as its argument, it is to print the facts that depend on it and return T. If the fact was the hypothesis, WHY should say so. If neither, WHY should return NIL.

Project: The deduction systems described, both forward and backward, say nothing about how certain their conclusions are. Read about certainty factors in *Artificial Intelligence* and extend the system given here to calculate and report how certain its conclusions are.

Summary

■ Identification world illustrates how if-then systems work.

■ Facts and rules can be represented easily.

■ Forward chaining means working from facts to conclusions.

References

For more information on if-then rules and production systems, see Chapters 5, 9, and 15 of *Artificial Intelligence*, by Patrick H. Winston [1977].

Newell and Simon established production systems as a way of looking at human problem solving in their definitive book [1972].

The *blackboard model* is a problem-solving idea that generalizes some of the production-system notions. For its application in speech understanding, see Reddy [1976] and Hayes-Roth and Lesser [1977].

For other work on production systems, see Davis [1979a, 1979b], Davis, Buchanan, and Shortliffe [1977], Duda *et al.* [1978], Hart, Duda, and Einaudi [1979], and Vere [1977].

19
INTERPRETING
AUGMENTED
TRANSITION
NETWORKS

In the previous chapter, we showed how LISP can be used to interpret the rules of an if-then system. The purpose of this chapter is to be more precise about how LISP can be used to implement other languages via the interpretation process. Specifically, we look at an interpreter for augmented transition networks. English interfaces to data bases are built on the same kind of technology. In the next chapter, we will take a second look at language implementation by looking at a so-called compiler as well.

Augmented Transition Networks Capture English Syntax

ATN is short for augmented transition network. The ATN formalism is intended to facilitate sentence analysis by capturing word-order regularities. Figure 19-1 exhibits a simple ATN that captures some of the regularities involved in English noun groups.

■ Any given ATN consists of nodes linked by arcs labeled with names for word classes like noun, verb, adjective, preposition, determiner, and the like. Analysis of a word sequence is accomplished in the course of driving a path through the network, using the word classes as instructions for what arcs to take. Legitimate sequences lead to so-called terminal nodes.

■ Several smaller ATNs may be linked together into one larger system through a convention by which some arcs require successful traversal of subordinate ATNs rather than just the consumption of single words. For example, a noun group ATN may have a preposition-group arc and a preposition group may have a noun-group arc, thus giving a recursive flavor to the formalism.

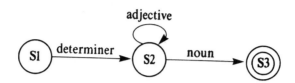

Figure 19-1: A simple Augmented Transition Network representing the structure of simple noun groups. Indeed, this transition network is so simple, it is not at all augmented.

■ There may be more action taking place on the arcs than just recognition of word classes and movement down a sentence. The word *augmented* in augmented transition network means that it is permitted to make notes as arcs are traversed and to refer to them later. One might, for example, make a note that a noun group is surely singular in moving over the determiner arc with the word *a*. A later test could check that conclusion when the noun is encountered.

■ The process of syntactic analysis is called *parsing*. The objective is to describe how the discovered sentence pieces fit together. The resulting description is called a *parse tree*.

Sometimes a combination of node and next word is encountered that allows more than one exit to another node, some of which may lead to a reasonable interpretation with others going toward dead ends. A full-capability ATN system should have some way of coping with this branching. Usually depth-first search with automatic backup is specified on the ground of relative simplicity.

Warning: the automatic backup feature is not to be implemented here. There are two reason: first, there is considerable doubt about the wisdom of depth-first search and stronger alternatives are under development; and second, omitting the search permits greater simplicity, albeit with some loss of power.

Satisfying an Augmented Transition Network Constitutes a Kind of Match

From a certain point of view, an augmented transition network is a generalized pattern of the sort seen already. The changes are considerable however:

■ In ATN "matches," any word feature can be tested, not just the word itself.

■ In ATN "patterns," subpatterns can be specified by reference to allied networks. These references can be recursive.

■ In ATN "execution," progress can be guided by making notes and referring to them.

Making LISP from Augmented Transition Networks is Easy

Given that automatic backup is not to be implemented, translating basic transition-network descriptions into function form is straightforward, but one must choose among a number of ways to do things. The development given here was chosen for relative transparency rather than for speed or size considerations. Note that since no backup is to be done, no alternatives from a node can be considered once an arc is traversed.

Each node in the transition net to be copied will have an associated PROG tag in the function form. Assume for now that REMAINING-WORDS is a variable whose value is a list of words remaining to be analyzed and CURRENT-WORD is a variable whose value is the current word, the one that is the CAR of REMAINING-WORDS. Then the following function fragment would look for a determiner followed by any number of adjectives followed by a noun.

```
  .
  .
  .
S1 (COND ((MEMBER 'DETERMINER (GET CURRENT-WORD 'FEATURES))
          (SETQ REMAINING-WORDS (CDR REMAINING-WORDS))
          (SETQ CURRENT-WORD (CAR REMAINING-WORDS))
          (GO S2))
         (T (RETURN NIL)))
S2 (COND ((MEMBER 'ADJECTIVE (GET CURRENT-WORD 'FEATURES))
          (SETQ REMAINING-WORDS (CDR REMAINING-WORDS))
          (SETQ CURRENT-WORD (CAR REMAINING-WORDS))
          (GO S2))
         ((MEMBER 'NOUN (GET CURRENT-WORD 'FEATURES))
          (SETQ REMAINING-WORDS (CDR REMAINING-WORDS))
          (SETQ CURRENT-WORD (CAR REMAINING-WORDS))
          (RETURN T))
         (T (RETURN NIL)))
  .
  .
  .
```

From this it is clear that the classification type of a word appears on the property list of the word under the property name FEATURES. Other features such as SINGULAR, for singular, or IMPERATIVE, for imperative verb, may appear on the same list with the type feature.

Getting to the features is such a common activity that the temptation to define a simple function to do this chore is overwhelming. We succumb to this temptation here, defining both GETF and TESTF, but the temptation will be resisted in general so as to avoid a need to remember the particulars of too many subordinate bookkeeping functions. Note that TESTF can handle either a single feature or a list of features. It returns T only if the given node has all of the given features:

```
(DEFUN GETF (X) (GET X 'FEATURES))

(DEFUN TESTF (NODE FEATURES)
       (COND ((NULL FEATURES))
             ((ATOM FEATURES)
              (SETQ FEATURES (LIST FEATURES))))
       (EQUAL (LENGTH FEATURES)
              (LENGTH (INTERSECTION FEATURES (GETF NODE)))))
```

Now it is time to see what the noun-group fragment is embedded in. It is assumed that several objectives are to be met by the instructions that set things up and provide for return:

■ There are to be specialists for the various group types. PARSE-NOUN-GROUP is the noun-group specialist.

■ A new atom is created for each newly discovered word group. PARSE-NOUN-GROUP-3 would be a typical name for a noun group. This new atom can have a FEATURES property for holding information about the corresponding group.

■ The relationship between any noun group and the higher-level group of which it is a part must be remembered. This is accomplished by passing the name of the higher-level group to the specialist function as an argument and by using PUTPROP to create and modify appropriate CHILDREN properties if everything works out.

■ A group may be rejected if it does not have certain features. These are prescribed through a nonNIL value for the FEATURES argument of the specialist.

■ If the search for a group fails somewhere, then the REMAINING-WORDS and CURRENT-WORD variables must be restored to their values on entry.

The following framework accomplishes these objectives by way of entry and
exit instructions. Note that (RETURN T) and (RETURN NIL) instructions in the
previous fragment are to be replaced by (GO WIN) and (GO LOSE).

```
(DEFUN PARSE-NOUN-GROUP (PARENT-NODE FEATURES)
       (PROG (THIS-NODE HOLD)
             (SETQ HOLD REMAINING-WORDS)
             (SETQ CURRENT-WORD (CAR REMAINING-WORDS))
             (SETQ THIS-NODE (GENNAME 'PARSE-NOUN-GROUP))
             S1
             .
             .
             .
             WIN
             (COND ((NOT (TESTF THIS-NODE FEATURES)) (GO LOSE)))
             (ATTACH THIS-NODE PARENT-NODE)
             (SETQ LAST-PARSED THIS-NODE)
             (RETURN THIS-NODE)
             LOSE
             (SETQ REMAINING-WORDS HOLD)
             (SETQ CURRENT-WORD (CAR REMAINING-WORDS))
             (RETURN NIL)))
```

Several points need to be mentioned. First, the variable LAST-PARSED will be
used frequently to hold on to the last node created by a successful ATN. Second,
ATTACH and GENNAME need explanation. ATTACH connects nodes by way of
placing appropriate values on a property list. ATTACH looks like this:

```
(DEFUN ATTACH (C P)
       (PUTPROP C P 'PARENT)        ;Work on child.
       (PUTPROP P                   ;Work on parent.
                (APPEND (GET P 'CHILDREN) (LIST C))
                'CHILDREN))
```

GENNAME generates a unique new atom each time it is evaluated. When the value
of the argument of GENNAME is PARSE-NOUN-GROUP as above, then the new atom
is of the form PARSE-NOUN-GROUP-n where the number n increases by one each
time the function is used with PARSE-NOUN-GROUP as the value of its argument.
GENNAME is not a standard LISP function, but it can be defined using EXPLODE
and IMPLODE. Also, GENSYM could be used instead, albeit with some loss of
clarity in the resulting trees.

After placing the fragment that actually defines a noun group, we have this:

```
(DEFUN PARSE-NOUN-GROUP (PARENT-NODE FEATURES)
      (PROG (THIS-NODE HOLD)
            (SETQ HOLD REMAINING-WORDS)
            (SETQ CURRENT-WORD (CAR REMAINING-WORDS))
            (SETQ THIS-NODE (GENNAME 'PARSE-NOUN-GROUP))
            S1 (COND ((MEMBER 'DETERMINER (GET CURRENT-WORD 'FEATURES))
                      (SETQ REMAINING-WORDS (CDR REMAINING-WORDS))
                      (SETQ CURRENT-WORD (CAR REMAINING-WORDS))
                      (GO S2))
                     (T (GO LOSE)))
            S2 (COND ((MEMBER 'ADJECTIVE (GET CURRENT-WORD 'FEATURES))
                      (SETQ REMAINING-WORDS (CDR REMAINING-WORDS))
                      (SETQ CURRENT-WORD (CAR REMAINING-WORDS))
                      (GO S2))
                     ((MEMBER 'NOUN (GET CURRENT-WORD 'FEATURES))
                      (SETQ REMAINING-WORDS (CDR REMAINING-WORDS))
                      (SETQ CURRENT-WORD (CAR REMAINING-WORDS))
                      (GO WIN))
                     (T (GO LOSE)))
            WIN
            (COND ((NOT (TESTF THIS-NODE FEATURES)) (GO LOSE)))
            (ATTACH THIS-NODE PARENT-NODE)
            (SETQ LAST-PARSED THIS-NODE)
            (RETURN THIS-NODE)
            LOSE
            (SETQ REMAINING-WORDS HOLD)
            (SETQ CURRENT-WORD (CAR REMAINING-WORDS))
            (RETURN NIL)))
```

This function becomes more simple and hence more transparent if a word specialist assumes the duty of testing words and doing bookkeeping when expected ones are identified. The variable LAST-PARSED gets set to the word inside the word specialist.

```
(DEFUN PARSE-NOUN-GROUP (PARENT-NODE FEATURES)
      (PROG (THIS-NODE HOLD)
            (SETQ HOLD REMAINING-WORDS)
            (SETQ CURRENT-WORD (CAR REMAINING-WORDS))
            (SETQ THIS-NODE (GENNAME 'PARSE-NOUN-GROUP))
            S1 (COND ((PARSE-WORD PARENT-NODE '(DETERMINER))
                      (GO S2))
                     (T (GO LOSE)))
```

```
S2 (COND ((PARSE-WORD PARENT-NODE '(ADJECTIVE))
          (GO S2))
         ((PARSE-WORD PARENT-NODE '(NOUN))
          (GO WIN))
         (T (GO LOSE)))
   WIN
   (COND ((NOT (TESTF THIS-NODE FEATURES)) (GO LOSE)))
   (ATTACH THIS-NODE PARENT-NODE)
   (SETQ LAST-PARSED THIS-NODE)
   (RETURN THIS-NODE)
   LOSE
   (SETQ REMAINING-WORDS HOLD)
   (SETQ CURRENT-WORD (CAR REMAINING-WORDS))
   (RETURN NIL)))
```

Note that LAST-PARSED is given a new value as PARSE-NOUN-GROUP concludes
its work. Thus LAST-PARSED, by convention, always holds on to the last node
created. The word-group specialist that has appeared can be defined as follows.
The style is a bit odd because it will prove useful to force it into the same general
form as that used for PARSE-NOUN-GROUP.

```
(DEFUN PARSE-WORD (PARENT-NODE FEATURES)
    (PROG (THIS-NODE HOLD)
          (SETQ HOLD REMAINING-WORDS)
          (SETQ CURRENT-WORD (CAR REMAINING-WORDS))
          (SETQ THIS-NODE (GENNAME 'PARSE-WORD))
          S1 (COND (T (SETQ THIS-NODE CURRENT-WORD)
                      (SETQ REMAINING-WORDS (CDR REMAINING-WORDS))
                      (COND (REMAINING-WORDS
                                (SETQ CURRENT-WORD (CAR REMAINING-WORDS)))
                            (T (SETQ CURRENT-WORD NIL)))
                      (GO WIN))
                   (T (GO LOSE)))
          WIN
          (COND ((NOT (TESTF THIS-NODE FEATURES)) (GO LOSE)))
          (ATTACH THIS-NODE PARENT-NODE)
          (SETQ LAST-PARSED THIS-NODE)
          (RETURN THIS-NODE)
          LOSE
          (SETQ REMAINING-WORDS HOLD)
          (SETQ CURRENT-WORD (CAR REMAINING-WORDS))
          (RETURN NIL)))
```

Since the value of THIS-NODE is made to be the word under inspection, the word must have the features given to PARSE-WORD as its second argument. Thus the following application of PARSE-WORD will succeed only if the next word on REMAINING-WORDS is a determiner:

```
(PARSE-WORD <name of parent> '(DETERMINER))
```

Here is what PARSE-NOUN-GROUP and PARSE-WORD specialists do if the value of REMAINING-WORDS is (A BIG RED BLOCK):

ATOM	PROPERTY	VALUE
<noun group name>	CHILDREN	(A BIG RED BLOCK)

An ATN Interpreter Follows a Retained Description

We have succeeded in converting PARSE-NOUN-GROUP and PARSE-WORD from graphs into working LISP functions. The resulting functions, however, are not particularly easy to read. It would be nice to have some notation that explicitly captures the idea of nodes and transitions.

We now invent such a notation. Having done so, we will then create a program that can follow it one step at a time.

■ An *interpeter* is a program that follows a procedure description one step at a time, doing what the procedure description specifies.

To a large extent the notational details are a matter of taste and invention. The following for a one-exit node is therefore only one of many possibilities:

```
(<node name> (IF <test> --> <new node>))
```

The test can be any LISP expression. The arrow is intended to stir up the transition image. More transitions simply add more arrow-containing node-change descriptions. If transition is to be accompanied by side effects, those side effects are specified by a LISP expression following the suggestive atom AFTER:

```
(<node name> (IF <test> --> <new node> AFTER <side effects>))
```

Using this syntax, we will soon be able to define PARSE-NOUN-GROUP and PARSE-WORD this way:

```
(RECORD PARSE-NOUN-GROUP
        (S1 (IF (PARSE-WORD THIS-NODE 'DETERMINER) --> S2))
        (S2 (IF (PARSE-WORD THIS-NODE 'ADJECTIVE) --> S2)
            (IF (PARSE-WORD THIS-NODE 'NOUN) --> WIN)))

(RECORD PARSE-WORD
        (S1 (IF T --> WIN
                AFTER
                (SETQ THIS-NODE CURRENT-WORD)
                (SETQ REMAINING-WORDS (CDR REMAINING-WORDS))
                (COND (REMAINING-WORDS (SETQ CURRENT-WORD
                                             (CAR REMAINING-WORDS)))
                      (T (SETQ CURRENT-WORD NIL))))))
```

First, however, we will work toward the description of an auxiliary function named INTERPRET that works by maintaining the proper values for certain variables we have used before, notably PARENT-NODE, FEATURES, THIS-NODE and HOLD.

Importantly, INTERPRET will also have NETWORK, an atom whose value is the network described using the newly invented syntax. For the moment, assume that NETWORK has this value:

```
((S1 (IF (PARSE-WORD THIS-NODE 'DETERMINER) --> S2))
 (S2 (IF (PARSE-WORD THIS-NODE 'ADJECTIVE) --> S2)
     (IF (PARSE-WORD THIS-NODE 'NOUN) --> WIN)))
```

Further assume that value of NEWSTATE is always the name of some node. Then the sensible value for the atom named STATE-DESCRIPTION is obtained by this:

```
(SETQ STATE-DESCRIPTION (ASSOC NEWSTATE NETWORK))
```

For example, if NEWSTATE is S2, then STATE-DESCRIPTION becomes:

```
(S2 (IF (PARSE-WORD THIS-NODE 'ADJECTIVE) --> S2)
    (IF (PARSE-WORD THIS-NODE 'NOUN) --> WIN))
```

With this in hand, it is easy to bind RULE to the first of the transition descriptions:

```
(SETQ STATE-DESCRIPTION (CDR STATE-DESCRIPTION))
(SETQ RULE (CAR STATE-DESCRIPTION))
```

Hence RULE becomes:

```
(IF (PARSE-WORD THIS-NODE 'ADJECTIVE) --> S2)
```

The transition should happen if the result of evaluating (CADR RULE) is not NIL. Then the next node will be (CADDDR RULE), namely S2. The following PROG fragment is a loop that does these things on the successive transition descriptions given by STATE-DESCRIPTION. Note that the value of NEWSTATE defaults to LOSE if STATE-DESCRIPTION becomes NIL, indicating that no transition descriptions are satisfactory. Note also the MAPCAR-EVAL combination that causes any side effects following an AFTER to be executed.

```
TEST-TRANSITION-RULE
(COND ((SETQ STATE-DESCRIPTION (CDR STATE-DESCRIPTION))
       (SETQ RULE (CAR STATE-DESCRIPTION)))
      (T (SETQ OLDSTATE NEWSTATE)
         (SETQ NEWSTATE 'LOSE)
         (GO GET-STATE-DESCRIPTION)))
(COND ((EVAL (CADR RULE)) (SETQ OLDSTATE NEWSTATE)
                          (SETQ NEWSTATE (CADDDR RULE))
                          (COND ((CDDDDR RULE)
                                 (MAPCAR 'EVAL (CDR (CDDDDR RULE)))))
                          (GO GET-STATE-DESCRIPTION))
      (T (GO TEST-TRANSITION-RULE)))
```

Given the loop, all that remains is to set up other variables and to do the right thing on success or failure. The following definition of INTERPRET includes the needed additions. It takes three arguments: a network description, a parent node, and a list of required features. It maintains certain free variables, REMAINING-WORDS, CURRENT-WORD, and LAST-PARSED.

```
(DEFUN INTERPRET (NETWORK PARENT-NODE FEATURES)
     (PROG (NEWSTATE OLDSTATE STATE-DESCRIPTION RULE HOLD THIS-NODE)
           (SETQ HOLD REMAINING-WORDS)
           (SETQ CURRENT-WORD (CAR REMAINING-WORDS))
           (SETQ THIS-NODE (GENNAME (CAR NETWORK)))
           (SETQ NETWORK (CDR NETWORK))
           (SETQ NEWSTATE (CAAR NETWORK))
     GET-STATE-DESCRIPTION
           (COND ((EQUAL NEWSTATE 'WIN) (GO WIN))
                 ((EQUAL NEWSTATE 'LOSE) (GO LOSE))
                 (T (SETQ STATE-DESCRIPTION (ASSOC NEWSTATE NETWORK))))
     TEST-TRANSITION-RULE
           (COND ((SETQ STATE-DESCRIPTION (CDR STATE-DESCRIPTION))
                  (SETQ RULE (CAR STATE-DESCRIPTION)))
                 (T (SETQ OLDSTATE NEWSTATE)
                    (SETQ NEWSTATE 'LOSE)
                    (GO GET-STATE-DESCRIPTION)))
```

```
(COND ((EVAL (CADR RULE))
       (SETQ OLDSTATE NEWSTATE)
       (SETQ NEWSTATE (CADDDR RULE))
       (COND ((CDDDDR RULE)
              (MAPCAR 'EVAL (CDR (CDDDDR RULE)))))
       (GO GET-STATE-DESCRIPTION))
      (T (GO TEST-TRANSITION-RULE)))
WIN
(COND ((NOT (TESTF THIS-NODE FEATURES)) (GO LOSE)))
(ATTACH THIS-NODE PARENT-NODE)
(SETQ LAST-PARSED THIS-NODE)
(RETURN THIS-NODE)
LOSE
(SETQ REMAINING-WORDS HOLD)
(SETQ CURRENT-WORD (CAR REMAINING-WORDS))
(RETURN NIL)))
```

Now we are close to what we want. But to see if the value of REMAINING-WORDS starts with, say, a noun group, we must evaluate the following expression:

```
(INTERPRET <noun-group description> <parent node> NIL)
```

We would prefer to arrange for PARSE-NOUN-GROUP to have a definition such that the following does the right thing:

```
(PARSE-NOUN-GROUP <parent node> NIL)
```

It is easy to define PARSE-NOUN-GROUP, especially if we hang the noun-group description under the NETWORK property:

```
(DEFUN PARSE-NOUN-GROUP (PARENT-NODE FEATURES)
       (INTERPRET (GET 'PARSE-NOUN-GROUP 'NETWORK)
                  PARENT-NODE
                  FEATURES))

(PUTPROP 'PARSE-NOUN-GROUP
         '(PARSE-NOUN-GROUP
           (S1 (IF (PARSE-WORD THIS-NODE 'DETERMINER) --> S2))
           (S2 (IF (PARSE-WORD THIS-NODE 'ADJECTIVE) --> S2)
               (IF (PARSE-WORD THIS-NODE 'NOUN) --> WIN)))
         'NETWORK)
```

It is convenient to define still another function that does jobs of both the DEFUN and the PUTPROP. This works:

```
(DEFUN RECORD FEXPR (X)
        (PUTPROP (CAR X) X 'NETWORK)
        (EVAL (SUBST (CAR X) 'NAME
                     '(DEFUN NAME (PARENT-NODE FEATURES)
                             (INTERPRET (GET 'NAME 'NETWORK)
                                        PARENT-NODE
                                        FEATURES)))))
```

Now PARSE-NOUN-GROUP can be defined for interpretation as follows:

```
(RECORD PARSE-NOUN-GROUP
        (S1 (IF (PARSE-WORD THIS-NODE 'DETERMINER) --> S2))
        (S2 (IF (PARSE-WORD THIS-NODE 'ADJECTIVE) --> S2)
            (IF (PARSE-WORD THIS-NODE 'NOUN) --> WIN)))
```

Satisfyingly, the interpreter just described and the so-called compiler of the next chapter are compatible: RECORD, which uses INTERPRET, and COMPILE create definitions that can be freely intermingled. A clause network interpreted by INTERPRET can call a noun-group network function created by COMPILE or vice versa.

Problems

Problem 19-1: Modify the interpreter so that if the variable DEBUG is nonNIL, it prints the name of each ATN entered and the name of each node traversed. In general it is easier to add debugging features to interpreters than to compilers.

Problem 19-2: It is annoying that each ATN function requires THIS-NODE as its first argument so that inside it will have the proper value for PARENT-NODE. By appropriate modification of RECORD and INTERPRET, this first argument can be dropped. Assume that the modification to INTERPRET is minimal: the argument list is changed from (NETWORK PARENT-NODE FEATURES) to (FEATURES). Modify RECORD so that the proper values for THIS-NODE and PARENT-NODE are maintained anyway. If THIS-NODE is unbound when an ATN function is called, have PARENT-NODE get UNIVERSAL-TOP as its value. Think of using a lambda expression and the BOUNDP function.

Registers Add Power to ATN Descriptions

The noun-group description used for illustration so far is puny. The fancier version below makes notes and refers to them. Abstractly, notes are written in places called *registers*. Concretely, the registers are represented as properties of the corresponding node.

```
(RECORD PARSE-NOUN-GROUP
        (S1 (IF (PARSE-WORD THIS-NODE 'DETERMINER)
                --> S2
                AFTER
                (SETR 'NUMBER (SELECT '(SINGULAR PLURAL)
                                      (GETF LAST-PARSED)))
                (SETR 'DETERMINER (SELECT '(DEFINITE INDEFINITE)
                                          (GETF LAST-PARSED)))))
        (S2 (IF (PARSE-WORD THIS-NODE 'ADJECTIVE)
                --> S2
                AFTER
                (ADDR 'ADJECTIVES LAST-PARSED))
            (IF (PARSE-WORD THIS-NODE 'NOUN)
                --> WIN
                AFTER
                (SETR 'NUMBER (SELECT '(SINGULAR PLURAL)
                                      (GETF LAST-PARSED)))
                (SETR 'NOUN LAST-PARSED))))
```

Now this is what PARSE-NOUN-GROUP and PARSE-WORD specialists do if the value of REMAINING-WORDS is (A BIG RED BLOCK):

ATOM	PROPERTY	VALUE
<noun group name>	CHILDREN	(A BIG RED BLOCK)
	DETERMINER	INDEFINITE
	NUMBER	SINGULAR
	ADJECTIVES	(RED)
	NOUN	BLOCK

Registers require the introduction of three new functions. SETR and GETR place and retrieve, using THIS-NODE as a free variable. ADDR uses SETR and GETR to add a new element to a register.

```
(DEFUN SETR (REGISTER VALUE)
       (PUTPROP THIS-NODE VALUE REGISTER)
       VALUE)

(DEFUN GETR (REGISTER)
       (GET THIS-NODE REGISTER))

(DEFUN ADDR (REGISTER VALUE)
       (SETR REGISTER (CONS VALUE (GETR REGISTER))))
```

SELECT takes two lists. It returns the first thing in the first list that is also in the second.

Problems

Problem 19-3: Define SELECT.

Problem 19-4: Define GENNAME.

Problem 19-5: Generalize the noun group ATN so that noun groups without determiners are accepted. Show your answer to this and similar problems in two ways, first by adding and/or deleting nodes, arcs, and LISP fragments, as necessary, on a diagram, and second, by showing the modified LISP-like ATN description.

Problem 19-6: Improve the noun group ATN so that it complains if the number indicated by the noun clashes with that indicated by the determiner.

Problem 19-7: Generalize the noun group ATN so that numbers are accepted as in the fragment "the three big red blocks." You may assume a representation for numbers produced as follows for three:

(DEFPROP THREE (NUMBER) FEATURES)

(DEFPROP THREE 3 NUMBER)

Your answer must be such that "a three big red blocks" and "the three five big red blocks" and "the big three red blocks" all fail. For "the three big red blocks" the revised noun group ATN must produce this:

ATOM	PROPERTY	VALUE
<noun group name>	DETERMINER	DEFINITE
	NUMBER	3.
	ADJECTIVES	(RED BIG)
	NOUN	BLOCKS

Problem 19-8: The noun-group function cannot handle both "the deep blue river" and "the deep blue" given that the word blue has both NOUN and ADJECTIVE on its feature list. The reason is that blue will cause the adjective arc to be taken, even if it is really the noun of the noun group. Generalize the noun-group function so that both of the noun groups are correctly analyzed in spite of the lack of backup.

ATN Specifications may be Involved

It would be diversionary to discuss too much English syntax here. Therefore the following is offered without comment:

```
(RECORD PARSE-CLAUSE
    (S1 (IF (PARSE-NOUN-GROUP THIS-NODE NIL)
            --> S2
            AFTER
            (SETR 'SUBJECT LAST-PARSED)))
    (S2 (IF (PARSE-WORD THIS-NODE '(VERB TENSED))
            --> S3
            AFTER (SETR 'VERB LAST-PARSED)))
    (S3 (IF (AND (EQUAL LAST-PARSED 'BE)
                 (PARSE-WORD THIS-NODE 'PASTPARTICIPLE))
            --> S4
            AFTER
            (SETR 'OBJECT (GETR 'SUBJECT))
            (SETR 'SUBJECT NIL)
            (SETR 'VERB LAST-PARSED))
        (IF (AND (TESTF (GETR 'VERB) 'TRANSITIVE)
                 (PARSE-NOUN-GROUP THIS-NODE NIL))
            --> S4
            AFTER (SETR 'OBJECT LAST-PARSED))
        (IF (OR (TESTF (GETR 'VERB) 'INTRANSITIVE)
                (GETR 'OBJECT))
            --> S4))
    (S4 (IF (AND (GETR 'SUBJECT)
                 (NULL REMAINING-WORDS))
            --> WIN)
        (IF (AND (NOT (GETR 'SUBJECT))
                 (EQUAL CURRENT-WORD 'BY)
                 (PARSE-WORD THIS-NODE NIL))
            --> S5)
        (IF (NOT (GETR 'SUBJECT))
            --> S4
            AFTER
            (SETR 'SUBJECT 'SOMEONE)))
    (S5 (IF (PARSE-NOUN-GROUP THIS-NODE NIL)
            --> S4
            AFTER
            (SETR 'SUBJECT LAST-PARSED))))
```

The corresponding node-and-arc diagram is given in figure 19-2.

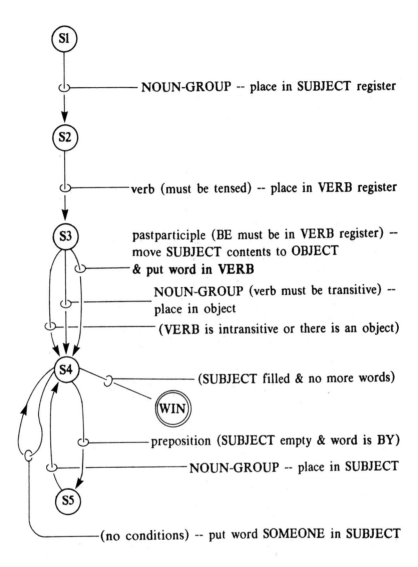

Figure 19-2: An Augmented Transition Network representing the structure of simple sentences. The program-like form is more precise. Arcs are tried in clockwise order, starting at 3 o'clock.

Summary

◨ Augmented transition networks capture English syntax.

◨ Satisfying an augmented transition network constitutes a kind of match.

◨ Making LISP from augmented transition networks is easy.

◨ An ATN interpreter follows a retained description.

◨ Registers add power to ATN descriptions.

◨ ATN specifications may be involved.

References

For more information on augmented transition networks, see Chapter 6 of *Artificial Intelligence*, by Patrick H. Winston [1977]. See also Harris [1977], Kaplan [1972], and Woods, Kaplan, and Nash-Webber [1972].

20
COMPILING
AUGMENTED
TRANSITION
NETWORKS

The purpose of this chapter is to take a second look at language translation by implementing a so-called compiler for augmented transition networks to complement the interpreter of the previous chapter. Take note that we will be talking about compiling in a general sense meaning translating from one language into another, somehow useful one. This is different from the more restricted sense that implies that the translation is into some computer's basic instruction set.

ATN Networks can be Compiled from Transparent Specifications

Since translating ATN graphs into LISP functions is straightforward but tedious, the job should really be done by a program. We shall develop such a translation program. The result will be a compiler.

▪ A *compiler* is a program that translates procedure descriptions from one language into another.

The main job of the ATN compiler is to translate source-language descriptions into PROG tags and CONDs that can go into the same framework that was already established for ATNs in the previous chapter:

```
<node name>
(COND (<test> <side effect>
              .
              .
              .
              <side effect>
              (GO <new node>))
      (T (GO LOSE)))
```

Once the compiler is developed, the entire noun-group and word-specialist definitions can be written just as they were for the interpreter:

```
(COMPILE PARSE-NOUN-GROUP
         (S1 (IF (PARSE-WORD THIS-NODE 'DETERMINER) --> S2))
         (S2 (IF (PARSE-WORD THIS-NODE 'ADJECTIVE) --> S2)
             (IF (PARSE-WORD THIS-NODE 'NOUN) --> WIN)))

(COMPILE PARSE-WORD
         (S1 (IF T --> WIN
                 AFTER
                 (SETQ THIS-NODE CURRENT-WORD)
                 (SETQ REMAINING-WORDS (CDR REMAINING-WORDS))
                 (COND (REMAINING-WORDS (SETQ CURRENT-WORD
                                              (CAR REMAINING-WORDS)))
                       (T (SETQ CURRENT-WORD NIL))))))
```

Compilers Treat Programs as DATA

Now the problem is creating COMPILE, a LISP function that converts perspicuous descriptions into descriptions that LISP understands directly. Thankfully, the job involves nothing more than the symbol-manipulating flair so characteristic of LISP.

First, of course, each transition-specifying parcel must be ripped apart and reassembled into a COND clause. Then the several clauses for each node must be amalgamated into a single COND structure. Naturally, CARs, CDRs, CONSs, and APPENDs abound.

Assuming that CLAUSE has a value corresponding to one of the transition specifications, then the following identifications hold (the CDR–CDDDR combination is needed in our LISP since only four CARs and CDRs can be squashed together):

```
(CADR CLAUSE)              <test>
(CADDDR CLAUSE)            <new node>
(CDR (CDDDDR CLAUSE))      <side effects>
```

Figure 20-1 shows how these pieces go into a COND clause.

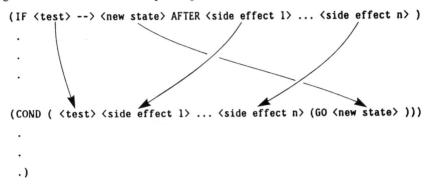

Figure 20-1: The ATN compiler splits up transition rules and reassembles them into COND clauses.

The construction can be done by this fragment:

```
(APPEND (LIST (CADR CLAUSE))
        (COND ((CDDDDR CLAUSE)
               (CDR (CDDDDR CLAUSE))))
        (LIST (LIST 'GO (CADDDR CLAUSE))))
```

Note that quite a menagerie of functions is needed to create the proper final list structure. Writing it of course is a job that demands interactive debugging. No one gets it right the first time.

Note that the buried test simply checks if side-effect descriptions are present and returns them if they are. If not, a NIL is returned that disappears when the APPEND is executed.

The COND clauses for a particular node are assembled together by a MAPCAR and LAMBDA combination operating on the list of transition specifications found in the value of the variable STATE, assumed to contain the complete description package.

```
(MAPCAR
 '(LAMBDA
   (CLAUSE)
   (APPEND (LIST (CADR CLAUSE))
           (COND ((CDDDDR CLAUSE)
                  (CDR (CDDDDR CLAUSE))))
           (LIST (LIST 'GO (CADDDR CLAUSE)))))
 (CDR STATE))
```

Once this is understood, then the required COND structure and all its clauses can be assembled as follows:

```
(LIST (CAR STATE)
      (CONS 'COND
            (APPEND
             (MAPCAR
              '(LAMBDA
                (CLAUSE)
                (APPEND (LIST (CADR CLAUSE))
                        (COND ((CDDDDR CLAUSE)
                               (CDR (CDDDDR CLAUSE))))
                        (LIST (LIST 'GO (CADDDR CLAUSE)))))
              (CDR STATE))
             '((T (GO LOSE)))))))
```

The grafting of (T (GO LOSE)) onto the end of the clause list allows the user to omit this implied default from his node transition descriptions. The atom COND is affixed to the other end, of course, and the whole package is then preceded by the node name as ferreted out by (CAR STATE).

The entire middle portion of the target LISP function is created by repeating the prescribed COND manufacture for each node specified by the body of the ATN description. Handling the repetition by a MAPCAR and LAMBDA arrangement yields the following somewhat complicated-looking result:

```
(SETQ
 MIDDLE
 (APPLY
  'APPEND
  (MAPCAR
   '(LAMBDA
     (STATE)
     (LIST (CAR STATE)
           (CONS 'COND
                 (APPEND
                  (MAPCAR
                   '(LAMBDA
                     (CLAUSE)
                     (APPEND (LIST (CADR CLAUSE))
                             (COND ((CDDDDR CLAUSE)
                                    (CDR (CDDDDR CLAUSE))))
                             (LIST (LIST 'GO (CADDDR CLAUSE)))))
                   (CDR STATE))
                  '((T (GO LOSE)))))))
   BODY)))
```

Thankfully, the entire translation is nearly complete because the middle portion of the target function is the only part that is very sensitive to the description given. In fact, the end portion is always the same and appears simply as a giant quoted list:

```
(SETQ END
      '(WIN (COND ((NOT (TESTF THIS-NODE FEATURES)) (GO LOSE)))
            (ATTACH THIS-NODE PARENT-NODE)
            (SETQ LAST-PARSED THIS-NODE)
            (RETURN THIS-NODE)
            LOSE
            (SETQ REMAINING-WORDS HOLD)
            (SETQ CURRENT-WORD (CAR REMAINING-WORDS))
            (RETURN NIL)))
```

The beginning is only a little more complicated. The quoted general form must be modified to get the name of the function into proper position inside the GENNAME function. The function SUBST can do the modification:

```
(SETQ BEGINNING
      (SUBST NAME
             'REPLACE
             '(PROG (THIS-NODE HOLD)
                    (SETQ HOLD REMAINING-WORDS)
                    (SETQ CURRENT-WORD (CAR REMAINING-WORDS))
                    (SETQ THIS-NODE (GENNAME 'REPLACE)))))
```

Having the beginning, middle, and end, the total function description is easy to get via (SETQ PROGRAM (APPEND BEGINNING MIDDLE END)).

The value of PROGRAM is exactly the ordinary LISP form of the LISP function desired. To effect the definition, the newly created LISP function must be combined with a name and argument list and placed together inside a DEFUN form:

```
(RETURN (LIST 'DEFUN NAME '(PARENT-NODE FEATURES) PROGRAM))
```

Everything is ready. COMPILE, the ATN compiler function, can be defined as a MACRO. The total result shows why COMPILE has been introduced in pieces:

```
(DEFUN COMPILE MACRO (DESCRIPTION)
  (PROG (NAME BODY PROGRAM BEGINNING MIDDLE END)
        (SETQ NAME (CADR DESCRIPTION))
        (SETQ BODY (CDDR DESCRIPTION))
        (SETQ BEGINNING
              (SUBST NAME
                     'REPLACE
                     '(PROG (THIS-NODE HOLD)
                            (SETQ HOLD REMAINING-WORDS)
                            (SETQ CURRENT-WORD (CAR REMAINING-WORDS))
                            (SETQ THIS-NODE (GENNAME 'REPLACE)))))
        (SETQ
         MIDDLE
         (APPLY
          'APPEND
          (MAPCAR
           '(LAMBDA
             (STATE)
             (LIST (CAR STATE)
                   (CONS 'COND
                         (APPEND
                          (MAPCAR
                           '(LAMBDA
                             (CLAUSE)
                             (APPEND (LIST (CADR CLAUSE))
                                     (COND ((CDDDDR CLAUSE)
                                            (CDR (CDDDDR CLAUSE))))
                                     (LIST (LIST 'GO (CADDDR CLAUSE)))))
                           (CDR STATE))
                          '((T (GO LOSE)))))))
           BODY)))
        (SETQ END
              '(WIN (COND ((NOT (TESTF THIS-NODE FEATURES)) (GO LOSE)))
                    (ATTACH THIS-NODE PARENT-NODE)
                    (SETQ LAST-PARSED THIS-NODE)
                    (RETURN THIS-NODE)
                    LOSE
                    (SETQ REMAINING-WORDS HOLD)
                    (SETQ CURRENT-WORD (CAR REMAINING-WORDS))
                    (RETURN NIL)))
        (SETQ PROGRAM (APPEND BEGINNING MIDDLE END))
        (RETURN (LIST 'DEFUN NAME '(PARENT-NODE FEATURES) PROGRAM))))
```

Of course many improvements and extensions suggest themselves. Error-handling, reporting, and debugging features, for example, are missing.

Compilers are usually Harder to Make than Interpreters

Compilers translate programs from a source language to a target language. When the compiled program runs, neither the source-language version nor the compiler is around to help figure things out. Once compiled, a program is on its own. For example, in the compiled ATNs, the specifications about what node to jump to are present only implicitly in the GOs.

Interpreters follow programs in a source language step-by-step. The source-language program is always there to refer to. For example, in working with interpreted ATNs, specifications about what node to jump to are always present in their original form. No implicit representation of that information is necessary.

Generally, it is easier to write an interpreter. Compiled programs, on the other hand, generally run faster.

Compilers are usually Major Undertakings

In the ATN example, LISP is both the compiler's implementation language and the compilation's target language. Creating the compiler was straightforward because compiling is a symbol-manipulating task for which LISP is eminently suited. Often compilers translate from source languages into assembler-level languages to achieve high running speed. Working with such compilers is much harder, especially if the compiler itself must be written in an assembler language, again for reasons of speed.

LISP Itself is either Compiled or Interpreted

First we used a LISP program to interpret ATN descriptions. Then we used another LISP program to compile ATN descriptions into LISP programs.

Of course LISP programs themselves are descriptions of procedures, and as such, they can be interpreted by a program written using the basic machine instructions of a computer or they can be compiled into programs written in those basic instructions.

This makes for the curious set of possibilities shown in figure 20-2. The translation of LISP into basic instructions is a symbol-manipulation job. Hence it is nicely accomplished by a program written in LISP. Said another way, LISP is a good language for writing a LISP compiler. But then the LISP compiler itself is a LISP program which can be compiled. Once compiled, the compiler can compile itself. Indeed the first program a new LISP compiler usually compiles is itself, relying on an interpreter or a previous compiler until the self-compilation is done!

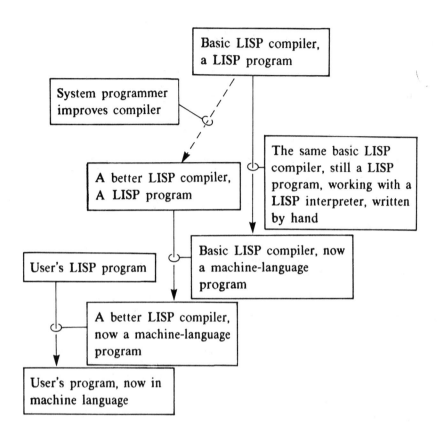

Figure 20-2: Each new version of the LISP compiler is compiled by the previous version. At the very beginning, the original compiler is compiled using the combined talents of the compiler itself and an interpreter. User programs are either run by the current version of the interpreter or compiled by the last compiler in the chain. One compiler is better than another if it runs faster or if it produces faster or smaller programs or if it handles more of the language it is compiling.

Problems

Problem 20-1: Suppose a LISP compiler is available. Is it possible to gain extra speed improvements by going from ATN descriptions to basic instructions in two steps?

Summary

■ ATN networks can be compiled from transparent specifications.

■ Compilers treat programs as data.

■ Compilers are usually harder to make than interpreters.

■ Compilers are usually major undertakings.

■ LISP itself is either compiled or interpreted.

References

Further information on compilers for the MACLISP version of LISP can be found in Golden [1970], Steele [1977b, 1979], and Greenberg [1977].

21
PROGRAM
WRITING
PROGRAMS
AND
NATURAL
LANGUAGE
INTERFACES

Certainly LISP programs can write programs. We have seen an example of this already since a compiler takes one program as input and produces another as output. The purpose of this chapter is to show that a problem-solving program also may write its own programs and evaluate them in the normal course of problem solving.

The particular system developed here deals with the tool world, answering a user's English-stated questions about what tools there are and how many. It illustrates the principles behind commercial English data-base interfaces.

Tool World is an Illustrative Domain

Suppose tool world consists in part of a few screwdrivers lying around on a workbench or hanging on a pegboard. The system to be developed is then demonstrated by these interactions:

```
(REQUEST: IDENTIFY THE LARGE SCREWDRIVERS)
   THE RESULTS ARE: S1 S2 S3

(REQUEST: IDENTIFY THE LARGE RED SCREWDRIVERS)
   THE RESULTS ARE: S2 S3

(REQUEST: IDENTIFY A LONG SCREWDRIVER)
   THE RESULT IS: S1

(REQUEST: COUNT THE SCREWDRIVERS)
   THERE ARE 3.
```

```
(REQUEST: COUNT THE LARGE RED SCREWDRIVERS)
  THERE ARE 2.
```

Answering Requests is done in Four Steps

Figure 21-1 shows the shape of the request-answering system.

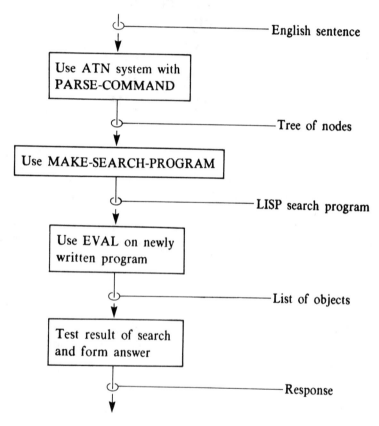

Figure 21-1 The structure of a system that answers English questions about some data base. Note that one program writes another and then executes that program.

■ The first step in answering a request is to convert the English question into a parse tree using an ATN to do the analysis.

■ Next the parse tree guides the manufacture of a search function that can look for the sought-after items in the data base.

■ Then the search function is evaluated producing the names of the sought-after items.

■ Finally, the items are listed or their number is announced.

Let us skip over the first step, producing a parse tree, and return to it later, noting only that the syntactic features used are as follows for the sample sentences:

ATOM	PROPERTY	VALUE
A	FEATURES	(DETERMINER SINGULAR INDEFINITE)
THE	FEATURES	(DETERMINER DEFINITE)
LARGE	FEATURES	(ADJECTIVE)
RED	FEATURES	(ADJECTIVE)
LONG	FEATURES	(ADJECTIVE)
SCREWDRIVER	FEATURES	(NOUN SINGULAR)
SCREWDRIVERS	FEATURES	(NOUN PLURAL)
SCREWDRIVERS	SINGULAR-FORM	SCREWDRIVER

The result of parsing is a parse tree as in this example:

(REQUEST: IDENTIFY THE LARGE SCREWDRIVERS)

ATOM	PROPERTY	VALUE
G0034	CHILDREN	(IDENTIFY PARSE-NOUN-GROUP-61)
	COMMAND	ENUMERATE
	NOUN-GROUP	PARSE-NOUN-GROUP-61
PARSE-NOUN-GROUP-61	CHILDREN	(THE LARGE SCREDRIVERS)
	DETERMINER	DEFINITE
	NUMBER	PLURAL
	ADJECTIVES	(LARGE)
	NOUN	SCREWDRIVERS

Simple Programs can Count and Enumerate Description-matching Objects

Translation of a parse tree into a search function exploits other atom properties that hold semantic information. The first step in actually doing the search is to get a list of all the possibilities using the singular form of the noun in the noun group. This means that something like (GET 'SCREWDRIVER 'INSTANCE) must appear in the search function and therefore must be produced by the translator. Here are a few of the INSTANCE property values:

ATOM	PROPERTY	VALUE
TOOL	INSTANCE	(HAMMER SCREWDRIVER SAW WRENCH)
HAMMER	INSTANCE	(H1)
SCREWDRIVER	INSTANCE	(S1 S2 S3 S4 S5)
SAW	INSTANCE	(SAW1)
WRENCH	INSTANCE	(W1 W2)

The second step in doing the search is to filter the possibilities generated in the first step, leaving only the ones that fit the adjectives. The adjectives themselves supply predicates that enable this filtering:

ATOM	PROPERTY	VALUE
LARGE	ADJECTIVE-FUNCTION	LARGEP
RED	ADJECTIVE-FUNCTION	REDP
LONG	ADJECTIVE-FUNCTION	LONGP

```
(DEFUN LARGEP (OBJECT) (EQUAL (GET OBJECT 'SIZE) 'LARGE))

(DEFUN REDP (OBJECT) (EQUAL (GET OBJECT 'COLOR) 'RED))

(DEFUN LONGP (OBJECT) (GREATERP (OR (GET OBJECT 'LENGTH) 0.) 6.0))
```

Thus, given all the screwdrivers, the large ones are isolated by using LARGEP along with a MAPCAN that does a filtering accumulation:

```
(MAPCAN '(LAMBDA (CANDIDATE)
                 (COND ((LARGEP CANDIDATE) (LIST CANDIDATE))
                       (T NIL)))
        <a list of all the screwdrivers>)
```

From this, S1, S2 and S3 emerge, given this data base of property values:

ATOM	PROPERTY	VALUE
S1	SIZE	LARGE
S2	SIZE	LARGE
S3	SIZE	LARGE
S4	SIZE	SMALL
S5	SIZE	SMALL
S1	COLOR	BLUE
S2	COLOR	RED
S3	COLOR	RED
S1	LENGTH	7.

If other adjectives were present, other filtering steps, using other predicates, would handle them.

The last step in doing the search verifies that there is no clash between the determiner and number features of the noun group and the number of items discovered. If the user asks the system to identify the large screwdriver and there are many, there is no way the system can know which one the user has in mind. Consequently, a request should lead to an answer only if the determiner and number features mesh with the number of items that pass the filter or filters. For the example, there will be compatibility if the following holds:

```
(GREATERP <number of items surviving filters> 1.)
```

Putting all of this together, the system is to start with an English request handed to the function REQUEST:

```
(REQUEST: IDENTIFY THE LARGE SCREWDRIVERS)
```

It must then analyze the sentence to build a parse tree:

ATOM	PROPERTY	VALUE
G0034	CHILDREN	(IDENTIFY PARSE-NOUN-GROUP-61)
	COMMAND	ENUMERATE
	NOUN-GROUP	PARSE-NOUN-GROUP-61
PARSE-NOUN-GROUP-61	CHILDREN	(THE LARGE SCREDRIVERS)
	DETERMINER	DEFINITE
	NUMBER	PLURAL
	ADJECTIVES	(LARGE)
	NOUN	SCREWDRIVERS

Then it must use the parse tree to construct a search function with three parts: candidate finding, candidate filtering, and result testing:

```
(PROG (OBJECTS)
      (SETQ OBJECTS (GET 'SCREWDRIVER 'INSTANCE))
      (SETQ OBJECTS
            (MAPCAN '(LAMBDA (CANDIDATE)
                             (COND ((LARGEP CANDIDATE) (LIST CANDIDATE))
                                   (T NIL)))
                    OBJECTS))
      (COND ((GREATERP (LENGTH OBJECTS) 1.) (RETURN OBJECTS))
            (T (RETURN NIL))))
```

Then the system must run the function, producing (S1 S2 S3) as the result.
Finally it must enumerate the items in the result, as commanded:

THE RESULTS ARE: S1 S2 S3

For further illustration, consider this:

(REQUEST: COUNT THE LARGE RED SCREWDRIVERS)

The parse tree looks like this:

ATOM	PROPERTY	VALUE
G0088	CHILDREN	(COUNT PARSE-NOUN-GROUP-23)
	COMMAND	COUNT
	NOUN-GROUP	PARSE-NOUN-GROUP-23
PARSE-NOUN-GROUP-23	CHILDREN	(THE LARGE RED SCREWDRIVERS)
	DETERMINER	DEFINITE
	NUMBER	PLURAL
	ADJECTIVES	(LARGE RED)
	NOUN	SCREWDRIVERS

The search function has two filters:

```
(PROG (OBJECTS)
     (SETQ OBJECTS (GET 'SCREWDRIVER 'INSTANCE))
     (SETQ OBJECTS
          (MAPCAN '(LAMBDA (CANDIDATE)
                         (COND ((REDP CANDIDATE) (LIST CANDIDATE))
                               (T NIL)))
                OBJECTS))
     (SETQ OBJECTS
          (MAPCAN '(LAMBDA (CANDIDATE)
                         (COND ((LARGEP CANDIDATE) (LIST CANDIDATE))
                               (T NIL)))
                OBJECTS))
     (COND ((GREATERP (LENGTH OBJECTS) 1.) (RETURN OBJECTS))
          (T (RETURN NIL))))
```

The search function returns (S2 S3). The answer given is this:

THERE ARE 2.

The Question-answering Program Builds a Program and then Executes It

REQUEST is actually straightforward, since most of the interesting work is done by the PARSE-COMMAND and MAKE-SEARCH-PROGRAM functions inside it. The printing function P is the one defined in the printing and reading chapter.

```
(DEFUN REQUEST: FEXPR (REMAINING-WORDS)
  (PROG (TREE PROGRAM RESULTS NOUN-GROUP)
    (SETQ TREE (PARSE-COMMAND (GENSYM) NIL))         ;Analyze English.
    (SETQ PROGRAM (MAKE-SEARCH-PROGRAM (GET TREE 'NOUN-GROUP))) ;Construct function.
    (SETQ RESULTS (EVAL PROGRAM))                    ;Run it.
    (COND ((EQUAL (GET TREE 'COMMAND) 'COUNT)        ;Use answer.
          (COND ((CDR RESULTS) (P '(THERE ARE) (LENGTH RESULTS)))
                (RESULTS (P '(THERE IS) 1))
                (T (P '(SORRY THE REQUEST AND DATA BASE CLASH)))))
         ((EQUAL (GET TREE 'COMMAND) 'ENUMERATE)
          (COND ((CDR RESULTS) (P '(THE RESULTS ARE:) RESULTS))
                (RESULTS (P '(THE RESULT IS:) RESULTS))
                (T (P '(SORRY THE REQUEST AND DATA BASE CLASH)))))))))
```

Note carefully the use of MAKE-SEARCH-PROGRAM to make the search function and the subsequent execution of that function in the next line. Now let us look at how MAKE-SEARCH-PROGRAM does its job.

Search Programs can be Written Automatically

MAKE-SEARCH-PROGRAM builds the search function in three parts and then appends them together. The first part consists of the atom PROG, the parameter list, and the instance-retrieval expression:

```
(PROG (OBJECTS)
      (SETQ OBJECTS (GET 'NOUN 'INSTANCE)))
```

To get the right noun into this, a SUBST helps. It goes to the noun register of the value of NODE to find the noun:

```
(SUBST (PROG (NOUN)
             (SETQ NOUN (GET NODE 'NOUN))
             (RETURN (COND ((MEMBER 'PLURAL (GET NOUN 'FEATURES))
                            (GET NOUN 'SINGULAR-FORM))
                           (T NOUN))))
       'NOUN
       '(PROG (OBJECTS)
              (SETQ OBJECTS (GET 'NOUN 'INSTANCE)))))
```

Next, MAKE-SEARCH-PROGRAM must build filtering expressions. Each will have the form below, but proper expressions must be substituted for the predicate:

```
(SETQ OBJECTS
      (MAPCAN
       '(LAMBDA (CANDIDATE)
                (COND ((PREDICATE CANDIDATE) (LIST CANDIDATE))
                      (T NIL)))
       OBJECTS))
```

Again, SUBST does the substitution:

```
(SUBST (GET ADJECTIVE 'ADJECTIVE-FUNCTION)
       'PREDICATE
       '(SETQ OBJECTS
              (MAPCAN
               '(LAMBDA (CANDIDATE)
                        (COND ((PREDICATE CANDIDATE) (LIST CANDIDATE))
                              (T NIL)))
               OBJECTS)))
```

Since there may be many adjectives, this may need to be repeated many times. A MAPCAR gets it done once for each adjective found on the value of NODE. This completes the second part of the search-function construction:

```
(MAPCAR
 '(LAMBDA (ADJECTIVE)
          (SUBST (GET ADJECTIVE 'ADJECTIVE-FUNCTION)
                 'PREDICATE
                 '(SETQ OBJECTS
                        (MAPCAN
                         '(LAMBDA (CANDIDATE)
                                  (COND ((PREDICATE CANDIDATE)
                                         (LIST CANDIDATE))
                                        (T NIL)))
                         OBJECTS))))
 (GET NODE 'ADJECTIVES))
```

The last thing MAKE-SEARCH-PROGRAM does is generate a test expression that
compares the number of items found with what the determiner and number
features allow. This last part of MAKE-SEARCH-PROGRAM is long only because
there are many combinations to look for:

```
(SUBST (PROG (DETERMINER NUMBER)
             (SETQ DETERMINER (GET NODE 'DETERMINER))
             (SETQ NUMBER (GET NODE 'NUMBER))
             (RETURN
              (COND ((EQUAL DETERMINER 'DEFINITE)
                     (COND ((EQUAL NUMBER 'SINGULAR)
                            '(EQUAL (LENGTH OBJECTS) 1))
                           ((EQUAL NUMBER 'PLURAL)
                            '(GREATERP (LENGTH OBJECTS) 1))))
                    ((EQUAL DETERMINER 'INDEFINITE)
                     (COND ((EQUAL NUMBER 'SINGULAR)
                            '(GREATERP (LENGTH OBJECTS) 0))))
                    ((NUMBERP NUMBER)
                     (LIST 'GREATERP '(LENGTH OBJECTS) NUMBER)))))
       'TEST
       '((COND (TEST (RETURN OBJECTS))
               (T (RETURN NIL)))))
```

It is time to put it all together. MAKE-SEARCH-PROGRAM is just an APPEND
working on three pieces:

```
(DEFUN MAKE-SEARCH-PROGRAM (NODE)
     (APPEND
      (SUBST (PROG (NOUN)
                   (SETQ NOUN (GET NODE 'NOUN))
                   (RETURN (COND ((MEMBER 'PLURAL (GET NOUN 'FEATURES))
                                  (GET NOUN 'SINGULAR-FORM))
                                 (T NOUN))))
             'NOUN
             '(PROG (OBJECTS)
                    (SETQ OBJECTS (GET 'NOUN 'INSTANCE))))
      (MAPCAR
       '(LAMBDA (ADJECTIVE)
                (SUBST (GET ADJECTIVE 'ADJECTIVE-FUNCTION)
                       'PREDICATE
                       '(SETQ OBJECTS
                              (MAPCAN
                               '(LAMBDA (CANDIDATE)
                                        (COND ((PREDICATE CANDIDATE)
                                               (LIST CANDIDATE))
                                              (T NIL)))
                               OBJECTS))))
       (GET NODE 'ADJECTIVES))
      (SUBST (PROG (DETERMINER NUMBER)
                   (SETQ DETERMINER (GET NODE 'DETERMINER))
                   (SETQ NUMBER (GET NODE 'NUMBER))
                   (RETURN
                    (COND ((EQUAL DETERMINER 'DEFINITE)
                           (COND ((EQUAL NUMBER 'SINGULAR)
                                  '(EQUAL (LENGTH OBJECTS) 1))
                                 ((EQUAL NUMBER 'PLURAL)
                                  '(GREATERP (LENGTH OBJECTS) 1))))
                          ((EQUAL DETERMINER 'INDEFINITE)
                           (COND ((EQUAL NUMBER 'SINGULAR)
                                  '(GREATERP (LENGTH OBJECTS) 0))))
                          ((NUMBERP NUMBER)
                           (LIST 'GREATERP '(LENGTH OBJECTS) NUMBER)))))
             'TEST
             '((COND (TEST (RETURN OBJECTS))
                     (T (RETURN NIL))))))))
```

A Simple ATN Determines how to Build the Guiding Parse Tree

In this demonstration, only identify-type and count-type sentences are involved.
Consequently the ATN that is used is simple:

```
(COMPILE PARSE-COMMAND
        (S1 (IF (AND (EQUAL CURRENT-WORD 'COUNT)
                     (PARSE-WORD THIS-NODE '()))
                --> S2
                AFTER
                (SETR 'COMMAND 'COUNT))
            (IF (AND (EQUAL CURRENT-WORD 'IDENTIFY)
                     (PARSE-WORD THIS-NODE '()))
                --> S2
                AFTER
                (SETR 'COMMAND 'ENUMERATE)))
        (S2 (IF (AND (PARSE-NOUN-GROUP THIS-NODE NIL)
                     (NULL REMAINING-WORDS))
                --> WIN
                AFTER
                (SETR 'NOUN-GROUP LAST-PARSED)))))
```

Properties are not quite Enough

The predicate REDP uses the COLOR property of the object it is testing:

```
(DEFUN REDP (OBJECT) (EQUAL (GET OBJECT 'COLOR) 'RED))
```

A similar function could be written for METALP:

```
(DEFUN METALP (OBJECT) (EQUAL (GET OBJECT 'MATERIAL) 'METAL))
```

Objects would be identified as metallic through their individual property lists. But this is often wastefully redundant, since all screws, for example, are metallic. In the next chapter, we will see how to identify all screws as metallic using mechanisms that enable information about specific objects to be inherited from descriptions that hold for all objects of the same type.

Problems

Project: Generalize the system to take a wider variety of requests.

Summary

■ Tool world is an illustrative domain.

■ Answering requests is done in four steps.

■ Simple programs can count and enumerate description-matching objects.

■ The question-answering program builds a program and then executes it.

■ Search programs can be written automatically.

■ A simple ATN determines how to build the guiding parse tree.

■ Properties are not quite enough.

References

For more information on natural language interfaces to data bases, see Chapter 6 of *Artificial Intelligence*, by Patrick H. Winston [1977].

See also Codd [1974], Grishman and Hirschman [1978], Harris [1977], Hendrix *et al.* [1978], Minker, Fishman, and McSkimin [1972], Petrick [1976], and Waltz [1978].

22
IMPLEMENTING
FRAMES

The purpose of this chapter is to see how to implement fancy data bases that have features beyond those offered by basic LISP. In particular, we look at an implementation of a set of functions that captures some of the ideas in Marvin Minsky's original paper on frames. The functions are slightly simplified versions of those in FRL, the frames-representation language designed and implemented by Ira Goldstein and Bruce Roberts.

A Frame is a Generalized Property List

Using DEFPROP and GET, it is easy to say quite a lot about any given symbol. For example, in describing some person named Henry, we might do the following:

```
(DEFPROP HENRY MAN AKO)
```

```
(DEFPROP HENRY 178 HEIGHT)
```

```
(DEFPROP HENRY 75 WEIGHT)
```

```
(DEFPROP HENRY (JOGGING SKIING) HOBBIES)
```

These few lines explicitly establish that Henry is a man of a particular height and weight with certain hobbies. Eventually, however, properties and property values are not enough. There may be a need, for example, for the following information about Paul, about whom little is known:

◻ A default value. If no one has explicitly given Paul's weight assume it is 57 kilograms by default.

◻ A function activated by placing a value. If Paul's weight ever goes above 60, he should be told to go on a diet.

◻ A function activated to compute a needed value. If no one has explicitly given Paul's weight, or even a default, then multiply his height in meters times 33 since he is a man.

Such information can be conveniently captured if the notion of property list is generalized.

◻ In part, a *frame* is a generalized property list because there is room in a frame to specify more than property values. In part, a frame is a generalized property list because it is possible for a frame to inherit information from another, related frame.

Frames can be Represented as Nested Association Lists

Let us review association lists. An association list is a list of elements, each of which can be identified and extracted from the list using its so-called key. In the following example, the value of A-LIST becomes a short, two-element association list. The keys are WEIGHT and HOBBIES, and the elements are the lists (WEIGHT 75) and (HOBBIES JOGGING SKIING) that contain both keys and keyed information.

```
(SETQ A-LIST '((WEIGHT 75) (HOBBIES JOGGING SKIING)))
```

The association list is simple to extend using CONS or APPEND:

```
(SETQ A-LIST (CONS '(HEIGHT 178) A-LIST))
```

```
(SETQ A-LIST (APPEND '((AKO MAN)) A-LIST))
```

The standard function for using association lists is ASSOC. It looks for a given key on a given association list and returns the element whose CAR is equal to the key. If there is no such element, NIL is returned. For example, consider this:

```
(ASSOC 'WEIGHT A-LIST)
  (WEIGHT 75)
```

```
(ASSOC 'EYE-COLOR A-LIST)
  NIL
```

Now one way to represent a frame is as a nested association list. On the highest level, the frame structure looks like this:

```
(<frame name> (<slot name 1> ...) (<slot name 2> ...) ...)
```

The CDR of the structure is an association list in which the keys are *slot* names. One level deeper, the slot-keyed elements have the same sort of structure:

```
(<slot name> (<facet name 1> ...) (<facet name 2> ...) ...)
```

Now the CDR is again an association list, but the keys are *facet* names. We will look at functions that use the VALUE, DEFAULT, IF-NEEDED, IF-ADDED, and IF-REMOVED facets.

Finally, still one level more, the facet-keyed elements look like this:

```
(<facet name> (<value 1>) (<value 2>) ...)
```

Thus a frame can have any number of slots. The slots can have any number of facets. And the facets can have any number of *values*. Putting it all together, we have this:

```
(<frame name> (<slot 1> (<facet 1> (<value 1>)
                                   (<value 2>)
                                      .
                                   . )
                       (<facet 2> (<value 1>) . . )
                                   .
                                . )
              (<slot 2> (<facet 1> (<value 1>) . . ) . .)
                 .
              . )
```

The frame representing the facts known about Henry, previously stored as a set of properties on the property list of Henry or on an ordinary association list, can be stuck into a frame:

```
(HENRY (AKO (VALUE (MAN)))
       (HEIGHT (VALUE (178)))
       (WEIGHT (VALUE (75)))
       (HOBBIES (VALUE (JOGGING) (SKIING))))
```

This structure has the desirable feature of uniformity at every level. There remains the question of where the structure should be stored. One idea would be to make it the value of HENRY. Another is to make a long list of all the frames and make that list the value of the atom FRAMES. Still another idea, and the one we use here, is to store the structure on the property list of HENRY under the property FRAME.

Given this structure for frames, we will eventually implement the following functions:

■ FGET fetches information. The user supplies an access path consisting of a frame, a slot, and a facet.

■ FPUT places information. As with FGET, the user supplies a frame-slot-facet access path.

■ FREMOVE removes information. As with FGET and FPUT, the user supplies a frame-slot-facet access path.

■ FGET-V-D fetches information. The user supplies an access path consisting only of a frame and a slot. The VALUE facet is inspected first. If nothing is found, then the DEFAULT facet is also inspected.

■ FGET-I fetches information. The user supplies a frame-slot access path. If nothing is found in the VALUE facet, then the function looks at frames found in the given frame's AKO slot under the VALUE facet. This enables a frame to inherit information from frames it is related to by the AKO relation, an abbreviation for a-kind-of.

■ FGET-N and FGET-Z fetch information. They use values, defaults, and value-finding functions, not only as found in the given frame but also in the frames it is related to by the AKO relation.

FGET, FPUT, and FREMOVE are the Basic Frame-handling Functions

The following simple function could retrieve information, given a frame-slot-facet access path:

```
(DEFUN FGET (FRAME SLOT FACET)
       (MAPCAR 'CAR
               (CDR (ASSOC FACET
                      (CDR (ASSOC SLOT
                             (CDR (GET FRAME 'FRAME)))))))))
```

Note that the function requires the CAR and CDR of NIL to be NIL, as they are in the LISP we are using. A MAPCAR is used to package up the final answer. To see why, suppose the following request is given:

```
(FGET 'HENRY 'HOBBIES 'VALUE)
```

The answer should be this:

```
(JOGGING SKIING)
```

Now the second argument to the MAPCAR is ((JOGGING) (SKIING)). It would seem sensible to run these together using an APPEND to produce the final, desired result, (JOGGING SKIING). The MAPCAR is used instead to enable a possible generalization of the frame structures in the direction of allowing comments to be attached to values by still another nesting. Assuming that FGET is to ignore such comments, the MAPCAR is needed.

FGET was fairly easy to do. It is a pity, but FPUT and FREMOVE will be harder to understand, partly because they do list-structure surgery using RPLACD.

The general strategy for FPUT is this: probe into the frame structure just like FGET does; however, if at any stage a key is not found, add a new element. Thus, if the given frame structure has nothing on its slot list corresponding to a new addition, then the slot list is enlarged. If a slot structure has nothing on its facet list corresponding to a new addition, then the facet list is enlarged. And if the given value is not there, then it too is similarly installed.

Suppose, for example, that the HENRY frame is to be augmented with the following application of FPUT:

```
(FPUT 'HENRY 'OCCUPATION 'VALUE 'TEACHING)
```

Since the HENRY frame has no OCCUPATION slot, the first step is to create one:

```
(HENRY (AKO (VALUE (MAN)))
       (HEIGHT (VALUE (178)))
       (WEIGHT (VALUE (75)))
       (HOBBIES (VALUE (JOGGING) (SKIING)))
       (OCCUPATION))
```

Next, since the OCCUPATION slot has no VALUE facet, it is created too:

```
(HENRY (AKO (VALUE (MAN)))
       (HEIGHT (VALUE (178)))
       (WEIGHT (VALUE (75)))
       (HOBBIES (VALUE (JOGGING) (SKIING)))
       (OCCUPATION (VALUE)))
```

And finally, the actual value is placed:

```
(HENRY (AKO (VALUE (MAN)))
       (HEIGHT (VALUE (178)))
       (WEIGHT (VALUE (75)))
       (HOBBIES (VALUE (JOGGING) (SKIING)))
       (OCCUPATION (VALUE (TEACHING))))
```

At this point, the following FPUT application encounters no need to create new structure until it hits the value level:

```
(FPUT 'HENRY 'OCCUPATION 'VALUE 'RESEARCH))))
```

The result is this:

```
(HENRY (SEX (VALUE (MAN)))
       (HEIGHT (VALUE (178)))
       (WEIGHT (VALUE (75)))
       (HOBBIES (VALUE (JOGGING) (SKIING)))
       (OCCUPATION (VALUE (TEACHING) (RESEARCH))))
```

Since association list inspection and enlargement are critical to FPUT, we consider it first:

```
(DEFUN FASSOC (KEY A-LIST)
       (COND ((ASSOC KEY (CDR A-LIST)))          ; Key is present?
             (T (CADR (RPLACD (LAST A-LIST)      ; If not, put it in.
                              (LIST (LIST KEY)))))))
```

If the key is found on the list, then FASSOC acts just like ASSOC, returning the element whose CAR is the given key. Otherwise, somehow, it adds an element whose CAR is the key to the end of the list. The addition is surgical. The RPLACD replaces the CDR of its first argument with its second argument by altering existing list structure, not by building entirely new structure.

Given FASSOC, the following will do for FPUT. Note that FPUT returns the value if the value is not already in the given place and NIL otherwise.

```
(DEFUN FPUT (FRAME SLOT FACET VALUE)
       (COND ((MEMBER VALUE (FGET FRAME SLOT FACET)) NIL)     ; Value there?
             (T (FASSOC VALUE                                  ; If not, put it in.
                        (FASSOC FACET
                                (FASSOC SLOT
                                        (FGETFRAME FRAME))))
                VALUE)))
```

FPUT uses FGETFRAME to get an existing frame structure if there is one; if there is none, FGETFRAME makes one.

```
(DEFUN FGETFRAME (FRAME)
      (COND ((GET FRAME 'FRAME))                    ;Frame already made?
            (T (PUTPROP FRAME (LIST FRAME) 'FRAME))))    ;If not, make one.
```

To complete the basic frame functions, we add FREMOVE to complement FGET and
FPUT. It works by first finding the slot, facet, and value structures if they are
indeed present. Then it deletes the value, if it exists. If this leaves the facet or
slot lists empty, they are deleted too. Note that the function DELETE attacks
existing list structure to do its job.

```
(DEFUN FREMOVE (FRAME SLOT FACET VALUE)
      (PROG (SLOTS FACETS VALUES TARGET)
            (SETQ SLOTS (FGETFRAME FRAME))          ;Find everything.
            (SETQ FACETS (ASSOC SLOT (CDR SLOTS)))
            (SETQ VALUES (ASSOC FACET (CDR FACETS)))
            (SETQ TARGET (ASSOC VALUE (CDR VALUES)))
            (DELETE TARGET VALUES)                  ;Purge what's there.
            (COND ((NULL (CDR VALUES))
                   (DELETE VALUES FACETS)))
            (COND ((NULL (CDR FACETS))
                   (DELETE FACETS SLOTS)))
            (RETURN (NOT (NULL TARGET))))))
```

Problems

Problem 22-1: Define FCHECK, a function of four arguments:

```
(FCHECK <frame> <slot> <facet> <value>)
```

It is to return T if the given value is in the given facet of the given slot of the
given frame and NIL otherwise.

Problem 22-2: Define FCLAMP, a function of three arguments:

```
(FCLAMP <frame 1> <frame 2> <slot>)
```

Its purpose is to tie together the two frames so that anything that goes into the
given slot by way of either frame goes automatically into the other. You will
need to use a dangerous, list-structure-altering function. You may assume that the
first frame has nothing in the given slot at the time FCLAMP is used.

Simple Programs can Exploit Defaults and If-needed Demons

Using FGET, it is easy to write a function that first looks in the VALUE facet of a given slot and then in the DEFAULT facet if nothing is found in the VALUE facet:

```
(DEFUN FGET-V-D (FRAME SLOT)
       (COND ((FGET FRAME SLOT 'VALUE))
             ((FGET FRAME SLOT 'DEFAULT))))
```

Next we add a feature that causes any function found in the IF-NEEDED facet to be executed if neither the VALUE or DEFAULT facets help:

```
(DEFUN FGET-V-D-F (FRAME SLOT)
       (COND ((FGET FRAME SLOT 'VALUE))
             ((FGET FRAME SLOT 'DEFAULT))
             (T (MAPCAN 'FUNCALL                    ;Use functions.
                        (FGET FRAME SLOT 'IF-NEEDED)))))
```

The if-needed functions are assumed to have no arguments. Furthermore, they are to return a list of values, possibly empty. They may, of course, use the variables FRAME and SLOT.

■ Functions that are activated automatically in response to the need for a value are called *demons*. Functions that are activated automatically when a value is placed or removed are also called demons. Thus there are if-needed, if-added, and if-removed demons.

The following function, ASK, could be a very popular occupant of the IF-NEEDED facet of a slot:

```
(DEFUN ASK ()
       (PRINT (APPEND '(PLEASE SUPPLY A LIST FOR THE)
                      (LIST SLOT)
                      '(SLOT IN THE)
                      (LIST FRAME)
                      '(FRAME)))
       (READ))
```

For calculating Paul's weight, if it is not given explicitly or by default, the following function would supply a result if there is a height or default height:

```
(DEFUN CALCULATE-WEIGHT ()
    (PROG (RESULT)
        (RETURN (COND ((SETQ RESULT (FGET-V-D FRAME 'HEIGHT))
                    (LIST (FPUT FRAME
                            'WEIGHT
                            'VALUE
                            (TIMES 33 (CAR RESULT)))))))))
```

Note that CALCULATE-WEIGHT both inserts its conclusion into the frame and returns the conclusion as its value. The function would be put in place like this:

```
(FPUT 'PAUL 'WEIGHT 'IF-NEEDED 'CALCULATE-WEIGHT)
```

Inheritance Works through the AKO Slot

Instead of looking at the DEFAULT or IF-NEEDED facets of a slot if the VALUE facet has nothing, it is possible instead to look for values in frames that the given frame is related to. For this we work through the AKO slot. FGET-I is one function that does this. It uses FGETCLASSES, a function that returns a list of all frames that a given frame is linked to by an AKO path.

```
(DEFUN FGET-I (FRAME SLOT)
    (PROG (CLASSES RESULT)
        (SETQ CLASSES (FGETCLASSES FRAME))
        LOOP
        (COND ((NULL CLASSES) (RETURN NIL))        ;Give up?
                ((SETQ RESULT                        ;Got something?
                    (FGET (CAR CLASSES) SLOT 'VALUE))
                 (RETURN RESULT))
                (T (SETQ CLASSES (CDR CLASSES))       ;Climb tree.
                 (GO LOOP)))))
```

Other possibilities immediately come to mind to complement FGET-I. For example, FGET-N does N-inheritance: it first follows AKO relations looking for values only; finding none, it starts over at the beginning, looking this time for defaults as it moves through the AKO relations; and finally, if both other possibilities fail, it looks for if-needed functions. FGET-Z is similar in that it looks for values, defaults, and if-needed functions. It is different in that it exhausts each frame in the AKO chain before moving up. Note the mnemonic use of the letters I, N, and Z: FGET-I makes one trip up the AKO chain looking only at values; FGET-N goes up once, then starts over and goes up again, forming an N if the path is drawn on paper; and FGET-Z goes up only once, as does GET-I, but it looks at defaults and functions, as well as values, following a sort of zig-zag pattern.

These new functions make it possible to put values, defaults, and if-needed functions in the most general places possible. For example, it is no longer necessary to place the CALCULATE-WEIGHT if-needed function in the PAUL frame and in every other man frame. Instead it is placed in the MAN frame where it is accessible whenever any effort is made to find the weight of a man using FGET-N or FGET-Z:

```
(FPUT 'MAN 'WEIGHT 'IF-NEEDED 'CALCULATE-WEIGHT)
```

Problems

Problem 22-3: Define FGETCLASSES, a function that returns a list of all frames that a given frame is linked to by an AKO path. Be sure that no frame in the list is returned more than once.

Problem 22-4: Define FGET-Z.

Problem 22-5: Define FGET-N.

FPUT+ and FREMOVE+ Activate Demons

If-needed functions are useful when a value is wanted, yet no value or default is explicitly given. If-added and if-removed functions are useful when the addition or removal of a value should cause some secondary action. Suppose, for example, that Paul's weight should be calculated whenever her height is specified. This could be arranged by way of using CALCULATE-WEIGHT as an if-added function. Before it was thought of as an if-needed function residing in the IF-NEEDED facet of the WEIGHT slot. Now we can think of it as an if-added function residing in the IF-ADDED facet of the HEIGHT slot:

```
(FPUT 'PAUL 'HEIGHT 'IF-ADDED 'CALCULATE-WEIGHT)
```

It would make more sense, however, to put the function in the MAN frame, if indeed the calculation makes sense for men in general:

```
(FPUT 'MAN 'HEIGHT 'IF-ADDED 'CALCULATE-WEIGHT)
```

Thus it is reasonable to activate the corresponding functions found by following AKO paths. Hence, the following function for using if-added functions makes sense:

```
(DEFUN FPUT+ (FRAME SLOT FACET VALUE)
     (COND ((FPUT FRAME SLOT FACET VALUE)
           (MAPCAR '(LAMBDA (E)              ;Use functions.
                         (MAPCAR 'FUNCALL
                                (FGET E SLOT 'IF-ADDED)))
                   (FGETCLASSES FRAME))
           VALUE)))
```

Again assume FGETCLASSES finds all frames that the given frame is linked to by an AKO path. Needless to say, the definition of FREMOVE+ would be very similar.

Problems

Problem 22-6: Define FREMOVE+.

Project: Connect the English interface of the previous chapter to a frame system.

Summary

◻ A frame is a generalized property list.

◻ Frames can be represented as nested association lists.

◻ FGET, FPUT, and FREMOVE are the basic frame-handling functions.

◻ Simple programs can exploit defaults and if-needed demons.

◻ Inheritance works through the AKO slot.

◻ FPUT+ and FREMOVE+ activate demons.

References

The paper that popularized frames is by Minsky [1975]. For more on frames and frame-like representations see Bobrow et al. [1977], Bruce [1975], Charniak [1978], and Roberts and Goldstein [1977a, 1977b]. Much of Schank's work can be viewed as in the spirit of and predating the work on frames. See Schank and Abelson [1977] for an overview.

23
LISP
IN
LISP

The best way of describing a procedure often is to give its definition in LISP. Since the evaluation of LISP functions surely is a procedure, it is reasonable to conclude that LISP itself might be usefully described in terms of a LISP. The purpose of this chapter is to show how this can be done. In particular, it presents an interpreter for MICRO, a sort of primitive, LISP-like language.

A Simple Symbol-manipulation Language can be Interpreted Easily

To keep things straight, let us begin with some naming conventions:

■ All names of functions in MICRO begin with M-. Thus M-CAR, M-CDR, and M-CONS are the MICRO analogs to CAR, CDR, and CONS in LISP.

■ All names of LISP-defined functions needed to implement MICRO begin with MICRO-. Thus MICRO-EVAL, MICRO-APPLY, and MICRO-R-E-P are all functions defined in LISP in order to interpret MICRO s-expressions.

MICRO-EVAL, MICRO-APPLY, and MICRO-R-E-P are the key functions of the interpreter. They will be explained first by short overview paragraphs and then by longer explanations accompanied by the function definitions:

■ MICRO-EVAL gets two arguments, an s-expression and an association list of variable values. The job of MICRO-EVAL is to classify the s-expression and to decide how it should be evaluated. If the s-espression is an atom, it uses the association list to find a value. Otherwise, it assumes the s-expression is a function with arguments and evaluates the arguments in the way that is appropriate for the function. Most functions require MICRO-EVAL to get help from MICRO-APPLY.

■ MICRO-APPLY gets three arguments, a function name or description, a list of arguments, and an association list of variable values. The job of MICRO-APPLY is to classify functions and to arrange for their proper application. MICRO-APPLY handles some simple functions directly. For others, MICRO-APPLY augments the association list of variable values and appeals to MICRO-EVAL for help. MICRO-APPLY often has to retrieve function definitions from the association list of variable values.

■ MICRO-R-E-P reads expressions to be evaluated, evaluates them, and prints the results. MICRO-R-E-P also arranges for function definitions to be stored on an association list to be supplied to MICRO-EVAL.

Now let us consider MICRO-EVAL in more detail. If the s-expression given to MICRO-EVAL is an atom other than T, NIL, or a number, its value is found on the association list of variable values and returned. If the s-expression begins with M-QUOTE, then the thing quoted is returned. If the s-expression begins with M-COND, evaluation is handled by an auxiliary function, MICRO-EVALCOND. Otherwise MICRO-EVAL evaluates all of the elements in the s-expression after the first, in left-to-right order, and passes them to MICRO-APPLY, along with a function name or description and the association list of variable values.

```
(DEFUN MICRO-EVAL (S ENVIRONMENT)
  (COND ((ATOM S)                                    ;Test for simple cases.
         (COND ((EQUAL S T) T)
               ((EQUAL S NIL) NIL)
               ((NUMBERP S) S)
               (T (MICRO-VALUE S ENVIRONMENT))))     ;Get value from environment.
        ((EQUAL (CAR S) 'M-QUOTE) (CADR S))
        ((EQUAL (CAR S) 'M-COND)                     ;Quoted?
         (MICRO-EVALCOND (CDR S) ENVIRONMENT))       ;Conditional?
        (T (MICRO-APPLY (CAR S)                       ;Apply function
                        (MAPCAR '(LAMBDA (X)          ;to evaluated arguments.
                                   (MICRO-EVAL X ENVIRONMENT))
                                (CDR S))
                        ENVIRONMENT)))))
```

The test for M-QUOTE in MICRO-EVAL is needed because MICRO needs something equivalent to QUOTE in LISP. M-QUOTE is the answer because unlike other functions, it refuses to evaluate its argument, thus protecting expressions in the same way LISP's QUOTE does.

If MICRO-APPLY is handed an expression whose first element is a primitive function like M-CAR, M-CDR, or M-CONS, it does the appropriate thing directly. If it is handed an expression whose first element is some other function name, it fetches a definition from the association list of values and recurses on itself. If it is handed an expression whose first element is a function definition, signaled by the atom M-DEFINITION, it augments the association list of values using MICRO-BIND and hands the baton back to MICRO-EVAL.

```
(DEFUN MICRO-APPLY (FUNCTION ARGS ENVIRONMENT)
  (COND ((ATOM FUNCTION)
         (COND ((EQUAL FUNCTION 'M-CAR) (CAAR ARGS))       ;Do basic things.
               ((EQUAL FUNCTION 'M-CDR) (CDAR ARGS))
               ((EQUAL FUNCTION 'M-CONS) (CONS (CAR ARGS) (CADR ARGS)))
               ((EQUAL FUNCTION 'M-ATOM) (ATOM (CAR ARGS)))
               ((EQUAL FUNCTION 'M-NULL) (NULL (CAR ARGS)))
               ((EQUAL FUNCTION 'M-EQUAL) (EQUAL (CAR ARGS) (CADR ARGS)))
               ((EQUAL FUNCTION 'M-TIMES) (TIMES (CAR ARGS) (CADR ARGS)))
               (T (MICRO-APPLY
                   (MICRO-EVAL FUNCTION ENVIRONMENT)       ;Get definition.
                   ARGS
                   ENVIRONMENT))))
        ((EQUAL (CAR FUNCTION) 'M-DEFINITION)              ;Use definition.
         (MICRO-EVAL (CADDR FUNCTION)
                     (MICRO-BIND (CADR FUNCTION) ARGS ENVIRONMENT)))))
```

From now on, it will be convenient to call a collection of variables and variable values an *environment*. Here we have implemented environments using association lists. The MICRO interpretation functions bind the atom ENVIRONMENT to such association lists.

The R-E-P in MICRO-R-E-P is a mnemonic for read-eval-print. If the expression read is a function definition, signaled by M-DEFUN, a function definition is placed in the environment. Otherwise, the expression is handed to MICRO-EVAL for evaluation.

```
(DEFUN MICRO-R-E-P ()
  (PROG (S ENVIRONMENT)
    LOOP
    (SETQ S (READ))
    (COND ((ATOM S)                                    ;S is an atom.
           (PRINT (MICRO-EVAL S ENVIRONMENT)))
          ((EQUAL (CAR S) 'M-DEFUN)                    ;S is a definition.
           (SETQ ENVIRONMENT                           ;Store definition.
                 (CONS (LIST (CADR S)
                             (CONS 'M-DEFINITION
                                   (CDDR S)))
                       ENVIRONMENT))
           (PRINT (CADR S)))
          (T (PRINT (MICRO-EVAL S ENVIRONMENT))))      ;Evaluate s.
    (GO LOOP)))                                        ;Repeat.
```

To see how all this fits together, let us define a function in MICRO and walk through an example using it. To keep things simple, our function will be equivalent to M-CAR, simply returning the first element of a list supplied as an argument. First we activate the read-eval-print loop by calling MICRO-R-E-P. Then we supply the definition for M-1ST:

```
(MICRO-R-E-P)

(M-DEFUN M-1ST (L) (M-CAR L))
  M-1ST
```

Recognizing a function definition, MICRO-R-E-P, adds it to the value of ENVIRONMENT, which now has exactly one element:

```
((M-1ST (M-DEFINITION (L) (M-CAR L))))
```

Now suppose we try using M-1ST:

```
(M-1ST (M-QUOTE (A B C)))
```

Seeing that this is not a function definition, MICRO-R-E-P hands it off to MICRO-EVAL. The arguments to MICRO-EVAL are the s-expression to be evaluated and the environment supplied by the read-eval-print loop:

```
S:           (M-1ST (M-QUOTE (A B C)))

ENVIRONMENT: ((M-1ST (M-DEFINITION (L) (M-CAR L))))
```

Since the s-expression to be evaluated is neither an atom nor a special case, MICRO-EVAL hands things over to MICRO-APPLY, after evaluating the argument, (M-QUOTE (A B C)). Thus MICRO-APPLY gets these arguments:

FUNCTION: M-1ST

ARGS: (A B C)

ENVIRONMENT: ((M-1ST (M-DEFINITION (L) (M-CAR L))))

MICRO-APPLY does not recognize M-1ST as a primitive it knows how to handle. It therefore looks up the value of M-1ST in the environment and recursively calls itself, this time with these arguments:

FUNCTION: (M-DEFINITION (L) (M-CAR L))

ARGS: (A B C)

ENVIRONMENT: ((M-1ST (M-DEFINITION (L) (M-CAR L))))

Now MICRO-APPLY, recognizing that the value of FUNCTION is a function definition, augments the value of ENVIRONMENT to record that L is bound to (A B C). Having done so, MICRO-EVAL is called. The s-expression handed to MICRO-EVAL is the body of the definition of M-1ST and the environment is the newly augmented value of ENVIRONMENT:

S: (M-CAR L)

ENVIRONMENT: ((L (A B C))
                 (M-1ST (M-DEFINITION (L) (M-CAR (M-CDR L)))))

MICRO-EVAL finds the value for L in the environment, and hands these arguments back to MICRO-APPLY:

FUNCTION: M-CAR

ARGS: (A B C)

ENVIRONMENT: ((L (A B C))
                 (M-1ST (M-DEFINITION (L) (M-CAR (M-CDR L)))))

Finally, something can be done directly. MICRO-APPLY recognizes the M-CAR primitive and returns A. This is passed all the way up and returned as the value of the original s-expression. The PRINT in MICRO-R-E-P prints it.

Having seen a simple example, it is time to present the auxiliary functions. One handles the special syntax of M-COND, one pairs variables with values and augments an association list, and one retrieves values from an association list:

```
(DEFUN MICRO-EVALCOND (CLAUSES ENVIRONMENT)
       (COND ((NULL CLAUSES) NIL)
             ((MICRO-EVAL (CAAR CLAUSES) ENVIRONMENT)
              (MICRO-EVAL (CADAR CLAUSES) ENVIRONMENT))
             (T (MICRO-EVALCOND (CDR CLAUSES) ENVIRONMENT))))

(DEFUN MICRO-BIND (KEY-LIST VALUE-LIST A-LIST)
       (COND ((OR (NULL KEY-LIST) (NULL VALUE-LIST)) A-LIST)
             (T (CONS (LIST (CAR KEY-LIST) (CAR VALUE-LIST))
                      (MICRO-BIND (CDR KEY-LIST) (CDR VALUE-LIST) A-LIST)))))

(DEFUN MICRO-VALUE (KEY A-LIST)
       (CADR (ASSOC KEY A-LIST)))
```

Note that the definition of MICRO-EVALCOND permits M-CONDs to have only clauses with exactly two elements.

This concludes the basic development of MICRO. From here, more and more power can be developed by bootstrapping, using MICRO's own function-defining mechanism. M-APPEND, for example, can be defined in terms of the primitives:

```
(M-DEFUN M-APPEND (L1 L2)
         (M-COND ((M-NULL L1) L2)
                 (T (M-CONS (M-CAR L1)
                            (M-APPEND (M-CDR L1) L2)))))
```

Both Dynamic and Lexical Variable Binding may be Arranged

In MICRO, the values of all variables in the body of a function are determined by the current environment. The environment is constantly changing as it is passed back and forth between MICRO-APPLY and MICRO-EVAL. The way the changes take place determine whether MICRO functions have so-called dynamic free variables or so-called lexical free variables.

Before defining these terms and explaining the difference, it is helpful to develop an example that requires two new features. The first new feature makes M-SETQ possible. It requires an addition to MICRO-EVAL and the definition of MICRO-SETQ (see Problem 23-1). The addition to MICRO-EVAL looks like this:

```
.
.
((EQUAL (CAR S) 'M-SETQ)
 (MICRO-SETQ (CADR S) (CADDR S) ENVIRONMENT))
.
.
```

The second feature enables function definition through M-LAMBDA expressions. It also requires an addition to MICRO-EVAL:

```
.
.
((EQUAL (CAR S) 'M-LAMBDA)                          ;temporary addition
 (LIST 'M-DEFINITION (CADR S) (CADDR S)))
.
.
```

The M-LAMBDA feature makes it possible to define M-DO-IT-TWICE, a function that has two arguments, the first being an M-LAMBDA expression. M-DO-IT-TWICE uses the function defined by the M-LAMBDA expression on the second argument and then uses the function again on the result:

```
(M-DEFUN M-DO-IT-TWICE (F X) (F (F X)))
  M-DO-IT-TWICE
```

Now we can use the function to get the following results:

```
(M-SETQ Y 3)
  3

(M-DO-IT-TWICE (M-LAMBDA (N) (M-TIMES N Y)) 2)
  18

(M-DO-IT-TWICE (M-LAMBDA (L) (M-CONS Y L)) NIL)
  (3 3)
```

These are sensible results. In the first example the M-LAMBDA expression called for multiplication by 3 and it was done twice, once to 2 and once to the result of 3 times 2. In the second example, the M-LAMBDA expression called for adding 3 to the front of a list and it was done twice, once to the empty list and once to the result of adding 3 to the empty list.

Why then do we get different results by just changing the Ys to Xs?

```
(M-SETQ X 3)
  3
```

```
(M-DO-IT-TWICE (M-LAMBDA (N) (M-TIMES N X)) 2)
   8
```

```
(M-DO-IT-TWICE (M-LAMBDA (L) (M-CONS X L)) NIL)
   (NIL NIL)
```

The answer has to do with the fact that X appears as a parameter in the definition of M-DO-IT-TWICE, but Y does not. By the time the bodies of the M-LAMBDA expressions are evaluated, M-DO-IT-TWICE has added (X 2) to the front of ENVIRONMENT, preventing MICRO-VALUE from getting to that part of ENVIRONMENT where X is associated with 3.

It is generally agreed that this is bad. The free-variable values in force when the body of the M-LAMBDA expression is evaluated should be those in force when the M-LAMBDA expression was first encountered. Thankfully, it is easy to arrange for this with two small changes. The first is to MICRO-EVAL. Instead of converting M-LAMBDA expressions into M-DEFINITION definitions, they are converted into M-CLOSURE definitions with the current value of ENVIRONMENT attached as a fourth element:

```
   .
   .
 ((EQUAL (CAR S) 'M-LAMBDA)
  (LIST 'M-CLOSURE (CADR S) (CADDR S) ENVIRONMENT))
   .
   .
```

The second change is to MICRO-APPLY, enabling the recognition of the new M-CLOSURE definitions. When one is recognized, its fourth-element association list is used instead of the current value of ENVIRONMENT by MICRO-BIND:

```
   .
   .
 ((EQUAL (CAR FUNCTION) 'M-CLOSURE)
  (MICRO-EVAL (CADDR FUNCTION)
              (MICRO-BIND (CADR FUNCTION) ARGS (CADDDR FUNCTION))))
   .
   .
```

Now the examples with M-DO-IT-TWICE work no matter what free variables are used in the M-LAMBDA expression given as the first argument. This is because the M-LAMBDA expression was immediately converted into a M-CLOSURE definition when it was first encountered. The M-CLOSURE definition has the current value of ENVIRONMENT attached.

■ Insuring that a functional argument gets the correct environment when it is applied is called the *functional argument problem* or the *funarg problem*.

■ Attaching an environment to a function definition is called *closure*.

■ When function closure is done at definition time, the function is said to have *lexical free variables*.

■ When function closure is done at evaluation time, the function is said to have *dynamic free variables*.

When a function has lexical free variables, the value of a particular free variable is always found in one place, given our association list implementation. This is because the environment attached to the function definition never becomes longer or shorter. When a function has dynamic free variables, however, the value of a particular variable is not necessarily found in one place. This is because the environment grows and shrinks.

As now arranged, MICRO functions defined by M-DEFUN have dynamic free variables because the functions are implicitly closed at evaluation time. On the other hand, MICRO functions defined by M-LAMBDA have lexical free variables because the functions are explicitly closed at the time the M-LAMBDA expressions are encountered and converted into M-CLOSURE definitions.

MICRO-EVAL and MICRO-APPLY now look like this:

```
(DEFUN MICRO-EVAL (S ENVIRONMENT)
       (COND ((ATOM S)
                   (COND ((EQUAL S T) T)
                         ((EQUAL S NIL) NIL)
                         ((NUMBERP S) S)
                         (T (MICRO-VALUE S ENVIRONMENT))))
             ((EQUAL (CAR S) 'M-QUOTE) (CADR S))
             ((EQUAL (CAR S) 'M-COND)
              (MICRO-EVALCOND (CDR S) ENVIRONMENT))
             ((EQUAL (CAR S) 'M-SETQ)
              (MICRO-SETQ (CADR S) (CADDR S) ENVIRONMENT))
             ((EQUAL (CAR S) 'M-LAMBDA)
              (LIST 'M-CLOSURE (CADR S) (CADDR S) ENVIRONMENT))
             (T (MICRO-APPLY (CAR S)
                      (MAPCAR '(LAMBDA (X)
                                        (MICRO-EVAL X ENVIRONMENT))
                              (CDR S))
                      ENVIRONMENT))))
```

```
(DEFUN MICRO-APPLY (FUNCTION ARGS ENVIRONMENT)
  (COND ((ATOM FUNCTION)
         (COND ((EQUAL FUNCTION 'M-CAR) (CAAR ARGS))
               ((EQUAL FUNCTION 'M-CDR) (CDAR ARGS))
               ((EQUAL FUNCTION 'M-CONS) (CONS (CAR ARGS) (CADR ARGS)))
               ((EQUAL FUNCTION 'M-ATOM) (ATOM (CAR ARGS)))
               ((EQUAL FUNCTION 'M-NULL) (NULL (CAR ARGS)))
               ((EQUAL FUNCTION 'M-EQUAL) (EQUAL (CAR ARGS) (CADR ARGS)))
               ((EQUAL FUNCTION 'M-TIMES) (TIMES (CAR ARGS) (CADR ARGS)))
               (T (MICRO-APPLY (MICRO-EVAL FUNCTION ENVIRONMENT)
                               ARGS
                               ENVIRONMENT))))
        ((EQUAL (CAR FUNCTION) 'M-DEFINITION)
         (MICRO-EVAL (CADDR FUNCTION)
                     (MICRO-BIND (CADR FUNCTION) ARGS ENVIRONMENT)))
        ((EQUAL (CAR FUNCTION) 'M-CLOSURE)
         (MICRO-EVAL (CADDR FUNCTION)
                     (MICRO-BIND (CADR FUNCTION) ARGS (CADDDR FUNCTION)))))))
```

Problems

Problem 23-1: Implement MICRO-SETQ. Be sure that it works even if the variable to be set is not yet in the environment.

Problem 23-2: Modify MICRO-EVAL so that it recognizes M-CLOSE, a function that converts a procedure definition from dynamic to lexical form. Given the name of a previously defined function, M-CLOSE is to change the entry for the function in the environment, converting

(M-DEFINITION <parameters> <body>)

into

(M-CLOSURE <parameters> <body> <environment>)

The actual work is to be done by the function MICRO-CLOSE. It finds the function definition in the environment supplied, alters it to begin with M-CLOSURE, and establishes the environment supplied as the one to be used for free variable values.

Problem 23-3: As it stands now, closure of MICRO's dynamic functions is done implicitly at evaluation time. Alter MICRO-APPLY so that the closure is explicit.

Problem 23-4: Why should functions defined by M-DEFUN have dynamic free variables?

LISP is Best Defined in LISP

It may seem weird, but MICRO could be made into a language much like LISP itself. This means that LISP can be described using LISP. But keep in mind that functions describe processes. Since LISP interpretation is a process and since LISP itself is a clear, transparent language, the LISP evaluation process might just as well be described by a set of functions in LISP!

▪ Describing how LISP works using LISP as a tool is like the way a dictionary defines words in terms of other, presumably simpler words. LISP can be defined in terms of a small number of core functions whose definitions are primitives.

That this can be done using only EVAL, APPLY, and a few other simple functions is suggestive, for it means that a primitive LISP can be created by implementing a few functions in another, lower-level implementation language using the LISP descriptions as a guide.

Fancy Control Structures Usually Start out as Basic LISP Interpreters

Inserting a layer of interpretation is the first step toward implementing fancy control structures. An interpreter interposed between the standard LISP evaluation procedure and a user's function provides the programming-language surgeon with a place to make incisions. There is no need to tamper with the offered version of a LISP interpreter. Instead, it is possible to frolic at will in the more exposed LISP-level implementation. This is the way many very-high-level languages are first implemented and tested. There is usually a severe price to pay, however. The extra layer of interpretation generally brings along a grotesque reduction in speed.

Summary

▪ A simple symbol-manipulation language can be interpreted easily.

▪ Both dynamic and lexical variable binding may be arranged.

▪ LISP is best defined in LISP.

◘ Fancy control structures usually start out as basic LISP interpreters.

References

For a sparklingly clear treatment of the funarg problem, see Moses [1970]. For a sparklingly clear treatment of LISP interpretation in LISP, see Steele and Sussman [1978].

ANSWERS
TO THE
PROBLEMS

Solutions to Problems in Chapter 2

Answer 2-1:

ATOM	atom, s-expression
(THIS IS AN ATOM)	list, s-expression
(THIS IS AN S-EXPRESSION)	list, s-expression
((A B) (C D))	list, s-expression
3	atom, s-expression
(3)	list, s-expression
(LIST 3)	list, s-expression
(QUOTIENT (ADD1 3) (SUB1 3))	list, s-expression
)(	malformed expression
((()))	list, s-expression
(() ())	list, s-expression

```
((())                      malformed expression

())(                       malformed expression

((ABC                      malformed expression
```

Answer 2-2:

```
(QUOTIENT (ADD1 3) (SUB1 3))
  2

(TIMES (MAX 3 4 5) (MIN 3 4 5))
  15

(MIN (MAX 3 1 4) (MAX 2 7 1))
  4
```

Answer 2-3:

```
(CAR '(P H W))
  P

(CDR '(B K P H))
  (K P H)

(CAR '((A B) (C D)))
  (A B)

(CDR '((A B) (C D)))
  ((C D))

(CAR (CDR '((A B) (C D))))
  (C D)

(CDR (CAR '((A B) (C D))))
  (B)

(CDR (CAR (CDR '((A B) (C D)))))
  (D)

(CAR (CDR (CAR '((A B) (C D)))))
  B
```

Answer 2-4:

```
(CAR (CDR (CAR (CDR '((A B) (C D) (E F)))))))
   D

(CAR (CAR (CDR (CDR '((A B) (C D) (E F)))))))
   E

(CAR (CAR (CDR '(CDR ((A B) (C D) (E F)))))))
  (A B)

(CAR (CAR '(CDR (CDR ((A B) (C D) (E F)))))))
   ERROR

(CAR '(CAR (CDR (CDR ((A B) (C D) (E F)))))))
   CAR

'(CAR (CAR (CDR (CDR ((A B) (C D) (E F)))))))
  (CAR (CAR (CDR (CDR ((A B) (C D) (E F))))))
```

Answer 2-5:

```
(CAR (CDR (CDR '(APPLE ORANGE PEAR GRAPEFRUIT))))

(CAR (CAR (CDR '((APPLE ORANGE) (PEAR GRAPEFRUIT)))))

(CAR (CAR (CDR (CDR (CAR '(((APPLE) (ORANGE) (PEAR) (GRAPEFRUIT)))))))))

(CAR (CAR (CAR (CDR (CDR '(APPLE (ORANGE) ((PEAR)) (((GRAPEFRUIT))))))))))

(CAR (CAR (CDR (CDR '((((APPLE))) ((ORANGE)) (PEAR) GRAPEFRUIT)))))

(CAR (CDR (CAR '(((((APPLE) ORANGE) PEAR) GRAPEFRUIT))))
```

Answer 2-6:

```
(SET 'TOOLS (LIST 'HAMMER 'SCREWDRIVER))
  (HAMMER SCREWDRIVER)

(CONS 'PLIERS TOOLS)
  (PLIERS HAMMER SCREWDRIVER)
```

```
TOOLS
  (HAMMER SCREWDRIVER)

(SET 'TOOLS (CONS 'PLIERS TOOLS))
  (PLIERS HAMMER SCREWDRIVER)

TOOLS
  (PLIERS HAMMER SCREWDRIVER)

(APPEND '(SAW WRENCH) TOOLS)
  (SAW WRENCH PLIERS HAMMER SCREWDRIVER)

TOOLS
  (PLIERS HAMMER SCREWDRIVER)

(SET 'TOOLS (APPEND '(SAW WRENCH) TOOLS))
  (SAW WRENCH PLIERS HAMMER SCREWDRIVER)

TOOLS
  (SAW WRENCH PLIERS HAMMER SCREWDRIVER)
```

Answer 2-7:

```
(LENGTH '(PLATO SOCRATES ARISTOTLE))
  3

(LENGTH '((PLATO) (SOCRATES) (ARISTOTLE)))
  3

(LENGTH '((PLATO SOCRATES ARISTOTLE)))
  1

(REVERSE '(PLATO SOCRATES ARISTOTLE))
  (ARISTOTLE SOCRATES PLATO)

(REVERSE '((PLATO) (SOCRATES) (ARISTOTLE)))
  ((ARISTOTLE) (SOCRATES) (PLATO))

(REVERSE '((PLATO SOCRATES ARISTOTLE)))
  ((PLATO SOCRATES ARISTOTLE))
```

Answer 2-8:

```
(LENGTH '((CAR CHEVROLET) (DRINK COKE) (CEREAL WHEATIES)))
  3

(REVERSE '((CAR CHEVROLET) (DRINK COKE) (CEREAL WHEATIES)))
  ((CEREAL WHEATIES) (DRINK COKE) (CAR CHEVROLET))

(APPEND '((CAR CHEVROLET) (DRINK COKE))
        (REVERSE '((CAR CHEVROLET) (DRINK COKE))))
  ((CAR CHEVROLET) (DRINK COKE) (DRINK COKE) (CAR CHEVROLET))
```

Answer 2-9:

```
(SUBST 'OUT 'IN '(SHORT SKIRTS ARE IN))
  (SHORT SKIRTS ARE OUT)

(SUBST 'IN 'OUT '(SHORT SKIRTS ARE IN))
  (SHORT SKIRTS ARE IN)

(LAST '(SHORT SKIRTS ARE IN))
  (IN)
```

Answer 2-10:

```
(SETQ METHOD1 'PLUS)
  PLUS

(SETQ METHOD2 'DIFFERENCE)
  DIFFERENCE

(SETQ METHOD METHOD1)
  PLUS

METHOD
  PLUS

(EVAL METHOD)
  ERROR

(SETQ METHOD 'METHOD1)
  METHOD1
```

```
METHOD
   METHOD1

(EVAL METHOD)
   PLUS

(EVAL (EVAL '(QUOTE METHOD)))
   METHOD1
```

Solutions to Problems in Chapter 3

Answer 3-1:

```
(DEFUN FIRST (S)
       (CAR S))

(DEFUN REST (S)
       (CDR S))

(DEFUN INSERT (ELEMENT S)
       (CONS ELEMENT S))
```

Answer 3-2:

```
(DEFUN ROTATE-L (L)
       (APPEND (CDR L) (LIST (CAR L))))
```

Answer 3-3:

```
(DEFUN ROTATE-R (L)
       (APPEND (LAST L) (REVERSE (CDR (REVERSE L)))))
```

Answer 3-4:

```
(DEFUN PALINDROMIZE (L)
       (APPEND L (REVERSE L)))
```

Answer 3-5:

```
(DEFUN F-TO-C (TEMPERATURE)
       (DIFFERENCE (QUOTIENT (PLUS TEMPERATURE 40)
                             1.8)
                   40))

(DEFUN C-TO-F (TEMPERATURE)
       (DIFFERENCE (TIMES (PLUS TEMPERATURE 40)
                          1.8)
                   40))
```

Answer 3-6:

```
(DEFUN ROOTS (A B C)
       (LIST (QUOTIENT (PLUS (MINUS B)
                             (SQRT (DIFFERENCE (TIMES B B)
                                               (TIMES 4.0 A C))))
                       (TIMES 2.0 A))
             (QUOTIENT (DIFFERENCE (MINUS B)
                                   (SQRT (DIFFERENCE (TIMES B B)
                                                     (TIMES 4.0 A C))))
                       (TIMES 2.0 A))))
```

Answer 3-7:

```
(DEFUN EVENP (N)
       (ZEROP (REMAINDER N 2)))
```

Answer 3-8:

```
(DEFUN PALINDROMEP (L)
       (EQUAL L (REVERSE L)))
```

Answer 3-9:

```
(DEFUN RIGHTP (H S1 S2)
       (LESSP (ABS (DIFFERENCE (TIMES H H)
                               (PLUS (TIMES S1 S1)
                                     (TIMES S2 S2))))
              (TIMES .02 H H)))
```

Answer 3-10:

```
(DEFUN COMPLEXP (A B C)
       (LESSP (DIFFERENCE (TIMES B B)
                          (TIMES 4.0 A C)) 0))
```

Or, even simpler:

```
(DEFUN COMPLEXP (A B C)
       (LESSP (TIMES B B) (TIMES 4.0 A C)))
```

Answer 3-11:

```
(DEFUN NILCAR (S)
       (COND ((NULL S) NIL)
             (T (CAR S))))

(DEFUN NILCDR (S)
       (COND ((NULL S) NIL)
             (T (CDR S))))
```

Answer 3-12:

```
(DEFUN CHECK-TEMPERATURE (X)
       (COND ((GREATERP X 100.) 'RIDICULOUSLY-HOT)
             ((LESSP X 0) 'RIDICULOUSLY-COLD)
             (T 'OK)))
```

Answer 3-13:

```
(DEFUN CIRCLE (RADIUS)
       (LIST (TIMES 2 PI RADIUS)
             (TIMES PI RADIUS RADIUS)))
```

Solutions to Problems in Chapter 4

Answer 4-1:

It computes the depth to which a given s-expression is nested.

Answer 4-2:

It returns a copy of the s-expression it is given.

Answer 4-3:

```
(DEFUN SQUASH (S)
       (COND ((NULL S) NIL)
             ((ATOM S) (LIST S))
             (T (APPEND (SQUASH (CAR S))
                        (SQUASH (CDR S)))))))
```

Answer 4-4:

```
(DEFUN FIBONACCI (N)
       (FIBONACCI-AUX 1 1 1 N))

(DEFUN FIBONACCI-AUX (FO FN I N)
       (COND ((EQUAL I N) FN)                    ;Terminating condition.
             (T (FIBONACCI-AUX FN               ;f(n-1)
                        (PLUS FO FN)            ;f(n) + f(n-1)
                        (ADD1 I)                ;Count up
                        N))))                   ;until i = n.
```

Answer 4-5:

```
(DEFUN UNION (X Y)
       (COND ((NULL X) Y)
             ((MEMBER (CAR X) Y) (UNION (CDR X) Y))
             (T (CONS (CAR X) (UNION (CDR X) Y)))))
```

Answer 4-6:

```
(DEFUN INTERSECTION (X Y)
       (COND ((NULL X) NIL)
             ((MEMBER (CAR X) Y)
              (CONS (CAR X) (INTERSECTION (CDR X) Y)))
             (T (INTERSECTION (CDR X) Y))))
```

Answer 4-7:

```
(DEFUN LDIFFERENCE (IN OUT)
       (COND ((NULL IN) NIL)
             ((MEMBER (CAR IN) OUT) (LDIFFERENCE (CDR IN) OUT))
             (T (CONS (CAR IN) (LDIFFERENCE (CDR IN) OUT)))))
```

Answer 4-8:

The function INTERSECT will do the job. The following is a solution which does a little less work:

```
(DEFUN INTERSECTP (A B)
       (COND ((NULL A) NIL)
             ((MEMBER (CAR A) B) T)
             (T (INTERSECTP (CDR A) B))))
```

Answer 4-9:

Here is a simple solution using LDIFFERENCE defined in the previous exercise:

```
(DEFUN SAMESETP (A B)
       (NOT (OR (LDIFFERENCE A B)
                (LDIFFERENCE B A))))
```

Next, we show a solution using SUBSETP, a predicate which checks whether one set contains another:

```
(DEFUN SAMESETP (A B) (AND (SUBSETP A B)
                           (SUBSETP B A)))

(DEFUN SUBSETP (A B)
       (COND ((NULL A) T)
             ((MEMBER (CAR A) B) (SUBSETP (CDR A) B))
             (T NIL)))
```

Finally, we have a solution which uses FLUSH to remove atoms of one set from the other:

```
(DEFUN SAMESETP (A B)
       (COND ((NULL A) (NULL B))
             ((NULL B) (NULL A))
             (T (SAMESETP (CDR A)
                          (FLUSH (CAR A) B)))))
```

```
(DEFUN FLUSH (E S)
       (COND ((NULL S) NIL)
             ((EQUAL E (CAR S)) (CDR S))
             (T (CONS (CAR S) (FLUSH E (CDR S)))))))
```

Naturally there are many more ways to solve this problem.

Answer 4-10:

```
(DEFUN MOBILEP (M)
       (COND ((ATOM M) M)                        ;Simple case.
             (T (MOBILEP-AUX (CAR M)
                            (MOBILEP (CADR M))
                            (MOBILEP (CADDR M)))))))

(DEFUN MOBILEP-AUX (BEAM LEFT RIGHT)
       (AND LEFT                                 ;Left sub-mobile must be balanced.
            RIGHT                                ;Right sub-mobile must be balanced.
            (EQUAL LEFT RIGHT)                   ;The two must weight the same.
            (PLUS BEAM LEFT RIGHT)))             ;Total weight is the sum.
```


Answer 4-11:

```
(DEFUN COMPILE (S)
       (COMPILE-AUX 1 S))

(DEFUN COMPILE-AUX (R S)
       (COND ((ATOM S) (LIST (LIST 'MOVE R S)))
             (T (APPEND (COMPILE-AUX R (CADR S))
                       (COMPILE-AUX (ADD1 R) (CADDR S))
                       (LIST (LIST (OPCODE (CAR S)) R (ADD1 R)))))))

(DEFUN OPCODE (OP)
       (COND ((EQUAL OP '+) 'ADD)
             ((EQUAL OP '-) 'SUB)
             ((EQUAL OP '*) 'MUL)
             ((EQUAL OP '//) 'DIV)
             (T 'ERR)))
```

In some implementations of LISP, / is the "quoting" character used to suppress
any special significance of the following character. For this reason, we must use
//, where the effect of / is desired.

Answer 4-12:

```
(DEFUN WEIGHT (TREE)
      (COND ((ATOM TREE) 1)                          ;Easy case.
            (T (WEIGHT-AUX (WEIGHT (CADR TREE))      ;Left sub-tree.
                          (WEIGHT (CADDR TREE))))))) ;Right sub-tree.

(DEFUN WEIGHT-AUX (A B)
      (COND ((EQUAL A B) (ADD1 A))                   ;When weights are equal
            (T (MAX A B))))                          ;When they are unequal.
```

Answer 4-13:

```
(DEFUN COMPILE (S)
      (COMPILE-AUX 1 S))

(DEFUN COMPILE-AUX (R S)
      (COND ((ATOM S) (LIST (LIST 'MOVE R S)))
            ((GREATERP (WEIGHT (CADDR S))
                       (WEIGHT (CADR S)))
             (APPEND (COMPILE-AUX R (CADDR S))
                     (COMPILE-AUX (ADD1 R) (CADR S))
                     (LIST (LIST (OPCODE (CAR S)) (ADD1 R) R))
                     (LIST (LIST 'COPY R (ADD1 R)))))
            (T (APPEND (COMPILE-AUX R (CADR S))
                       (COMPILE-AUX (ADD1 R) (CADDR S))
                       (LIST (LIST (OPCODE (CAR S)) R (ADD1 R)))))))
```

Answer 4-14:

```
(DEFUN PLOT-LINE (LENGTH ANGLE)
      (CONNECT-LINE (PLUS X-OLD (TIMES LENGTH (COS ANGLE)))
                    (PLUS Y-OLD (TIMES LENGTH (SIN ANGLE)))))

(DEFUN CONNECT-LINE (X-NEW Y-NEW)
      (LINE X-OLD Y-OLD X-NEW Y-NEW)
      (SETQ X-OLD X-NEW Y-OLD Y-NEW))
```

Answer 4-15:

```
(DEFUN PSEUDO-SIN (N)
      (COND ((MINUSP N) (MINUS (PSEUDO-SIN (MINUS N))))
            ((GREATERP N 7) (PSEUDO-SIN (REMAINDER N 8)))
            ((GREATERP N 3) (MINUS (PSEUDO-SIN (DIFFERENCE N 4))))
            ((ZEROP N) 0.0)
            ((EQUAL N 1) SQRT-2)
            ((EQUAL N 2) 1.0)
            ((EQUAL N 3) SQRT-2)))
```

Here it is assumed that SQRT-2 is a free variable whose value is $2^{1/2}$.

Answer 4-16:

```
(DEFUN DRAGON-CURVE (LENGTH ANGLE SIGN)
      (COND ((LESSP LENGTH MIN-LENGTH) (PLOT-LINE LENGTH ANGLE))
            (T (DRAGON-CURVE (QUOTIENT LENGTH (SQRT 2.0))
                             (PLUS ANGLE (TIMES SIGN
                                               (QUOTIENT PI 4.0)))
                     +1.0)
               (DRAGON-CURVE (QUOTIENT LENGTH (SQRT 2.0))
                             (DIFFERENCE ANGLE (TIMES SIGN
                                                     (QUOTIENT PI 4.0)))
                     -1.0))))
```


Answer 4-17:

```
(DEFUN REWRITE (L)
      (COND ((ATOM L) L)
            ((EQUAL (CAR L) 'NAND)
             (LIST 'NAND
                   (REWRITE (CADR L))
                   (REWRITE (CADDR L))))
            ((EQUAL (CAR L) 'NOT)
             (REWRITE (LIST 'NAND (CADR L) T)))
            ((EQUAL (CAR L) 'AND)
             (REWRITE (LIST 'NOT
                           (LIST 'NAND (CADR L) (CADDR L)))))
            ((EQUAL (CAR L) 'OR)
             (REWRITE (LIST 'NAND
                           (LIST 'NOT (CADR L))
                           (LIST 'NOT (CADDR L)))))      ;Continued -->
```

```
            ((EQUAL (CAR L) 'XOR)
             (REWRITE (LIST 'AND
                            (LIST 'OR (CADR L) (CADDR L))
                            (LIST 'OR
                                  (LIST 'NOT (CADR L))
                                  (LIST 'NOT (CADDR L)))))))
            (T (LIST 'ERROR L))))
```

Answer 4-18:

```
(DEFUN DYNAMIC-RANGE (NUMBERS)
       (QUOTIENT (APPLY 'MAX NUMBERS)
                 (APPLY 'MIN NUMBERS)))
```

Answer 4-19:

```
(DEFUN FACTORIAL (N)
       (PROG (RESULT COUNTER)
             (SETQ RESULT 1)
             (SETQ COUNTER N)
             LOOP
             (COND ((ZEROP COUNTER) (RETURN RESULT)))
             (SETQ RESULT (TIMES COUNTER RESULT))
             (SETQ COUNTER (SUB1 COUNTER))
             (GO LOOP)))
```

Answer 4-20:

```
(DEFUN COALESCE (CLASSES)                          ;Equivalence classes.
       (PROG ()
             (COND ((NULL CLASSES) (RETURN NIL)))   ;Done?
             LOOP
             (COND ((OVERLAP (CAR CLASSES)          ;Expand first class?
                             (CDR CLASSES))
                    (SETQ CLASSES (COMBINE (CAR CLASSES)
                                          (CDR CLASSES)))
                    (GO LOOP))                       ;Yes, then start again.
                   (T (RETURN (CONS (CAR CLASSES)    ;No, work on rest.
                                    (COALESCE (CDR CLASSES)))))))))
```

```
(DEFUN OVERLAP (A CLASSES)                    ;Do classes overlap?
       (COND ((NULL CLASSES) NIL)             ;Done?
             ((INTERSECTP A (CAR CLASSES)))   ;Intersect with this class?
             (T (OVERLAP A (CDR CLASSES)))))   ;No, try other classes.

(DEFUN COMBINE (A CLASSES)                    ;Combine two classes.
       (COND ((NULL CLASSES) NIL)             ;Done (Error actually)
             ((INTERSECTP A (CAR CLASSES))    ;Is this the one?
              (CONS (UNION A (CAR CLASSES))   ;Yes, combine them.
                    (CDR CLASSES)))
             (T (CONS (CAR CLASSES)           ;No, try rest of classes.
                      (COMBINE A (CDR CLASSES))))))
```

Solutions to Problems in Chapter 5

Answer 5-1:

```
(DEFUN CONNECT (A B)
       (COND ((MEMBER B (GET A 'NEIGHBORS)) NIL)
             (T (PUTPROP A
                         (CONS B (GET A 'NEIGHBORS))
                         'NEIGHBORS)
                (CONNECT B A)
                T)))
```

Answer 5-2:

```
(DEFUN GRANDFATHER (X)
       (COND ((GET X 'FATHER)
              (GET (GET X 'FATHER) 'FATHER))))
```

Answer 5-3:

```
(DEFUN ADAM (X)
       (COND ((GET X 'FATHER)
              (ADAM (GET X 'FATHER)))
             (T X)))
```

Answer 5-4:

```
(DEFUN ANCESTORS (X)
       (COND ((NOT X) NIL)
             (T (CONS X (APPEND (ANCESTORS (GET X 'FATHER))
                                (ANCESTORS (GET X 'MOTHER)))))))
```

Answer 5-5:

```
(DEFUN DISTANCE (N1 N2)
       (SQRT (PLUS (SQUARE (DIFFERENCE (GET N1 'X) (GET N2 'X)))
                   (SQUARE (DIFFERENCE (GET N1 'Y) (GET N2 'Y))))))

(DEFUN SQUARE (X) (TIMES X X))
```

Answer 5-6:

```
(DEFUN FETCH (KEY A-LIST)
       (PROG (RESULT)
             (SETQ RESULT (ASSOC KEY A-LIST))
             (RETURN (COND (RESULT (CADR RESULT))
                           (T '?)))))
```

Note that the program has only one use of ASSOC for the sake of efficiency.

Answer 5-7:

```
(DEFUN LISTKEYS (A-LIST)
       (MAPCAR 'CAR A-LIST))
```

Answer 5-8:

```
(DEFUN TREND (OLD NEW)
       (SETQ NEW (ABS (DIFFERENCE (FETCH 'TEMPERATURE NEW) 98.6)))
       (SETQ OLD (ABS (DIFFERENCE (FETCH 'TEMPERATURE OLD) 98.6)))
       (COND ((GREATERP NEW OLD) 'SINKING)
             ((LESSP NEW OLD) 'IMPROVING)
             (T 'STABLE)))
```

Answer 5-9:

```
(DEFUN STUFF-MATRIX (L)
        (ARRAY MATRIX T (LENGTH L) (LENGTH (CAR L)))        ;Set up array.
        (STUFF-MATRIX-AUX 0. L))

(DEFUN STUFF-MATRIX-AUX (I L)
        (COND ((NULL L))
               (T (STUFF-ROW I 0. (CAR L))                  ;Go fill one row.
                  (STUFF-MATRIX-AUX (ADD1 I) (CDR L)))))

(DEFUN STUFF-ROW (I J SL)
        (COND ((NULL SL))
               (T (STORE (MATRIX I J) (CAR SL))             ;One element.
                  (STUFF-ROW I (ADD1 J) (CDR SL)))))
```

Solutions to Problems in Chapter 6

Answer 6-1:

```
(DEFUN PRESENTP (ITEM S)
        (COND ((EQUAL S ITEM) T)
               ((ATOM S) NIL)
               (T (APPLY 'OR (MAPCAR '(LAMBDA (E)
                                              (PRESENTP ITEM E))
                               S)))))
```

Solutions to Problems in Chapter 7

Answer 7-1:

```
(DEFUN MOVE-DISK (FROM TO)
        (PRINT (LIST 'MOVE (CAR (EVAL FROM))        ;Print out number,
                     'FROM FROM                     ;from pin,
                     'TO TO))                        ;and to pin.
        (COND ((NULL (EVAL FROM))
               (PRINT (LIST FROM 'EMPTY)))          ;No disks on pin.
              ((OR (NULL (EVAL TO))                 ;Either pin is empty
                   (GREATERP (CAR (EVAL TO))        ;or has larger disk
                             (CAR (EVAL FROM))))    ;than one moved.
                                                    ;Continued -->
```

```
          (SET TO (CONS (CAR (EVAL FROM))
                        (EVAL TO)))              ;Add to new stack.
          (SET FROM (CDR (EVAL FROM))))          ;Remove from old.
          (T (PRINT (LIST 'CANT 'MOVE            ;Illegal move.
                          (CAR (EVAL FROM))
                          'ONTO
                          (CAR (EVAL TO))))))
      (LIST (LIST 'MOVE (CAR (EVAL TO))          ;Number of disk
                  'FROM FROM                     ;moved from pin
                  'TO TO)))                       ;to this pin.

(DEFUN TOWER-OF-HANOI ()
      (TRANSFER 'A 'B 'C (LENGTH A)))
```

Answer 7-2:

```
(DEFUN ECHO1 ()
      (PROG ()
            LOOP
            (PRINT (READ))
            (GO LOOP)))

(DEFUN ECHO2 ()
      (PROG ()
            LOOP
            (PRINT (EVAL (READ)))
            (GO LOOP)))
```

Answer 7-3:

Using SQUASH, as defined in a previous problem, we have:

```
(DEFUN P (MESSAGE)
      (PRINT (SQUASH MESSAGE)))

(DEFUN PC (TRIGGER MESSAGE)
      (COND (TRIGGER (P MESSAGE))))

(DEFUN RQ (MESSAGE)
      (P MESSAGE)
      (EVAL (READ)))
```

Answer 7-4:

```
(DEFUN P1 (MESSAGE)
       (PROG ()
             (SETQ MESSAGE (SQUASH MESSAGE))
             (TERPRI)
             LOOP
             (COND (MESSAGE (PRINC (CAR MESSAGE))
                            (PRINC '| |)
                            (SETQ MESSAGE (CDR MESSAGE))
                            (GO LOOP))
                   (T (RETURN T)))))
```

Answer 7-5:

```
(DEFUN BOOKPRINT (MESSAGE)
             (TERPRI)
             (PRINC '| |)
             (PRIN1 MESSAGE))
```

Answer 7-6:

```
(DEFUN ATOMCAR (X)
       (CAR (EXPLODE X)))


(DEFUN ATOMCDR (X)
       (IMPLODE (CDR (EXPLODE X))))
```

Answer 7-7:

```
(DEFUN PRINT-MATRIX (N M)
       (PROG (I J)
             (SETQ I 0.)
             ROW-LOOP
             (COND ((EQUAL I N) (RETURN NIL)))
             (TERPRI)
             (SETQ J 0.)
             COLUMN-LOOP
             (COND ((EQUAL J M) (GO NEXT-ROW)))            ;Continued -->
```

```
                    (PRINC (MATRIX I J))
                    (PRINC '| |)
                    (SETQ J (ADD1 J))
                    (GO COLUMN-LOOP)
                    NEXT-ROW
                    (SETQ I (ADD1 I))
                    (GO ROW-LOOP)))
```

Answer 7-8:

```
(DEFUN FORM-ENTRY (FORM)
        (PROG (ROW COLUMN)
                (TOP-OF-SCREEN)                             ;Clear screen.
                (SETQ ROW 0. COLUMN 0.)                     ;Initialize.
                LOOP
                (COND ((NULL FORM) (RETURN NIL)))           ;See if all done.
                (GO-DOWN (CADAR FORM))                       ;Go to row.
                (GO-ACROSS (CADDAR FORM))                    ;Go to column.
                (COND ((ATOM (CAAR FORM))
                        (READ-WORD (CAAR FORM) (READ)))      ;Accept data.
                      (T (PRINT-WORDS (CAAR FORM))))         ;Print words.
                (SETQ FORM (CDR FORM))                       ;Advance to next.
                (GO LOOP)))

(DEFUN GO-DOWN (NEW-ROW)
        (COND ((GREATERP NEW-ROW ROW)
                (TERPRI)
                (SETQ ROW (ADD1 ROW)
                        COLUMN 0.)
                (GO-DOWN NEW-ROW))))

(DEFUN GO-ACROSS (NEW-COLUMN)
        (COND ((GREATERP NEW-COLUMN COLUMN)
                (PRINC '| |)
                (SETQ COLUMN (ADD1 COLUMN))
                (GO-ACROSS NEW-COLUMN))))

(DEFUN READ-WORD (NAME INFO)
        (SETQ COLUMN
                (PLUS COLUMN
                        (ADD1 (LENGTH (EXPLODE INFO)))))
        (SET NAME INFO))
```

```
(DEFUN PRINT-WORDS (WORDS)
    (COND ((NULL WORDS))
        (T (PRINC (CAR WORDS))
           (PRINC '| |)
           (SETQ COLUMN
               (PLUS COLUMN
                   (ADD1 (LENGTH (EXPLODE (CAR WORDS))))))
           (PRINT-WORDS (CDR WORDS))))))
```

Answer 7-9:

```
(DEFUN PRETTYPRINT (S) (PPAUX S 0 T))

(DEFUN PPAUX (S-EXP S-EXP-START NEWLINE)
    (PROG (ARG-START)
        (COND (NEWLINE (TERPRI) (SETQ COLUMN 0)))   ;Do carriage return?
        NEXTSPACE
        (COND ((LESSP COLUMN S-EXP-START)           ;Move out to starting place.
            (PRINC SP)
            (SETQ COLUMN (ADD1 COLUMN))
            (GO NEXTSPACE)))
        (COND ((ATOM S-EXP)                         ;If S is an atom, print it
            (PRINC S-EXP)
            (SETQ COLUMN                            ;and increase COLUMN.
                (PLUS COLUMN
                    (LENGTH (EXPLODE S-EXP)))))
           (T (PRINC LP)                            ;Print left paren.
              (SETQ COLUMN (ADD1 COLUMN))           ;Increment COLUMN.
              (PPAUX (CAR S-EXP) COLUMN NIL)        ;Prettyprint first element.
              (COND ((CDR S-EXP)                    ;If more,
                  (PRINC SP)                        ;print space
                  (SETQ COLUMN (ADD1 COLUMN))       ;increment COLUMN
                  (SETQ ARG-START COLUMN)           ;assign ARG-START
                  (PPAUX (CADR S-EXP) ARG-START NIL) ;prettyprint next
                  (MAPCAR '(LAMBDA (E)              ;and the rest
                               (PPAUX E ARG-START T))
                         (CDDR S-EXP))))            ;on new lines.
              (PRINC RP)                            ;Print right paren.
              (SETQ COLUMN (ADD1 COLUMN))))
        (RETURN S-EXP)))

(SETQ LP '|(|)
(SETQ RP '|)|)
(SETQ SP '| |)
```

Solutions to Problems in Chapter 8

Answer 8-1:

```
(DEFUN DEFINE FEXPR (DEFINITION)
       (EVAL (APPEND (LIST 'DEFUN
                           (CAAR DEFINITION)
                           (CDAR DEFINITION))
                     (CDR DEFINITION)))))
```

Answer 8-2:

```
(DEFUN DEFINE MACRO (DEFINITION)
       (APPEND (LIST 'DEFUN
                     (CAADR DEFINITION)
                     (CDADR DEFINITION))
               (CDDR DEFINITION)))
```

Answer 8-3:

```
(DEFUN FIRST MACRO (S)
       (CONS 'CAR (CDR S)))

(DEFUN REST MACRO (S)
       (CONS 'CDR (CDR S)))

(DEFUN INSERT MACRO (S)
       (CONS 'CONS (CDR S)))
```

Answer 8-4:

```
(DEFUN DOWHILE MACRO (X)
       (SUBST (CADDR X) 'ACTIVITY
              (SUBST (CADR X) 'TEST
                     '(PROG (RESULT)
                        START
                        (COND (TEST (SETQ RESULT ACTIVITY)
                                    (GO START))
                              (T (RETURN RESULT)))))))
```

The version shown here will work unless there is a variable conflict involving the variable RESULT. If RESULT is a variable in the expressions evaluated by DOWHILE, it will have the local, wrong value, instead of the value outside the PROG.

The potential variable conflict can be fixed by using a new atom instead of RESULT. This can by done by adding (SUBST (GENSYM) 'RESULT ... right after the (DEFUN DOWHILE MACRO (X) .... The answer to the next problem uses this method.

Answer 8-5:

```
(DEFUN DOUNTIL MACRO (X)
       (SUBST (GENSYM) 'RESULT
              (SUBST (CADDR X) 'ACTIVITY
                     (SUBST (CADR X) 'TEST
                            '(PROG (RESULT)
                                   START
                                   (COND (TEST (RETURN RESULT))
                                         (T (SETQ RESULT ACTIVITY)
                                            (GO START)))))))))
```

Answer 8-6:

```
(DEFUN FACTORIAL (N)
       (PROG (R)
             (SETQ R N)
             (DOUNTIL (ZEROP (SETQ N (SUB1 N)))
                      (SETQ R (TIMES R N)))
             (RETURN R)))
```

Answer 8-7:

```
(DEFUN LOGAND MACRO (X)
       (SUBST (CADR X) 'A (SUBST (CADDR X) 'B '(BOOLE 1 A B))))

(DEFUN LOGOR MACRO (X)
       (SUBST (CADR X) 'A (SUBST (CADDR X) 'B '(BOOLE 7 A B))))

(DEFUN LOGXOR MACRO (X)
       (SUBST (CADR X) 'A (SUBST (CADDR X) 'B '(BOOLE 6 A B))))
```

Answer 8-8:

```
(DEFUN PUSH MACRO (X)
       (LIST 'SETQ
             (CADDR X)
             (LIST 'CONS (CADR X) (CADDR X))))

(DEFUN POP MACRO (X)
       (LIST '(LAMBDA (FIRST SECOND) FIRST)
             (LIST 'CAR (CADR X))
             (LIST 'SETQ
                   (CADR X)
                   (LIST 'CDR (CADR X)))))
```

Answer 8-9:

```
(DEFUN LET MACRO (S)
       (CONS (CONS 'LAMBDA
                   (CONS (MAPCAR 'CAR
                                 (CADR S))
                         (CDDR S)))
             (MAPCAR 'CADR
                     (CADR S))))
```

Solutions to Problems in Chapter 9

Answer 9-1:

```
(DEFUN ENQUEUE MACRO (X)
       (LIST 'SETQ
             (CADDR X)
             (LIST 'NCONC
                   (CADDR X)
                   (LIST 'LIST
                         (CADR X)))))

(DEFUN DEQUEUE MACRO (X)
       (LIST '(LAMBDA (FIRST SECOND) FIRST)
             (LIST 'CAR
                   (CADR X))
             (LIST 'SETQ
                   (CADR X)
                   (LIST 'CDR
                         (CADR X)))))
```

Solutions to Problems in Chapter 10

Answer 10-1:

```
(DEFUN ORIENTATION (N M)                              ;n rows & m columns.
      (PROG (C-O-A I0 J0 A B C I J SUM)
            (SETQ C-O-A (CENTER N M)                  ;Find center of area first.
                  I0 (CAR C-O-A)
                  J0 (CADR C-O-A))
            (SETQ A 0 B 0 C 0 SUM 0)                  ;Reset sum accumulators.
            (SETQ I 0)
            LOOP-ROW
            (COND ((EQUAL I N) (GO FINISH)))          ;Done last row?
            (SETQ J 0)
            LOOP-COLUMN
            (COND ((EQUAL J M) (GO NEXT-ROW)))        ;Done last in row?
            (COND ((ZEROP (IMAGE I J)))               ;Ignore 0's in image.
                  (T (SETQ SUM (ADD1 SUM)
                           A (PLUS A (TIMES I I))
                           B (PLUS B (TIMES 2 I J))
                           C (PLUS C (TIMES J J)))))
            (SETQ J (ADD1 J))
            (GO LOOP-COLUMN)
            NEXT-ROW
            (SETQ I (ADD1 I))
            (GO LOOP-ROW)
            FINISH
            (SETQ A (DIFFERENCE A (TIMES SUM I0 I0))
                  B (DIFFERENCE B (TIMES 2 SUM I0 J0))
                  C (DIFFERENCE C (TIMES SUM J0 J0)))
            (COND ((AND (ZEROP B) (EQUAL A C))        ;Check if symmetrical.
                   (RETURN (APPEND C-O-A
                                  '(SYMMETRICAL)))))
            (RETURN (APPEND C-O-A                      ;Compute orientation.
                           (LIST (QUOTIENT (ATAN B
                                           (DIFFERENCE A C))
                                    2.0)))))))
```

Answer 10-2:   (see next page)

```
(DEFUN PROJECT (N M)
      (PROG (I J)
            (ARRAY ROW T N)                          ;Row sums.
            (ARRAY COLUMN T M)                       ;Column sums.
            (SETQ I 0)
            LOOP-ROW
            (COND ((EQUAL I N) (RETURN NIL)))
            (SETQ J 0)
            LOOP-COLUMN
            (COND ((EQUAL J M) (GO NEXT-ROW)))
            (COND ((ZEROP (IMAGE I J)))              ;Ignore 0's in image.
                (T (STORE (ROW I) (ADD1 (ROW I)))
                   (STORE (COLUMN J) (ADD1 (COLUMN J)))))
            (SETQ J (ADD1 J))
            (GO LOOP-COLUMN)
            NEXT-ROW
            (SETQ I (ADD1 I))
            (GO LOOP-ROW)))

(DEFUN CENTER (N M)
      (PROG (I J SUM-R SUM-C SUM-I SUM-J)
            (PROJECT N M)                            ;Row and column sums.
            (SETQ I 0 SUM-R 0 SUM-I 0)
            LOOP-ROW
            (COND ((EQUAL I N) (GO FINISH-ROW)))
            (SETQ SUM-R (PLUS SUM-R (ROW I))         ;Add up rows.
                  SUM-I (PLUS SUM-I (TIMES I (ROW I)))
                  I (ADD1 I))
            (GO LOOP-ROW)
            FINISH-ROW
            (SETQ J 0 SUM-C 0 SUM-J 0)
            LOOP-COLUMN
            (COND ((EQUAL J M) (GO FINISH-COLUMN)))
            (SETQ SUM-C (PLUS SUM-C (COLUMN J))      ;Add up columns.
                  SUM-J (PLUS SUM-J (TIMES J (COLUMN J)))
                  J (ADD1 J))
            (GO LOOP-COLUMN)
            FINISH-COLUMN
            (COND ((ZEROP SUM-R) (RETURN 'NO-OBJECT))
                  ((NOT (EQUAL SUM-R SUM-C)) (RETURN 'COUNTING-ERROR)))
            (RETURN (LIST (QUOTIENT (FLOAT SUM-I)
                                    (FLOAT SUM-R))
                          (QUOTIENT (FLOAT SUM-J)
                                    (FLOAT SUM-C)))))))
```

Answer 10-3:

```
(DEFUN ORIENTATION (N M)
        (PROG (C-O-A I0 J0 I J K SUM SUM-II SUM-IJ SUM-JJ SUM-KK)
             (SETQ C-O-A (CENTER N M)
                   I0 (CAR C-O-A)
                   J0 (CADR C-O-A))
             (SETQ I 0 SUM-II 0)
             LOOP-ROW
             (COND ((EQUAL I N) (GO FINISH-ROW)))
             (SETQ SUM-II (PLUS SUM-II (TIMES I I (ROW I)))
                   I (ADD1 I))
             (GO LOOP-ROW)
             FINISH-ROW
             (SETQ J 0 SUM-JJ 0)
             LOOP-COLUMN
             (COND ((EQUAL J M) (GO FINISH-COLUMN)))
             (SETQ SUM-JJ (PLUS SUM-JJ (TIMES J J (COLUMN J)))
                   J (ADD1 J))
             (GO LOOP-COLUMN)
             FINISH-COLUMN
             (SETQ K 0 SUM 0 SUM-KK 0)
             LOOP-DIAGONAL
             (COND ((EQUAL K (SUB1 (PLUS N M))) (GO FINISH-DIAGONAL)))
             (SETQ SUM (PLUS SUM (DIAGONAL K))
                   SUM-KK (PLUS SUM-KK (TIMES K K (DIAGONAL K)))
                   K (ADD1 K))
             (GO LOOP-DIAGONAL)
             FINISH-DIAGONAL
             (SETQ SUM-IJ (DIFFERENCE SUM-KK (PLUS SUM-II SUM-JJ)))
             (SETQ SUM-II (DIFFERENCE SUM-II (TIMES SUM I0 I0))
                   SUM-IJ (DIFFERENCE SUM-IJ (TIMES 2 SUM I0 J0))
                   SUM-JJ (DIFFERENCE SUM-JJ (TIMES SUM J0 J0)))
             (COND ((AND (ZEROP SUM-IJ) (EQUAL SUM-II SUM-JJ))
                    (RETURN (APPEND C-O-A
                                    '(SYMMETRICAL)))))
             (RETURN (APPEND C-O-A
                             (LIST (QUOTIENT (ATAN (FLOAT SUM-IJ)
                                                   (FLOAT (DIFFERENCE SUM-II
                                                                      SUM-JJ)))
                                             2.0)))))))
```

Answer 10-4:

```
(DEFUN IMAGE (I J)
       (LSH (LSH (PACKED I (QUOTIENT J 36.))
                 (REMAINDER J 36.))
            -35.))
```

Alternatively, using BOOLE, a function which computes the bit-wise logical AND of its second and third argument, when given a first argument of 1:

```
(DEFUN IMAGE (I J)
       (BOOLE 1
              1
              (LSH (PACKED I (QUOTIENT J 36.))
                   (DIFFERENCE (REMAINDER J 36.) 35.)))))
```

Answer 10-5:

```
(DEFUN DISTANCE (A B)
       (COND ((AND (NULL A) (NULL B)) 0.0)
             ((OR (NULL A) (NULL B)) (PRINT 'ERROR))
             (T (PLUS (TIMES (DIFFERENCE (CAR A) (CAR B))
                             (DIFFERENCE (CAR A) (CAR B)))
                      (DISTANCE (CDR A) (CDR B))))))
```

Answer 10-6:

If the stored feature lists are altered to contain pairs of mean and variance, DISTANCE can be easily changed as follows:

```
(DEFUN DISTANCE (A B)
       (COND ((AND (NULL A) (NULL B)) 0.0)
             ((OR (NULL A) (NULL B)) (PRINT 'ERROR))
             (T (PLUS (QUOTIENT (TIMES (DIFFERENCE (CAAR A) (CAR B))
                                       (DIFFERENCE (CAAR A) (CAR B)))
                                (CADAR A))
                      (DISTANCE (CDR A) (CDR B))))))
```

Answer 10-7:

```
(DEFUN MAKE-TABLE (L)                              ;Next & equivalent.
        (ARRAY MAPPING T (ADD1 (CAR L)))           ;Setup lookup table.
        (FILL-TABLE (COALESCE (CADR L))))          ;Fill using equivalences.

(DEFUN FILL-TABLE (CLASSES)                        ;Place result in table.
    (COND ((NULL CLASSES))                         ;Done?
          (T (FILL-CLASS (CAAR CLASSES)            ;First is representative.
                         (CAR CLASSES))            ;Rest labelled same.
             (FILL-TABLE (CDR CLASSES)))))         ;Then do other classes.

(DEFUN FILL-CLASS (N CLASS)                        ;Mapping for one class.
    (COND ((NULL CLASS))                           ;Done?
          (T (STORE (MAPPING (CAR CLASS)) N)       ;Put entry in table.
             (FILL-CLASS N (CDR CLASS)))))         ;Then do other elements.
```

The difficult part is making a set of equivalence classes for the labels using all the pairwise equivalences noted during the labelling process. Fortunately, we already solved that problem with COALESCE, defined in a problem near the end of Chapter 4.

Solutions to Problems in Chapter 11

Answer 11-1:

```
(DEFUN HILL (START FINISH)
    (PROG (QUEUE EXPANSION)
          (SETQ QUEUE (LIST (LIST START)))
          TRYAGAIN
          (COND ((NULL QUEUE) (RETURN NIL))
                ((EQUAL FINISH (CAAR QUEUE))
                 (RETURN (REVERSE (CAR QUEUE)))))
          (SETQ EXPANSION (EXPAND (CAR QUEUE)))
          (SETQ QUEUE (CDR QUEUE))
          (SETQ QUEUE (APPEND (SORT EXPANSION 'CLOSERP) QUEUE))
          (GO TRYAGAIN)))
```

Answer 11-2:

We can use the solution to the previous problem here if we just change the last four lines to read:

```
(SETQ EXPANSION (EXPAND (CAR QUEUE)))
(SETQ QUEUE (CDR QUEUE))
(SETQ QUEUE (SORT (APPEND EXPANSION QUEUE)
                  'SHORTERP))
(GO TRYAGAIN)))
```

where SHORTERP is defined as follows:

```
(DEFUN SHORTERP (P1 P2)
    (LESSP (PATHLENGTH P1) (PATHLENGTH P2)))

(DEFUN PATHLENGTH (L)
    (COND ((NULL (CDR L)) 0)
          (T (PLUS (DISTANCE (CAR L) (CADR L))
                   (PATHLENGTH (CDR L))))))
```

Answer 11-3:

Again, a simple change suffices; just replace the last four lines with:

```
(SETQ EXPANSION (MAPCAN 'EXPAND (FIRSTN QUEUE N)))
(SETQ QUEUE (SORT EXPANSION 'CLOSERP))
(GO TRYAGAIN)))
```

where FIRSTN is defined as follows:

```
(DEFUN FIRSTN (S N)
    (COND ((ZEROP N) NIL)
          ((NULL S) NIL)
          (T (CONS (CAR S) (FIRSTN (CDR S) (SUB1 N))))))
```

Answer 11-4:

RADIX-SORT does the right thing when the bit in the position sorted on is zero in all numbers or one in all numbers. In this case only one recursive call takes place; the array is not split in two. To speed up the handling of the case when BOTTOM equals TOP, one can add right after the PROG:

```
(COND ((EQUAL BOTTOM TOP) (RETURN NIL)))
```

Answer 11-5:

```
(DEFUN SORT-MERGE (L)
       (COND ((NULL (CDR L)) L)                          ;Only one element.
             (T (MERGE (SORT-MERGE (FIRST-HALF L))        ;Sort first half.
                       (SORT-MERGE (LAST-HALF L)))))))    ;Sort second half.


(DEFUN MERGE (A B)
       (COND ((NULL A) B)                                 ;Easy cases first.
             ((NULL B) A)                                 ;Easy cases first.
             ((LESSP (CAAR A) (CAAR B))                   ;Pick smaller of the
              (CONS (CAR A) (MERGE (CDR A) B)))           ;elements at front of
             (T (CONS (CAR B) (MERGE A (CDR B)))))))      ;the two lists.

(DEFUN FIRST-HALF (L)                         ;Get first half of list
       (HEAD L (QUOTIENT (LENGTH L) 2)))

(DEFUN LAST-HALF (L)                                      ;Get second half of list.
       (TAIL L (QUOTIENT (LENGTH L) 2)))

(DEFUN HEAD (L N)
       (COND ((ZEROP N) NIL)
             (T (CONS (CAR L) (HEAD (CDR L) (SUB1 N))))))

(DEFUN TAIL (L N)
       (COND ((ZEROP N) L)
             (T (TAIL (CDR L) (SUB1 N)))))
```

Answer 11-6:

```
(DEFUN SPLICEIN (ELEMENT S PREDICATE)
       (COND ((NULL S) (LIST ELEMENT))
             ((FUNCALL PREDICATE ELEMENT (CAR S))
              (CONS ELEMENT S))
             (T (CONS (CAR S) (SPLICEIN ELEMENT
                                        (CDR S)
                                        PREDICATE)))))
```

```
(DEFUN SORT (S PREDICATE)
      (COND ((NULL S) NIL)
            (T (SPLICEIN PREDICATE
                      (CAR S)
                      (SORT (CDR S) PREDICATE)))))
```

Answer 11-7:

```
(DEFUN WATER-CROCK-OPTIMUM (A B C)
      (WATER-CROCK-AUX (WATER-CROCK A B C)
                      (WATER-CROCK B A C)))

(DEFUN WATER-CROCK-AUX (SEQ-A SEQ-B)
      (COND ((NOT (GREATERP (LENGTH SEQ-A) (LENGTH SEQ-B))) SEQ-A)
            (T (SUBST 'B 'Z (SUBST 'A 'B (SUBST 'Z 'A SEQ-B))))))
```

Answer 11-8:

```
(DEFUN QUEEN (SIZE)
      (PROG (N M BOARD)
            (SETQ N 1)                              ;First row.
            LOOP-N
            (SETQ M 1)                              ;First column.
            LOOP-M
            (COND ((CONFLICT N M BOARD) (GO UN-DO-M)))  ;Check for conflict.
            (SETQ BOARD (CONS (LIST N M) BOARD))       ;Add queen to board.
            (COND ((GREATERP (SETQ N (ADD1 N)) SIZE)    ;Advance to next row.
                  (PRINT (REVERSE BOARD))))            ;Print if N placed.
            (GO LOOP-N)                               ;Go try find column.
            UN-DO-N
            (COND ((NULL BOARD) (RETURN 'FINISHED))    ;Tried all possibilities.
                  (T (SETQ M (CADAR BOARD)             ;Undo last decision
                        N (CAAR BOARD)                ;by removing queen
                        BOARD (CDR BOARD))))           ;placed last.
            UN-DO-M
            (COND ((GREATERP (SETQ M (ADD1 M)) SIZE)    ;Advance to next column.
                  (GO UN-DO-N))
                  (T (GO LOOP-M)))))
```

Answer 11-9:

```
(DEFUN BOARD-PRINT (BOARD)
      (PROG (SIZE)
            (SETQ SIZE (LENGTH BOARD))
            (BOARD-PRINT-AUX BOARD)))

(DEFUN BOARD-PRINT-AUX (BOARD)
      (TERPRI)
      (COND ((NULL BOARD))
            (T (BOARD-PRINT-SUB (CADAR BOARD) 1)
               (BOARD-PRINT-AUX (CDR BOARD)))))

(DEFUN BOARD-PRINT-SUB (COLUMN N)
      (COND ((GREATERP N SIZE))
            (T (COND ((EQUAL COLUMN N) (PRINC 'Q))
                     (T (PRINC '|.|)))
               (PRINC '| |)
               (BOARD-PRINT-SUB COLUMN (ADD1 N)))))
```

Solutions to Problems in Chapter 12

Answer 12-1:

```
(DEFUN PRE-TO-INF (L)
      (COND ((NULL L) NIL)
            ((ATOM L) L)                             ;Simple case.
            (T (LIST (PRE-TO-INF (CADR L))           ;Translate part.
                     (OPSYMBOL (CAR L))              ;Look up symbol.
                     (PRE-TO-INF (CADDR L))))))       ;Translate rest.

(DEFUN OPSYMBOL (X)                                  ;Get symbol
      (COND ((EQUAL X 'SETQ) '=)                      ;given LISP function.
            ((EQUAL X 'PLUS) '+)
            ((EQUAL X 'DIFFERENCE) '-)
            ((EQUAL X 'TIMES) '*)
            ((EQUAL X 'QUOTIENT) '//)
            ((EQUAL X 'REMAINDER) '\)
            ((EQUAL X 'EXPT) '^)
            (T X)))
```

Answer 12-2:

```
(DEFUN PRE-TO-INF (L WIN)
       (PROG (WOUT)
             (COND ((NULL L) (RETURN L))
                   ((ATOM L) (RETURN (LIST L))))
             (SETQ WOUT (PRECEDENCE (CAR L)))
             (RETURN (COND ((LESSP WOUT WIN)            ;Compare weights.
                            (LIST
                             (APPEND (PRE-TO-INF (CADR L) WOUT)
                                     (LIST (OPSYMBOL (CAR L)))
                                     (PRE-TO-INF (CADDR L) WOUT))))
                           (T (APPEND (PRE-TO-INF (CADR L) WOUT)
                                      (LIST (OPSYMBOL (CAR L)))
                                      (PRE-TO-INF (CADDR L) WOUT)))))))

(DEFUN PRECEDENCE (X)                                   ;Find weight
       (COND ((EQUAL X 'SETQ) 0)                        ;given LISP function.
             ((EQUAL X 'PLUS) 1)
             ((EQUAL X 'DIFFERENCE) 1)
             ((EQUAL X 'TIMES) 2)
             ((EQUAL X 'QUOTIENT) 3)
             ((EQUAL X 'REMAINDER) 3)
             ((EQUAL X 'EXPT) 4)
             (T 5)))
```

This version has a second parameter, WIN, which should be some larger number when the function is first called.

Answer 12-3:

```
            STUFF
            (COND (TRACE-FLG (PRINT (LIST 'AE AE))))
            (COND (TRACE-FLG (PRINT (LIST 'OPERATORS OPERATORS))))

            SCAN
            (COND (TRACE-FLG (PRINT (LIST 'AE AE))))
            (COND (TRACE-FLG (PRINT (LIST 'OPERANDS OPERANDS))))
```

Answer 12-4:

Simply replace (NOT (LESSP ... by (GREATERP ...

Answer 12-5:

Simply insert after the first COND following the label SCAN:

```
(COND ((AND AE                              ;Not at end of AE
             (OR (NOT (ATOM (CAR AE)))      ;and sub-list
                 (EQUAL (WEIGHT (CAR AE)) 4)))  ;or not operator.
          (SETQ AE (CONS '* AE)) (GO SCAN)))    ;Insert '*', go on.
```

Answer 12-6:

```
(DEFPROP DUMMY -1 WEIGHT)
(DEFPROP =  0 WEIGHT)
(DEFPROP +  1 WEIGHT)
(DEFPROP -  1 WEIGHT)
(DEFPROP *  2 WEIGHT)
(DEFPROP // 2 WEIGHT)
(DEFPROP \  2 WEIGHT)
(DEFPROP ^  3 WEIGHT)

(DEFPROP DUMMY DUMMY OPCODE)
(DEFPROP =  SETQ OPCODE)
(DEFPROP +  PLUS OPCODE)
(DEFPROP -  DIFFERENCE OPCODE)
(DEFPROP *  TIMES OPCODE)
(DEFPROP // QUOTIENT OPCODE)
(DEFPROP \  REMAINDER OPCODE)
(DEFPROP ^  EXPT OPCODE)

(DEFUN WEIGHT (OPERATOR) (GET OPERATOR 'WEIGHT))

(DEFUN OPCODE (OPERATOR) (GET OPERATOR 'OPCODE))
```

Answer 12-7:

In LISP implementations that use | to surround atom names containing break or separator characters one has to use /| as shown below:

```
(DEFPROP DUMMY -1 WEIGHT)
(DEFPROP =  0 WEIGHT)
(DEFPROP /| 1 WEIGHT)
(DEFPROP &  2 WEIGHT)
(DEFPROP <  3 WEIGHT)
```

```
(DEFPROP >  3 WEIGHT)
(DEFPROP +  4 WEIGHT)
(DEFPROP -  4 WEIGHT)
(DEFPROP *  5 WEIGHT)
(DEFPROP // 5 WEIGHT)
(DEFPROP \  5 WEIGHT)
(DEFPROP ^  6 WEIGHT)

(DEFPROP DUMMY DUMMY OPCODE)
(DEFPROP =  SETQ OPCODE)
(DEFPROP /| OR OPCODE)
(DEFPROP &  AND OPCODE)
(DEFPROP <  LESSP OPCODE)
(DEFPROP >  GREATERP OPCODE)
(DEFPROP +  PLUS OPCODE)
(DEFPROP -  DIFFERENCE OPCODE)
(DEFPROP *  TIMES OPCODE)
(DEFPROP // QUOTIENT OPCODE)
(DEFPROP \  REMAINDER OPCODE)
(DEFPROP ^  EXPT OPCODE)
```

Answer 12-8:

```
(DEFUN SPARSE-V-COMPONENT (V N)
       (COND ((NULL V) 0.0)
             ((GREATERP (CAAR V) N) 0.0)
             ((LESSP (CAAR V) N) (SPARSE-V-COMPONENT (CDR V) N))
             (T (CADAR V))))
```

Answer 12-9:

Simply add the following to the COND, just before the T-clause:

```
((ZEROP (PLUS (CADAR A) (CADAR B)))
 (SPARSE-V-PLUS (CDR A) (CDR B)))
```

Answer 12-10:

No. They could be negative too. In fact the indices could be floating point numbers! The only thing that matters is that they are ordered, so that the program can tell which list to proceed in when indices at the head of the two lists are not equal.

Answer 12-11:

```
(DEFUN SPARSE-M-PRINT (M)
       (COND ((NULL M) (TERPRI))
             (T (PRINT (CAR M))
                (SPARSE-M-PRINT (CDR M)))))
```

Answer 12-12:

Because of what may appear to be a superfluous extra layer of parentheses around the vectors representing the rows, it is easy to modify the function SPARSE-V-PLUS to add matrices instead of vectors. Simply change all calls to SPARSE-V-PLUS to SPARSE-M-PLUS, and all calls to PLUS to SPARSE-V-PLUS:

```
(DEFUN SPARSE-M-PLUS (A B)
       (COND ((NULL A) B)
             ((NULL B) A)
             ((LESSP (CAAR A) (CAAR B))
              (CONS (CAR A)
                    (SPARSE-M-PLUS (CDR A) B)))
             ((LESSP (CAAR B) (CAAR A))
              (CONS (CAR B)
                    (SPARSE-M-PLUS (CDR B) A)))
             (T (CONS (LIST (CAAR A)
                            (SPARSE-V-PLUS (CADAR A) (CADAR B)))
                      (SPARSE-M-PLUS (CDR A) (CDR B))))))
```

Answer 12-13:

```
(DEFUN SPARSE-M-TIMES-V (M V)
       (COND ((NULL M) NIL)
             (T (CONS (LIST (CAAR M)
                            (SPARSE-DOT-PRODUCT (CADAR M) V))
                      (SPARSE-M-TIMES-V (CDR M) V)))))
```

For example:

```
(SETQ MATRIX-A '((1. ((1. 2.0) (3. 4.0)))
                 (3. ((2. 1.0) (3. 4.0) (4. -5.0) (5. 7.0)))
                 (5. ((1. 0.5) (2. 3.0) (4. 9.0)))))

(SETQ VECTOR-A '((1. 3.0) (3. -1.0) (4. 2.0)))
```

```
(SPARSE-M-TIMES-V MATRIX-A VECTOR-A)
  ((1 2.0) (3 -14.0) (5 19.5))
```

Note, however, that this straightforward solution may lead to the inclusion of zero
elements when the dotproduct is zero.

Answer 12-14:

One way to find the transpose is to first expand the list representing the matrix
into one that is more symmetrical in the row and column indices:

```
(M-EXPAND '((1 ((2 1.2) (4 1.4)))
            (3 ((1 3.1) (5 3.5) (6 3.6)))
            (4 ((2 4.2) (3 4.3)))))
  ((1 2 1.2) (1 4 1.4) (3 1 3.1) (3 5 3.5) (3 6 3.6) (4 2 4.2) (4 3 4.3))

(DEFUN M-EXPAND (L)
      (COND ((NULL L) NIL)
            (T (APPEND (M-EXPAND-AUX (CAAR L) (CADAR L))
                       (M-EXPAND (CDR L))))))

(DEFUN M-EXPAND-AUX (I L)
      (COND ((NULL L) NIL)
            (T (CONS (LIST I (CAAR L) (CADAR L))
                     (M-EXPAND-AUX I (CDR L))))))
```

The function M-COMPRESS performs the inverse operation:

```
(DEFUN M-COMPRESS (L)
      (PROG (I ROW RESULT)
            OUTER-LOOP
            (COND ((NULL L) (RETURN (REVERSE RESULT))))
            (SETQ I (CAAR L)
                  ROW (LIST (CDAR L))
                  L (CDR L))
            ROW-LOOP
            (COND ((NULL L) (GO END-ROW))
                  ((NOT (EQUAL I (CAAR L))) (GO END-ROW)))
            (SETQ ROW (CONS (CDAR L) ROW)
                  L (CDR L))
            (GO ROW-LOOP)
            END-ROW
            (SETQ RESULT (CONS (LIST I (REVERSE ROW)) RESULT))
            (GO OUTER-LOOP)))
```

The row and column indices can be switched around using M-ALTER-FLIP:

```
(DEFUN M-ALTER-FLIP (L)
        (COND ((NULL L) NIL)
               (T (CONS (LIST (CADAR L) (CAAR L) (CADDAR L))
                        (M-ALTER-FLIP (CDR L))))))
```

Next, it is necessary to sort on the new row indices:

```
(DEFUN M-ALTER-SORT (L)
        (PROG (FINISH-FLG)
               LOOP
               (COND (FINISH-FLG (RETURN L)))
               (SETQ FINISH-FLG T
                     L (M-ALTER-AUX L))
               (GO LOOP)))
```

```
(DEFUN M-ALTER-AUX (L)
        (COND ((NULL (CDR L)) L)
               (T (M-ALTER-SUB (CAR L)
                               (M-ALTER-AUX (CDR L))))))
```

```
(DEFUN M-ALTER-SUB (E L)
        (COND ((GREATERP (CAR E) (CAAR L))
                (SETQ FINISH-FLG NIL)
                (CONS (CAR L) (CONS E (CDR L))))
               (T (CONS E L))))
```

Finally, all of this can be put together:

```
(DEFUN SPARSE-M-TRANSPOSE (L)
        (M-COMPRESS (M-ALTER-SORT (M-ALTER-FLIP (M-EXPAND L)))))
```


Answer 12-15:

```
(DEFUN SPARSE-M-TIMES (A B)
        (SPARSE-M-TRANSPOSE (SPARSE-M-TIMES-AUX A (SPARSE-M-TRANSPOSE B))))
```

```
(DEFUN SPARSE-M-TIMES-AUX (A B)
        (COND ((NULL B) NIL)
               ((CONS (LIST (CAAR B)
                            (SPARSE-M-TIMES-V A (CADAR B)))
                      (SPARSE-M-TIMES-AUX A (CDR B))))))
```

Answer 12-16:

It works just as well. Typically an answer is returned after 5 to 10 iterations. A zero argument must be tested for by adding the following to the conditional in SQUARE-ROOT:

```
((ZEROP Y) Y)
```

Answer 12-17:

The solution shown uses y as an initial estimate instead of 1 as did SQUARE-ROOT. This solution also will not work for some floating point arguments. These require a test for the condition $x_{n+2} = x_n$.

```
(DEFUN CUBE-ROOT (Y)
        (COND ((ZEROP Y) Y)
              (T (CUBE-ROOT-AUX Y
                                Y
                                (QUOTIENT (PLUS Y
                                                Y
                                                (QUOTIENT 1 Y))
                                          3)))))
```

```
(DEFUN CUBE-ROOT-AUX (Y XO XN)
       (COND ((EQUAL XN XO) XN)
             ((EQUAL XN (QUOTIENT Y (TIMES XO XO))) XN)
             (T (CUBE-ROOT-AUX Y
                               XN
                               (QUOTIENT (PLUS XN
                                               XN
                                               (QUOTIENT Y (TIMES XN XN)))
                                         3)))))
```

Answer 12-18:

```
(DEFUN C-SQRT (L)
       (C-SQRT-PUNT (CAR L)                          ;Real part.
                    (CADR L)                         ;Imaginary part.
                    (SQRT (PLUS (TIMES (CAR L)       ;Modulus.
                                       (CAR L))
                                (TIMES (CADR L)
                                       (CADR L)))))))
```

```
(DEFUN C-SQRT-PUNT (C D R)
      (COND ((MINUSP D)
              (LIST (SQRT (QUOTIENT (PLUS R C)                ;Real part.
                                    2.0))
                    (MINUS (SQRT (QUOTIENT (DIFFERENCE R C)   ;Imaginary.
                                           2.0)))))
            (T (LIST (SQRT (QUOTIENT (PLUS R C)              ;Real part.
                                     2.0))
                     (SQRT (QUOTIENT (DIFFERENCE R C)        ;Imaginary.
                                     2.0)))))))
```


Answer 12-19:

```
(DEFUN C-PLUS (A B)
      (LIST (PLUS (CAR A) (CAR B))
            (PLUS (CADR A) (CADR B))))

(DEFUN C-INVERSE (A)
      (C-INVERSE-AUX (CAR A)
                     (CADR A)
                     (PLUS (TIMES (CAR A) (CAR A))
                           (TIMES (CADR A) (CADR A)))))

(DEFUN C-INVERSE-AUX (R I S)
      (COND ((ZEROP S) (PRINT 'DIVISION-BY-ZERO))
            (T (LIST (QUOTIENT R S)
                     (MINUS (QUOTIENT I S))))))
```


Answer 12-20:

```
(DEFUN ADMITTANCE (CIRCUIT OMEGA)
      (C-INVERSE (IMPEDANCE CIRCUIT OMEGA)))
```


Answer 12-21:

```
(DEFUN CURT (X)
      (CURT-ITER (COND ((MINUSP X)
                        (MINUS (EXP (QUOTIENT (LOG (MINUS X)) 3.0))))
                       ((ZEROP X) 0.0)
                       (T (EXP (QUOTIENT (LOG X) 3.0))))
                 X))
```

```
(DEFUN CURT-ITER (X Y)
        (QUOTIENT (PLUS X X (QUOTIENT Y (TIMES X X)))
                   3.0))
```

Answer 12-22:

```
(DEFUN MAKE-POLY (ROOTS)                            ; List of roots is given.
        (POLY-AUX (LIST '(1.0 0.0)                  ; Linear seed polynomial.
                         (C-MINUS (CAR ROOTS)))
                  (CDR ROOTS)))                      ; Rest of the roots.
```

The next function multiplies a polynomial represented by its coefficients by the linear term $(x-r)$, where the list of coefficients is represented by COEFF and r is the first root in the list ROOTS. The result is a new, larger list of coefficients.

```
(DEFUN POLY-AUX (COEFF ROOTS)
        (COND (ROOTS (POLY-AUX (CONS (CAR COEFF)
                                     (POLY-IT COEFF
                                              (CAR ROOTS)))
                               (CDR ROOTS)))
              (T COEFF)))
```

Note that here a polynomial is multiplied by a single linear term. Finally we get to the function that does all the work.

```
(DEFUN POLY-IT (COEFF ROOT)
        (COND ((CDR COEFF)
               (CONS (C-DIFFERENCE (CADR COEFF)
                                   (C-TIMES (CAR COEFF) ROOT))
                     (POLY-IT (CDR COEFF) ROOT)))
              (T (LIST (C-TIMES (CAR COEFF)
                                (C-MINUS ROOT))))))
```

To do this we need a few functions to manipulate complex numbers represented as lists of real and imaginary parts.

```
(DEFUN C-MINUS (L)                                  ; Negate a complex number.
        (LIST (MINUS (CAR L))
                     (MINUS (CADR L))))
```

```
(DEFUN C-DIFFERENCE (L M)                           ; Take the difference.
        (LIST (DIFFERENCE (CAR L) (CAR M))
              (DIFFERENCE (CADR L) (CADR M))))
```

```
(DEFUN C-TIMES (L M)                              ;Multiply two complex numbers.
     (LIST (DIFFERENCE (TIMES (CAR L) (CAR M))
                       (TIMES (CADR L) (CADR M)))
           (PLUS (TIMES (CAR L) (CADR M))
                 (TIMES (CADR L) (CAR M))))))
```

Answer 12-23:

```
(DEFUN POLY-VALUE (COEFF L)
     (POLY-VALUE-AUX (REVERSE COEFF) L))

(DEFUN POLY-VALUE-AUX (COEFF L)                   ;Now low order first.
     (COND ((CDR COEFF)
            (C-PLUS (CAR COEFF)
                    (C-TIMES L
                             (POLY-VALUE-AUX (CDR COEFF)
                                             L))))
           (T (LIST (CAR COEFF) 0.0))))

(DEFUN C-PLUS (L M)                               ;Add two complex numbers.
     (LIST (PLUS (CAR L) (CAR M))
           (PLUS (CADR L) (CADR M))))
```

Answer 12-24:

```
(DEFUN CUBIC-S (A B C D)
     (COND ((ZEROP A) (QUADRATIC-S B C D))
           ((ZEROP D) (MAX 0.0 (QUADRATIC-S A B C)))
           ((MINUSP A) (CUBIC-S (MINUS A) (MINUS B) (MINUS C) (MINUS D)))
           (T (CUBIC-SUB-S A
                           B
                           (PLUS (TIMES 2.0 B B B)
                                 (TIMES 9.0
                                        A
                                        (DIFFERENCE (TIMES 3.0 A D)
                                                    (TIMES B C))))
                           (EXPT (DIFFERENCE (TIMES B B)
                                             (TIMES 3.0 A C)) 3)))))

(DEFUN CUBIC-SUB-S (A B P Q)                      ;Check discriminant.
     (CUBIC-PUNT-S A B P Q (DIFFERENCE (TIMES P P)
                                       (TIMES 4 Q))))
```

```
(DEFUN CUBIC-PUNT-S (A B P Q DET)
       (COND ((AND (ZEROP P) (ZEROP Q)) (CUBIC-REAL-S A B 0.0 0.0))
             ((OR (MINUSP DET)
                  (ZEROP DET)) (CUBIC-REAL-S A
                                             B
                                             (SQRT Q)
                                             (ATAN (SQRT (MINUS DET))
                                                   (MINUS P))))
             ((MINUSP P) (CUBIC-CONJUG-S A B (DIFFERENCE (SQRT DET) P) Q))
             (T (CUBIC-CONJUG-S A B (MINUS (PLUS (SQRT DET) P)) Q))))

(DEFUN CUBIC-CONJUG-S (A B RAT Q)
       (QUOTIENT (DIFFERENCE (PLUS (CURT (QUOTIENT RAT 2.0))
                                  (CURT (QUOTIENT (TIMES 2.0 Q) RAT)))
                            B)
                 (TIMES 3.0 A)))

(DEFUN CUBIC-REAL-S (A B R THETA)
       (QUOTIENT (DIFFERENCE (TIMES 2.0
                                   (CURT R)
                                   (COS (QUOTIENT THETA 3.0)))
                            B)
                 (TIMES A 3.0)))
```

Here, QUADRATIC-S, computes the most positive root of a quadratic equation.

Solutions to Problems in Chapter 14

Answer 14-1:

```
(DEFUN PUTON (OBJECT SUPPORT)
       (PROG (PLACE PLAN)
             (COND ((EQUAL OBJECT SUPPORT)
                    (BREAK '(PUTON CANNOT PUT SOMETHING ON ITSELF))))
             (COND ((SETQ PLACE (FINDSPACE SUPPORT OBJECT))
                    (PUTAT OBJECT PLACE))
                   ((SETQ PLACE (MAKESPACE SUPPORT OBJECT))
                    (PUTAT OBJECT PLACE))
                   ((BREAK '(PUTON CANNOT FIND A PLACE FOR THE OBJECT))))
             (RETURN (REVERSE PLAN))))
```

Answer 14-2:

```
(DEFUN BREAK2 (MESSAGE TEST)
      (PROG (QUERY)
            (COND ((NOT TEST) (RETURN NIL)))
            (PRINT MESSAGE)
            LOOP
            (PRINT '>)
            (SETQ QUERY (READ))
            (COND ((AND (NOT (ATOM QUERY))
                        (EQUAL (CAR QUERY) 'RETURN))
                   (RETURN (EVAL (CADR QUERY))))
                  (T (PRINT (EVAL QUERY))))
            (GO LOOP)))
```

Solutions to Problems in Chapter 15

Answer 15-1:

```
(DEFUN HOW (SITUATION)
      (PROG (QUEUE PROGENY)
            (SETQ QUEUE (LIST 'HISTORY))
            TRYAGAIN
            (COND ((NULL QUEUE) (RETURN NIL))
                  ((EQUAL SITUATION
                          (GET (CAR QUEUE) 'SITUATION))
                   (MAPCAR '(LAMBDA (E) (PRINT (GET E 'SITUATION)))
                           (GET (CAR QUEUE) 'CHILDREN))
                   (RETURN T)))
            (SETQ PROGENY (GET (CAR QUEUE) 'CHILDREN))
            (SETQ QUEUE (CDR QUEUE))
            (SETQ QUEUE (APPEND PROGENY QUEUE))
            (GO TRYAGAIN)))
```

Answer 15-2:

```
(DEFUN WHY (SITUATION)
      (PROG (QUEUE PROGENY)
            (SETQ QUEUE (LIST 'HISTORY))
```

;Continued -->

```
               TRYAGAIN
               (COND ((NULL QUEUE) (RETURN NIL))
                     ((EQUAL SITUATION
                            (GET (CAR QUEUE) 'SITUATION))
                      (PRINT (GET (GET (CAR QUEUE) 'PARENT) 'SITUATION))
                      (RETURN T)))
               (SETQ PROGENY (GET (CAR QUEUE) 'CHILDREN))
               (SETQ QUEUE (CDR QUEUE))
               (SETQ QUEUE (APPEND PROGENY QUEUE))
               (GO TRYAGAIN)))
```

Answer 15-3:

```
(DEFUN WHEN (SITUATION)
       (PROG (QUEUE PROGENY USER-COMMANDS TOP-COMMAND)
             (SETQ USER-COMMANDS (GET 'HISTORY 'CHILDREN))
             OUTER-LOOP
             (COND ((NULL USER-COMMANDS) (RETURN NIL)))
             (SETQ TOP-COMMAND (CAR USER-COMMANDS))
             (SETQ QUEUE (LIST TOP-COMMAND))
             (SETQ USER-COMMANDS (CDR USER-COMMANDS))
             TRYAGAIN
             (COND ((NULL QUEUE) (GO OUTER-LOOP))
                   ((EQUAL SITUATION
                          (GET (CAR QUEUE) 'SITUATION))
                    (PRINT (GET TOP-COMMAND 'SITUATION))
                    (RETURN T)))
             (SETQ PROGENY (GET (CAR QUEUE) 'CHILDREN))
             (SETQ QUEUE (CDR QUEUE))
             (SETQ QUEUE (APPEND PROGENY QUEUE))
             (GO TRYAGAIN)))
```

Answer 15-4:

```
(DEFUN DEFUN+ FEXPR (X)
       (APPLY 'DEFUN
              (LIST (CAR X)
                    (CADR X)
                    (LIST
                     (APPEND '(LAMBDA (PARENT CHILD)
                                      (ATTACH CHILD PARENT))
                             (CONS
```

```
                        (LIST 'PUTPROP
                              'CHILD
                              (LIST 'CONS
                                    (LIST 'QUOTE (CAR X))
                                    (CONS 'LIST (CADR X)))
                              ''SITUATION)
                        (CDDR X)))
                  '(COND ((BOUNDP 'CHILD) CHILD) (T 'HISTORY))
                  '(GENSYM)))))
```

Answer 15-5:

```
(DEFUN
 TRACE1 (NAME)
 (PROG
  (PARAMETERS LAMBDA-EXPRESSION)
  (SETQ LAMBDA-EXPRESSION (GET NAME 'EXPR))
  (SETQ PARAMETERS (CADR LAMBDA-EXPRESSION))
  (PUTPROP NAME LAMBDA-EXPRESSION 'TRACED-EXPR)
  (PUTPROP
   NAME
   (SUBST
    (CONS 'LIST PARAMETERS) 'LIST-PARAMETERS
    (SUBST
     PARAMETERS 'PARAMETERS
     (SUBST
      NAME 'NAME
      '(LAMBDA PARAMETERS
               ((LAMBDA (TRACE-RESULT TRACE-DEPTH EVALUATED-ARGUMENTS)
                        (INDENT-PRINT TRACE-DEPTH
                                      (APPEND '(ENTERING NAME)
                                              EVALUATED-ARGUMENTS))
                        (SETQ TRACE-RESULT (APPLY (GET 'NAME 'TRACED-EXPR)
                                                  EVALUATED-ARGUMENTS))
                        (INDENT-PRINT TRACE-DEPTH
                                      (LIST 'EXITING
                                            'NAME
                                            TRACE-RESULT))
                        TRACE-RESULT)
                NIL
                (ADD1 TRACE-DEPTH)
                LIST-PARAMETERS)))))
    'EXPR)
  (RETURN NAME)))
```

Answer 15-6:

```
(DEFUN INDENT-PRINT (N MESSAGE)
       (PROG ()
             (TERPRI)
             LOOP
             (SETQ N (SUB1 N))
             (COND ((ZEROP N)
                    (PRINC MESSAGE)
                    (RETURN T)))
             (PRINC '| |)
             (GO LOOP)))
```

Answer 15-7:

```
(DEFUN TRACE FEXPR (FUNCTIONS)
       (MAPCAN '(LAMBDA (E)
                        (COND ((MEMBER E TRACED-FUNCTIONS) NIL)
                              (T (TRACE1 E)
                                 (SETQ TRACED-FUNCTIONS
                                       (CONS E TRACED-FUNCTIONS))
                                 (LIST E))))
               FUNCTIONS))

(DEFUN UNTRACE FEXPR (FUNCTIONS)
       (MAPCAN '(LAMBDA (E)
                        (COND ((MEMBER E TRACED-FUNCTIONS)
                               (PUTPROP E (GET E 'TRACED-EXPR) 'EXPR)
                               (SETQ TRACED-FUNCTIONS
                                     (DELETE E TRACED-FUNCTIONS))
                               (LIST E))
                              (T NIL)))
               (COND ((NULL FUNCTIONS) TRACED-FUNCTIONS)
                     (T FUNCTIONS)))))
```

Solutions to Problems in Chapter 16

Answer 16-1:

```
(DEF2N AREA (OBJECT)
       (FUNCALL (GET (GET OBJECT 'TYPE)
                     'AREA-FUNCTION)
                OBJECT))
```

```
(DEFUN PERIMETER (OBJECT)
       (FUNCALL (GET (GET OBJECT 'TYPE)
                     'PERIMETER-FUNCTION)
               OBJECT))

(DEFPROP CIRCLE
         (LAMBDA (OBJECT)
                 (TIMES PI (EXPT (GET OBJECT 'RADIUS) 2)))
         AREA-FUNCTION)

(DEFPROP CIRCLE
         (LAMBDA (OBJECT)
                 (TIMES PI 2 (GET OBJECT 'RADIUS)))
         PERIMETER-FUNCTION)

(DEFPROP SQUARE
         (LAMBDA (OBJECT)
                 (TIMES (EXPT (GET OBJECT 'LENGTH) 2)))
         AREA-FUNCTION)

(DEFPROP SQUARE
         (LAMBDA (OBJECT)
                 (TIMES (GET OBJECT 'LENGTH) 4))
         PERIMETER-FUNCTION)
```

Answer 16-2:

```
(DEFUN D2 (E X)
       (COND ((ATOM E) (COND ((EQUAL E X) 1)
                             (T 0)))
             (T (FUNCALL (GET (FUNC E) 'D2FUNCTION) E X))))

(DEFPROP PLUS
         (LAMBDA (E X) (LIST 'PLUS
                             (D2 (ARG1 E) X)
                             (D2 (ARG2 E) X)))
         D2FUNCTION)

(DEFPROP TIMES
         (LAMBDA (E X) (LIST 'PLUS
                             (LIST 'TIMES
                                   (ARG1 E)
                                   (D2 (ARG2 E) X))          ;Continued -->
```

```
                        (LIST 'TIMES
                              (ARG2 E)
                              (D2 (ARG1 E) X))))
            D2FUNCTION)
```

Solutions to Problems in Chapter 17

Answer 17-1:

```
(DEFUN ADD (PATTERN)
       (COND ((MEMBER PATTERN ASSERTIONS) NIL)
             (T (SETQ ASSERTIONS (CONS PATTERN ASSERTIONS)) T)))
```

Answer 17-2:

```
(DEFUN FETCH (PATTERN)
       (FETCH1 ASSERTIONS))

(DEFUN FETCH1 (POSSIBILITIES)
       (COND ((NULL POSSIBILITIES) NIL)
             ((MATCH PATTERN (CAR POSSIBILITIES))
              (CONS (CAR POSSIBILITIES)
                    (FETCH1 (CDR POSSIBILITIES))))
             (T (FETCH1 (CDR POSSIBILITIES)))))
```

Answer 17-3:

```
(DEFUN FLUSH (PATTERN)
       (PROG (SWITCH)
             (SETQ ASSERTIONS (FLUSH1 ASSERTIONS))
             (RETURN SWITCH)))

(DEFUN FLUSH1 (POSSIBILITIES)
       (COND ((NULL POSSIBILITIES) NIL)
             ((MATCH PATTERN (CAR POSSIBILITIES))
              (SETQ SWITCH T)
              (FLUSH1 (CDR POSSIBILITIES)))
             (T (CONS (CAR POSSIBILITIES)
                      (FLUSH1 (CDR POSSIBILITIES))))))
```

Answer 17-4:

```
(DEFUN INF-TO-PRE (E)
      (PROG (V L R)
           (RETURN
            (COND ((ATOM E) E)
                  ((MATCH '(>V) E)
                   (INF-TO-PRE V))
                  ((MATCH '(+L (RESTRICT > ONEPLUS) +R) E)
                   (LIST 'PLUS (INF-TO-PRE L) (INF-TO-PRE R)))
                  ((MATCH '(+L - +R) E)
                   (LIST 'DIFFERENCE (INF-TO-PRE L) (INF-TO-PRE R)))
                  ((MATCH '(+L * +R) E)
                   (LIST 'TIMES (INF-TO-PRE L) (INF-TO-PRE R)))
                  ((MATCH '(+L / +R) E)
                   (LIST 'QUOTIENT (INF-TO-PRE L) (INF-TO-PRE R)))
                  ((MATCH '(+L ^ +R) E)
                   (LIST 'EXPT (INF-TO-PRE L) (INF-TO-PRE R)))
                  ((MATCH '(- +R) E)
                   (LIST 'MINUS (INF-TO-PRE R)))
                  (T E)))))
```

ONEPLUS and the restriction are needed because the + for plus would be confused with the match-any-string symbol recognized by MATCH.

Answer 17-5:

```
(DEFUN TRANSLATE (E)
      (PROG (V L R)
           (RETURN
            (COND ((MATCH '(+L IS +R) E)
                   (LIST 'EQUAL (TRANSLATE L) (TRANSLATE R)))
                  ((MATCH '(THE DIFFERENCE BETWEEN +L AND +R) E)
                   (LIST 'DIFFERENCE (TRANSLATE L) (TRANSLATE R)))
                  ((MATCH '(THE SUM OF +L AND +R) E)
                   (LIST 'PLUS (TRANSLATE L) (TRANSLATE R)))
                  ((MATCH '((RESTRICT >V NUMBERP) PERCENT +R) E)
                   (TRANSLATE (APPEND (LIST (QUOTIENT V 100.0)) R)))
                  ((MATCH '(+L TIMES +R) E)
                   (LIST 'TIMES (TRANSLATE L) (TRANSLATE R)))    ;Continued -->
```

```
((MATCH '(TWICE +R) E)
 (LIST 'TIMES 2. (TRANSLATE R)))
((MATCH '((RESTRICT >V NUMBERP) OF +R) E)
 (LIST 'TIMES V (TRANSLATE R)))
((MATCH '(THE SQUARE OF +R) E)
 (LIST 'EXPT (TRANSLATE R) 2.))
((MATCH '(+L SQUARED) E)
 (LIST 'EXPT (TRANSLATE L) 2.))
((MATCH '((RESTRICT >V NUMBERP)) E) V)
(E)))))
```

Answer 17-6:

```
(DEFUN DOCTOR ()
      (PROG (L MOTHER S)
            (PRINT '(SPEAK UP!))
            LOOP
            (SETQ S (READ))
            (COND ((MATCH '(I AM WORRIED +L) S)
                   (PRINT (APPEND '(HOW LONG HAVE YOU BEEN WORRIED)
                                  L)))
                  ((MATCH '(+ MOTHER +) S)
                   (SETQ MOTHER T)
                   (PRINT '(TELL ME MORE ABOUT YOUR FAMILY)))
                  ((MATCH '(+ COMPUTERS +) S)
                   (PRINT '(DO MACHINES FRIGHTEN YOU)))
                  ((OR (MATCH '(NO) S) (MATCH '(YES) S))
                   (PRINT '(PLEASE DO NOT BE SO SHORT WITH ME)))
                  ((MATCH '(+ (RESTRICT > BADWORD) +) S)
                   (PRINT '(PLEASE DO NOT USE WORDS LIKE THAT)))
                  (MOTHER (SETQ MOTHER NIL)
                          (PRINT '(EARLIER YOU SPOKE OF YOUR MOTHER)))
                  (T (PRINT '(I AM SORRY OUR TIME IS UP))
                     (RETURN 'GOODBYE)))
            (GO loop)))
```

Note that READ and PRINT establish communication with the user. Note also that if a sentence containing MOTHER is encountered, the variable MOTHER is set to T. Then later on, if nothing else in the conditional is triggered, the response of (EARLIER YOU SPOKE OF YOUR MOTHER) seems very judicious.

Solutions to Problems in Chapter 18

Answer 18-1:

```
(DEFUN INIF (FACT)
       (MAPCAN '(LAMBDA (R)
                        (COND ((IFP FACT R)
                               (LIST R))))
               RULES))

(DEFUN IFP (FACT RULE)
       (MEMBER FACT (CADDR RULE)))
```

Answer 18-2:

```
(DEFUN TRYRULE (RULE)
       (COND ((AND (TESTIF RULE) (USETHEN RULE))
              (SETQ RULESUSED (CONS RULE RULESUSED))
              T)))

(DEFUN USEDP (RULE)
       (PROG (POSSIBILITIES)
             (SETQ POSSIBILITIES RULESUSED)
             LOOP
             (COND ((NULL POSSIBILITIES) (RETURN NIL))
                   ((EQUAL RULE (CADAR POSSIBILITIES))
                    (RETURN T)))
             (SETQ POSSIBILITIES (CDR POSSIBILITIES))
             (GO LOOP)))
```

Answer 18-3:

```
(DEFUN HOW (FACT)
       (PROG (POSSIBILITIES SUCCESS)
             (SETQ POSSIBILITIES RULESUSED)
             LOOP
             (COND ((NULL POSSIBILITIES)
                    (COND (SUCCESS (RETURN T))
                          ((RECALL FACT)
                           (P FACT '|was given.|)
                           (RETURN T))
```

;Continued -->

```
                      (T (P FACT '|is not established.|)
                         (RETURN NIL))))
              ((THENP FACT (CAR POSSIBILITIES))
               (SETQ SUCCESS T)
               (P FACT '|demonstrated by:|)
               (MAPCAR '(LAMBDA (A) (P A))
                       (CDADDR (CAR POSSIBILITIES)))))
          (SETQ POSSIBILITIES (CDR POSSIBILITIES))
          (GO LOOP)))
```

Answer 18-4:

```
(DEFUN WHY (FACT)
       (PROG (POSSIBILITIES SUCCESS)
             (SETQ POSSIBILITIES RULESUSED)
             LOOP
             (COND ((NULL POSSIBILITIES)
                    (COND (SUCCESS (RETURN T))
                          ((RECALL FACT)
                           (P FACT '|was hypothesis.|)
                           (RETURN T))
                          (T (P FACT '|is not established.|)
                             (RETURN NIL))))
                   ((IFP FACT (CAR POSSIBILITIES))
                    (SETQ SUCCESS T)
                    (P FACT '|needed to show:|)
                    (MAPCAR '(LAMBDA (A) (P A))
                            (CDR (CADDDR (CAR POSSIBILITIES))))))
             (SETQ POSSIBILITIES (CDR POSSIBILITIES))
             (GO LOOP)))
```

Solutions to Problems in Chapter 19

Answer 19-1:

Add, as the first thing in the PROG of the function INTERPRET:

```
(COND (DEBUG (PRINT (APPEND '(ENTERING THE NETWORK)
                            (LIST (CAR NETWORK)))))))
```

Directly after the tag GET-STATE-DESCRIPTION, add:

```
(COND (DEBUG (PRINT (APPEND '(ENTERING THE STATE)
                            (LIST NEWSTATE)))))
```

Answer 19-2:

```
(DEFUN RECORD FEXPR (X)
       (PUTPROP (CAR X) X 'NETWORK)
       (EVAL (SUBST (CAR X) 'NAME
                    '(DEFUN NAME (FEATURES)
                           ((LAMBDA (PARENT-NODE)
                                    (INTERPRET (GET 'NAME 'NETWORK)
                                               FEATURES))
                            (COND ((BOUNDP 'THIS-NODE) THIS-NODE)
                                  (T 'UNIVERSAL-TOP)))))))
```

Answer 19-3:

```
(DEFUN SELECT (X Y)
       (COND ((NULL X) NIL)
             ((MEMBER (CAR X) Y) (CAR X))
             (T (SELECT (CDR X) Y))))
```

Answer 19-4:

```
(DEFUN GENNAME (NAME)
       (PROG (N)
             (COND ((SETQ N (GET NAME 'NAMECOUNTER)))
                   (T (SETQ N 1)))
             (PUTPROP NAME (ADD1 N) 'NAMECOUNTER)
             (RETURN (IMPLODE (APPEND (EXPLODE NAME)
                                      (EXPLODE N))))))
```

Answer 19-5:

```
(RECORD PARSE-NOUN-GROUP
        (S1 (IF (PARSE-WORD THIS-NODE 'DETERMINER)
                --> S2
                AFTER                                 ;Continued -->
```

```
                    (SETR 'NUMBER (SELECT '(SINGULAR PLURAL)
                                        (GETF LAST-PARSED)))
                    (SETR 'DETERMINER (SELECT '(DEFINITE INDEFINITE)
                                            (GETF LAST-PARSED))))
            (IF T --> S2))
        (S2 (IF (PARSE-WORD THIS-NODE 'ADJECTIVE)
                --> S2
                AFTER
                (ADDR 'ADJECTIVES LAST-PARSED))
            (IF (PARSE-WORD THIS-NODE 'NOUN)
                --> WIN
                AFTER
                (SETR 'NUMBER (SELECT '(SINGULAR PLURAL)
                                    (GETF LAST-PARSED)))
                (SETR 'NOUN LAST-PARSED))))
```

Answer 19-6, 19-7 & 19-8:

To save space, the version of PARSE-NOUN-GROUP shown, incorporates all the
changes suggested in these three problems.

```
(RECORD PARSE-NOUN-GROUP
        (S1 (IF (PARSE-WORD THIS-NODE 'DETERMINER)
                --> S2A
                AFTER
                (SETR 'NUMBER (SELECT '(SINGULAR PLURAL)
                                    (GETF LAST-PARSED)))
                (SETR 'DETERMINER (SELECT '(DEFINITE INDEFINITE)
                                        (GETF LAST-PARSED))))
            (IF T --> S2A))
        (S2A (IF (PARSE-WORD THIS-NODE 'NUMBER)
                --> S2
                AFTER
                (COND ((EQUAL 'SINGULAR (GETR 'NUMBER))
                        (PRINT 'TILT-DETERMINER-NUMBER)))
                (SETR 'NUMBER (GET LAST-PARSED 'NUMBER)))
            (IF T --> S2))
        (S2 (IF (AND REMAINING-WORDS
                    (SELECT '(ADJECTIVE NOUN)
                            (GETF (CADR REMAINING-WORDS)))
                    (PARSE-WORD THIS-NODE 'ADJECTIVE))
                --> S2
                AFTER
                (ADDR 'ADJECTIVES LAST-PARSED))
```

```
(IF (PARSE-WORD THIS-NODE 'NOUN)
    --> WIN
    AFTER
    (COND ((EQUAL
              (LENGTH (INTERSECTION '(SINGULAR PLURAL)
                                    (CONS (GETR 'NUMBER)
                                          (GETF LAST-PARSED))))
             2)
            (PRINT 'TILT-DETERMINER-NOUN))
           ((AND (NUMBERP (GETR 'NUMBER))
                 (MEMBER 'SINGULAR (GETF LAST-PARSED)))
            (PRINT 'TILT-NUMBER-NOUN)))
     (COND ((NOT (NUMBERP (GETR 'NUMBER)))
            (SETR 'NUMBER (SELECT '(SINGULAR PLURAL)
                                  (GETF LAST-PARSED)))))
     (SETR 'NOUN LAST-PARSED))))
```

Solutions to Problems in Chapter 20

Answer 20-1:

Yes, but only if COMPILE is available. INTERPRET does not help because it never translates ATN descriptions into LISP, and LISP programs are the only things the LISP compiler knows how to work with.

Solutions to Problems in Chapter 22

Answer 22-1:

```
(DEFUN FCHECK (FRAME SLOT FACET VALUE)
       (COND ((MEMBER VALUE (FGET FRAME SLOT FACET)) T)
             (T NIL)))
```

Answer 22-2:

```
(DEFUN FCLAMP (FRAME1 FRAME2 SLOT)
       (RPLACD (FASSOC SLOT (FGETFRAME FRAME1))
               (CDR (FASSOC SLOT (FGETFRAME FRAME2))))
       SLOT)
```

Answer 22-3:

```
(DEFUN FGETCLASSES (FRAME)
     (PROG (QUEUE PROGENY CLASSES)
           (SETQ QUEUE (LIST FRAME))
           TRYAGAIN
           (COND ((NULL QUEUE) (RETURN (REVERSE CLASSES)))
                 ((NOT (MEMBER (CAR QUEUE) CLASSES))
                  (SETQ CLASSES (CONS (CAR QUEUE) CLASSES))))
           (SETQ PROGENY (FGET (CAR QUEUE) 'AKO 'VALUE))
           (SETQ QUEUE (CDR QUEUE))
           (SETQ QUEUE (APPEND QUEUE PROGENY))
           (GO TRYAGAIN)))
```

Answer 22-4:

```
(DEFUN FGET-Z (FRAME SLOT)
     (PROG (CLASSES RESULT)
           (SETQ CLASSES (FGETCLASSES FRAME))
           LOOP
           (COND ((NULL CLASSES) (RETURN NIL))
                 ((SETQ RESULT
                      (OR (FGET-V-D (CAR CLASSES) SLOT)
                          (MAPCAN '(LAMBDA (E) (APPLY E NIL))
                                  (FGET (CAR CLASSES) SLOT 'IF-NEEDED))))
                  (RETURN RESULT))
                 (T (SETQ CLASSES (CDR CLASSES))
                    (GO LOOP)))))
```

Answer 22-5:

```
(DEFUN FGET-N (FRAME SLOT)
     (PROG (CLASSES RESULT)
           (SETQ CLASSES (FGETCLASSES FRAME))
           LOOP1
           (COND ((NULL CLASSES)
                  (SETQ CLASSES (FGETCLASSES FRAME))
                  (GO LOOP2))
                 ((SETQ RESULT (FGET (CAR CLASSES) SLOT 'VALUE))
                  (RETURN RESULT))
                 (T (SETQ CLASSES (CDR CLASSES))
                    (GO LOOP1)))
```

```
LOOP2
(COND ((NULL CLASSES)
         (SETQ CLASSES (FGETCLASSES FRAME))
         (GO LOOP3))
        ((SETQ RESULT (FGET (CAR CLASSES) SLOT 'DEFAULT))
         (RETURN RESULT))
        (T (SETQ CLASSES (CDR CLASSES))
           (GO LOOP2)))
LOOP3
(COND ((NULL CLASSES) (RETURN NIL))
        ((SETQ RESULT (MAPCAN '(LAMBDA (E) (APPLY E NIL))
                              (FGET (CAR CLASSES)
                                    SLOT
                                    'IF-NEEDED)))
         (RETURN RESULT))
        (T (SETQ CLASSES (CDR CLASSES))
           (GO LOOP3)))))
```

Answer 22-6:

```
(DEFUN FREMOVE+ (FRAME SLOT FACET VALUE)
      (COND ((FREMOVE FRAME SLOT FACET VALUE)
             (MAPC '(LAMBDA (E)
                            (MAPC '(LAMBDA (F) (APPLY F NIL))
                                  (FGET E SLOT 'IF-REMOVED)))
                   (FGETCLASSES FRAME))
             VALUE)))
```

Solutions to Problems in Chapter 23

Answer 23-1:

```
(DEFUN MICRO-SETQ (VARIABLE VALUE A-LIST)
      (PROG (ENTRY)
            (SETQ ENTRY (ASSOC VARIABLE A-LIST))
            (SETQ RESULT (MICRO-EVAL VALUE A-LIST))
            (COND (ENTRY (RPLACA (CDR ENTRY) RESULT))
                  (T (RPLACD (LAST A-LIST) (LIST (LIST VARIABLE RESULT)))))
            (RETURN RESULT)))
```

Answer 23-2:

Add the following to MICRO-EVAL:

```
((EQUAL (CAR S) 'M-CLOSE)
 (MICRO-CLOSE (CADR S) ENVIRONMENT))
```

Also define MICRO-CLOSE:

```
(DEFUN MICRO-CLOSE (FUNCTION-NAME ENVIRONMENT)
       (RPLACD (CDDR (RPLACA (MICRO-VALUE FUNCTION-NAME ENVIRONMENT)
                             'M-CLOSURE))
               (LIST ENVIRONMENT))
       FUNCTION-NAME)
```

Answer 23-3:

One solution is to replace the following in MICRO-APPLY

```
((EQUAL (CAR FUNCTION) 'M-DEFINITION)
 (MICRO-EVAL (CADDR FUNCTION)
             (MICRO-BIND (CADR FUNCTION) ARGS ENVIRONMENT)))
```

by

```
((EQUAL (CAR FUNCTION) 'M-DEFINITION)
 (MICRO-APPLY (MICRO-EVAL (CONS 'M-LAMBDA (CDR FUNCTION)) ENVIRONMENT)
              ARGS
              ENVIRONMENT))
```

thereby tricking MICRO-APPLY into thinking it stumbled into an M-LAMBDA expression.

Answer 23-4:

Otherwise they would not be able to refer to other functions defined by M-DEFUN later in time.

BIBLIOGRAPHY

Abramowitz, M. and I. A. Stegan (editors) (1964) *Handbook of Mathematical Functions with Formulas, Graphs, and Mathematical Tables*, pp. 17—18, National Bureau of Standards, United States Department of Commerce.

Aho, Alfred V., John E. Hopcroft, and Jeffrey D. Ullman (1974) *The Design and Analysis of Computer Algorithms*, Addison-Wesley, Reading, Massachusetts. Reprinted 1976.

Allen, John (1978) *Anatomy of LISP*, McGraw-Hill, New York.

Allen, John (1979) "An Overview of LISP," *Byte*, Vol. 4, No. 8, pg. 10, August 1979.

Auslander, M. A. and H. R. Strong (1976) "Systematic Recursion Removal," Report RC 5841, IBM Research Center, Yorktown Heights, New York, February 1976.

Backus, John (1978) "Can Programming be Liberated from the Von Neumann Style? A Functional Style and Its Algebra of Programs," *Communications of the ACM*, Vol. 21, No. 8, pp. 613—641, August 1978.

Baird, Michael (1978) "SIGHT-I: A Computer Vision System for Automated IC Chip Manufacture," *IEEE Transactions on Systems, Man and Cybernetics*, Vol. SMC-8, No. 2, February 1978.

Baker, Henry G., Jr. and Carl Hewitt (1977) "The Incremental Garbage Collection of Processes," Memo No. 454, Artificial Intelligence Laboratory, MIT, Cambridge, Massachusetts, December 1977.

Baker, Henry G., Jr. (1978a) "List Processing in Real Time on a Serial Computer," *Communications of the ACM*, Vol. 21, No. 4, pp. 280—293, April 1978.

Baker, Henry G., Jr. (1978b) "Shallow Binding in LISP 1.5," *Communications of the ACM*, Vol. 21, No. 7, pp. 565—569, July 1978. Also in *Artificial Intelligence: An MIT Perspective*, Volume 2, edited by Patrick H. Winston and Richard H. Brown, pp. 377—387, 1979.

Baker, Henry G., Jr. (1979) "Optimizing Allocation and Garbage Collection of Spaces," in *Artificial Intelligence: An MIT Perspective*, Volume 2, edited by Patrick H. Winston and Richard H. Brown, pp. 391—395.

Bauer, M. A. (1979) "Programming by Examples," *Artificial Intelligence*, Vol. 12, No. 1, pp. 1—22, May 1979.

Bawden, Alan, Richard Greenblatt, John Holloway, Tom Knight, David Moon, and Daniel Weinreb (1977) "LISP Machine Progress Report," Memo No. 444, Artificial Intelligence Laboratory, MIT, Cambridge, Massachusetts. August 1977. Also in *Artificial Intelligence: An MIT Perspective*, Volume 2, edited by Patrick H. Winston and Richard H. Brown, pp. 347—373, 1979.

Berkeley, E. C. and Daniel G. Bobrow (editors) (1964) *The Programming Language LISP: Its Operation and Applications*, Information International Incorporated, Cambridge, Massachusetts. Also, Second Edition, The MIT Press, Cambridge, Massachusetts, 1966.

Berliner, Hans J. (1978) "A Chronology of Computer Chess and its Literature," *Artificial Intelligence*, Vol. 10, No. 2, pp. 201—214, April 1978.

Berliner, Hans J. (1979) "The B* Tree-search Algorithm: A Best-first Proof Procedure," *Artificial Intelligence*, Vol. 12, No. 1, pp. 23—40, May 1979.

Black, F. (1964) "A Deductive Question-Answering System," Ph. D. Thesis, Harvard University. Also in *Semantic Information Processing*, pp. 354—402, edited by Marvin Minsky, 1968.

Blair, Fred W. and R. D. Jenks (1970) "LPL — LISP Programming Language," Report RC 3062, IBM Research Center, Yorktown Heights, New York, September 1970.

Blair, Fred W. (1979) "LISP/370 Concepts and Facilities," Report RC 7771, IBM Research Center, Yorktown Heights, New York, August 1979.

Bledsoe, W. W. (1977) "Non-resolution Theorem Proving," *Artificial Intelligence*, Vol. 9, No. 1, pp. 1—35, August 1977.

Bobrow, Daniel G. (1962) "A Question-Answerer for Algebra Word Problems," Memo No. 45, Artificial Intelligence Project, Computation Center and Research Laboratory of Electronics, MIT, Cambridge, Massachusetts.

Bobrow, Daniel G. (1963) "METEOR: A LISP Interpreter for String Transformations," Memo No. 51, Artificial Intelligence Project, Computation Center and Research Laboratory of Electronics, MIT, Cambridge, Massachusetts.

Bobrow, Daniel G. and Bertram Raphael (1964) "A Comparison of List-Processing Languages," *Communications of the ACM*, Vol. 7, No. 4, pp. 231—240, April 1964.

Bobrow, Daniel G. (1964) "Natural Language Input for a Computer Problem-Solving System," Memo No. 66, Artificial Intelligence Project, Computation Center and Research Laboratory of Electronics, MIT, Cambridge, Massachusetts, September 1964. Also in *Semantic Information Processing*, edited by Marvin Minsky, pp. 146—226, 1968.

Bobrow, Daniel G., L. D. Darley, D. L. Murphy, C. Solomon, and W. Teitelman (1966) "The BBN-LISP System," AFCRL-66-180, Bolt, Beranek and Newman, Cambridge, Massachusetts, February 1966.

Bobrow, Daniel G. and D. Murphy (1967) "The Structure of a LISP System Using Two-level Storage," *Communications of the ACM*, Vol. 10, No. 3, pp. 155—159, March 1967.

Bobrow, Daniel G. (1972) "Requirements for Advanced Programming Systems for List Processing," *Communications of the ACM*, Vol. 15, No. 7, pp. 618—627, July 1972.

Bobrow, Daniel G. and Ben Wegbreit (1973) "A Model and Stack Implementation of Multiple Environments," *Communications of the ACM*, Vol. 16, No. 10, pp. 591—603, October 1973.

Bobrow, Daniel G. and B. Raphael (1974) "New Programming Languages for Artificial Intelligence Research," *ACM Computing Surveys*, Vol. 6, No. 3, pp. 153—174, September 1974.

Bobrow, Daniel G. and Allan Collins (editors) (1975) *Representation and Understanding*, Academic Press, New York.

Bobrow, Daniel G., R. M. Kaplan, M. Kay, D. A. Norman, H. Thompson, and T. Winograd (1977) "GUS, A Frame-driven Dialog System," *Artificial Intelligence*, Vol. 8, No. 2, pp. 155—173, April 1977.

Bobrow, Daniel G. and Douglas W. Clark (1979) "Compact Encoding of List Structure," *ACM TOPLAS*, Vol. 1, No. 2, October 1979.

Bobrow, R. J., R. R. Burton, J. M. Jacobs, and D. Lewis (1973) "UCI LISP Manual," Technical Report 21, Department of Information and Computer Science, University of California, Irvine, California.

Boden, M. A. (1977) *Artifical Intelligence and Natural Man*, Basic Books, New York.

Bolce, J. F. (1968) "LISP/360: A Description of the University of Waterloo LISP 1.5 Interpreter for the IBM/360," University of Waterloo, Waterloo, Ontario, Canada.

Boyer, R. S. and J. S. Moore (1975) "Proving Theorems about LISP Functions," *Journal of the ACM*, Vol. 22, No. 1, pp. 129—144, January 1975.

Braffort, P. and D. Hirshberg (editors) (1963) *Computer Programming and Formal Systems*, North Holland, Amsterdam, pp. 33—70.

Brown, W. S. (1971) "On Euclid's Algorithm and the Computation of Polynomial Greatest Common Divisors," *Journal of the ACM*, Vol. 18, No. 4, pp. 478—504, October 1971.

Bruce, B. (1975) "Case Systems for Natural Language," *Artificial Intelligence*, Vol. 6, No. 4, pp. 327—360, Winter 1975.

Buchanan, Bruce G. and Edward A. Feigenbaum (1978) "Dendral and Meta-dendral: Their Applications Dimension," *Artificial Intelligence*, Vol. 11, No. 1-2, pp. 5—24, August 1978.

Burge, W. H. (1975) *Recursive Programming Techniques*, Addison-Wesley, Reading, Massachusetts.

Burington, R. S. (1973) *Handbook of Mathematical Tables and Formulas*, Fifth Edition, pp. 12—15, McGraw-Hill, New York.

Burstall, R. M., J. S. Collins, and R. J. Popplestone (1971) *Programming in POP-2*, Edinburgh University Press, Edinburgh, Scotland.

Burstall, R. M. and John Darlington, (1977) "A Transformation System for Developing Recursive Programs," *Journal of the ACM*, Vol. 24, No. 1, pp. 44—67, January 1977.

Chaitin, Gregory J. (1976) "A Toy Version of the LISP Language," Report RC 5924, IBM Research Center, Yorktown Heights, New York, March 1976.

Chang, C. L. and J. R. Slagle (1979) "Using Rewriting Rules for Connection Graphs to Prove Theorems," *Artificial Intelligence*, Vol. 12, No. 2, pp. 159—178, August 1979.

Charniak, Eugene (1978) "On the Use of Framed Knowledge in Language Comprehension," *Artificial Intelligence*, Vol. 11, No. 3, pp. 225—266, December 1978.

Charniak, Eugene, C. Riesbeck and D. McDermott (1979) *Artificial Intelligence Programming*, Lawrence Erlbaum Associates, Hillsdale, New Jersey.

Cheney, C. J. (1970) "A Nonrecursive List Compacting Algorithm," *Communications of the ACM*, Vol. 13, No. 11, pp. 677—678, November 1970.

Church, Alonzo (1941) "The Calculi of Lambda-Conversion," *Annals of Mathematical Studies*, Vol. 6, Princeton University Press, Princeton, New Jersey (Reprinted by Klaus Reprints, New York, 1965).

Ciccarelli, E. (1977) "An Introduction to the EMACS Editor," Memo No. 447, Artificial Intelligence Laboratory, MIT, Cambridge, Massachusetts, November 1977.

Codd, E. F. (1974) "Seven Steps to Rendezvous with the Casual User," in *Data Base Management*, edited by J. W. Klimbie and K. I. Koffeman.

Cohen, Donald and G. Levitt (1965) "Sort by Exchange on Linked Lists," Report P-3122, Rand Corporation, April 1965.

Conrad, William R. (1974) "A Compactifying Garbage Collector for ECL's Non-Homogeneous Heap," Technical Report 2-74, Center for Research in Computing Technology, Harvard University, Cambridge, Massachusetts, February 1974.

Conte, S. D. and C. de Boor (1972) *Elementary Numerical Analysis — an Algorithmic Approach*, Second Edition, McGraw-Hill, New York.

Darlington, J. and R. M. Burstall (1976) "A System Which Automatically Improves Programs," *Acta Informatica*, Vol. 6, pp. 41—60.

Davis, Randall, Bruce Buchanan, and E. Shortliffe (1977) "Production Rules as a Representation for a Knowledge-based Consultation Program," *Artificial Intelligence*, Vol. 8, No. 1, pp. 15—4646, February 1977.

Davis, Randall (1979a) "Interactive Transfer of Expertise: Acquisition of New Inference Rules," *Artificial Intelligence*, Vol. 12, No. 2, pp. 121—158, August 1979.

Davis, Randall (1979b) "Applications of Meta Level Knowledge to the Construction, Maintenance, and Use of Large Knowledge Bases," Ph. D. Thesis, Stanford University, Stanford, California. Also in *Knowledge-Based Systems in Artificial Intelligence*, Randall Davis and Douglas Lenat, 1980.

Davis Randall and Douglas Lenat (1980) *Knowledge-Based Systems in Artificial Intelligence*, McGraw-Hill, New York.

Deutsch, E. S. (1972) "Thinning Algorithms on Rectangular, Hexagonal, and Triangular Arrays," *Communications of the ACM*, Vol. 15, No. 9, pp. 827—837, September 1972.

Deutsch, L. P. and E. Berkeley (1964) "The LISP Implementation for the PDP-1 Computer," in *The Programming Language LISP: Its Operation and Applications*, edited by E. C. Berkeley and Daniel G. Bobrow.

Deutsch, L. P. and B. W. Lampson (1965) "Reference Manual, 930 LISP," University of California, Berkeley, California.

Deutsch, L. P. (1973) "A Lisp Machine With Very Compact Programs," *Proceedings of the 3rd International Joint Conference on Artificial Intelligence.* pp. 697—703, Stanford, California, 20-23 August 1973. Available from Stanford Research Institute, Menlo Park, California.

Deutsch, P. (1979) "Experience with a Microprogrammed Interlisp System," *IEEE Transactions on Computers*, Vol. C-28, No. 10, October 1979.

Dodd, George, D., and Lothar Rossol (editors) (1979) *Computer Vision and Sensor-Based Robotics*, Plenum Press, New York.

Duda, Richard O. and Peter E. Hart (1973) *Pattern Recognition and Scene Analysis*, Wiley, New York.

Duda, Richard O., Peter E. Hart, Nils J. Nilsson, and G. L. Sutherland (1978) "Semantic Network Representations in Rule-Based Inference Systems," in *Pattern Directed Inference Systems*, edited by D. A. Waterman and F. Hayes-Roth.

Duda, Richard O., Peter E. Hart, P. Barrett, John G. Gaschnig, K. Konolige, R. Reboh, and J. Slocum (1978) "Development of the Prospector Consultation System for Mineral Exploration," Final Report, SRI Projects 5821 and 6415, SRI International, Menlo Park, California, October 1978.

Eastlake, Donald, Richard Greenblatt, Jack Holloway, Thomas Knight and Steward Nelson (1969) "ITS 1.5 Reference Manual," Memo No. 161A, Artificial Intelligence Laboratory, MIT, Cambridge, Massachusetts, July 1969.

Eastlake, Donald (1972) "ITS Status Report," Memo No. 238, Artificial Intelligence Laboratory, MIT, Cambridge, Massachusetts, April 1972.

Ejiri, Masakazu, Tekeshi Uno, Michihiro Mese, and Sadahiro Ikeda (1973) "A Process for Detecting Defects in Complicated Patterns," *Computer Graphics and Image Processing*, Vol. 2, No. 3, pp. 326—339.

Ernst, G. W. and A. Newell (1967) *Generality and GPS*, Carnegie Institue of Technology, Pittsburgh, Pennsylvania.

Ericson, Lars Warren (1979) "Translation of Programs from MACLISP to INTERLISP," MTR-3874, MITRE Corporation, Bedford, Massachusetts, November 1979.

Ernst, G. W. and A. Newell (1969) *GPS: A Case Study in Generality and Problem Solving*, Academic Press, New York.

Evans, A. Jr. (1972) "The Lambda Calculus and its Relation to Programming Languages," *Proceedings of the ACM Annual Conference*, Association for Computing Machinery, New York, pp. 714—716.

Evans, Thomas G. (1962) "A Heuristic Program to Solve Geometric-Analogy Problems," Memo No. 46, Artificial Intelligence Project, Computation Center and Research Laboratory of Electronics, MIT, Cambridge, Massachusetts, October 1962. Also in *Semantic Information Processing*, edited by Marvin Minsky, pp. 271—353, 1968.

Fahlman, Scott E. (1974) "A Planning System for Robot Construction Tasks," *Artificial Intelligence*, Vol. 5, No. 1, pp. 1—49. Spring 1974.

Feigenbaum, Edward, A. and Julian Feldman (editors) (1963) *Computers and Thought*, McGraw-Hill, New York.

Fenichel, R. R. and J. C. Yochelson (1969) "A LISP Garbage-Collector for Virtual-Memory Computer Systems," *Communications of the ACM*, Vol. 12, No. 11, pp. 611—612, November 1969.

Fenichel, R. R. (1970) "A New List-Tracing Algorithm," Technical Report 19, Project MAC, MIT, Cambridge, Massachusetts.

Fikes, Richard E. and Nils J. Nilsson (1971) "STRIPS: A New Approach to the Application of Theorem Proving to Problem Solving," *Artificial Intelligence*, Vol. 2, No. 3-4, pp. 189—208, Winter 1971.

Fikes, Richard E., Peter E. Hart, and Nils J. Nilsson (1972) "Learning and Executing Generalized Robot Plans," *Artificial Intelligence*, Vol. 3, No. 4, pp. 251—288, Winter 1972.

Findler, N. V. and B. Meltzer (editors) (1971) *Artifical Intelligence and Heuristic Programming*, American Elsevier, New York.

Firestone, Roger M. (1980) "An Experimental LISP System for the Sperry Univac 1100 Series," *ACM SIGPLAN Notices*, Vol. 15, No. 1, pp. 117—129, January 1980.

Foderaro, John K. (1979) "The FRANZ LISP Manual," University of California, Berkeley, California.

Foster, J. M. (1967) *List Processing*, American Elsevier, New York.

Frey, Peter W. (1977) *Chess Skill in Man and Machine*, Springer Verlag, New York.

Friedman, D. (1974) *The Little LISPer*, Science Research Associates, Palo Alto, California.

Galley, S. W. and Greg Pfister (1975) *The MDL Language*, Document SYS.11.01, Laboratory for Computer Science, MIT, Cambridge, Massachusetts, November 1975.

Gelernter, H. (1963) "Realization of a Geometry Theorem-Proving Machine," *Proceedings Internatinal Conference Information Processing* UNESCO House, Paris, pp. 273—282. Also in *Computers and Thought*, edited by Edward A. Feigenbaum and Julian Feldman, pp. 134—152, 1963.

Gilmore, P. C. (1963) "An Abstract Computer with a LISP-like Machine Language without a LABEL operator," in *Computer Programming and Formal Systems*, edited by P. Braffort and D. Hirshberg, pp. 71—86, 1963.

Gillogly J. J. (1972) "The Technology Chess Program," *Artificial Intelligence*, Vol. 3, No. 4, pp. 145—163, Winter 1972.

Gleason, Gerald J. and Gerald J. Agin (1979) "A Modular Vision System for Sensor-Controlled Manipulation and Inspection," Technical Note 178, Artificial Intelligence Center, SRI International, Menlo Park, California, February 1979.

Golay, M. J. E. (1969) "Hexagonal Parallel Pattern Transformations," *IEEE Transactions on Computers*, Vol. C-18, No. 8, pp. 733—740, August 1969.

Golden, Jeffrey P. (1970) "A User's Guide to the A.I. Group LISCOM LISP Compiler: Interim Report," Memo No. 210, Artificial Intelligence Laboratory, MIT, Cambridge, Massachusetts, December 1970.

Goldstein, Ira P. (1973) "Pretty-Printing — Converting List to Linear Structure, Memo No. 279, Artificial Intelligence Laboratory, MIT, Cambridge, Massachusetts, February 1973.

Goldstein, Ira P. (1978) "Developing a Computational Representation for Problem Solving Skills," Memo No. 495, Artificial Intelligence Laboratory, MIT, Cambridge, Massachusetts, November 1978.

Goto, Eiichi (1974) "Monocopy and Associative Algorithms in an Extended LISP," Information Science Laboratory, University of Tokyo, May 1974.

Gray, S. B. (1971) "Local Properties of Binary Images in Two Dimensions," *IEEE Transactions on Computers*, Vol. C-20, No. 5, pp. 551—561, May 1971.

Green, Cordell, and David Barstow (1978) "On Program Synthesis Knowledge," *Artificial Intelligence*, Vol. 10, No. 3, pp. 241—280, November 1978.

Greenberg, Bernard S. (1976) *Notes on the Programming Language LISP*, Student Information Processing Board, MIT, Cambridge, Massachusetts, Revised 1978.

Greenberg, Bernard S. (1977) "The Multics MACLISP Compiler — the Basic Hackery," unpublished paper, Honeywell Information Systems, Cambridge, Massachusetts, December 1977.

Greenberg, Bernard S. and Katie Kissel (1979) *EMACS Text Editor Users' Guide*, Order Number CH27-00, Honeywell, Waltham, Massachusetts, December 1979.

Greenblatt, Richard (1974) "The LISP Machine," Working Paper 79, Artificial Intelligence Laboratory, MIT, Cambridge, Massachusetts, November 1974.

Greenblatt, Richard, Tom Knight, John Holloway, and David Moon (1979) *The LISP Machine*, Artificial Intelligence Laboratory, MIT, Cambridge, Massachusetts.

Greussay, P. (1976) "Iterative Interpretation of Tail-Recursive LISP Procedures," Technical Report 20-76, University of Vincennes, Paris.

Grishman, R. and L. Hirschman (1978) "Question Answering from Natural Language Data Bases," *Artificial Intelligence*, Vol. 11, No. 1-2, pp. 25—44, August 1978.

Griss, M. L. and M. R. Swanson (1977) "MBALM/1700: A Microprogrammed LISP-Machine for the Burroughs B1726," UUCS-77-109, Computer Science, Utah University, Salt Lake City, Utah, April 1977.

Hamming, R. W. (1962) *Numerical Methods for Scientists and Engineers*, McGraw-Hill, New York.

Hansen, Wilfred J. (1969) "Compact List Representation: Definition, Garbage Collection, and System Implementation," *Communications of the ACM*, Vol. 12, No. 9, pp. 499—507, September 1969.

Hanson, A. R. and E. M. Riseman (editors) (1978) *Computer Vision Systems*, Academic Press, New York.

Harris, Larry R. (1977) "A High Performance Natural Language Processor for Data Base Query," *ACM SIGART Newsletter 61*, February 1977.

Harrison, M. C. (1970) "BALM — An Extensible List-Processing Language," *Proceedings of AFIPS Spring Joint Computer Conference*, Vol. 36, pp. 507—511.

Hart, Peter E., Richard O. Duda and M. T. Einaudi (1979) "A Computer-Based Consultation System for Mineral Exploration," in *Computer Methods for the 80's*, edited by Michel David, Society of Mining Engineers.

Hart, T. P. (1963) "MACRO Definitions in LISP," Memo No. 57, Artificial Intelligence Project, Computation Center and Research Laboratory of Electronics, MIT, Cambridge, Massachusetts, October 1963.

Hart, T. P. and T. G. Evans (1964) "Notes on Implementing LISP for the M-460 Computer," *The Programming Language LISP: Its Operation and Applications*, edited by E. C. Berkeley and Daniel G. Bobrow, pp. 191—203.

Hayes-Roth, Frederick, and Victor R. Lesser (1977) "Focus of Attention in the Hearsay-II Speech Understanding System," *Proceedings of the 5th International Joint Conference on Artificial Intelligence*, Cambridge, Massachusetts, 22—25 August 1977, pp. 27—35. Available from Department of Computer Science, Carnegie-Mellon University, Pittsburgh, Pennsylvania.

Hearn, Anthony C. (1966) "Standard LISP," *ACM SIGPLAN Notices*, Vol. 4, No. 9, September 1966.

Hearn, Anthony C. (1969) "Standard LISP," AIM-90, Artificial Intelligence Project, Stanford University, Stanford, California, March 1969.

Hearn, Anthony C. (1971) "A Program and Language for Algebraic Manipulation," *Proceedings of the Second Symposium on Symbolic and Algebraic Manipulation*, ACM, New York, pp. 128—133.

Hearn, Anthony C. (1974) "REDUCE 2 Symbolic Mode Primer," Operating Note No. UPC-5.1, Computational Physics, University of Utah, Salt Lake City, Utah, October 1974.

Hearn, Anthony C. and Arthur C. Norman (1979) "A One-pass Prettyprinter," *ACM SIGPLAN Notices*, Vol. 14, No. 12, pp. 50—58, December 1979.

Hedrick, C. L (1976) "Learning Production Systems from Examples," *Artificial Intelligence*, Vol. 7, No. 1, pp. 21—50, Spring 1976.

Hendrix, Gary G., Earl D. Sacerdoti, Daniel Sagalowicz, and Jonathan Slocum (1978) "Developing a Natural Language Interface to Complex Data," *ACM Transactions on Database Systems*, Vol. 3, No. 2, June 1978.

Hewitt, Carl (1977) "Viewing Control Structures as Patterns of Passing Messages," *Artificial Intelligence*, Vol. 8, No. 3, pp. 324—364, June 1977.

Hildebrand, F. B. (1974) *Introduction to Numerical Analysis*, Second Edition, McGraw-Hill, New York.

Holland, S. W., L. Rossol and M. R. Ward (1979) "CONSIGHT-1: A Vision-controlled Robot System for Transferring Parts From Belt Conveyors," in *Computer Vision and Sensor-Based Robotics*, edited by George D. Dodd and Lothar Rossol, pp. 81—100.

Horn, Berthold K. P. (1970) "Shape-from-Shading: A Method for Obtaining the Shape of a Smooth Opaque Object from One View," Technical Report 79, Project MAC, MIT, Cambridge, Massachusetts, November 1970. Also in *The Psychology of Computer Vision*, edited by Patrick H. Winston, pp. 115—155, April 1975.

Horn, Berthold K. P. (1974) "Determining Lightness from an Image," *Computer Graphics and Image Processing*, Vol. 3, No. 1, pp. 277—299, December 1974.

Horn, Berthold K. P. and Patrick H. Winston (1975) "Personal Computers," *Datamation*, pp. 111—115, May 1975.

Horn, Berthold K. P. (1977) "Understanding Image Intensities," *Artificial Intelligence*, Vol. 8, No. 2, pp. 201—231, April 1977.

Horn, Berthold K. P. (1979) "Artificial Intelligence and the Science of Image Understanding," in *Computer Vision and Sensor-Based Robots*, edited by George G. Dodd and Lothar Rossol, pp. 69—77.

Horn, Berthold K. P. (1980) "Derivation of Invariant Scene Characteristics from Images," *Proceedings of AFIPS National Computer Conference*, Vol. 49, pp. 245—250, 19-23 May 1980.

Hunt, Earl, B. (1975) *Artificial Intelligence*, Academic Press, New York.

IBM (1978) "LISP/370 Program Description/Operations Manual," Program Number: 5796-PKL, Manual Number: SN20-2076-0, IBM, Detroit.

Iyanga, S. and Y. Kawada (editors) (1977) *Encyclopedic Dictionary of Mathematics*, pp. 38—39 in Vol. 1 and p. 1396 in Vol. 2 (English tranlation), The MIT Press, Cambridge, Massachusetts.

Jackson, Philip, C. (1974) *Introduction to Artificial Intelligence*, Mason and Liscomb, New York.

Johnson, E. S. and R. F. Rosin (1965) "SLIP: A Symmetric List Processor," Computing Center, Yale University, New Haven, Connecticut, May 1965.

Kameny, S. L. (1965) *LISP 1.5 Reference Manual for Q-32*, TM-2337/101/0, System Development Corporation, August 1965.

Kaplan, R. M. (1972) "Augmented Transition Networks as Psychological Models of Sentence Comprehension," *Artificial Intelligence*, Vol. 3, No. 4, pp. 77—100, Winter 1972.

Kent, J. (1966) "LISP 3600: User's Manual," Norwegian Defense Research Establishment, Catalogue L2 KCIN LISP, Kjeller, Norway.

Kleene, Stephen Cole (1950) *Introduction to Metamathematics*, Von Nostrand, Princeton.

Klimbie, J. W. and K. I. Koffeman (editors) (1974) *Data Base Management*, North-Holland, Amsterdam.

Knight, Thomas, (1974) "The CONS Microprocessor," Working Paper 80, Artificial Intelligence Laboratory, MIT, Cambridge, Massachusetts, November 1974.

Knight, Tom, David Moon, John Holloway, and Guy Steele (1979) "CADR," Memo No. 528, Artificial Intelligence Laboratory, MIT, Cambridge, Massachusetts, June 1979.

Knuth, Donald E. (1968) *The Art of Computer Programming, Volume 1, Fundamental Algorithms*, Addison-Wesley, Reading, Massachusetts.

Knuth, Donald E. (1969) *The Art of Computer Programming, Volume 2, Seminumerical Algorithms*, Addison-Wesley, Reading, Massachusetts.

Knuth, Donald E. (1973) *The Art of Computer Programming, Volume 3, Sorting and Searching*, Addison-Wesley, Reading, Massachusetts.

Knuth, Donald E. (1974) "Structured Programming with GO-TO Statements," *ACM Computing Surveys*, Vol. 6, No. 4, pp. 261—302, December 1974.

Kornfeld, William A. (1979) "Pattern-directed Invocation Languages," *Byte*, Vol. 4, No. 8, pg. 34, August 1979.

Kung, H. T. and S. W. Song (1977) "An Efficient, Parallel Garbage Collection System and its Correctness Proof," Department of Computer Science, Carnegie-Mellon University, Pittsburgh, Pennsylvania, September 1977.

Landin, P. (1964) "The Mechanical Evaluation of Expressions," *Computer Journal*, Vol. 6, No. 4, pp. 308—320.

Landin, P. (1965) "A Correspondence between ALGOL 60 and Church's LAMBDA-Notation," *Communications of the ACM*, Vol. 8, No. 2, pp. 89—101, February 1965, and Vol. 8, No. 3, pp. 158—165, March 1965.

LeFaivre, R. (1978) *Rutgers/UCI LISP Manual*, Rutgers University.

Lenat, Douglas B. (1976) "AM: An Artificial Intelligence Approach to Discovery in Mathematics as Heuristic Search," STAN-CS-76-570, Computer Science Department, Stanford University Stanford, California. Also in *Knowledge-Based Systems in Artificial Intelligence*, Randall Davis and Douglas Lenat, 1980.

Lenat, Douglas B. (1977) "The Ubiquity of Discovery," *Artificial Intelligence*, Vol. 9, No. 3, pp. 257—286, December 1977.

Levialdi, S. (1972) "On Shrinking Binary Picture Patterns," *Communications of the ACM*, Vol. 15, No. 1, pp. 7—10, January 1972.

Lewis, V. Ellen (1977a) "User Aids for MACSYMA," *Proceedings of the MACSYMA User's Conference*, NASA, Berkeley, California, 27—29 July 1977, pp. 277—290.

Lewis, V. Ellen (1977b) "An Introduction to ITS for the MACSYMA User," Laboratory for Computer Science, MIT, Cambridge, Massachusetts, September 1977. Revised January 1979.

Lieberman, Henry and Carl Hewitt (1980) "A Real Time Garbage Collector that can Recover Temporary Storage Quickly," Memo No. 569, Artificial Intelligence Laboratory, MIT, Cambridge, Massachusetts, April 1980.

Lozano-Perez, Tomas (1980) "Spatial Planning with Polyhedral Models" Ph. D. Thesis, MIT, Cambridge, Massachusetts, June 1980.

Luckham, D., and Nils J. Nilsson (1971) "Extracting Information from Resolution Proof Trees," *Artificial Intelligence*, Vol. 2, No. 1, pp. 27—54, Spring 1971.

Maekilae, K. and T. Risch (1975) "PL360-LISP — A LISP 1.5 Interpreter written in PL360," FOA Report C10041-M3(E5), Foervarets Forskninganstalt, Stockholm, Sweden.

Manove, M. (1965) "INTEGRATE: A Program for the Machine Computation of the Indefinite Integral of Rational Functions," TM-4204, MITRE Corporation, Bedford, Massachusetts, April 1965.

Marti, J., A. C. Hearn, M. L. Griss, and C. Griss (1979) "Standard LISP Report," *ACM SIGPLAN Notices*, Vol. 14, No. 10, pp. 48-68, October 1979.

Martin, William A. and Tim Hart (1963) "Revised User's Version, Time Sharing LISP for CTSS," Memo No. 67, Artificial Intelligence Project, Computation Center and Research Laboratory of Electronics, MIT, Cambridge, Massachusetts.

Martin, William A. (1967) "Symbolic Mathematical Laboratory," Report No. MAC-TR-36, Project MAC, MIT, Cambridge, Massachusetts, January 1967.

Maurer, W. D. (1973) *A Programmer's Introduction to LISP*, American Elsevier, New York.

McCarthy, John (1958) "Programs with Common Sense," *Mechanisation of Thought Processes, Proceedings Symposium National Physics Laboratory*, Vol. 1, pp. 77—84, Her Majesty's Stationary Office, London. Also in *Semantic Information Processing*, edited by Marvin Minsky, 1968, pp. 403—410.

McCarthy, John (1960) "Recursive Functions of Symbolic Expressions and their Computation by Machine, Part I," *Communications of the ACM*, Vol. 3, No. 4, pp. 185—195, April 1960.

McCarthy, John, R. Brayton, D. Edwards, P. A. Fox, L. Hodes, D. Luckham, K. Maling, D. Park, and S. Russell (1960) "LISP 1 Programmer's Manual," Artifical Intelligence Group, Computation Center and Research Laboratory of Electronics, MIT, Cambridge, Massachusetts, March 1960.

McCarthy, John (1961a) "A Basis for a Mathematical Theory of Computation," *Proceedings of the Western Joint Computer Conference*, corrected version in *Computer Programming and Formal Systems*, edited by P. Braffort and D. Hirshberg, pp. 33—70, 1963.

McCarthy, John (1961b) "Computer Program for Checking Mathematical Proofs," *Proceedings of the American Mathematical Society on Recursive Function Theory*, New York, April 1961.

McCarthy, John, P. W. Abrahams, D. J. Edwards, T. P. Hart, and M. I. Levin (1962) *LISP 1.5 Programmer's Manual*, The MIT Press, Cambridge, Massachusetts.

McCarthy, John (1978) "A Micromanual for LISP — Not the Whole Truth," *ACM SIGPLAN Notices*, Vol. 13, No. 8, pp. 215—216, August 1978.

McCarthy, John (1978) "History of LISP," *ACM SIGPLAN Notices*, Vol. 13, No. 8, pp. 217—223, August 1978.

McDermott, Drew V. and Gerald Jay Sussman (1974) "The CONNIVER Reference Manual," Memo No. 259A, Artificial Intelligence Laboratory, MIT, Cambridge, Massachusetts, January 1974.

McDermott, Drew V. (1975) "Very Large PLANNER-type Data Bases," Memo No. 339, Artificial Intelligence Laboratory, MIT, Cambridge, Massachusetts,

September 1975.

McCorduck, P. (1979) *Machines Who Think*, W. H. Freeman, San Fransisco.

Meehan, J. R. (1979) *New UCI LISP Manual*, Lawrence Erlbaum Associates, Hillsdale, New Jersey.

Metcalfe, R. M. and D. R. Boggs (1976) "ETHERNET: Distributed Packet Switching for Local Computer Networks," *Communications of the ACM*, Vol. 19, No. 7, pp. 395-404, July 1976.

Minker, J., D. H. Fishman, and J. R. McSkimin (1972) "The Q* Algorithm — A Search Strategy for a Deductive Question-answering System," *Artificial Intelligence*, Vol. 4, No. 3-4, pp. 225—244, Winter 1973.

Minsky, Marvin (1963) "A LISP Garbage Collector Using Serial Secondary Storage," Memo No. 58, Artificial Intelligence Laboratory, MIT, Cambridge, Massachusetts, October 1963.

Minsky, Marvin (editor) (1968) *Semantic Information Processing*, The MIT Press, Cambridge, Massachusetts.

Minsky, Marvin and Seymour Papert (1969) *Perceptrons: An Introduction to Computational Geometry*, The MIT Press, Cambridge, Massachusetts.

Minsky, Marvin (1975) "A Framework for Representing Knowledge," in *The Psychology of Computer Vision*, edited by Patrick H. Winston, pp. 211—277.

Moon, David (1974) *MACLISP Reference Manual*, Version 0, Laboratory for Computer Science, MIT, Cambridge, Massachusetts, April 1974. Parts 1,2, and 3 revised 1978.

Moore, J. Strother (1976) "The INTERLISP Virtual Machine Specification," CSL-76-6, Xerox Corporation, Palo Alto Research Center, Palo Alto, California. September 1976.

Morris, F. Lockwood (1978) "A Time- and Space-Efficient Garbage Compaction Algorithm," *Communications of the ACM*, Vol. 21, No. 8, pp. 662—665, August 1978.

Moses, Joel and Robert Fenichel (1966) "A New Version of CTSS LISP," Memo No. 93, Artifical Intelligence Group, Computation Center and Research Laboratory of Electronics, MIT, Cambridge, Massachusetts.

Moses, Joel (1966) "Symbolic Integration," Memo No. 97, Artifical Intelligence Group, Computation Center and Research Laboratory of Electronics, MIT, Cambridge, Massachusetts, June 1966.

Moses, Joel (1970) "The Function of FUNCTION in LISP," *ACM SIGSAM Bulletin*, pp. 13—27, July 1970.

Moses, Joel (1974) "MACSYMA — The Fifth Year," *Proceedings of the EUROSAM Conference*, in *ACM SIGSAM Bulletin*, August 1974.

Mathlab Group, The (1977) *MACSYMA Reference Manual*, Laboratory for Computer Science, MIT, Cambridge, Massachusetts, Version 9, December 1977.

Nagy, George (1969) "Feature Extraction on Binary Patterns," *IEEE Transactions on Systems Science and Cybernetics*, Vol. SSC-5, No. 4, pp. 273—278, October 1969.

Newell, Allen (editor) (1961) *Information Processing Language V Manual*, Prentice Hall, Englewood Cliffs, New Jersey.

Newell, Allen and Herbert A. Simon (1972) *Human Problem Solving*, Prentice Hall, Englewood Cliffs, New Jersey.

Nilsson, Nils J. (1971) *Problem Solving Methods in Artificial Intelligence*, McGraw-Hill, New York.

Nilsson, Nils J. (1980) *Principles of Artificial Intelligence*, Tioga Publishing Company, Palo Alto, California.

Nordstroem, Mats, Erik Sandewall, and Diz Breslow (1975) "LISP F1: A FORTRAN Implementation of LISP 1.5," Department of Computer Science, Uppsala University. Uppsala, Sweden.

Norman, Eric (1978) *LISP Reference Manual for the UNIVAC 1108*, Computing Center, University of Wisconsin, October 1978.

Oppen, Derek C. (1979) "Pretty Printing," STAN-CS-79-770, Department of Computer Science, Stanford University, Stanford, California.

Organick, E. I., A. I. Forsythe, and R. D. Plummer (1978) *Programming Language Structures*, Chapter 7, Academic Press, New York.

Osman, E. (1971) "DDT Reference Manual," Memo No. 147A, Artificial Intelligence Laboratory, MIT, Cambridge, Massachusetts, September 1971.

Petrick, S. R. (1976) "On Natural Language Based Computing Systems," *IBM Journal of Research and Development*, Vol. 20, No. 4.

Postma, Stefan Willem (1979) "A Critical Evaluation of the Programming Language LISP with Suggestions for Possible Improvements," M. Sc. Dissertation, Computer Science, Randse Afrikaanse Universiteit, Johannesburg.

Pratt, T. W. (1975) *Programming Languages: Design and Implementation*, Chapters 7 and 14, Prentice Hall, Englewood Cliffs, New Jersey.

Pratt, Vaughan R. (1976) "CGOL — An Alternative External Respresentation for LISP Users," Working Paper 121, Artificial Intelligence Laboratory, MIT, Cambridge, Massachusetts, March 1976.

Pratt, Vaughan R. (1979) "A Mathematician's View of LISP," *Byte*, Vol. 4, No. 8, pg. 162, August 1979.

Preston, K. (1971) "Feature Extraction by Golay Hexagonal Pattern Transforms," *IEEE Transaction on Computers*, Vol. C-20, No. 9, pp. 1007—1014, September 1971.

Quam, L. and W. Diffie (1972) *Stanford LISP 1.6 Manual*, Operating Note 28.7, Artificial Intelligence Laboratory, Stanford University, Stanford, California.

Raphael, Bertram (1976) *The Thinking Computer: Mind Inside Matter*, W. H. Freeman, San Francisco.

Reboh, R. and Earl Sacerdoti (1973) "A Preliminary QLISP Manual," Technical Note 81, Artificial Intelligence Center, Stanford Research Institute, Menlo Park, California.

Reddy, Raj (1976) "Speech Recognition by Machine: a Review," *Proceedings of the IEEE*, Vol. 64, No. 4, April 1976.

Ribbens, D. (1970) *Programmation Non Numerique, LISP 1.5*, Dunod, Paris.

Roberts, R. Bruce and Ira P. Goldstein (1977a) "The FRL Primer," Memo No. 408, Artificial Intelligence Laboratory, MIT, Cambridge, Massachusetts, July 1977.

Roberts, R. Bruce and Ira P. Goldstein (1977b) "The FRL Manual," Memo No. 409, Artificial Intelligence Laboratory, MIT, Cambridge, Massachusetts, June 1977.

Robinson, J. A. (1965) "A Machine-Oriented Logic Based on the Resolution Principle," *Journal of the ACM*, Vol. 12, pp. 23—41, January 1965.

Rogers, Hartley, Jr. (1967) *Theory of Recursive Functions and Effective Computability*, McGraw-Hill, New York.

Rulifson, J. F., J. A. Derksen, and R. J. Waldinger (1972) "QA4: A Procedural Calculus for Intuitive Reasoning," Technical Note 73, Artificial Intelligence Center, Stanford Research Institute, Menlo Park, California, November 1972.

Sacerdoti, Earl D. (1974) "Planning in a Hierarchy of Abstraction Spaces," *Artificial Intelligence*, Vol. 5, No. 2, pp. 115—135, Summer 1974.

Sacerdoti, Earl D. (1976) "QLISP — A Language for the Interactive Development of Complex Systems," *Proceedings of AFIPS National Computer Conference*, pp. 349—356.

Samuel, A. L. (1959) "Some Studies in Machine Learning Using the Game of Checkers," *IBM Journal of Research and Development*, Vol. 3, pp. 211—229. Also in *Computers and Thought*, edited by Edward A. Feigenbaum and Julian Feldman, pp. 71—105, 1963.

Samson, Peter (1966) "PDP-6 LISP," Memo No. 98, Artifical Intelligence Group, Computation Center and Research Laboratory of Electronics, MIT, Cambridge, Massachusetts, June 1966.

Sandewall, Erik (1971) "A Proposed Solution to the FUNARG Problem," *ACM SIGSAM Bulletin*, Vol. 17, pp. 29—42, January 1971.

Sandewall, Erik (1975) "Ideas About Management of LISP Data Bases," *Advance Papers of the Fourth International Conference on Artificial Intelligence*, Artificial Intelligence Laboratory, MIT, Cambridge, Massachusetts.

Sandewall, Erik (1977) "Some Observations on Conceptual Programming," in *Machine Intelligence 8*, edited by E. W. Elcock and Donald Michie, Ellis Horwood, Chichester, distributed by Halstead Press, a division of John Wiley, New York.

Sandewall, Erik (1978) "Programming in the Interactive Environment: The LISP Experience," *ACM Computing Surveys*, Vol. 10, No. 1, pp. 35—72, March 1978.

Saunders, Robert A. (1964) "The LISP System for the Q-32 Computer," in *The Programming Language LISP: Its Operation and Applications*, edited by E. C. Berkeley and Daniel G. Bobrow.

Schank, Roger C., and Kenneth Colby (1973) *Computer Models of Thought and Language*, W. H. Freeman, San Francisco.

Schank, Roger C., and Chuck Rieger (1974) "Inference and the Computer Understanding of Natural Language," *Artificial Intelligence*, Vol. 5, No. 4, pp. 373—412, Winter 1974.

Schank, Roger C., and Robert P. Abelson (1977) *Scripts, Plans, Goals, and Understanding*, Lawrence Erlbaum Associates, Hillsdale, New Jersey, distributed by Halstead Press, a division of John Wiley, New York.

Schorr, H. and W. M. Waite (1967) "An Efficient Machine-Independent Procedure for Garbage Collection in Various List Structures," *Communications of the ACM*, Vol. 10, No. 8, pp. 501—506, August 1967.

Shannon, C. E. (1950) "Programming a Computer for Playing Chess," *Philosophical Magazine*, Series 7, Vol. 41, pp. 256—275.

Shapiro, S. C. (1979) *Techniques of Artificial Intelligence*, Van Nostrand, New York.

Shortliffe, E. H. (1976) *Computer Based Medical Consultations: MYCIN*, American Elsevier, New York.

Siklossy, Laurent, A. Rich, and V. Marinov (1973) "Breadth-first Search: Some Surprising Results," *Artificial Intelligence*, Vol. 4, No. 1, pp. 1—27, Spring 1973.

Siklossy, Laurent, and J. Roach (1975) "Model Verification and Improvement using DISPROVER," *Artificial Intelligence*, Vol. 6, No. 1, pp. 41—52, Spring 1975.

Siklossy, Laurent (1976) *Let's Talk LISP*, Prentice-Hall, Englewood Cliffs, New Jersey.

Siemens (1976) "SIEMENS INTERLISP 4004 Users Manual," Siemens Datenverarbeitung, Munich, Germany.

Simon, Herbert A., and J. B. Kadane (1975) "Optimal Problem-solving Search: All-or-none Solutions," *Artificial Intelligence*, Vol. 6, No. 3, pp. 235—247, Fall 1975.

Slagle, James R. (1963) "A Heuristic Program that Solves Symbolic Integration Problems in Freshman Calculus," *Journal of the ACM*, Vol. 10, pp. 507—520, October 1963. Also in *Computers and Thought*, edited by Edward A. Feigenbaum and Julian Feldman, pp. 191—206, 1963.

Slagle, J. R. (1971) *Artificial Intelligence: The Heuristic Programming Approach*, McGraw-Hill, New York.

Smith, David C. (1970) "MLISP," AIM-135, Artificial Intelligence Project, Stanford University, Stanford, California, October 1970.

Smith, David C. and H. J. Enea (1973) "MLISP2," AIM-195, Artificial Intelligence Project, Stanford University, Stanford, California, May 1973.

Stallman, Richard M. and Gerald Jay Sussman (1977) "Forward Reasoning and Dependency-directed Backtracking in a System for Computer-aided Circuit Analysis," *Artificial Intelligence*, Vol. 9, No. 2, pp. 135—196, October 1977. Also in *Artificial Intelligence: An MIT Perspective*, Volume 1, edited by Patrick H. Winston and Richard H. Brown, pp. 31—91.

Stallman, Richard, M. (1979) "EMACS — The Extensible, Customizable, Self-Documenting Display Editor," Memo No. 519, Artificial Intelligence Laboratory, MIT, Cambridge, Massachusetts, June 1979.

Steele, Guy Lewis, Jr. (1975) "Multiprocessing Compactifying Garbage Collection," *Communications of the ACM*, Vol. 18, No. 9, pp. 495-508, September 1975.

Steele, Guy Lewis, Jr. (1976) "LAMBDA — The Ultimate Imperative," Memo No. 353, Artificial Intelligence Laboratory, MIT, Cambridge, Massachusetts, March 1976.

Steele, Guy Lewis, Jr. (1977a) "Data Representation in LISP," Memo No. 420, Artificial Intelligence Laboratory, MIT, Cambridge, Massachusetts. Also in *Proceedings of the MACSYMA User's Conference*, NASA, Berkeley, California, 27—29 July 1977.

Steele, Guy Lewis, Jr. (1977b) "Fast Arithmetic in MACLISP," Memo No. 421, Artificial Intelligence Laboratory, MIT, Cambridge, Massachusetts. Also in *Proceedings of the MACSYMA User's Conference*, NASA, Berkeley, California, pp. 215—224, 27—29 July 1977.

Steele, Guy Lewis, Jr. (1977c) "Debunking the 'Expensive Procedure Call' Myth," *Proceedings ACM National Conference*, Seattle, Washington, October 1977, pp. 153—162. Revised as Memo No. 443, Artificial Intelligence Laboratory, MIT, Cambridge, Massachusetts, October 1977.

Steele, Guy Lewis, Jr. and Gerald Jay Sussman (1978a) "The Revised Report on SCHEME: A Dialect of LISP," Memo No. 452, Artificial Intelligence Laboratory, MIT, Cambridge, Massachusetts, January 1978.

Steele, Guy Lewis, Jr. and Gerald Jay Sussman (1978b) "The Art of the Interpreter, or, The Modularity Complex," Memo No. 453, Artificial Intelligence Laboratory, MIT, Cambridge, Massachusetts, May 1978.

Steele, Guy Lewis, Jr. (1979) "Compiler Optimization Based on Viewing LAMBDA as RENAME plus GOTO," in *Artificial Intelligence: An MIT Perspective*, Volume 2, edited by Patrick H. Winston and Richard H. Brown, pp. 401—431.

Steele, Guy Lewis, Jr. and Gerald Jay Sussman (1979) "Design of LISP-Based Processors," Memo No. 514, Artificial Intelligence Laboratory, MIT, Cambridge, Massachusetts, March 1979.

Stefanelli, R. and A. Rosenfeld (1971) "Some Parallel Thinning Algorithms for Digital Pictures," *Journal of the ACM*, Vol. 18, No. 2, pp. 255—264, April 1971.

Stockman, G. C. (1979) "A Minimax Algorithm Better than Alpha-beta?" *Artificial Intelligence*, Vol. 12, No. 2, pp. 179—196, August 1979.

Sussman, Gerald, Terry Winograd, and Eugene Charniak (1971) "MICRO-PLANNER Reference Manual," Memo No. 203A, The Artificial Intelligence Laboratory, MIT, Cambridge, Massachusetts, December 1971.

Sussman, Gerald Jay and Drew V. McDermott (1972) "Why Conniving is Better than Planning," Memo No. 255A, Artificial Intelligence Laboratory, MIT, Cambridge, Massachusetts, April 1972.

Sussman, Gerald Jay and Guy Lewis Steele, Jr. (1975) "SCHEME: An Interpreter for Extended Lambda Calculus," Memo No. 349, Artificial Intelligence Laboratory, MIT, Cambridge, Massachusetts, December 1975.

Szolovits, Peter and Stephan G. Pauker (1978) "Categorical and Probabilistic Reasoning in Medical Diagnosis," *Artificial Intelligence*, Vol. 11, No. 1-2, pp. 115—144, August 1978.

Teitelman, Warren (1974) *INTERLISP Reference Manual*, Xerox Corporation, Palo Alto Research Center, Palo Alto, California, and Bolt, Beranek and Newman, Cambridge, Massachusetts, revised October 1978.

Thacker, C. P., E. M. McCreight, B. W. Lampson, R. F. Sproull, and D. R. Boggs (1979) "ALTO: A Personal Computer," CSL-79-11 Xerox Corporation, Palo Alto Research Center, Palo Alto, California, August 1979.

Touretzky, David S. (1979) *A Summary of MACLISP Functions and Flags*, Carnegie-Mellon University, Pittsburgh, Pennsylvania, August 1979.

Urmi, Jaak (1976a) "INTERLISP/370 Reference Manual," Department of Mathematics, Linkoeping University, Linkoeping, Sweden.

Urmi, Jaak (1976b) "A Shallow Binding Scheme for Fast Environment Changing in a 'Spaghetti Stack' LISP System," Report 76-18, Department of Mathematics, Linkoeping University, Linkoeping, Sweden.

Urmi, Jaak (1978) "A Machine Independent LISP Compiler and its Implications for Ideal Hardware," Report 78-22, Department of Mathematics, Linkoeping University, Linkoeping, Sweden.

Vere, S. A. (1977) "Relational Production Systems," *Artificial Intelligence*, Vol. 8, No. 1, pp. 47—68, February 1977.

Waltz, David (1978) "An English Language Front End for a Large Relational Data Base," *Communications of the ACM*, Vol. 21, No. 7.

Wang, Hao (1960) "Towards Mechanical Mathematics," *IBM Journal of Research and Development*, Vol. 4, pp. 2—22.

Warren, David H. D. and Luis Pereira (1977) "PROLOG: The Language and Its Implementation Compared with LISP," *Proceedings of the Symposium on Artificial Intelligence and Programming Languages*, Rochester, New York, *ACM SIGPLAN Notices* Vol. 12, No. 8, pp. 109—115. August 1977.

Waterman, D. A. (1970) "Generalization Learning Techniques for Automating the Learning of Heuristics," *Artificial Intelligence*, Vol. 1, No. 1-2, pp. 121—170.

Waterman D. A. and F. Hayes-Roth (editors) (1978) *Pattern Directed Inference Systems*, Academic Press, New York.

Weinreb, Daniel and David Moon (1978) *Lisp Machine Manual*, Artificial Intelligence Laboratory, MIT, Cambridge, Massachusetts, revised January 1979.

Weinreb, Daniel L. (1979) "A Real-Time Display-Oriented Editor for the LISP Machine," S. B. Thesis, Department of Electrical Engineering and Computer Science, MIT, January 1979.

Weiss, S. M., C. A. Kulikowski, S. Amarel, and A. Safir (1978) "A Model-based Method for Computer-aided Medical Decision-making," *Artificial Intelligence*, Vol. 11, No. 1-2, pp. 145—172, August 1978.

Weissman, Clark (1967) *LISP 1.5 Primer*, Dickenson Publishing Company, Belmont, California.

Weizenbaum, Joseph (1962) "Knotted List Structures," *Communications of the ACM*, Vol. 5, No. 3, pp. 161-165, March 1962.

Weizenbaum, Joseph (1963) "Symmetric List Processor," *Communications of the ACM*, Vol. 6, No. 10, January 1963.

Weizenbaum, Joseph (1965) "ELIZA — A Computer Program for the Study of Natural Language Communication between Man and Machine," *Communications of the ACM*, Vol. 9, No. 1, January 1965.

White, John L. (1967) "PDP-6 LISP (Lisp 1.6) Revised," Memo No. 116A, Artificial Intelligence Laboratory, MIT, Cambridge, Massachusetts, April 1967.

White, John L. (1970) "An Interim LISP User's Guide," Memo No. 190, Artificial Intelligence Laboratory, MIT, Cambridge, Massachusetts, March 1970.

White, Jon L. (1977a) "Lisp: Program is Data — A Historical Perspective on MACLISP," *Proceedings of the MACSYMA User's Conference*, NASA, Berkeley, California, pp. 181—189, 27—29 July 1977.

White, Jon L. (1977b) "Lisp: Data is Program — A Tutorial in LISP," *Proceedings of the MACSYMA User's Conference*, NASA, Berkeley, California, pp. 190—199, 27—29 July 1977.

White, Jon L. (1978) "LISP/370: A Short Technical Description of the Implementation," *ACM SIGSAM Bulletin*, Vol. 48, pp. 23—27, November 1978.

White, Jon L. (1979) "NIL — A Perspective," *Proceedings of the MACSYMA User's Conference*, Washington, D. C. pp. 190—199, 20 June 1979. Available from Laboratory for Computer Science, MIT, Cambridge, Massachusetts.

Wilber, B. M. (1976) "A QLISP Reference Manual," Technical Note 118, Artificial Intelligence Center, Stanford Research Institute, Menlo Park, California,

Wilks, Yorick and Eugene Charniak (1976) *Computational Semantics*, North Holland, Amsterdam.

Winograd, Terry (1972) *Understanding Natural Language*, Academic Press, New York.

Winston, Patrick Henry (1970) "Learning Structural Descriptions from Examples," Technical Report 76, Project MAC, MIT, Cambridge, Massachusetts, September 1970. Also in *The Psychology of Computer Vision*, edited by Patrick H. Winston, pp. 157–209, April 1975.

Winston, Patrick Henry (1972) "The M.I.T. Robot," in *Machine Intelligence 7*, edited by B. Meltzer and D. Michie, pp. 431–463, Edinburgh University Press, Edinburgh, Scotland.

Winston, Patrick Henry (1974) "New Progress in Artificial Intelligence," Technical Report 310, Artificial Intelligence Laboratory, MIT, Cambridge, Massachusetts.

Winston, Patrick Henry (1975) *The Psychology of Computer Vision*, McGraw-Hill, New York.

Winston, Patrick Henry (1977) *Artificial Intelligence*, Addison-Wesley, Reading, Massachusetts.

Winston, Patrick Henry (1978) "Learning by Creating and Justifying Transfer Frames," *Artificial Intelligence*, Vol. 10, No. 2, pp. 147–172, April 1978.

Winston, Patrick H. and Richard H. Brown (editors) (1979a) *Artificial Intelligence: An MIT Perspective*, Volume 1 (Expert Problem Solving, Natural Language Understanding and Intelligent Computer Coaches, Representation and Learning), The MIT Press, Cambridge, Massachusetts.

Winston, Patrick H. and Richard H. Brown (editors) (1979b) *Artificial Intelligence: An MIT Perspective*, Volume 2 (Understanding Vision, Manipulation and Productivity Technology, Computer Design and Symbol Manipulation), The MIT Press, Cambridge, Massachusetts.

Winston, Patrick Henry (1979) "Learning by Understanding Analogies," Memo No. 520, Artificial Intelligence Laboratory, MIT, Cambridge, Massachusetts, April 1979.

Woods, William A. and R. M. Kaplan, and B. Nash-Webber (1972) "The Lunar Sciences Natural Language Information System: Final Report," BBN Report No. 2378, Bolt Beranek and Newman, Cambridge, Massachusetts.

Yasuhara, A. (1971) *Recursive Function Theory and Logic*, Academic Press, New York.

APPENDIX 1:
INTERLISP

Two of the principal dialects of LISP are MACLISP and INTERLISP. In this book we discuss MACLISP, confining our attention mostly to a limited repertoire of functions commonly found in other versions of LISP as well. In this appendix we point out the major differences between INTERLISP and MACLISP as far as these commonly used functions are concerned, so that the reader with access to an INTERLISP system will be able to do the exercises. The comparison is arranged in order of appearance of the functions in this book. The most important differences are highlighted by indentation.

INTERLISP distinguishes lower case from upper case in symbolic atoms; MACLISP does not, lower case is translated to upper case on input.

The arithmetic functions PLUS, TIMES, MAX, and MIN are the same in INTERLISP. DIFFERENCE and QUOTIENT, which can be used with any number of arguments in MACLISP, are restricted to two arguments in INTERLISP. The functions ADD1 and SUB1 can be used with integer arguments only in INTERLISP. SQRT, EXPT, MINUS, ABS and GCD are the same. The function REMAINDER can be used with floating point arguments as well in INTERLISP. FLOAT, is the same in both dialects.

■ The function FIX truncates its floating point argument in INTERLISP. Thus given a negative argument, it returns a negative integer whose magnitude is less than or equal to the magnitude of the argument. So (FIX -8.2) returns -8 in INTERLISP, while it returns -9 in MACLISP.

The functions CAR, CDR, QUOTE, and CONS are the same. Both dialects provide all twenty-eight shorthand combinations of CAR and CDR, such as CADADR. SET is the same.

■ SETQ can only take two arguments in INTERLISP. Multiple assignments have to be handled by separate SETQs.

APPEND and LIST can take multiple arguments in both dialects. However, if APPEND is given a single argument, MACLISP returns that argument, while INTERLISP makes a copy. One way to get a copy of a list in MACLISP is to use (APPEND <list> NIL). LENGTH and REVERSE are the same, except that in INTERLISP, REVERSE does not complain if given an argument that is not a list. It simply returns its argument. All three arguments to SUBST may be s-expressions in both dialects. LAST is similar, except that INTERLISP does not complain if LAST is given an atom. In that case it just returns NIL.

EVAL is essentially the same. CAR of an s-expression is never evaluated, and it should be an atom with a function definition or a lambda-type expression. There are four types of functions in INTERLISP, providing for all combinations of evaluated versus unevaluated arguments and fixed versus variable number of arguments. These are related to the three types available in MACLISP as follows:

MACLISP	INTERLISP	arguments	number
EXPR	EXPR	evaluated	fixed
----	FEXPR	unevaluated	fixed
LEXPR	EXPR*	evaluated	variable
FEXPR	FEXPR*	unevaluated	variable

The arguments are said to be spread, for a function with a fixed number of arguments, and unspread, for a function with a variable number of arguments. Giving a function the wrong number of arguments, by the way, does not constitute an error in INTERLISP; missing arguments are filled in with NIL, while extra arguments are discarded.

■ DEFINEQ takes the place in INTERLISP of DEFUN in MACLISP, with a somewhat different syntax. First of all, DEFINEQ allows one to define several functions at once. DEFINEQ is given a list, each element of which is either of the form (<name> <definition>) or (<name> <parameters> <body>). Here, <definition> is a list starting with LAMBDA or NLAMBDA depending on whether the arguments are to be evaluated or not (EXPR versus FEXPR). Further, <parameters> is either a list of parameters or a single atom depending on whether the function takes a fixed or variable number of arguments (spread versus unspread).

Therefore instead of:

```
(DEFUN SUM-SQUARES (A B)
       (PLUS (TIMES A A) (TIMES B B)))
```

one could use in INTERLISP:

```
(DEFINEQ ((SUM-SQUARES (A B)
                (PLUS (TIMES A A) (TIMES B B)))))
```

There is another version of this function, called DEFINE, which evaluates its argument.

Function definitions in INTERLISP are stored in the function definition cell and are accessible via GETD. In MACLISP function definitions are attached to the EXPR, FEXPR or LEXPR property and can be retrieved using GET.

Arguments to an INTERLISP function of type EXPR* are evaluated and can be retrieved using the function ARG. This is similar to the method used to retrieve arguments of LEXPRs in MACLISP. In INTERLISP, however, ARG takes two arguments: the first is the name of the single atomic parameter of the given EXPR* function, while the second is the number of the argument to be located.

Normally, what the user types is read by READ, handed off to EVAL, and the result returned is then printed using PRINT. A peculiarity of INTERLISP is that it permits user input at the top level to be in an older, so-called EVALQUOTE form. Using this feature, the user may enter <function> (<arg1> <arg2> ...), instead of typing (<function> '<arg1> '<arg2> ...).

The predicates ATOM, BOUNDP, EQUAL, EQ, NULL, MEMBER, and NUMBERP are the same. GREATERP and LESSP take only two arguments in INTERLISP however. MINUSP, is the same.

■ ZEROP cannot be used on floating point numbers in INTERLISP. Instead of (ZEROP <number>) use (EQUAL <number> 0.0).

AND, OR, and NOT are the same. In both dialects, (AND) returns T and (OR) returns NIL. Also, COND is the same. Instead of FUNCALL use APPLY* in INTERLISP.

FUNCTION in MACLISP is just like QUOTE, except that it tells the compiler that a function follows. *FUNCTION in INTERLISP produces a FUNARG, a function with an environment pointer (FUNCTION is more powerful in INTERLISP, taking two arguments, a function and an environment. The latter is either NIL, a list of variables used free in the function, or an atom. A closure is created by bundling up the function definition with an environment. The result returned is a list starting with the atom FUNARG. This form is recognized by EVAL and APPLY).

UNION, INTERSECTION, and LDIFFERENCE, each defined in a problem here, exist in INTERLISP.

■ The syntax of MAPCAR is different. If only two arguments are given, these are simply reversed. So, while one uses (MAPCAR <function> <list>) in MACLISP, in INTERLISP one must employ (MAPCAR <list> <function>).

The MACLISP version of MAPCAR allows for additional lists from which arguments can be drawn when the function takes more than one argument. The INTERLISP version provides instead for an optional third argument used to specify how to step through the given list. The default is to use CDR to obtain the next, shorter version at each iteration.

The function MAPCAN described in this book, is called MAPCONC in INTERLISP. Both use NCONC-like operations to build the result, thus altering existing list structure.

APPLY is essentially the same. PROG is similar. The parameter list in a PROG, however, can contain items of the form (<atom> <expression>) in INTERLISP. This is used to initialize variables to values other than the standard value, NIL. PROGN is the same in both dialects, while INTERLISP has PROG1, which returns the value of the first argument, and MACLISP has PROG2, which returns the value of the second argument. GO and RETURN are the same.

MACLISP supports iterative computations using a function called DO, while INTERLISP provides a simpler, less flexible facility called RPT.

GET is called GETPROP in INTERLISP.

■ The last two arguments to PUTPROP are reversed. While one uses (PUTPROP <atom> <value> <property>) in MACLISP, in INTERLISP on must employ (PUTPROP <atom> <property> <value>).

While REMPROP is the same, there is no equivalent to DEFPROP. One has to use PUTPROP, quote all three arguments, and remember that the value returned will be different.

The function ASSOC has the same definition in both dialects.

■ ARRAY in INTERLISP can create only one dimensional arrays. The arguments are also rearranged. What would be (ARRAY <name> T <size>) in MACLISP becomes (SETQ <name> (ARRAY <size> NIL NIL)) in INTERLISP. The value returned is an array pointer to be used in manipulating the array. To access a cell in the array one uses (ELT <name> <index>), while storing a value in the array can be accomplished using (SETA <name> <index> <value>).

In both dialects, the arguments to ARRAY make it possible to specify other information, such as whether the entries in the array will be arbitrary s-expression or just numbers. This information is used to select efficient storage methods appropriate to the type of data indicated.

Both dialects support SORT, although the INTERLISP version does not sort arrays. Both modify existing list structures when applied to lists. (In fact the original list structure no longer contains useful information when the sort has been done.) The INTERLISP sorting method for lists and the MACLISP sorting method for arrays are not stable. That is, the order of elements that are equal may be different in the result from what it was in the input. MACLISP also has

SORTCAR, which sorts on the CAR of the items in the given list or array.

The value of (PRINT <message>) is <message> in INTERLISP, not T as in MACLISP. In both dialects, an optional second argument specifies a file to which output is to be directed. The form of this argument is different in the two dialects, since it reflects details of the file structure supported by the operating system. TERPRI and READ are similar in the two dialects and also take an optional second argument. The function READCH for reading one character is called READC in INTERLISP. The "quoting" character, used to allow break and separator characters in atom names, is % rather than / as in MACLISP. The function PRIN1 (which is like PRINT, but does not start a new line) is called PRIN2 in INTERLISP. The function PRINC (which is like PRIN1, but does not insert "quoting" characters to hide break and separator characters in weird atom names) is called PRIN1 in INTERLISP.

GENSYM behaves similarly, with the default first character being X in INTERLISP rather than G as in MACLISP. In both dialects an optional argument can be used to specify an alternate first character. EXPLODE is called UNPACK in INTERLISP, while IMPLODE is called PACK. EXPLODE is not restricted to atomic arguments in either dialect.

■ There are considerable differences in the macro facilities. INTERLISP provides so-called compiler macros, and a special program package, MACROTRAN, is needed to permit interpretive use. Macros can be debugged using EXPANDMACRO, which types the expanded expression on the user's terminal. Macros are defined by placing the macro definition on the property list of the an atom under the MACRO property. When the CAR of a expression being evaluated has a MACRO property, the macro is used in place of the expression.

There are three types of macros in INTERLISP: open, computed, and substitution. Of these, computed macros are most like the macros in MACLISP. A computed macro definition begins with an atom other than LAMBDA, NLAMBDA, or NIL. The CDR of the expression being evaluated is bound to this atom. The expression following the atom is then evaluated and the result used in place of the expression.

What would appear in MACLISP as:

```
(DEFUN ADD1 MACRO (X)
       (LIST 'PLUS (CADR X) 1))
```

could be written in INTERLISP as:

```
(PUTPROP 'ADD1 'MACRO '(X (LIST 'PLUS (CAR X) 1)))
```

Note that in INTERLISP macros are passed only the argument list; in MACLISP they are passed the function name as well.

■ MACLISP comments can occur anywhere in a program. They start with a ; and stop at the end of the line. A comment in INTERLISP has to be enclosed in a list with * as the first element. That is, (* <text>) will be ignored by the interpreter except in so far as that a useless value will be returned. Consequently, INTERLISP comments can occur only in PROGs and other places where a value returned is ignored. The same problem occurs in MACLISP when a list is used which starts with the atom COMMENT (Note that in MACLISP the asterisk is used to denote multiplication).

NCONC, RPLACA, and RPLACD are the same.

DELETE in MACLISP uses EQUAL for comparisons. There is no exact equivalent in INTERLISP. A MACLISP function not discussed so far, DELQ, uses EQ for comparisons instead and is the same as DREMOVE in INTERLISP. Both modify existing list structures. In INTERLISP there is an alternative that copies list structures and uses EQUAL for comparisons called REMOVE. We defined this function as an example in the section in which DELETE is discussed. All of this is summarized in the following table:

MACLISP	INTERLISP	comparison	list structure
DELETE	-	EQUAL	modified
DELQ	DREMOVE	EQ	modified
-	REMOVE	EQUAL	copied

Trigonometric functions take an optional extra argument in INTERLISP specifying whether the computation is to be performed using radians or degrees. The default is to assume that the argument is given in degrees. Other than that, SIN and COS are the same, and ATAN in MACLISP corresponds to ARCTAN2 in INTERLISP. LOG is the same, while EXP is called ANTILOG in INTERLISP. All of these mathematical functions will work on fixed point as well as the more commonly used floating point arguments. Instead of LSH in MACLISP, one uses LLSH in INTERLISP. Both perform logical shifts, left or right, depending on the whether the second argument is positive or negative. The function LSH in INTERLISP performs an arithmetic shift instead.

■ Bit-wise logical operations can be performed using BOOLE in MACLISP, while LOGAND, LOGOR, and LOGXOR are used in INTERLISP. Both forms can handle two or more arguments.

Both dialects have breaking and tracing features. BREAK in MACLISP corresponds to BREAK1 in INTERLISP, except that the first and third argument are interchanged. In both cases, the second argument (if present) is evaluated. A break occurs if the value returned is nonNIL. In MACLISP the first argument specifies a message to be printed, while the third argument serves this purpose in INTERLISP. In the INTERLISP version, the first argument specifies a function to be evaluated.

BREAK, and BREAKIN in INTERLISP are used to insert BREAK1s into functions, while UNBREAK is used to remove such modifications. There are no equivalents in MACLISP, although similar effects can be achieved using TRACE. At the level of detail covered in this book, the two versions of TRACE are similar. To UNTRACE a function in INTERLISP, use UNBREAK. Both dialects have many additional features for controlling debugging such as BAKTRACE, a function which prints information about the series of functions calls leading to the current environment.

Programs can be read in from a file using LOAD (described briefly in Appendix 3), although there are some differences due to differences in the file structures of the two systems. Control can be returned to the operating system using QUIT (described in Appendix 3) in MACLISP, while LOGOUT serves a similar function in INTERLISP.

Both MACLISP and INTERLISP have numerous functions not discussed here. Some of these deal with other, newer types of data such as the so-called strings and hunks. Some are convenient, but redundant, combinations of simpler functions already described. Others allow interfacing with the operating system in which LISP is embedded. We have restricted ourselves to a basic set here that is sufficient for most purposes and common to several dialects.

Also, what the user sees is a whole programming environment, including text editors, debugging tools, file management systems, and the operating system. Usually the LISP system itself contains such tools as pretty printers, debugging packages, compilers, editors, indexers, spelling correctors, infix to prefix translators, and automatic file updaters. DWIM is the INTERLISP facility for dealing with user typing errors, while CLISP allows translation from the usual arithmetic statement format, typical of other computer languages, to normal LISP format. These types of software facilities were not described in this book, because there is little standardization.

Typically LISP is supported by a highly interactive set of tools that vary from installation to installation and which is therefore difficult to discuss except in general terms. It cannot be overemphasized how important this program development environment is in making a language exciting to use.

References

A technical report by Ericson [1979] describes software aids for translating from MACLISP to INTERLISP.

There are definitive manuals for the principle LISP dialects. The following are particularly noteworthy: MACLISP, Moon [1974]; LISP Machine LISP, Weinreb and Moon [1978]; Franz LISP, Foderaro [1979]; INTERLISP, Teitelman [1975]; INTERLISP/370, Urmi [1976a]; LISP/370, Blair [1979]; Stanford LISP, Quam and Diffie [1972]; UCI LISP, Meehan [1979]; and UNIVAC 1108 LISP, Norman [1978].

APPENDIX 2: BASIC LISP FUNCTIONS

All of the basic LISP functions introduced in the book are listed here. The page number on which they are first described is given, as is the function type, which indicates how the arguments are treated. A SUBR takes a fixed number of arguments and evaluates them, while a FSUBR takes a variable number which may not be evaluated, and a LSUBR takes a variable number of arguments which are evaluated. These function types for LISP-supplied functions are analogous to EXPR, FEXPR, and LEXPR types for interpreted functions. Some information about the allowable arguments is also provided. Here, number means either fixed or floating point number, while s-expression means atom or list. Items in parentheses are less commonly used, while those in brackets are optional. Some of these optional arguments were not discussed in this book, but are included here for completeness.

FUNCTION NAME	PAGE	TYPE	NUMBER OF ARGUMENTS	TYPE
ABS	16	SUBR	1	number
ADD1	15-16	SUBR	1	fix (or float)
AND	42-43	FSUBR	0 or more	NIL or nonNIL
APPEND	23-24, 110	LSUBR	0 or more	lists
APPLY	64	LSUBR	2 or 3	function, argument list, [environ]
ARG	423	SUBR	1	fix (or NIL)
ARRAY	75	FSUBR	3 or more	name, type, dimensions
ASSOC	73-74	SUBR	2	atom, a-list
ATAN	125	SUBR	2	float (or fix)
ATOM	38	SUBR	1	s-expression

FUNCTION NAME	PAGE	TYPE	NUMBER OF ARGUMENTS	TYPE
BAKTRACE	196	LSUBR	0 or 1	[PDL pointer]
BOOLE	101, 150	LSUBR	3 or more	0-15, fix
BOUNDP	38	SUBR	1	atom
BREAK	191-192	FSUBR	1 to 3	message, [predicate], [s-expression]
CAR	18-19, 22	SUBR	1	list
CDR	18-19, 22	SUBR	1	list
COMMENT	406	FSUBR	0 or more	arbitrary text
COND	43, 45	FSUBR	0 or more	clauses
CONS	24-25, 106	SUBR	2	s-expression, list
COS	172	SUBR	1	(fix or) float
DEFPROP	72	FSUBR	3	atom, value, property
DEFUN	33-34	FSUBR	3 or 4	name, [type], parameter list, body
DELETE	114-115	LSUBR	2 or 3	atom, list, [number]
DELQ	406	LSUBR	2 or 3	atom, list, [number]
DIFFERENCE	15-16	LSUBR	0 or more	numbers
EQ	118-119	SUBR	2	atoms, (or numbers, lists)
EQUAL	38, 118	SUBR	2	s-expressions
EVAL	29-31	LSUBR	1 or 2	s-expression, [environ]
EXP	174	SUBR	1	(fix or) float
EXPLODE	90-91	SUBR	1	atom (or list)
EXPT	16	SUBR	2	numbers
FIX	19, 418	SUBR	1	(fix or) float
FLOAT	19, 418	SUBR	1	fix (or float)
FUNCALL	48-49	LSUBR	1 or more	function, arguments
FUNCTION	80	FSUBR	1	function
GCD	151	SUBR	2	fix
GENSYM	91	LSUBR	0 or 1	[atom (or fix)]
GET	71-72	SUBR	2	atom, property
GO	68	FSUBR	1	atom (or s-expression)
GREATERP	40-41	LSUBR	2 or more	numbers
IMPLODE	91	SUBR	1	list of character atoms (or fix)
LAST	28	SUBR	1	list
LENGTH	27	SUBR	1	list
LESSP	40-41	LSUBR	2 or more	numbers
LIST	23-24	LSUBR	0 or more	s-expressions
LOG	174	SUBR	1	(fix or) float
LOAD	407, 416	SUBR	1	file specification
LSH	127	SUBR	2	fix
MAPCAN	83-85	LSUBR	2 or more	function, lists
MAPCAR	63-64	LSUBR	2 or more	function, lists
MAX	15-16	LSUBR	1 or more	numbers
MEMBER	39-40, 53	SUBR	2	atom, list

FUNCTION NAME	PAGE	TYPE	NUMBER OF ARGUMENTS	TYPE
MIN	15-16	LSUBR	1 or more	numbers
MINUS	16	SUBR	1	number
MINUSP	41	SUBR	1	number
NCONC	112-113	LSUBR	0 or more	lists
NOT	42	SUBR	1	NIL or nonNIL
NULL	39	SUBR	1	NIL or nonNIL
NUMBERP	40	SUBR	1	s-expression
OR	42-43	FSUBR	0 or more	NIL or nonNIL
PLUS	13, 15-16	LSUBR	0 or more	numbers
PRIN1	91-92	LSUBR	1 or 2	s-expression, [file specification]
PRINC	91-92	LSUBR	1 or 2	s-expression, [file specification]
PRINT	87-88	LSUBR	1 or 2	s-expression, [file specification]
PROG	67, 68	FSUBR	0 or more	variable-list, tags & expressions
PROG2	68	LSUBR	2 or more	expressions
PROGN	68	LSUBR	0 or more	expressions
PUTPROP	72	SUBR	3	atom, value, property
QUIT	407, 416	LSUBR	0 or 1	fix
QUOTE	21, 105	FSUBR	1	s-expression
QUOTIENT	15-16,417	LSUBR	0 or more	numbers
READ	88	LSUBR	0 to 2	[file specification], [e-o-f arg]
READCH	92	LSUBR	0 to 2	[file specification], [e-o-f arg]
REMAINDER	417	SUBR	2	fix
REMPROP	72	SUBR	2	atom, property
RETURN	67	SUBR	1	s-expression
REVERSE	27	SUBR	1	list
RPLACA	113	SUBR	2	list, s-expression
RPLACD	113-114	SUBR	2	list, s-expression
SET	23	SUBR	2	s-expressions
SETQ	29	FSUBR	2 or more	atom, value
SIN	172	SUBR	1	(fix or) float
SORT	147, 150	SUBR	2	list or array, predicate
SORTCAR	405	SUBR	2	list or array, predicate
SQRT	16	SUBR	1	(fix or) float
STORE	75	FSUBR	2	array reference, value
SUB1	15-16	SUBR	1	fix (or float)
SUBST	27-28	SUBR	3	s-expression, s-expression, list
TRACE	193-195	FSUBR	0 or more	atoms (or trace specifications)
TERPRI	91	LSUBR	0 or 1	[file specification]
TIMES	15-16	LSUBR	0 or more	numbers
UNTRACE	195	FSUBR	0 or more	atoms (or trace specifications)
ZEROP	41	SUBR	1	number

The following are not LISP functions but are atoms which have special significance when seen by EVAL.

APPENDIX 3: USING MACLISP

The way one interacts with MACLISP at a terminal has changed considerably over the years and is likely to continue to change in the future. We therefore must be content to give a short skeletal scenario to give the feel of what happens as of this writing.

There are several implementations of MACLISP. First of all, there is a version running on the Incompatible Time Sharing system (ITS) developed at the Artificial Intelligence Laboratory of MIT. Second, there is a version available on the Honeywell MULTICS system developed by the Laboratory of Computer Science of MIT. Thirdly, there is a version available for the DEC PDP10 TOPS-10 system, which can also be used under the BBN TENEX operating system using a TOPS-10 emulator. Also note that Franz Lisp on VAX UNIX is compatible with MACLISP. The LISP Machine, a dedicated personal computer, runs a LISP which is essentially upward compatible with MACLISP while providing many new features. There are reputed to be other implementations of MACLISP.

The following would be typical for users doing ordinary things using MACLISP on the ITS system. Text typed by the system is in upper case, while the users input is shown in lower case for clarity. (Implementations of MACLISP differ in their treatment of lower case input. The PDP10 versions convert all input to upper case, while the MULTICS version does not.) So-called *control characters* can be typed by holding down the control key while pressing another key. If the character z is typed in this fashion, this will be shown here as <control z>. Similarly, carriage return is shown as <CR>, while the escape character is indicated using <escape>.

<control z>   User walks up to free terminal and
                               gets system's attention.

`AI ITS 1163 DDT 1388 TTY 51`	System acknowledges request and may present the user with system messages if there are any.
`:login smith <CR>`	Log in with assigned user name.
`*`	System's prompt character appears after mail for the user is typed if there is any.
`:lisp <CR>`	Call up LISP.
`LISP 1861`	LISP announces version number.
`ALLOC?`	LISP asks if there are any special memory allocation arrangements desired.
`n`	The user indicates that none are by typing n.
`*`	LISP's prompt character.
`(plus 3.14 2.71)`	The user requests a simple addition.
`5.85`	LISP responds with the result.
`(car '(simple list))`	The user tries another example.
`SIMPLE`	LISP evaluates the expression and prints the result.
`(ledit demo >)`	More serious work requires that a file be created containing a few functions and some data for them to work on. This is conveniently done using the system's editing program. LEDIT calls up the editing program, asking it to get the most recent version of the file DEMO. If there is no such file, one will be created with version number 1.

`(defun sum-squares (a b)`
`     (plus (times a a`
`          (times b b))))`
	User enters function definition.

`<escape> z`	User marks this function, indicating that it is to be sent to LISP. Marked material in DEMO will be read by LISP when the user finally returns from the editor.

⟨control x⟩ z	When defining new functions and editing old ones is complete, it is time to go back to LISP. A new version of DEMO is written on mass storage. Also, new material in DEMO, marked by the user, is now read by LISP as if it had been typed in directly to LISP by the user.
;READING FROM LEDIT SUM-SQUARES ;EDIT COMPLETED	LISP announces that it is reading new stuff, and lists the names of functions read. LISP indicates that it has read everything.
⋆	LISP's prompt character.
(sum-squares 2.0 3.0)	The user tries his new function.
36.0	LISP returns result -- not what the user expected.
	Bugs will occur. TRACE and BREAK will probably help find them. There are a number of ways to get back to the editor to fix errant functions.
⟨control e⟩	One way to get back to the editor.
⟨control s⟩ (times a a	The user searches for place to fix the problem.
⟨escape⟩)	The user stops search, enters missing parenthesis.
⟨escape⟩ z	The function is marked so that it will be transmitted to LISP using a temporary file as before.
⟨control x⟩ z	Now return to LISP from editor.
;READING FROM LEDIT SUM-SQUARES ;EDIT COMPLETED	LISP announces that it is reading new stuff, and lists the names of functions read. LISP indicates that it has read everything.
⋆	LISP's prompt character.
(sum-squares 2.0 3.0)	The user tries the new version.
13.0	LISP returns result.
⋅ ⋅ ⋅	The LISP ... Editor ... LISP ... loop will no doubt be repeated many times.

Finally, it is time to get off the system.
Depending on whether the user is currently engaged
with LISP or the editor, one or the other
of the following commands can be used:

(quit)   One way to get out of LISP.

⟨control x⟩ ⟨control c⟩   One way to get out of the editor.

                                         To return to LISP or the editor at this point,
                                         simply type :continue ⟨CR⟩. Otherwise,

:logout ⟨CR⟩   Log off the system.

AI ITS 1163 CONSOLE 51 FREE   Console free message.

Next time Smith logs in, Smith will likely type the following to LISP so that LISP
will read all of the definitions previously prepared:

(load '(demo ⟩))

All of the above would be different on some other system supporting LISP, of
course.

References

For details about the Incompatible Time Sharing system (ITS) and its top-level
monitor, DDT or HACTRN, see Eastlake [1969], Osman [1971], Eastlake [1972],
and Lewis [1977a, 1977b].
    The editor invoked by the LEDIT command in MACLISP is called EMACS.
This powerful display oriented editor is described by Ciccarelli [1977] and Stallman
[1979]. Incidentally, the version of EMACS developed by Greenberg [1979] for the
Honeywell MULTICS system is written in MACLISP.
    Aspects of the LISP compiler used with MACLISP on ITS are described in
Golden [1970], Steele [1977b], and Steele [1979]. The MULTICS version of the
compiler is explained by Greenberg [1977].
    For details about the LISP Machine, see Greenblatt [1974], Bawden *et al.*
[1977], Weinreb and Moon [1978], Knight *et al.* [1979], and Greenblatt *et al.*
[1979]. For general ideas about why dedicated computers now make more sense
than time sharing systems, see Horn and Winston [1975] and Thacker *et al.* [1979].

APPENDIX 4:
NOTES

Note 1: LISP Handles Both Fixed and Floating Numbers

It is necessary to know something about one or two of the details of how computers handle numbers in order to understand certain seemingly strange results, such as the following:

```
(QUOTIENT 6.0 4.0)
  1.5

(QUOTIENT 6 4)
  1

(REMAINDER 6 4)
  2
```

Most larger computers have two ways to store numbers: one way is by using the fixed-point format; the other is by using the floating-point format.

Fixed point is useful if only integers are of interest. Numbers like 0, 3, and 1024 are fine, but .001, 3.14159, and 27.27 are not. *Floating point* is necessary when a number includes a fractional part. Floating point is also handy when dealing with very large numbers, although some versions of LISP have a third format specially for this purpose.

There are some simple conventions required so that LISP and LISP users can tell each other what sort of numbers are involved in any particular computation:

■ If there is no decimal point, a number is fixed point. If there is a decimal point, but nothing follows it, again a number is fixed point.

■ If there is a decimal point with something following it, a number is floating point.

■ Finally, if there is an E after a number, followed directly by a second number, then the number is floating point. The value represented equals the number before the E times 10 raised to the number after the E.

When a LISP arithmetic function gets mixed arguments, typically all are converted automatically to floating point and a floating-point answer is returned:

```
(PLUS 1 1.1)
   2.1
```

Because of the existence of two kinds of numbers, the use of QUOTIENT may give rise to bugs. The reason is that QUOTIENT insists on returning a fixed-point result if all of its arguments are fixed point. That is why (QUOTIENT 6 4) returns 1, which is the expected result with the fraction suppressed. REMAINDER, a function that only works on fixed-point numbers, returns what is left over. Thus (REMAINDER 6 4) returns 2.

Consequently, LISP programs sometimes have flourishes that force conversion of fixed-point numbers into floating-point and vice versa. FLOAT forcibly converts fixed-point number into floating-point ones. FIX goes the other way, producing the largest integer that is less than or equal to its argument. This illustrates:

```
(FLOAT 8)
   8.0
```

```
(FIX 8.8)
   8
```

```
(FIX -8.2)
   -9
```

```
(QUOTIENT 6 4)
   1
```

```
(QUOTIENT (FLOAT 6) 4)
   1.5
```

```
(QUOTIENT 6 (FLOAT 4))
   1.5
```

The reader should be warned that input and output of numbers in LISP does not necessarily have to be in decimal digits. Some versions of LISP in fact use octal notation until instructed to do otherwise by the user. In MACLISP one can take care of this problem as follows:

(SETQ BASE 10. IBASE 10.)

Note 2: LISP is Neither Call-by-reference nor Call-by-value

Atoms and lists are the objects that LISP deals with. They are passed as arguments to functions and returned as values. In LISP we say that an atom may be *bound* to such an object. Note that two atoms may be bound to the same object. Each LISP object has its individual identity; that is, we can test (using EQ) whether two objects are in fact one and the same. If two atoms are bound to the same object, changes in that object will affect both atoms.

Most other programming languages deal with variables that have values. Each variable can be in one of a number of different *states*. In the case of a fixed point variable, the possible states correspond to those integers which can be represented. We can ask whether two variables are in the same state. Changing the state of one variable does not cause a change of state in another variable. In such programming languages there are two ways to pass an argument when a function is called:

■ One can initialize the state of the function's parameter to be the same as the present state of the given argument. This is termed *call by value.*

■ One can use the parameter name as an alias for the argument name. Changing the state of the function's parameter changes the state of the argument. This is termed *call by reference.*

Note that call by value may involve copying some information. On the other hand, call by reference may lead to side effects on the variable used as the argument, possibly unexpectedly.

Strictly speaking, LISP can be neither call by value nor call by reference because the notion of what a LISP variable is does not correspond exactly to the notion of variable for which call by value and call by reference have a natural meaning.

■ In LISP, when the argument to a function is an atom, the function's parameter is bound to the value of the atomic argument. There is no other choice.

Note that there is no copying involved, which suggests that this method is like call by reference. At the same time, the value of the argument is not usually altered by changes to the value of the parameter. This behavior is like that of call by value. The value of the argument can change, however, if we use functions like RPLACA and RPLACD on the parameter. This is because these are the functions which can alter existing list structures.

The conclusion is that what LISP does corresponds most closely with call by reference, but that for most purposes it can be thought of as using call by value. The only time we can tell is when we use list structure altering primitives. Since LISP passes the object bound to the argument to the function being called, one might say that LISP uses *call-by-passing*.

The following example may help clarify:

```
(DEFUN DONOTHING (A) (SETQ A 1) B)
```

```
(SETQ B 0)
```

Executing (DONOTHING B) causes the value that was bound to A to be the value bound to B, namely 0. The immediate SETQ changes the value bound to A, but certainly, it does not change the value bound to B. The result of DONOTHING is 0, the original value bound to B, not 1, the value taken on by A.

In a programming language that uses the more usual notion of variable along with the call-by-reference convention, a function analogous to DONOTHING would produce different results. The parameter A would be treated as an alias for the argument B. Any changes to A would implicitly change B. The value of B would become 1 and the result of DONOTHING would be 1 as well.

In a programming language that used the more usual notion of variable along with the call-by-value convention, a function analogous to DONOTHING would produce the same results as LISP. Thus LISP works more like call by value than like call by reference in this particular situation.

Note 3: Free-variable Values are Determined Dynamically, not Lexically

Consider the following function, used in Chapter 3:

```
(DEFUN INCREMENT (PARAMETER)               ;PARAMETER is bound.
   (SETQ PARAMETER (PLUS PARAMETER FREE))  ;FREE is free.
   (SETQ OUTPUT PARAMETER))                ;OUTPUT is free.
 INCREMENT
```

Evidently INCREMENT is to add the value of FREE to its argument, returning the result after arranging for the result to be the value of OUTPUT. When using INCREMENT, it is necessary to have a value for the free variable FREE. Finding this value becomes a problem when functions are defined or used inside other functions.

An environment is a collection of bindings. We need to specify in which environment the binding of the free variable can be looked up.

■ A function is said to be defined or used in the *top-level environment* if its definition or use is directly demanded by a user, rather than indirectly by way of the evaluation of one or more other functions. The *global value* of an atom is the value in the top-level environment, the one a person gets by typing its name while LISP is not doing anything.

If INCREMENT is defined and used in the top-level environment, then the value for FREE used by INCREMENT must be the global value obtained from the top-level environment since no other environment is involved at either the time of definition or the time of use.

Things can be more complicated. Consider the situation depicted in figure A-1. The function DEFINE-1, when evaluated, uses DEFINE-2. When DEFINE-2 is evaluated, INCREMENT is defined. Later, some function named USE-1 uses USE-2, and USE-2 uses INCREMENT.

■ The environment in force when a function is defined determines the *definition environment*.

■ The environment in force when a function is used determines the *evaluation environment*.

In the new situation, the value that should be used for FREE is no longer clear. There are two possibilities: the value of FREE may be determined by looking at either the definition environment or the evaluation environment.

■ LISP uses *dynamic scoping*, and the values of free variables are determined by the evaluation environment.

In the example, using dynamic scoping means FREE has a value determined by USE-2 if FREE is a parameter of USE-2. Otherwise, FREE is determined by USE-1 if it is a parameter there. Otherwise, if FREE has a value at all, it is determined by the top-level environment.

■ If LISP used *lexical scoping* instead, then the values of free variables would be determined by the definition environment, the environment in force when the function requiring the free-variable values was defined.

In the example, this means FREE would have a value determined by DEFINE-2 or DEFINE-1, if FREE is a parameter of one of them, or by the top-level environment otherwise.

■ The LISP used in this book has dynamic scoping. Arranging for a LISP-like language to use lexical scoping is possible, but may cause some complications.

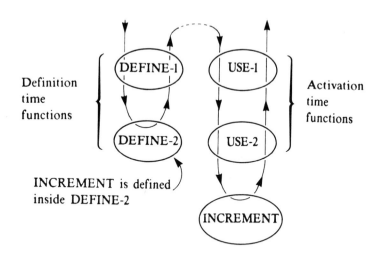

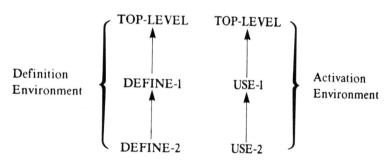

Figure A-1: The function INCREMENT is defined inside one nested sequence of calls and used inside another. These sequences determine the definition and activation environments. If dynamic scoping is used, a function's free variable values are determined by the activation environment. If lexical scoping is used, a function's free variables are determined by the definition environment.

Sometimes dynamic scoping leads to surprising *variable name conflicts.* To see why, consider one function that calculates the simple interest on money deposited and another that calculates an incremented balance:

```
(DEFUN INTEREST (BALANCE)
        (TIMES BALANCE INTEREST-RATE))

(DEFUN NEWBALANCE (BALANCE)
        (PLUS BALANCE (INTEREST BALANCE)))
```

Clearly these functions give the following result if the value of INTEREST-RATE is equal to 0.1:

```
(NEWBALANCE 100.0)
   110.0
```

Now suppose that X has been used all over the place rather than the more mnemonic names. Suppose, indeed, that we have foolishly let X be the parameter in NEWBALANCE as well as the interest rate used as a free variable in INTEREST:

```
(DEFUN INTEREST (BALANCE)
       (TIMES BALANCE X))

(DEFUN NEWBALANCE (X)
       (PLUS X (INTEREST X)))
```

With these definitions, dynamic scoping causes big trouble because NEWBALANCE can screw up the value of X used inside INTEREST:

```
(NEWBALANCE 100.0)
   10100.0
```

Evidently, the value of X desired inside the function INTEREST is temporarily put aside when NEWBALANCE is entered. The value of X becomes 100.0 instead. When the instance of TIMES inside INTEREST sees 100.0 as the value of both BALANCE and X, it produces a blunder, as it should.

References

Steele and Sussman [1978b] present a balanced discussion of the relative merits of dynamic and lexical scoping. Their paper on SCHEME [1979] describes a lexically-scoped dialect of LISP.

Note 4: A LEXPR is still another Function Form

FEXPRs were featured as functions that do not evaluate their arguments and that take any number of arguments. It is natural to suppose that it would be useful to disentangle these features, offering them individually. To complete the picture, then, LEXPRs are described. The treatment is brief.

LEXPRs are like FEXPRs in that they take any number of arguments. The number of arguments given becomes the value of an LEXPR's single parameter. The evaluated arguments are obtained by way of executing (ARG <number>) where the number specifies which argument is desired. LEXPRs are defined by using this syntax:

```
(DEFUN <function name> <single parameter> <body>)
```

The lack of parentheses around the parameter signals that a LEXPR is to be defined.

INDEX